gender-equal refs: XV, 44, 129, 137, 195,

on inequality in general: 81, 71, 152, 188, 19

religion refs: 10, 17

20 — liberalism's historic anti-religious/anti-clerical stance is important
25 — antiliberals like Maistre fought efforts to institutionalize individual
57 — me: both de Maistre's + Schmitt's antiliberalism emerges
     in the context of liberal victory — in the FR in the
     former case and in WWI in the ___ latter case.
71 — inequality as basic basic tenet of antiliberalism
     (me: might say traditional inequalities)

The Anatomy of Antiliberalism

The Anatomy of Antiliberalism

/ Stephen Holmes /

HARVARD UNIVERSITY PRESS

Cambridge, Massachusetts

London, England

1993

This book is printed on acid-free paper, and its binding materials have
been chosen for strength and durability.

Library of Congress Cataloging-in-Publication Data
Holmes, Stephen, 1948–
    The anatomy of antiliberalism / Stephen Holmes.
        p. cm.
    Includes bibliographical references and index.
    ISBN 0-674-03180-6
    1. Liberalism. I. Title
HM276.H744 1993
320.5'1—dc20   92-41387
                                                              CIP

To Alexa

Acknowledgments

For their heartening and chastening comments on an earlier draft of this book, I must thank Bruce Ackerman, Ann Davies, Jon Elster, Don Herzog, Albert Hirschman, Helge Høibraaten, Rumyana Kolarova, David Laitin, Charles Larmore, Susan Liebell, John McCormick, Richard Posner, Nancy Rosenblum, Marion Smiley, Cass Sunstein, David Wooton, and Bernard Yack. Without periodic editorial encouragement from Leon Wieseltier, many of these chapters would never have been written. Appreciation goes, too, to Joseph Cropsey, William Galston, Harvey Mansfield, and Nathan Tarcov—all of whom provided warm criticisms of Chapter 3. To the late Judith Shklar, whose readiness to dismantle long essays on short notice was unflagging, I owe an unrepayable debt. Nancy Maull has read and improved each chapter in successive incarnations, emboldened my sober side, and deplored the innumerable postponements. Thanks do not suffice. I am grateful to the Guggenheim Foundation for supporting a sabbatical leave during the calendar year 1988, which made it possible to gather together the materials on which this study is based. Finally, acknowledgment is due to the Russell Baker Scholar's Fund of the University of Chicago Law School for research support during the summer of 1991, and to the Wissenschaftskolleg zu Berlin, where the final manuscript was prepared.

Contents

Preface

On devra écraser tout ce qui subsiste du libéralisme
dans les esprits

—*Charles Maurras*

The disparagement of "liberalism" is not a passing fashion of the late twentieth century. It is a recurring feature of Western political culture at least since the French Revolution. Nineteenth-century enemies of the Enlightenment, from Joseph de Maistre to Friedrich Nietzsche, poured scorn on liberal ideas and aspirations. In Europe during the 1920s and 1930s implacable hostility to liberalism was the one attitude on which extreme rightists and extreme leftists could agree. Even today, in American universities, muted versions of this outlook continue to flourish. In the century of Hitler and Stalin, wise professors still brand liberalism as the Great Enemy.

Why would some of America's leading intellects revile a tradition devoted, among other things, to freedom of thought? A generation ago, Martin Heidegger's subterranean but hypnotic influence prepared the way for this odd development. His harsh indictment of "modernity" was adapted to the mental horizon of their new American audience by Hannah Arendt and Leo Strauss. Having been welcomed as immigrants to this country, they hesitated to announce that the "decline" of modern times was caused by a "forgetfulness of Being," in Heidegger's portentous phrase; that would have been wholly unintelligible to their culturally backward readers. Decadence resulted from our forgetting the Greek polis (Arendt) or losing sight of classical natural right (Strauss). Meanwhile Herbert Marcuse, Theodor Adorno, and other members of the Frankfurt school helped popularize Heidegger's suggestion that "modern man," having lost his primeval reverence for nature, has adopted a basically instrumental attitude toward the world. A penchant for instrumental thinking, they argued, is the principal sign of our fallen condition; habituated to thinking instrumentally about nature, we tend to think instrumentally about each other as well.

Heideggerian ideas of this sort, domesticated and desacralized in various ways, spread through American universities in the 1950s and 1960s. In the 1970s and 1980s the scene looked different. Attacks on "modernity" were largely replaced by attacks on "liberalism." The phraseology changed, but the underlying pattern of hostility, belittlement, and rebuke was the same. Take Alasdair MacIntyre's *After Virtue* or Roberto Unger's *Knowledge and Politics*. It is nearly impossible to locate these influential works (their notions have found their way to the op-ed pages) on a spectrum from left to right, but both express distaste and even disgust for liberal politics and ideals. MacIntyre is the more candid of the two about the religious sources of his antiliberalism; he increasingly derides "secular reason" while continuing to write admiringly of "authority" and disparagingly of the "democratic self." For his part, Unger has recently shed the traditionalist aspects of his early antiliberalism (including the longing for stability and security) and converted to a radically Nietzschean stress on open possibilities, human creativity, and untrammeled will. The writings of both these detractors of liberalism will be analyzed in detail below.[1] It must be said at the outset, however, that their main claims are far from new. Their thinking has an impressive historical pedigree. The forefathering of contemporary antiliberalism deserves stressing because contemporary antiliberals frequently neglect it. They typically furnish a stylized, even sanitized, genealogy for their central ideas. MacIntyre gladly invokes Aristotle or Aquinas, for instance, but omits the bitter attacks on liberal theory and institutions that have loomed so large in nineteenth- and twentieth-century political thought. This omission is characteristic.

Brilliant but now discredited fascist theorists, such as Giovanni Gentile and Carl Schmitt, violently assailed the liberal tradition. They excoriated liberalism for its atomistic individualism, its myth of the presocial individual, its scanting of the organic, its indifference to community, its denial that man belongs to a larger whole, its belief in the primacy of rights, its flight from "the political," its uncritical embrace of economic categories, its moral skepticism (or even nihilism), its decision to give abstract procedures and rules priority over substantive values and commitments, and its hypocritical reliance on the sham of judicial neutrality.[2] All of this sounds uncannily familiar.

Consider two specific examples. According to MacIntyre, liberals typically see "the social world as nothing but a meeting place for individual wills." In the same spirit, Unger criticizes "the liberal conception of society as an association of independent and conflicting individuals," and he blames liberalism for conceiving society as "a battleground of wills" where each person is "isolated from others." These claims are not unprecedented. Indeed, they cry out to be compared with various pronouncements by fascist writers—with, say, Gentile's remark that "the error of the old liberalism is the atomistic conception of society, understood as the accidental grouping and encounter of abstract individuals."[3]

Similarly, MacIntyre thinks he can refute liberal individualism simply by calling attention to the fact that "I confront the world as a member of this family, this household, this clan, this tribe, this city, this nation, this kingdom. There is no 'I' apart from these." Unger, too, believes that he can discredit the ideas of classic European liberals by noting that they "think of the subject as an individual, whose participation in groups is a secondary feature of his existence." MacIntyre's and Unger's tendentious invocations of man's social nature, however, were anticipated in almost every detail by, among others, the proto-fascist pamphleteer, Charles Maurras: "liberalism wants to disengage the individual from his natural or historical antecedents: it will emancipate him from family bonds, corporate bonds, and all the other social or traditional bonds."[4] According to Maurras, too, liberalism is an antisocial crusade against all moral and meaningful forms of human relatedness.

To juxtapose such citations is not to indulge in guilt by association. I am *not* insinuating that MacIntyre and Unger are quasi-fascists or fascist-sympathizers or fascists-with-a-human-face. I am saying, rather, that they have absorbed and reproduced rhetoric whose history and implications they have failed to ponder. I do not want to accuse contemporary antiliberals writing in America of harboring dangerous thoughts. I am not worried about the practical consequences of their ideas. (They benefit from historical circumstances that make them politically harmless.) I want to draw attention, instead, to the fundamentally ahistorical, and therefore unclear, character of their thinking. Antiliberals talk endlessly about rootedness and tradition, lamenting the deep lack of historical consciousness characteristic of modern times, but they nonchalantly disregard their own intellectual descent.

They could distinguish themselves fairly easily from their most unsavory precursors. (After all, they idealize "community," not the state or *das Volk*; they do not seek a leader to follow; they do not engage in specific scapegoating or a paranoiac search for real enemies to exterminate, and so forth.) But they make no clarifying effort to explain their differences from fascist philosophers whose rhetoric is often indistinguishable from their own. They thus leave readers perplexed. They blithely deplore what they consider the liberal individual's lack of "constitutive attachments," to pick another example, but they never mention that this complaint was long the centerpiece of antisemitic propaganda, of political attacks on "uprooted" and cosmopolitan Jews.[5]

Lack of attention to the origins and political abuse of their fondest ideas is not the only shortcoming of recent antiliberal writers. In studying individual antiliberals, of both the present and the past, I focus on two other defects as well: the unrealistic or unattractive nature of the political alternatives they propose and, most important, the internal incoherence of their arguments. Their criticisms of liberalism, while sometimes valid, are usually exaggerated. Liberal societies display numerous failings, to be sure. Works by liberal writers are also flawed. Nothing in the following analysis of antiliberal thought suggests that liberal institutions or liberal theories are beyond criticism. On the contrary: both liberal societies and liberal ideas should be criticized—separately and sequentially, not simultaneously, as in the antiliberal fashion.

To criticize liberalism effectively, one must distinguish sharply between two objects of criticism: liberal theories and liberal societies. This distinction is vital because liberalism will always be, to some extent, an unrealized aspiration. Liberal ideals are only imperfectly embodied in existing liberal societies. As a consequence, simultaneous criticism of idea and reality is profoundly confusing. Liberal theories and liberal societies are criticized best when criticized sequentially, each on its own terms. But this distinction itself is one that antiliberals resolutely refuse to draw. Indeed, the unwillingness to examine liberal theories and liberal societies separately is a trademark of antiliberal thought, for antiliberals assume that liberal societies perfectly embody liberal ideals. They conclude, therefore, that the obvious failings of liberal societies follow directly from the inadequacy of liberal principles. Liberal societies are defective because they have been successfully programmed with liberal ideas. Critics who think along these lines, of course, see no need to distinguish between the criticism of liberal texts and the criticism of liberal institutions. The two forms of criticism, they believe, are actually one and the same.

The casual mixture of theoretical and institutional criticism is confusing. At the same time it also has an unhappy practical result: it belittles the critical appraisal of liberal society in the light of liberal ideas. This is the most important form of assessment to which liberal societies are subject, however. Any approach that makes reform-minded criticism more difficult should be regarded with distrust. When a society calling itself liberal does not guarantee, say, equal voting rights or equality before the law, it acts in violation of liberal norms. If it excludes women or blacks or Jews from rights constitutionally guaranteed to all citizens, it is organized in a patently illiberal way. To point this out is one of the most vital tasks of political commentary. But criticism of this sort is possible only on the basis of a sharp distinction between norms and societies. Such *liberal* discontent with a purportedly liberal society is trivialized by antiliberals predisposed to see all social faults as logical consequences of liberal ideals.

Criticizing liberal theorists is no less necessary than criticizing liberal societies, and it, too, can be a perfectly liberal procedure. Think of Hume's attack on Locke's "original contract" theory, Mill's criticism of Bentham, or the mutual criticisms of Kantians and utilitarians. Liberal writers contradict themselves, as well as each other, and make all manner of logical and empirical mistakes. Moreover, ideas that were once largely persuasive can be rendered obsolete by the passage of time. (Most eighteenth-century works, for example, do not contain adequate answers to many pressing problems of the late twentieth century: overpopulation, mass immigration, violently contested borders, nuclear proliferation, international terrorism, destruction of the environment, depletion of natural resources, and so forth.) The antiliberals I examine below, however, are not critics of liberal theories or liberal texts in such an ordinary sense. They are not content with exposing liberalism's intellectual weak points or showing its irrelevance to a changed social scene. They are grander. They look at liberal theory not to find its intellectual weaknesses or reveal its obsolescence, but to discover *the origins of the contemporary crisis*. Rather than seeing liberalism, reasonably enough, as sometimes inadequate to the problems of the present, they view it as the unique source of the problems of the present. To comprehend our current dilemmas, they say, we must look to the flawed philosophical works that set modernity in motion. The interpretation of books along unfriendly lines, it seems, is a refined form of sociology. Indeed, the analysis of classical liberal theories is diagnostic of pathology on a social scale. The assumption that most important social pathologies arise from theoretical mistakes lends the antiliberals' highly abstract treatises a remarkable, though not wholly persuasive, aroma of political engagement.

Carl Schmitt and Leo Strauss, for all their differences, share this basic assumption. They also argue that liberalism is a hypertolerationist or "anything goes" ideology. Liberals take toleration to the point of capitulation, they charge. Liberals are wholly unable to defend itself when attacked—and so forth. On a modest scale, the present book is designed to refute this charge—to refute it in practice. Antiliberals sneer at liberalism and describe it as one vast mistake. My response is just as argumentative as their own writings. It is also, I hope, well-documented and fair. Contentious writers such as the ones I discuss, who, after all, declare the entire Western world except for themselves to be depraved and diseased, surely cannot complain about an adversarial rejoinder.

While trying to do for them what they have done for liberalism (to highlight their position's basic defects), I have not imitated their Manicheanism. I do not consider them devils or traitors, which is the way they often describe liberals. They are merely theorists who, despite some interesting and valid insights, are often inconsistent and wrong. My aim is to be critical, therefore, and not prosecutorial. I will have succeeded maximally if I convince the reader of nonmarxist antiliberalism's intellectual shortcomings. I will have succeeded minimally if I bring nonmarxist antiliberalism into focus as a unified subject for theoretical scrutiny and partisan debate.

The Anatomy of Antiliberalism

Introduction: What Is Antiliberalism?

Un jour viendra, et peut-être il n'est pas loin, où
Locke sera placé au nombre des écrivains qui ont fait
le plus de mal aux hommes.

—Maistre

Critics of liberal thought and practice cluster naturally into two distinct schools: marxist and nonmarxist. While Marxism has been exhaustively analyzed and researched, nonmarxist attacks on liberalism have seldom been studied from a primarily theoretical and critical point of view. Marxists generally denigrate liberal theory as the ideology of the business classes: all liberalism's defects, they say, follow from its role in justifying class privilege and power. Nonmarxist but still antiliberal writers take a different approach. They pay little attention to class, claiming instead that liberal ideology has infected and degraded all members of Western societies, employers as well as employees, rulers and ruled alike.

Marxists assert that bourgeois liberties are purely "formal"—privileges monopolized by a few and virtually useless to the disinherited majority. Nonmarxist antiliberals, by contrast, impugn the ideal of individual liberty itself, not its selective or incomplete realization. Marxist critics usually focus on the nineteenth century, when the ideology of individual rights was purportedly adopted by industrial elites to subjugate ordinary men and women. Nonmarxist critics are more likely to blur together nineteenth-century liberalism with its seventeenth- and eighteenth-century antecedents. Marxists are no less secular than liberals (they would eradicate religion, while liberals would depoliticize it). Nonmarxist antiliberals see secularism as a moral disaster. Like liberals, Marxists view ethnic identity and national solidarity as particularistic atavisms (they would eradicate ethnicity while liberals

1

would demilitarize it). Nonmarxist antiliberals, by contrast, see the cutting of ethnic roots as an unparalleled human catastrophe.

Other equally important distinctions can be added to these. Marxists extol science, technology, and economic development, for example. Nonmarxist antiliberals interpret the authority of science and the spread of materialistic attitudes as two of liberalism's most abhorrent sins. They do not present themselves as heirs to the French Revolution, as Marx emphatically did. In fact, antiliberals in my sense assert with one voice that Marxism and liberalism, while superficially opposed, share a common ancestry and are secretly allied. They are two offshoots of a single and spiritually hollow Enlightenment tradition.[1]

Antiliberalism as a Tradition

This book ignores Marxism. It is devoted exclusively to nonmarxist criticisms of liberal theory and institutions. (Socialist writers are mentioned in passing only when, like R. H. Tawney, they criticize liberal society on the basis of explicitly premodern customs and ideals.) Historians, to be sure, have long studied the communitarian longing to overturn "bourgeois society" and redeem the degenerate present through a spiritual revolution. The interwar search for a "third force"—with its associated slogan, "neither capitalism nor communism"—has been voluminously documented and discussed. Two exemplary monographs surveying the political culture of nonmarxist antiliberalism, in quite different national and historical contexts, are Zeev Sternhell's *Neither Right nor Left* and Andrzej Walicki's *The Slavophile Controversy*. As these richly informative works suggest, nonmarxist antiliberalism is a pan-European movement whose history stretches back at least two centuries.[2] Sometimes on the ascendant, sometimes in decline, this antiliberalism has never wholly vanished from the scene. (Reawakened by the collapse of Marxism, and a volatile mixture of economic chaos and ethnic hatred, the antiliberal spirit shows menacing signs of renewal today across the former communist world.)

Recrudescent tribalisms and fundamentalisms remind us that antiliberalism exists as a political force and a cultural atmosphere. But is it, or has it ever been, a philosophical tradition? Do its exponents advance any serious theoretical claims? Is it a single tradition at all or is the word merely a catch-all misused by defenders of liberalism (such as myself) to lump together a diverse set of critics who have little in common? An all-purpose label such as "antiliberal," of course, does not suffice to describe the theorists I analyze individually in subsequent chapters. It simply helps focus attention on a range of arguments and attitudes shared by some of liberalism's most important nonmarxist critics. Antiliberalism *is* a resilient, diverse, fairly consistent, unbroken—but theoretically understudied—intellectual tradition. Its unity does not consist in uniformity, to be sure, but in a handful of basic assumptions plus, above all, a common enemy. That various of antiliberalism's nonmarxist critics share a core of attitudes and beliefs is a fundamental premise of this book. Before anatomizing antiliberal theory and exploring its several variants, therefore, I must show that it exists. I must inventory and analyze the positions held by its several exponents and provide examples to convince skeptical readers that I am not imposing an arbitrary classification upon unruly historical material. I must also explain how antiliberal attacks on liberalism differ from standard socialist and conservative attacks, and from liberalism's criticisms of itself.

To enter into the perspective of antiliberal writers, we must first understand what they mean by the "liberalism" they aim to dispute and overthrow and why they view it with such disfavor. To weigh their arguments and respond to them fully, we must develop a concept of liberalism of our own.

What Is Liberalism?

Very briefly, liberalism is a political theory and program that flourished from the middle of the seventeenth to the middle of the nineteenth century. It had important antecedents, of course, and it continues to be a living tradition today. Among the classic liberal theorists must be counted Locke, Montesquieu, Adam Smith, Kant, Madison, and J. S. Mill. Liberal institutions and practices first developed in the seventeenth and eighteenth centuries, in the Netherlands, England and Scotland, the United States, and (less successfully) France. Liberal principles were articulated not only in theoretical texts but also in the English Habeas Corpus Act, Bill of Rights, and Act of Toleration (1679, 1688–89), the first ten Amendments to the American Constitution, and the *Déclaration des droits de l'homme* (both of 1789).

The core practices of a liberal political order are religious toleration, freedom of discussion, restrictions on police behavior, free elections, constitutional government based on a separation of powers, publicly inspectable state budgets to inhibit corruption, and economic policy committed to sustained growth on the basis of private ownership and freedom of contract. Liberalism's four core norms or values are *personal security* (the monopolization of legitimate violence by agents of the state who are themselves monitored and regulated by law), *impartiality* (a single system of law applied equally to all), *individual liberty* (a broad sphere of freedom from collective or governmental supervision, including freedom of conscience, the right to be different, the right to pursue ideals one's neighbor thinks wrong, the freedom to travel and emigrate, and so forth), and *democracy* or the right to participate in lawmaking by means of elections and public discussion through a free press. That public disagreement is a creative force may have been the most novel and radical principle of liberal politics.

Concerning equality, the liberal attitude is traditionalism turned upside down. In traditional societies, as liberals understood them, inherited inequalities were accepted, while new economic inequalities were unwelcome. Liberals wanted to reverse this pattern, banning aristocracy while considering new inequalities of wealth as perfectly legitimate.[3] The liberal societies they helped construct reject all claims to inherited monopoly, especially the authority of a few "great" families owning large tracts of land. But classical liberals were not militantly egalitarian because they thought that *poverty and dependency* were more pressing problems than economic inequality itself. Why? Liberals welcomed commercial society because they believed, correctly, that economic competition would create (along with economic inequalities) enough economic prosperity to increase the welfare, as well as the personal security and independence, of "the lowest ranks of the people."[4]

Liberalism's Wrongs

This thumbnail sketch of liberalism is excruciatingly brief and inadequate.[5] Even skimpy remarks can help prepare the ground for an introduction to liberalism's enemies, however. Of what crimes is such a philosophy or ideology charged by its nonmarxists detractors? What defects do they discern in liberal practices and institutions? What objections do they have to liberal values and norms? Why do antiliberals describe liberalism as a whole (theories and societies mixed promiscuously together) as one vast mistake?

These questions cannot be answered in a simple way, for antiliberalism is no more monolithic than liberalism itself. Nonmarxist antiliberalism comes in many stripes and the different versions need to be distinguished carefully from one another. Even antiliberals who belong to distinct and rival camps (such as Carl Schmitt, Leo Strauss, Alasdair MacIntyre, and Roberto Unger) share some themes in common, however. They all engage in *Kulturkritik*, for example, and their criticisms of modern culture follow a fairly standardized format whereby "disparagement of liberalism forms part of a general lamentation over the moral and spiritual degeneration of modern society."[6] Higher spiritual truths are endangered in contemporary societies, they all explain, and liberalism is centrally at fault.

Even at its most philosophical, admittedly, antiliberalism is as much a mindset as a theory. It is always a sensibility as well as an argument. Its exponents define themselves negatively, in opposition to liberalism. To comprehend those who belong to the antiliberal tradition, therefore, we must first take stock of the dangers, threats, or diabolical forces they earnestly warn us against. Their enmity is typically lavished on individualism, rationalism, humanitarianism, rootlessness, permissiveness, universalism, materialism, skepticism, and cosmopolitanism. These corrosive attitudes, they say—not the separation of powers, competitive elections, a free press, religious toleration, public budgets, or judicial controls on the police—represent the core of liberal politics. These attitudes are also the prime symptoms of cultural decay and moral disintegration in the modern world. To identify a given writer as an antiliberal, then, we must look to the objects of his revulsion. Attention must also be paid to style and stance so we can learn to recognize a work of antiliberal theory when we come across it. Here is a preliminary checklist of antiliberalism's distinguishing characteristics.

Basic Attitudes and Claims

Antiliberal writers often jolt their readers awake by identifying a culprit and conducting a trial. Alternatively, they present themselves as diagnostic pathologists: as doctors of disorder. They often write long commentaries on old books, but their guiding purpose is to decry and diagnose the rot of contemporary society. They denounce "the twentieth century's moral poverty" as they warn us about some impending danger—about "the political crisis of today's world and the oncoming spiritual crisis," for instance.

Different critics focus on different aspects of the underlying "crisis" of modern society. But most ring an alarm bell about the universal disintegration of society into atomized individuals—selfish, calculating, materialistic, each at war with all the rest. Human beings need roots and togetherness, but liberal society pulls them apart and condemns them to an agitated and rootless mobility.

Antiliberals also deplore the "deviation of the Enlightenment," which they consider to be "a disaster which is very much with us." They are referring, in this case, to "the calamity of an autonomous, irreligious humanistic consciousness." Secular humanism, they assert, lies at the origins of the liberal disease. In the early modern age "a total emancipation occurred from the moral heritage of Christian centuries," from "the heritage of the preceding one thousand years." Liberalism was the political offspring of this fatal emancipation.

So was Marxism. The critics discussed here unfailingly argue that liberalism and Marxism can be traced to a common root, ordinarily described as a normative commitment to "boundless materialism," the emancipation and development of human individuality, "freedom from religion," "an allegedly scientific approach to society," and an exclusive focus on mankind's "earthly happiness."

Nonmarxist or antimarxist antiliberals also identify liberalism with modernity, as if there were no significant illiberal strands in modern culture or illiberal movements in modern politics. As a result, they uniformly underestimate what any historian of the nineteenth and twentieth centuries could explain: the fragility and beleaguered state of the liberal tradition.

The malady of modern societies, they go on to claim, stems from a viral infection with liberal theory. The intellectual disaster occurred at some dramatic turning-point in the past, usually during the seventeenth century: "it was several centuries ago in Europe that this philosophy was born." That the modern "crisis" has intellectual origins is crucial for all antiliberals. A philosophical error or act of disobedience marks the onset of modern corruption: "the mistake must be at the root, at the very foundation of thought in modern times." This philosophical misstep is often described as a cover-up, or act of forgetting. Some important spiritual truth, well known to preliberal societies, was repressed or lost. Social amnesia, with catastrophic consequences, was philosophically induced.

Finally, nonmarxist antiliberals have a burning sense of mission. Readers who accept the root-and-branch criticism of liberalism are promised that they can take part in an unprecedented, world-reshaping struggle to revive forgotten wisdom. They can help pull humanity back from the brink. If the repressed truth can be retrieved, modern society will not only be diagnosed, it will also be miraculously or heroically cured.

The citations in the previous paragraphs are prototypically antiliberal in my sense. They have been drawn from two essays written by Alexander Solzhenitsyn.[7] The viewpoint expressed and even the vocabulary are astonishingly familiar. Indeed, Solzhenitsyn's lexicon is so similar to, say, Strauss's or MacIntyre's, that we cannot help thinking that a single antiliberal *Geist*, bridging national and religious traditions, is speaking through them all. Dissimilarities coexist with parallels, of course. Neither Strauss nor MacIntyre, for instance, seriously proposes purging his country of foreign influences or leading his people back to its roots, thereby saving it from the corruption of modern times. But the discourse of "crisis" and moral impoverishment, the pathogenetic approach to "modernity," the tracing of Marxism and liberalism to a common root, the assumption that disobedient philosophers are at fault, and the veiled promise of salvation are common to them all.

These claims or attitudes are recycled with impressive perseverance in numberless works, including contemporary ones. Found together, they constitute the unmistakable trademark of the antiliberal mind in action. Whenever a book, article, or public lecture contains this series of ideas, it belongs to *the antiliberal tradition* as I understand it. The important differences among the writers studied below, while important, also serve to make underlying commonalities stand out.

Origin and Structure of This Book

This work began as an examination of contemporary antiliberals writing in America during the 1970s and 1980s—in particular, MacIntyre and Unger. In following out their basic arguments, I found myself driven backwards through time to writers of a larger stature—first to Strauss and Schmitt, and eventually to one of the truly brilliant originators of the antiliberal movement, Joseph de Maistre. The criticisms of liberalism advanced by Maistre and Schmitt are bold and uncompromising. (A few of them strike me as valid or, at least, difficult to refute.) This cannot be said of the criticisms put forward by postwar antiliberals. In these more recent writings, the antiliberal approach has been mollified or diluted, and perhaps academicized. To understand why antiliberalism today assumes a rather anodyne form, in any case, we must look back to its earlier and harsher incarnations.

While I began my research with contemporary authors and worked backwards, in organizing this book I have taken the opposite path. In Part One I examine a series of distinctive antiliberal theorists, more or less chronologically, beginning with Maistre and traveling forward to MacIntyre and Unger. (Only because they differ importantly among themselves, of course, may separate chapters profitably be devoted to each.) My criticisms—and my aim is to be critical—are mostly internal. That is, I focus on the intellectual inconsistencies and confusions marring each of the works discussed, and on the inadequacy of the practical alternatives suggested. I conclude on a more general level, describing and criticizing the main theoretical fallacies of "communitarianism," the form of antiliberalism currently most popular in the United States.

In Part Two I turn to a more specialized topic, the historical account of liberalism promulgated in antiliberal works. I restate the most common antiliberal claims about the history of liberal thought and try to show why, in large measure, these claims are misguided. In my effort to correct the principal mistakes of antiliberal historiography, I assemble the elements of an alternative portrait of liberalism. This allows me to end the book on a somewhat more positive note. By way of an afterword, I return briefly to the variety of antiliberalisms studied, attempting to mark out more precisely the commonalities and differences among them; and I reconsider what we have learned about liberalism from studying its most unforgiving critics.

The chronological sequence in which I treat individual authors is largely a matter of convenience. I have not written a narrative history of antiliberal theory. In Part One my aim is to understand a handful of important antiliberals writing in diverse historical situations. Their similarities are all the more striking because they are reacting to such different conditions. I endeavor first to approach each antiliberal on his own terms and, secondarily, to establish parallelisms among them. Intellectual influence or lineage are of limited interest, though such relations are occasionally observed. This study as a whole, as a consequence, remains much more theoretical than historical. It certainly does not provide a comprehensive survey of a far-flung and apparently irrepressible tradition. It leaves out many important antiliberal writers who could and probably should have been included. What it offers, by way of compensation, is a relatively simple analytical framework for classifying and evaluating "dateless" antiliberal arguments. I have dug into the subsoil to unearth what I take to be the main lineaments of the antiliberal mind.

Maistre, Schmitt, Strauss, MacIntyre, and Unger display a healthy range of antiliberalisms. Whatever uniformity can be discovered among them is compatible with colorful variety. These particular writers were selected, in fact, because they are distinctive, intrinsically interesting, prominent in American debates, widely influential, and representative of broader trends. (I have intentionally excluded halfway communitarians, such as Michael Walzer, who are emphatically committed to individual autonomy, tolerance for diversity, and private rights.) Not even the writers chosen for detailed scrutiny are "pure" antiliberals, to be sure. All are eclectic to some degree and sometimes veer toward more moderate and defensible positions—such as Tory conservatism or Augustinian Christianity.

Unlike the antiliberal pamphleteers studied by Sternhell, moreover, the contemporary writers discussed below (such as MacIntyre and Unger) have never been associated personally with militant "cadres" or powerful social movements of rage. Fascist theorists, active between the world wars, advanced many of the same claims as present-day antiliberals in the United States. But fascism contained virulent elements (such as racism, obsession about "the enemy within," the *Führerprinzip*, soil worship, the cult of violence, and so forth) that went far beyond anything suggested by postwar antiliberals addressing a largely American audience. I have juxtaposed nonaggressive communitarians to fascists, therefore, not because their politics are comparable (communitarians, as mentioned, seem to have no politics), but because the cases they make against liberalism are surprisingly similar.

While recent antiliberals are almost wholly silent about the years of fascism, the fascist experience nevertheless reshaped the rhetoric they use. After 1945, for one thing, the communitarian attack on "bourgeois society" was radically demilitarized. The demand for patriotic sacrifice was played down. True, postwar antiliberal writings have not been totally purged of occasional appeals to manliness, martial glory, and the idea that warfare breeds "virtue."[8] But the militaristic residues in these works cannot be taken seriously. When MacIntyre or Unger suggest *en passant* that killing enemies or risking one's life in the carnage of battle provides a solution to the spiritual emptiness of commercial society, readers cringe but then rightly dismiss the literal implications of what they say. A prewar antiliberal, such as Schmitt, was obviously in greater earnest.

There are antiliberalisms and antiliberalisms, therefore. While sharing a common enemy, nonmarxist antiliberals attack it in diverse ways and quarrel heatedly among themselves. Despite their differences, however, the writers discussed below share a radical sensibility that invites a common treatment. None of them criticize liberalism, for example, in the name of universalistic or Enlightenment ideals. Assembled for a group portrait, they reveal the charming variety observable in any extended family. But they are certainly kindred spirits and, together, reveal to us the multiple faces of a single tradition. The most promising place to begin a case-by-case study of this powerful intellectual movement is with the Catholic reaction to the French Revolution.

Part I / The Antiliberals

1 / Maistre and the Antiliberal Tradition

The individual antiliberals analyzed and reappraised in the following chapters differ from one another in a number of important ways. They define their common enemy almost identically, however, as the secular humanism of the Enlightenment. And they display a uniform contempt for liberal institutions and ideas. Naively or artfully, they present themselves as iconoclasts, innovators, thinkers "against the grain." In reality, they adhere unswervingly to a larger tradition—a tradition they seldom openly discuss. To bring this underground tradition into the daylight is one of the principal purposes of this book.

What is the genealogy of antiliberalism? When did the antiliberal tradition first emerge? There could be no antiliberalism, first of all, before liberalism itself took shape. Although antiliberals may appeal to the authority of Plato or Augustine, the origins of antiliberalism as an intellectual movement should probably be located in the eighteenth century. At the very outset, it was Rousseau who helped popularize an "antibourgeois" sensibility that profoundly affected subsequent critics of liberal theory and society. A century later, Nietzsche combined his scorn for Kant and Mill with a scorching diagnosis of the pathologies of modern Europe. To help grasp the historical depth of antiliberalism, however, I have chosen to consider directly neither Rousseau nor Nietzsche, but Joseph de Maistre. Maistre devoted his life to execrating and pillorying "the horrible literature of the eighteenth century."[1] No early theorist pioneered so many central antiliberal ideas as he.

Maistre combatted liberal ideas and institutions without ever employing the word *liberalism*, which did not come into common usage until after his death in 1821. He was one of the first to attack liberal rights as fictions or abstractions, inadequate to the concrete richness

13

of human relationships. He argued that the genuine antonym of "legal" was not "arbitrary" but "concrete." He exposed the absurdity of the Déclarations des droits de l'homme, prefaced to the successive French constitutions of the 1790s, by pointing out that "there is no such thing as *man* in the world. I have seen, during my life, Frenchmen, Italians, Russians, etc. . . . But as far as *man* is concerned, I declare that I have never in my life met him; if he exists, he is unknown to me."[2] But sarcasm about human equality and constitutionally protected rights was not his only contribution to the antiliberal crusade. He also perfected and popularized the habit of blaming a conspiracy of progressive intellectuals for all the world's woes.

Long before Carl Schmitt, Maistre contended that Enlightenment skepticism toward the biblical God led to a violent hatred of political authority. Before Leo Strauss, he argued that ordinary men and women need to be anaesthetized by fairy tales and that, as a consequence, philosophers must hide their real thoughts. (He also referred to Bacon, Locke, and Hume as teachers of "evil."[3]) Before Alasdair MacIntyre, he derided the Enlightenment's atomistic conception of the person. He apotheosized national community and longed for the fusion of the individual into the group. And he strongly believed that atheistical reason breeds endless disagreement: if people think for themselves, their ideas will never converge. Before Christopher Lasch, Maistre treated modern science as an immoral power that drags mankind into unhappiness. Before Martin Heidegger, he identified the central sin of modern thought as the deification of the ego or the belief that the world can become wholly transparent to the sovereign human mind. And before Roberto Unger, he denied that liberal institutions could last: abstract rules cannot create a coherent order among individuals attached to purely personal values. Maistre wove all these strands into a single doctrine at the beginning of the nineteenth century. Isaiah Berlin may be exaggerating when he writes that "Maistre's deeply pessimistic vision is the heart of the totalitarianisms of both left and right, of the twentieth century."[4] But Maistre certainly deserves to be recognized as one of the principal shapers of the antiliberal mentality.

Maistre had no good models to imitate—no more than did the French revolutionaries to whom he was responding. He is therefore harder to classify than the theorists who wrote in his wake. Indeed, the originality and elusiveness—not to mention occasional frenzy—of his thought is quite remarkable. He is frequently described as a traditionalist or counterrevolutionary. But such conventional labels are misleading. To portray him as a staid spokesman for class-based conservatism is to distort and banalize his outlook. The eccentricity of his mind is papered over by Schmitt's prosaic remark that Maistre "took sides against the French Revolution because he thought it was wrong."[5] While partly true, this trite assessment is misleading. For Maistre personally welcomed the French Revolution. It gave him a chance to escape from the drudgery of life as a provincial magistrate. (He was already forty-six in 1789.) Like his intellectual descendants, he relished the opportunity to struggle with evil on the world stage, to pose as a knight of the faith locked in a last-ditch battle to deliver civilization from its enemies. Moreover, his personally positive attitude toward the Revolution spilled surprisingly into his theoretical works.

Analyzing the revolutionary wars, for example, Maistre remarked that Robespierre had rescued France from the brink of disaster and prevented its dismemberment by foreign armies. Of those who died during the Terror, he disturbingly continued, none were innocent. Almost all Frenchmen were implicated in the insurrection. The "moral degradation" of the eighteenth-century nobility was a principal cause of the Revolution. French nobles, therefore, had only themselves to blame for their misfortunes. Even Louis XVI had granted civil liberties to Protestants. So the guillotine's victims reaped what they had sown. The Parisian upheaval of 1789–94 was the political equivalent of the Lisbon earthquake; it struck in exactly the right place at exactly the right time. Describing the scaffold as a kind of "altar," Maistre displayed an eerily pious attitude toward the death penalty—even toward the death penalty inflicted on Louis XVI. Mankind in general deserves to suffer; eighteenth-century French elites were especially guilty. God has every reason to unleash a cosmic Reign of Terror. The 1790s were cruel and catastrophic; hence they were just. And, he adds, they were also "interesting" in a queerly aesthetic sense.[6] These are not standard counterrevolutionary claims echoed by most conservative pamphleteers. They divulge the startling unconventionality of Maistre's mind.

The justice of atrocious human suffering, admittedly, is only one of Maistre's themes. He actually advances three distinct interpretations of the Terror. First, he explains it as the causally necessary result of eighteenth-century anticlericalism, antiauthoritarianism, and abstract humanism. Second, he presents it as God's plan for revivifying religion in France. Third, he describes it as just another expression of the great law of mutual slaughter that dominates all human history. (According to this final view, the guillotining of thousands was not peculiarly modern, and it will not have any particularly agreeable side effects.) These strange and inconsistent explanations of the Terror are, however, accompanied by more straightforwardly antiliberal claims.

The Social Nature of Man

Maistre's basic stance is not unfamiliar. On a wide range of issues, he was an unwavering antiliberal.[7] He even defended the Spanish Inquisition and opposed the emancipation of Russia's serfs. He claimed to despise freedom of speech. The folly of allowing all ranks of people to communicate freely is destroying European society. Tolerance is political suicide, a regime's sickly refusal to attack its attackers. Public deliberation is wholly sterile. If a government is criticized, even slightly, it will utterly collapse: "to annihilate it or submit it to discussion by each individual amount to the same thing." And the postulate of civic equality is thoroughly incompatible with any form of stable rule: "there can be no government if the masses who are ruled consider themselves the equals of those who rule."[8]

Like most subsequent enemies of liberalism, Maistre was indifferent to the details of institutional design. He emphasized, therefore, a more fundamental, almost metaphysical argument, and one that left a permanent mark on the rhetoric of the entire antiliberal school. Together with Louis de Bonald, whom he greatly admired, he ridiculed liberalism for its defective understanding of the self.[9] Liberal theory—and, therefore, liberal institutions—are founded on a descriptively inaccurate theory of the person. Liberals assume that individuals, before they ever join society, have a firm grasp on their own needs and can strike mutually beneficial bargains to ensure their satisfaction. But the socially uninfluenced individual does not exist. As a result, "the social contract is a chimera." You cannot dig beneath society to uncover man's natural state for the simple reason that "society is coeval with man." Or, to put the point another way, "for mankind there has never been a time prior to society because, before the formation of political societies, man was not yet man." The "isolated man" is an unnatural perversion. Man is a thoroughly social animal. Therefore, inherited ways of life should be accepted unthinkingly, never questioned.[10]

Maistre was one of the first to brandish man's social nature as a decisive argument against liberal institutions. Liberals blindly deny the social nature of man. But how can asocial atoms deliberate collectively and decide to enter into relations of mutual restraint and civilized cooperation? What language, for a start, would they speak? Deliberation presupposes language, and language cannot exist without society. Liberal fairy tales about an original contract should thus be discarded and replaced by an empirical and anthropologically sound approach to human behavior. Illusions about voluntariness and consent should yield to a realistic awareness of heteronomy and cultural constraints. (Note that Maistre's persistent focus on the social constitution of the individual eventually brought him into some conflict with the Catholic Church. The dogmas of original sin and individual immortality are difficult to reconcile with a hypersocialized conception of the individual. But then again, he was never a conventional Christian.)

Maistre's trend-setting "discovery" that human beings, by nature, live in society is not wholly empirical. When he appeals to nature, he means to say that society is where God intends human beings to live: "it was God who made man sociable." God's edict is what gives universal sociality its morally binding force. Maistre views sociality theologically; this is why he considers it not only a universal fact but also a universal norm. Theological premises alone allow him to treat "the social" as a normative rather than merely descriptive or value-neutral category. He perceived the dissolution of social bonds in the Europe of his time as a deviation from the divine injunction of sociality. The breakdown of traditional ways of life was occasioned by sin, by human disobedience to God's will. The eighteenth-century slackening of social attachments resulted principally from the philosophical "war to the death" waged against religion.[11]

Why do our contemporary "communitarians" habitually treat "the social" as a moral obligation rather than an inevitable condition? Here is a partial response: the antiliberal style of reasoning, which seems illogical today, originally depended on theological premises that later dropped from sight. When no longer based on the idea of a divine injunction, however, the claim that man's sociality is morally binding becomes unintelligible, even though it may remain psychologically attractive to some. In Maistre's argument, however, communitarian and religious forms of antiliberalism were tightly linked.

Religion is the "cement" of society. Secular philosophy, by contrast, is not only "the greatest scourge of the universe," but also "the universal solvent." The rot began with the Reformation. Protestantism encouraged human pride to revolt against authority; obedience was replaced by discussion. Philosophy continued along the same path. It, too, "corroded the cement that unites people." As a result, "there are no longer any moral communities." Reason can destroy a community, but only religion can create one. (This asymmetry helps reconcile the seemingly inconsistent claims, also characteristic for later antiliberals, that Enlightenment reason is simultaneously impotent and pernicious.) As the political expression of humanistic doubt, the Revolution was a direct assault on man's sociality, "an antireligious and antisocial insurrection" or, more pointedly, "a rebellion against God." It was the logical consequence of "the horrifying project of extinguishing both Christianity and sovereignty in Europe." Divorce man from divinity, bring religion into question, and the public spirit expires.[12] Doubt looses atomism on society, and isolation, and selfishness.

Authoritative Decisions

Schmitt insists that "the immortal de Maistre" was a militantly "unromantic" thinker. Antiliberalism is austere, manly, tough, and realistic, uninfected by the dreamy self-indulgence of romanticism. Working in this illusionless tradition, Maistre was sober and fact-minded, Schmitt says, committed to institutional *fixité*, not emotionalism or personal expressiveness. He was certainly not nostalgic for some lost peasant paradise. His "resolute advocacy of the Church's right of control" was naturally rejected by romantics such as Schlegel. He was a diplomat and man of affairs "with his own responsibility." As a result, he had no tolerance for the evasiveness and dissipation of sissy types like Adam Müller. His allegiance to monarchism was "the consequence of a specifically legalistic and extremely unromantic need for a final authority." His nationalism was not romantic either. It was a logical corollary of his distaste for liberal-romantic bosh about "the brotherhood of man." Schmitt also agreed heartily with Maistre that man needs to be ruled from above and that a virulent hatred of authority is destroying the world. What he most admired, however, was Maistre's "reduction of the state to the moment of the decision, to a pure decision not based on reason and discussion and not justifying itself, that is, to an absolute decision created out of nothingness."[13] God-like authority, such as he and Maistre both revered, required a wholly uncommanded commander, a monocratic ruler, beyond all influence and all rules.

Schmitt's portrait of Maistre is partly accurate. Maistre did believe that unquestionable decision-making authority was indispensable to social order. Republican governments are suitable for small countries during brief periods. Otherwise, "all men are born for monarchy." It is ludicrous to assert that man is born free, while observing him everywhere in chains. History shows that human beings are destined to be subjects, created to live in a hierarchical society where political power is amassed at the top. A king is the center of society, its linchpin, and the source of its moral unity. Monarchy is natural because individuals are spontaneously defiant, cannot make any important decisions on their own, and must have their refractory wills broken by overwhelming force. The sovereign must be "infallible" in a purely practical or legal sense: no one can have the power to declare him mistaken.[14] "Authority" must be perceived as perfect and beyond criticism. (In private, it should be mentioned, Maistre unstintingly denounced the stupidity and incompetence of actual monarchs.)

Liberal theorists are deluded: "they brag of their enlightenment, but they know nothing because they do not know themselves." They fatuously believe that human beings are naturally good. This is why they deny the absolute necessity of a divinely sanctioned authority to punish wicked humanity and keep it under control. But there is no thesis more frequently confirmed by experience than the ineradicability of original sin. Man was born evil and remains so: "l'homme est mauvais, horriblement mauvais." Such incurably corrupt creatures cannot be perfected, or even bettered, by enlightenment and secular education. They must be brought to heel. They cannot live without an unlimited ruler whose decisions are beyond dispute.[15]

What could be more ridiculous, Maistre asks, than the liberal attempt to emancipate human beings from authority? This "liberation" seems desirable only because of an unsophisticated conception of human preferences. In truth, the mind is a chaotic tangle. Individuals are invariably "weak and blind." Their will is not steady, but "wavering and irresolute." This inborn unsteadiness has its roots in man's bifurcated nature: every individual is a small battlefield and replicates inwardly the cosmic struggle between the forces of good and evil. As a microcosm of universal chaos, man has neither stable nor consistent preferences: "he does not know what he wants, he wants what he does not want, he does not want what he wants." That is a capsule summary of Maistrean psychology. Conclusive proof of human irrationality, myopia, and weakness of will is that those who sincerely believe in the eternal torments of hellfire still do nothing to avoid sin. It is preposterous, in any case, to call a distracted, spellbound, and passion-tossed creature such as man "free" simply because he is liberated from political constraints and allowed to maximize his utility. An individual's utility changes from moment to moment. Once he is satisfied, he becomes dissatisfied again. He is "always discontent with what he has; he loves only what he does not have."[16] He has no steady grip on what his utility is. A creature who believes that the grass is always greener on the other side is not a rational maximizer. He is profoundly sick. His whole life is a disease.

Because they ignore all this, and especially the deep human need to be ruled from above, liberals advocate self-government. They favor such an unworkable arrangement from naive confidence in mankind's intrinsic goodness and susceptibility to improvement through education. Enlightenment humanism and rationalism are expressions of humanity's eternal rebelliousness. True, man is a born *frondeur:* "the human heart is continually in rebellion against authority, which constricts and annoys it." Nevertheless, mankind's inherently mutinous tendencies were seldom so brazenly expressed as they have been in modern times. An antipower ethos is now poisoning Europe.[17] This seditious impulse erupted during the Reformation, inspired Enlightenment impiety, and finally unleashed the murderousness of the Terror. (Maistre sometimes explains the bureaucratic slaughter of 1792–94, paradoxically, as the natural result of a distinctively modern hatred of power.)

Because they slight human depravity, liberals deny the necessity of a final decision-maker. Maistre bequeathed this diagnosis of liberalism to Schmitt, among others. He also taught subsequent antiliberals that hostility toward political authority is rooted in "hatred for divinity." Political predilections mirror underlying religious commitments: a polity without a sovereign replicates a universe without God. Seen from this perspective, liberalism is the secularized or politicized form of "theophobia." The philosophes attacked God because, psychologically, the Divinity is the most potent symbol of authority.[18] Democratic ideology is rooted in a revolt against heaven. If people believed sincerely in God, if they truly thought that the whole cosmos were governed autocratically by a wise and omnipotent deity, they would never feel attracted to a democratic organization of political life. Maistre defines democracy, in fact, as the absence of sovereignty, which makes it almost indistinguishable from anarchy.

Esotericism

Maistre's influence on Schmitt is fairly direct and easy to document. On Leo Strauss's thought, by contrast, he seems to have had little or no impact. (Given Strauss's atheism, this is no surprise.) Nevertheless, the parallels between the two theorists cry out for comment. According to Maistre, for instance, the few philosophical "initiates" of antiquity wisely kept their superior knowledge "secluded in the temples," hidden away from the many. And Maistre, too, is exceptionally fond of the argument, advanced in Plato's *Phaedrus*, that speaking is superior to writing because speakers can be more selective than writers about the recipients of their communications.[19] Indeed, Maistre makes it possible, for the first time, to see how Schmitt and Strauss, decisionism and esotericism, may be combined in a single theory.

Maistre actually seems less disturbed by the decay of authoritarian political institutions (a Schmittian theme), than by the erosion of religion (a Straussian one). He argues that "we have just seen the social state shaken to its foundations because there was too much liberty in Europe and not enough religion."[20] As Strauss might have said, secularization is the crisis of the West. The attempt to detach men from God is "le chemin du néant," a pathway into the abyss. Unbelief is what makes the eighteenth century, which has ended only on the calendar, one of the most shameful and unhappy periods of human history. Man cannot live without some opinions adopted prior to examination and rational justification: "there is nothing more important for him than prejudices." To behave properly, individuals need beliefs, not perplexities. Ordinary men and women should be painstakingly gulled into believing that the guilty suffer more than the innocent, even in this world. About the view that virtue is not rewarded, and vice not punished, until the afterlife, one of the characters in the *Soirées* says: "if this proposition is not false, it nevertheless seems to me extremely dangerous."[21] Only liberals would be foolish enough to deny the indispensability of mesmerizing dogmas and consoling lies.

The gravest error of the Enlightenment was to overestimate the human capacity to justify authority. Only institutions that are sacralized can survive: "no human institution is durable if it does not have a religious foundation." The origins of sovereignty must appear to lie beyond the sphere of human power. People must believe that "every form of sovereignty is the immediate result of the will of God" or that "all sovereignty comes from God." This is the meaning of Maistre's opaque phrase: "the power of sovereignty is entirely moral." The authority of rulers is based neither on reason nor on force, but (as Schmitt, too, would later say) on political theology. Without the Koran, the entire edifice of Ottoman power would collapse in the wink of an eye. Power must be consecrated because "human beings never respect what they have made themselves." When individuals make, or believe they make, institutions, they assume they can also unmake them. Who will obey a sovereign whom he can depose? Who will comply with a law he can revoke? Only an authority surrounded by a nimbus of inevitability will be consistently obeyed. The people will acquiesce in a government only when they sense that they can neither create nor destroy it. Law must therefore acquire the "character of sanctity and immutability."[22] Liberal advocates of elected government and citizen participation in lawmaking deny the mind-entrancing power of the sacred. Secularism has made them unspeakably obtuse about human nature and the psychological preconditions for social order.

From a deconsecrating or rational perspective, no government can be legitimate. Realistically, all sovereignty is usurped. The truth about power does not bear inspection. Thus only a self-ignorant society—"closed" in the Straussian sense—can prosper and survive. The most enduring and civilized nations of antiquity had thoroughly religious constitutions. The sunlight of reason evaporates the foundations of political obligation. Authority and subjection thrive in darkness. People will obey—as they must do, for their own good—only if their minds are stunned into abjectness and reverence by unintelligible arcana. The original illegitimacy of all sovereignty must therefore be shrouded in mystery.[23]

For Maistre, in other words, "that which we should not know is more important than what we should know." He presents this argument in a completely secular manner; it should appeal, he writes, even to those who mock the idea of God. (This is how it would have appealed to Strauss.) Social stability requires, in addition to reason and force, an unquestioning belief that laws cannot be changed, that things cannot be other than they are. False necessity is mankind's only hope. Any belief which is socially useful must be considered "true." Destabilizing suspicions of arbitrariness will disappear if people are raised to believe that divine action has established the present order, that is, if they imbibe as children "the dogma of a divine lawgiver." Disillusioned reason overturns dogmatic beliefs. It takes away our deepest moral convictions but puts nothing in their place. When natural reverence is effaced by skepticism, "all is lost."[24]

Acids of Science

Maistre's veneration of religion is matched by his aversion to science. The scientific theory that the earth is a fragment of solar matter drawn off by a passing comet millions of years ago, and now hurtling through empty space, if accepted as a serious alternative to the Creation story, has utterly nihilistic implications. The explanation of natural events by reference to atoms and molecules degrades and soils the human spirit. Science hardens man and desiccates his heart. Scientists make bad citizens and worthless statesmen. It is not surprising that men of low birth succeed in science just as well as the sons of fine families. The very language of science is mechanical and shallow. Squatting ignominiously over nature to scrutinize its regularities causes individuals to lose all sense of human dignity. The scientific approach to man himself, moreover, tends to reduce human beings to animals. As a result, civilization is being "degraded by science" and, Maistre adds, "it is the ultimate degree of degradation."[25] From a moral point of view, science is a deadly enemy.

True, Maistre seems proud that Providence has reserved the most glorious achievements in physical sciences to Christian nations; and he thinks that natural science can serve as a safety valve, keeping intellectuals amused and distracted from politics. But science is like fire; it is only useful if localized and withheld from general dissemination: "when contained, science is good; when widely known, it is a poison." Viewed from a religious perspective, the scientific mind seems insubordinate, swollen with pride, and irrationally attached to dogmatic faith in doubt. The only reason scientists talk about physical "laws" is to prevent people from praying. In general, science leaves human beings morally unhinged.[26]

Because of its incompatibility with traditional morality, modern philosophy, along with natural science, is responsible for the Terror. Locke's ideas, reproduced in the Parisian pressure-cooker, unleashed "the revolutionary monster who has devoured Europe." This claim is the *ur*-version of an argument which was to become very popular in the twentieth century. It can be called the dialectic of Enlightenment. In a first phase, the philosophical spokesmen for modern science erode the religion that makes social order possible. Then, once the social fabric is in shreds, science itself expires. That irreligious skepticism destroys the conditions for human creativity, including scientific creativity, is Providence's most bitterly ironic comment on philosophisme.

By eroding religion, the philosophes also shattered the immemorial taboos that had traditionally kept society's "scoundrels and wretches" under control. The Encyclopaedists, therefore, have more blood on their hands than do the brutes who manned the killing machines. Enlightenment thinkers talk about civilization and reason, but what they produce is brutality and irrationality. The Terror, in fact, was the ultimate expression of "learned barbarism," a shocking and unprecedented development.[27]

Maistre did as much as any early writer to determine the lineaments of the antiliberal mind. He cast himself as an anti-Voltaire in a dramatic showdown with powerful worldwide forces of corruption. The local skirmishes of his time have cosmic connotations. The world itself is an eternal battle. "If there is anything obvious for man, it is the existence of two opposed forces that struggle ceaselessly in the universe." This melodramatic and Manichaean view probably reflects Maistre's early involvement with the Freemasons; from them he also borrows the idea of a secret knowledge that can save mankind. Liberals are superficial and dangerous because they ignore *the* key to political rule. They overestimate the sufficiency of reason and force in the creation and maintenance of social order.[28] What they do not see is that man also needs myth. The antiliberal who can rekindle elite awareness of the need for myth may well rescue the world.

The notion that skepticism poses a massive threat to society has remained a commonplace among antiliberals since Maistre's time. It led Schmitt to embrace authoritative decisions. It drew Strauss toward esotericism. It spurred MacIntyre's flight into community and tradition. From Milton and Spinoza to Constant and Mill, by contrast, liberals welcomed public disagreement on the assumption that freewheeling debate makes a positive contribution toward intelligent and informed government. Liberals themselves, then, have uniformly denied what the antiliberals have just as uniformly affirmed: that "the clash of unsupervised individual opinions produces only skepticism which destroys everything."[29] One may argue who is more realistic here, the liberals or the antiliberals. But the latter certainly fear doubt more than the former. Antiliberals lack liberal confidence that public disagreements will yield workable agreement and compromise, that all disputes can either be depoliticized, brokered, or resolved.[30] Antiliberals fear skepticism more, it seems, because they are more skeptical themselves. They also assert, implausibly, that skepticism is the gravest of all threats to civilization. They exaggerate the danger of skepticism because, among other reasons, they make some highly dubious empirical assumptions. For instance, they misleadingly suggest that all unthinking dogmas and false certainties can be, or have been, erased from of the modern mind.

The Nullity of the Self

Man needs authority. And man needs religion. To these Maistre is very careful to add: man also needs community. By denying hereditary guilt, he argues, liberals aim to prise the individual away from family attachments. But individualism is a lie: "the individuals who compose nations, families, and even political bodies are *solidary:* this is a fact."[31] Progressive attempts to institutionalize individualism must be counteracted in two ways. The *moi* must be disciplined by the force of the sovereign, and the reason of the individual must "lose itself in the national reason." This melting of the individual into a larger group will, among its other benefits, release people from the painful contradictions of their inner lives. In the *Soirées,* Maistre wonders what will become of the "I" if it succumbs to a desire to submerge itself into a "mysterious unity" with others. (This is a difficult question, he says, because it threatens the Christian belief in an immortal individual soul.) After the Last Judgment, evil, disagreement, and inner conflict will be suppressed. At that point, survivors will belong to an ideal community "where all inhabitants, penetrated by the same spirit, will fuse with one another."[32] The smudge of subjectivity will be definitively erased.

Maistre's reflections on self-erasure sometimes lead him in a universalistic, rather than nationalistic, direction. Man's "nascent reason," he explains, "must lose itself in universal reason in order to transform its individual existence into a common existence. It will thus resemble a river that, flowing into the sea, still exists in the mass of water, but nameless and without separate reality."[33] The boundless sea of "universal reason" is nothing like a sharply delimited solidary group, of course. Maistre resents liberalism not only because it mocks authority, but also because it thwarts the longing for fusion with the nation or (in other passages) the related longing for faceless anonymity.

Man is a despicable fleck of nothing compared with God. Flight into community, therefore, is an understandable form of psychological consolation. It saves individuals from having to contemplate their sin-infected and worm-like selves, well on the way toward death. A life guided by society is a great relief, since the human individual, viewed realistically, is a nonentity. The revolutionaries who thought they were changing human history were helpless automatons in the hands of Providence. The individual can create nothing, in fact—not language, not society, not a new constitution. Given "the absolute nullity of human reason," Maistre asks, what could be more absurd, than a few scribblers gathering in a room and penning a document to regulate political life? A written constitution is nothing but a spider's web. Philosophes cannot purposefully lay down rules organizing political life. No one can govern behavior with ink.[34] A true constitution is certainly not, in Paine's phrase, something you can put in your pocket—not a written document, but the basic structure of a society's inherited customs, manners, and morals.

Given human disloyalty and undependableness, moreover, there is no such thing as a law enforced by those who must obey it.[35] Social cooperation is impossible over the long haul without an *external* enforcer. Nevertheless, liberals foolhardily dream about the self-regulation of society, about man's capacity first to give a law to himself and then to obey it. This is utterly illogical. For one thing, the will cannot bind itself. The power to bind implies the power to loose. Similarly, liberal constitutionalists cannot justify one generation's binding the wills of its successors. Binding the future is necessary for any constitution, but manifestly impossible on liberalism's own voluntarist premises. Committing subsequent generations becomes possible only if the lawgiver occupies a higher ontological plane than those who must obey the promulgated law. If one generation of lowly mortals makes the constitution of its own sweet will, why should a successor generation not whimsically untie the knot? An institutional framework can endure, once again, only if it appears to result from divine action, from the command of "a binding god." Maistre presents this argument as an a priori proof of the absurdity of liberal constitution-making.[36] Every genuine constitution comes, or must seem to come, from heaven.

France's successive constitutional failures of the 1790s were grist to Maistre's mill. But he also had to deal with the American Constitution. He reasonably points out that, unlike its French counterparts, the American Constitution was not a total innovation. It was based on republican institutions and traditions that had been imported from England and that had thrived in the colonial period when the colonists had *gradually* learned how to live without a king. But he finally concludes that the American experiment with constitutional design, too, is bound to fail. (Convinced that "human power can create nothing," he notoriously predicts that no city called Washington, D.C., will ever be built.[37])

Violence and War

Liberals, according to Maistre, are extraordinarily naive. They think human beings are self-disciplined enough to rule themselves and cannot understand the necessity of a final authority, capable of resolving bitter disputes by fiat. They do not see the importance of sustaining the grip of prejudices on humble minds. They fail to comprehend the social function of a popular belief in the Last Judgment. And they are insensible to the allure of communal oneness, of self-obliterating fusion with others. Maistre stressed all these failings of liberal thought. In so doing he helped mold as well as inspire the antiliberal movement. These themes do not exhaust his thought, however. He went further, much further.

The most decisive failure of liberalism, he wrote, is none of the above. Liberalism's greatest weakness is its inability to face the brutality and violence of human existence. This is the most idiosyncratic and least imitated aspect of his antiliberalism. Liberals are wholly unable to understand war. They expect peace, but this expectation is ludicrous, for "there is nothing but violence in the universe."[38] This deliberately shocking pronouncement sounds vaguely Schmittian, though it is even more extreme. Liberals, who avert their gaze from bitter reality, seem wholly unaware that history is a promenade across a field of corpses. Having cheerfully discarded the dogma of original sin, they cannot absorb what lies plainly before their eyes.

The theme of violence, of the unspeakable cruelty humanity afflicts upon itself, is the most radical point of Maistre's attack on the Enlightenment. His argument, in this case, has a ring of plausibility. Particularly irksome, he wrote, is the sunniness and complacency of the liberal view of human nature, as if truculence and cruelty had been left behind by progress. Liberals imagine that individuals originally quit the state of nature to avoid mutual decimation.[39] That is the gist of the social contract story, even when it is employed in a sophisticated way, as a mere expository device. Yet the model is illusory. Only when people are in a social state does genuine butchery begin. Wars kill more efficiently than atomistic muggers. Why then, on liberal grounds, would people leave a state of disorganized (and therefore relatively mild) war for a state of organized (and therefore more deadly) war? An antiliberal can say that man joins groups because he is a social animal and that, realistically, violent confrontation between rival groups is the most intense expression of mankind's inherent sociality. But what can a liberal say? One answer might be that individuals leave the state of nature to pursue glory, which can be won in battle. But Maistre does not accept this reply. Only the leaders receive any glory. Moreover, invoking glory merely displaces the question. It does not explain why mankind perceives war as glorious in the first place.

Warfare also explodes the liberal myth of the sovereign ego. Human beings never control the outcome of war. Victory, in truth, is utterly flukish. Battles that change the face of Europe are decided neither by *force majeure* nor by the tactical skills of masterful campaigners, but by unpredictable psychological phobias. Sometimes, in the midst of battle, one of the opposing generals will suddenly be seized by "the cold goddess," that is, by a kind of mental paralysis, an inexplicable emotion that causes him to freeze in his tracks. This is "true magic."[40] There is no explaining why a military commander gets cold feet. When this occurs, however, it can decide the outcome of a war that, in turn, will transform the lives of millions for generations.

Every page of the book of history is red with blood. Despite the work of humanists and philosophes, "reasoning Europe" remains hopelessly addicted to warfare. What is the explanation for the endless killing and being killed? Man is a compassionate creature, after all. He weeps for his fellows. Indeed, he contrives little stories to make himself shed tears, so tender and piteous is the human heart. Let the clarion be heard, however, and a young man will dash onto the battlefield to slaughter his enemies, "without knowing what he wants or what he is doing." He will kill and risk being killed without having any idea who the enemy is, indeed, without knowing what the word "enemy" means. Perfectly gentle in civilian life, the soldier will ignite on the battlefield and display an appalling "enthusiasme du carnage."[41] Peter the Great found it almost impossible to compel his subjects to shave their beards, but he had no trouble marching them into battle to hack to pieces neighbors who had never done them any harm.

Utterly contrary to reason and the instinct for self-preservation (stressed by liberals), the irresistible lure of war nevertheless dominates our lives. It is absurd to claim, as Enlightenment thinkers typically do, that war is foisted on people from above. The notion that war originates in *Kabinettspolitik* or the craft of courts is just another example of the vulgar conspiracy-mindedness of the philosophic movement. This is one of Maistre's favorite and most persuasive themes: "self-interest can abuse general beliefs, but it cannot create them." If the impulse to battle were not instinctive, elites would not be able to manipulate it for their own foul purposes. The suggestion that they could invent it is nonsense.[42]

For Maistre, "it is impossible to explain how war is humanly possible." He does not think that men rush into battle, baying for blood, to prove to an enemy that they are willing to risk their lives. Bellicosity has nothing to do with freedom. On the contrary, warfare is compulsive; it is both wholly inhuman and wholly human. It is therefore the perfect example of the unsolvable riddle of life. War resists all rationalist attempts to dispel darkness with light. Nonreligious writers have nothing to say on the subject. That Enlightenment thinkers cannot deal intelligently with war is an utterly damning commentary, for human history is the history of war.[43] The past is a string of bellicose crusades and confrontations.

The individual is not a rational actor, calculating efficient means to realize clearly formulated ends. He is a plaything at the mercy of larger forces he can neither guide nor understand. The idea of violent enmity, the notion that there is someone out there whom one must confront and kill, is thoroughly innate, instinctive, prerational. Rooted so deeply in the human personality, the friend/enemy patterning of social behavior remains unscathed by antimilitarist pamphleteering. Hatred storms through the individual without his comprehending it. One of the most baffling enigmas of human life is how people perform with relish what, on a different level, profoundly disgusts them. The same young man who would sob uncontrollably if he injured his sister's pet canary will, in battle, clamber atop of a pile of corpses "to get a better view." What fascinates Maistre are not the hewn-off limbs, the smashed skulls, or the moans of agony, but the ultimate unintelligibility of war from a rationalist point of view.

Similar considerations animate Maistre's famous discussion of the executioner. He indulges in a stomach-churning description of death on the rack, with a blow-by-blow account of "shrieking" bones, lacerated flesh, a mouth frothing with blood through which the victim begs piteously for death, and so on. And he caps his gruesome narrative by noting how the executioner gloats with pride in his craft. But neither this passage nor those depicting the intoxicating horrors of war should be misconstrued as an expression of Maistre's personal sadism. He is emphasizing, for polemical purposes, that squeamish rationalists cannot face an inwrought paradox of all human society.

Every political system depends on the existence of a punitive power, but when liberals look at capital punishment directly, it makes them sick to their stomachs. The executioner is "the horror and the bond of human community."[44] This is shocking and mysterious, especially from a rationalist or secular humanist point of view. The very existence of the executioner is a miracle. Who could possibly bear the public ignominy poured on the men who perform this job? Yet there are always executioners. Liberals need punitive institutions as much as anyone, but they cannot even discuss physical punishment frankly. Assuming the total transparency or intelligibility of the world, secular humanism desensitizes them to the astonishing and cryptic realities that lie before their eyes—to the fact that the ultimate guarantor of civilized coexistence, the executioner, makes them want to vomit, for example. To reawaken a sense of the indecipherable mystery of society, banished prematurely by the sunny and superficial Enlightenment, Maistre dwells obsessively on the incomprehensibility of the executioner, on the inscrutability of war.

Maistre's famed "realism" is highly selective, however. If he had been a consistent realist he would not have assumed without evidence that all religious delusions are always socially beneficial.[45] Sober fact-mindedness is no more characteristic of his thought than is conservative attachment to tradition. A brief comparison with Edmund Burke should make this clear. Burke firmly denounces the gallows-centric conception of society. Indeed, he associates the theory that the death penalty deters crime with the rationalistic Enlightenment. When Burke says that religion is the cement of society, he means to deny that social order depends upon the hangman.[46] The contrast between Burke and Maistre on this point is stunning. For the latter there is no conflict between a society integrated by religion and a society integrated by the executioner. Indeed, the two are identical. The executioner is the cornerstone of society not because the death penalty is a deterrent to crime, but because the executioner is the last archaic priest presiding over mankind's last sacrificial altar.

Most of Maistre's criticisms of Enlightenment rationalism are inaccurate or confused. But his claim that liberal theorists tend to be evasive about violence and cruelty has some validity. True, it would be implausible to suggest that Locke or Montesquieu ignored the problem of human cruelty. Bentham was speaking for all liberals when he asked: "what is history, but a collection of the absurdest animosities, the most useless persecutions?" But some liberals, such as Hume, did write as if violence and brutality were becoming a thing of the past.[47] Many liberals also have a difficult time thinking reasonably about war.[48] On the other hand, Maistre's extreme, not to say macabre, theory of the executioner-priest discloses a strain of near-dementia in his works.

It also leads him to pose one of his most revealing questions. Why is there nothing more honorable on earth than the innocent shedding of innocent blood? To revere the martial virtues, after all, is to honor the innocent shedding of innocent blood. One seemingly Maistrean explanation for war (as well as for the executioner) might be that man's heart seethes with murderous, demonic drives. Capable of crying pathetically over injured canaries, man is nevertheless a vicious beast, a born despot, like "the child who suffocates a bird in his hand for the pleasure of seeing that there exists in the universe a creature weaker than himself."[49] This, however, is not the explanation Maistre himself chooses to stress.

Murder, he writes instead, is simply the law of life. All of nature is a killing field. History is permanent carnage. The whole planet is a vast sacrificial altar, crying out for blood. It is not surprising, therefore, that man turns out to be a murdering animal. He is the king of the predators whose tables are laden with corpses. He kills nearly every living creature he comes across, sometimes for food and clothing, at other times merely for sport. He also kills for killing's sake: "il tue pour tuer." He does not stop there; he kills his fellows too.[50]

Maistre highlights the unfathomableness of humanity's proclivity to butcher itself with the following device.[51] Imagine a philosophical visitor from a foreign planet who has been informed that, on earth, there are two licensed killers. He knows that one, the soldier, kills the innocent, while the other, the executioner, kills the guilty; and he learns that there are many of the former and few of the latter. The extraterrestrial observer is then asked to guess: which one of the two is the most highly honored by human society? Being perfectly rational, he will give precisely the wrong answer. This shows the irrelevance of detached Enlightenment psychology to a realistic appraisal of mankind's scale of values. The relative status of the executioner and the soldier is another exemplary mystery of the human mind.

How are we to explain the suicidal mania of a self-murdering species? Maistre himself invokes "an occult and terrible law that demands human blood," or a great law of "the violent destruction of the human species." His so-called "laws" merely summarize historical events, however. They are in no sense explanations. God has simply implanted in our otherwise gentle souls an irresistible craving to shed innocent blood. The planetary abattoir, the unfailing slaughter that we call human life, remains a "horrible enigma."[52]

Nevertheless, "no nation has ever doubted that the spilling of blood contains an expiatory power."[53] All known cultures assume that the innocent alone can atone for the sins of the guilty. Hence all nations have practiced ritual sacrifice, particularly of weak and gentle creatures. The French Revolution assumes a new and unexpected significance in the light of this idea. The Terror itself was merely another *mise en scène* of mankind's primordial belief in expiation through ritual bloodshed. That is what made the revolutionary tribunals so "interesting" from Maistre's point of view. Christianity elevated a sacrificial story into its central belief. The Cross shows how Christianity is deeply rooted in the natural human situation.[54] The guillotine shows the same thing about the Terror. It is another universal symbol. Schmitt admired Maistre's classic sobriety, but "sober" is not the most obvious word to apply to this, the very heart of Maistre's thought. Indeed, his writings strongly suggest that there is nothing at all sober about seeing the world without illusions.

The Gnostic Strain

Sometimes Maistre represents the universe as disorderly and evil. At other times he depicts it as orderly and good. This confusion apparently results from his simultaneous commitment to two traditions: gnosticism (the belief that this world is hopelessly defiled) and Christian theodicy (or the belief that all worldly events, however painful from a human perspective, serve a higher good known to God). Carnage and suffering are an inexplicable enigma *and also* an efficient means to a rational end. Maistre explicitly says that the world is unredeemably corrupt—what gnostic writers call a "labyrinth," simultaneously a locked prison and a riot of disorder. In the great cosmic battle between good and evil, evil has won. (It is this gnostic aspect of his thinking that places him beyond both ordinary class-based conservatism and orthodox Christianity, and cuts him off from most of his antiliberal descendants.)

Maistre's radical providentialism, however, also implies total confidence in the cunning of reason, in the secular advantages to be reaped from torment and affliction. His belief that the world is irredeemably evil leads him to denounce repeatedly the naive optimism of the Enlightenment.[55] But he also affirms, like a reborn Pangloss, the ultimate utility of all apparent evils. The Revolution scattered the French clergy throughout Europe, for example, relocating them in Protestant lands and thus preparing the way for a future reunification of Christendom. After periods of cultural contraction and sterility, when people are plunged into listlessness, a good bloodbath can be rejuvenating. It will galvanize a civilization back into life. All great periods of cultural creativity have followed hideously cruel wars.[56] *Le salut par le sang* may sound heterodox, but it is also optimistic—too optimistic for Maistre in his bleaker moods.

Misfortune in general is useful, the Panglossian Maistre says, because it reminds people of mortality and of God and prevents them from becoming irreligiously attached to this world. On an even grander scale, Providence is a kind of cosmic breeder, eliminating genetic inferiors and using war to weed out the weak from the strong: "the human species can be conceived as a tree that an invisible hand ceaselessly trims and that often profits from this operation." In criticizing Voltaire's poem about the Lisbon earthquake, Maistre insists that natural disasters appear to be evil but are actually good because all human beings deserve to be punished. Perhaps the small children of Lisbon did not deserve to suffer their cruel fate—at the same time, the only way to punish a town, as all students of the art of siege know, is to penalize its inhabitants jointly. Why did God not remove the innocent to another place, where they could be protected, while He flayed the guilty? Well, says Maistre, that is exactly what He did. He punished the guilty (by killing them), while transporting the innocent children to heaven (by killing them).[57] This is remarkable logic. It can perhaps be summarized as "tout est bien" because "tout est mal."

With the same gift for inconsistency, Maistre compares the execution of Louis XVI not only to a ritual sacrifice but also to an accidental death caused by a heavy tile falling from a rooftop. Indeed, the most distressingly illiberal implication of his thought is that there is no injustice in the world, only misfortune—*le malheur.* "Is it an injustice when a good man is killed in war? No, it is a misfortune." Or again, "when an innocent person perishes, this is a misfortune like any other." The Hobbesian mind is afraid of violent death, death by stabbing, for example. From God's perspective, however, there is no difference between a stab wound and a stroke. Human beings will no doubt continue to dwell on such a superficial distinction: "but for God there is no such thing as violent death."[58]

The inconsistency of Maistre's discussion of this subject is mind-wrenching. Does God whip us because he loves us—for our own good—or because His own anger can be sated only by a river of blood? Maistre asserts that the sacrifice of the innocent redeems the sins of the guilty, for example. But he also insists, with equal fervor, that there are no innocents.[59] When a good man dies in battle, it is not an injustice, but merely a misfortune. Yet he immediately adds that all men are wicked and therefore deserve the cruelest possible fate. Is worldly suffering, then, a form of just retribution or just bad luck? The *Soirées* open with a discussion of the utter randomness of human pain and death. Evils of all sorts rain down on the human species like bullets upon an army, without distinguishing the good from the bad. The sense of arbitrariness is total. You do not have a certain disease; but you could have had it. You died in battle; but you might not have. No meaning attaches to human agony or satisfaction. Once having made this argument, however, Maistre lurches into reverse. All suffering is meaningful, he says. It is God's way of punishing us for our unpardonable trespasses.[60] The incoherence of this account of evil and suffering would seem bold if it did not appear so thoroughly inadvertent.

Isaiah Berlin once remarked that the "armoury of weapons" Maistre wielded "against liberalism" is "the most effective ever assembled." His "positive doctrine," however, is "unconvincing."[61] This is an understatement. Maistre's description of the role of violence and cruelty in history is accurate enough, but his account of the origins of gratuitous bloodshed, his whole theory of sacrifice, in fact, is obscure to the point of delirium. His simultaneous allegiance to gnosticism and theodicy leads him into a welter of contradictions. Ultimately, moreover, the colossal scope of his determinism is incompatible with any sort of political thinking, liberal or conservative. He says that the plans of God are unthwartable *and* that God is furious with human beings for having thwarted His plans. But what is the point of decrying present trends if an omnipotent God is completely in control of the course of history?

On a more prosaic level, Maistre has a wildly exaggerated idea of the noxious effects of skepticism. Doubt will remain politically useful so long as false certainties retain their unyielding grip on human minds. Liberalism and anarchism are quite distinct. Enlightenment rationalists knew perfectly well that binding agreements are precarious without an external enforcer. Religion is not the only possible "social cement." (Society can be held together by shared interests and secular norms; moreover, religion is often a divisive rather than a harmonizing force.) Social order does not depend on an unquestionable decision-maker. Public disagreement does not destroy the government's capacity to enforce the law. Chaos will not result if a legislative assembly today reconsiders decisions made by the executive yesterday. Constitutional rules can lead to more thoughtful and intelligent political decisions. As it turns out, stable government *can* be established by reflection and choice.[62] Constitutions "contrived" by a few Enlightenment scribblers can survive for centuries and help organize the political life of large nations. Citizens *will* obey laws they can revoke. They will also acquiesce in the decisions of rulers they can oust from office.

Maistre's empirical generalizations about liberal politics, in other words, were simply wrong. They have nevertheless been faithfully reproduced by his heirs.

Conclusion

To the existential pose of antiliberals, Maistre's greatest contribution may have been his blending of pessimism and optimism. The modern world is hopelessly rotten, he explained, but a chance for spiritual renewal lies just around the corner. He referred to the Revolution as "the great purification," as if he looked forward hopefully to the inauguration of a new order in which France would be purged of its former sinfulness.[63] He also wrote that human history has always been, and will always remain, an uninterrupted chain of gruesome calamities. Neither authority nor religion nor community can relieve man's miserable estate. This is a depressing thought. Maistre managed to rise above the woeful implications of his own diagnosis, however. In so doing, he set a trend. But how could he do this? How could he be both inconsolable and militant? Perhaps he sustained this paradoxical mood, as did many of his spiritual descendants, because he relished his struggle with liberalism even more than the chance to retire tranquilly in a postliberal world. This is true, at least, of Maistre's most original twentieth-century admirer, Carl Schmitt.

2 / Schmitt:
The Debility of Liberalism

La haine de l'autorité est le fléau de nos jours

—*Maistre*

Like Maistre, Carl Schmitt experienced the collapse of a national monarchy as a world-shaking crisis of authority. The breakdown of the Reich in 1918 and its replacement by a weak liberal regime was the principal occasion for, or inspiration behind, his antiliberalism. He first gained a reputation as a brilliant critic of liberal ideas and institutions in the 1920s, well before he joined the Nazi party. And that reputation continues to grow today. His debunking of parliamentary government and his exposés of liberal hypocrisy remain influential among leftists. Conservatives still applaud his characterization of liberal states as concessive and indecisive—appeaser regimes unable to defend themselves from attack. Even his fiercest critics treat him deferentially, as an intellect to be reckoned with. The leftish quarterly *Telos* recently devoted an entire issue to his work. According to one contributor, "the rehabilitation of Schmitt has begun." And the editors' introduction tantalizingly concludes: "in the present situation of political stalemate, the left can only benefit by learning from Carl Schmitt"[1] (*from*, not about).

Schmitt was born in the Sauerland in 1888 and raised as a Catholic. He eventually went on to study law and rose to a certain academic prominence in the 1920s, publishing an impressive series of scholarly and polemical works. The antiliberalism of these writings was unrelenting. He described the Weimar constitution as a symbol of Germany's capitulation before the enemy. It was "a standard-issue English suit," he ironized, foisted on the Germans in 1919.[2] In the same spirit, he expressed strong sympathy for Mussolini: "with ancient true-heartedness, the fascist state strives to be a state again." And in the early 1930s, before he joined the NSDAP (May 1933), he coauthored some of Hitler's early legislation "synchronizing" the states. After he enrolled in the party and assumed the post of Prussian state councilor, his writings became more extreme. (His unsavory career between 1933 and 1936 is, without a doubt, the main obstacle confronting his rehabilitators.) But his overtly Nazi writings built coherently upon his earlier works. Already in the 1920s he had remorselessly skewered liberalism as the hypocritical ideology of the Rheinland-seizing powers.

In the even more strident pamphlets he published between 1933 and 1936, Schmitt not only damned Weimar's liberal constitution as a foreign plot; he also celebrated the Third Reich as an intoxicating response to the humiliation of Versailles. He reiterated his claim that "the liberal freedoms of nineteenth-century constitutions were used by the allied powers to elevate the religious and class divisions of the German people into a fundamental law."[3] The victors in the Great War shrewdly weakened the German state with checks and balances in order to expose a defeated nation to self-destructive civil war. The task Schmitt set himself as a political publicist was to free the German spirit from its fatal attachment to a nefarious bourgeois constitutionalism imposed from abroad.

Once the Nazis seized power, he declared triumphantly that the liberal illusion was now doomed to disappear. Germans "have now realized that liberal constitutions are the typical disguise in which foreign domination appears." Perfidious Jewish writers smuggled liberal constitutional principles into Wilhelminian Germany, weakening the monarchy and preparing for the great disaster of 1918; now their noxious influence could be expunged. In his famous article defending the Röhm purge, Schmitt yet again asserted that liberalism had crippled the imperial regime, overprotecting the private sphere and preventing officials from crushing mutineers. At last, in 1933, German victimization had engendered its healthy opposite: "all moral indignation about the scandal of such a collapse has concentrated itself in Adolf Hitler."[4]

Schmitt's growing celebrity eventually provoked the envy of party hacks, particularly in the SS. Accused of being insincerely antisemitic, he redeemed himself by hosting a conference on "German jurisprudence at war with the Jewish spirit." Published on October 15, 1936, in the official *Deutsche Juristen-Zeitung*, Schmitt's closing speech was a masterful performance, *if* he was merely engaged, as his apologists contend, in a hypocritical attempt to please authorities. Holding Jews accountable for a moral crisis in the West, he described them as "the deadly enemy of every genuine productivity of every other people." To help sustain "the undamaged purity of the German people," law faculties must create "a German jurisprudence no longer infected by Jews." To avoid the "atrocious suggestion" that German students should use Jewish ideas, books by Jews must be yanked from the shelves and confined to a special section labeled "Judaica." Airy anti-semitic discussions, by which "no individual Jew feels himself person-ally touched," are ineffective. Only a detailed public register of Jewish scholars will permit a "cleansing" of German jurisprudence. Footnotes should read, for example: Kelsen, Hans, Jew. "The very mention of the word Jewish will be a wholesome exorcism."[5]

Still under attack from the party, Schmitt retained his chair at the University of Berlin only by the good graces of Hermann Göring. After 1936 he wrote less and less about domestic issues and focused instead on international law, justifying the Greater Reich, for example, by spinning a powerful analogy—embarrassing to Americans—with the Monroe Doctrine. Feeling unappreciated, however, he soured somewhat (but not completely) on the Nazi regime. He was arrested at the end of the war and modestly told his Nuremberg interrogator: "I am an intellectual adventurer." To put things into perspective, he added: "Christianity, too, resulted in the murder of millions of peo-ple."[6] Released without being charged, he lived a relatively uneventful life in West Germany for the next 40 years, publishing in moderation, making a few attempts at self-exculpation, and apparently never relin-quishing the belief that he was one of the misunderstood giants of the age. He died in 1985 at the age of 96.

Two Concepts of Enmity

Characteristic of Schmitt's artfully crafted prose is an unremitting oscillation between the cold and the feverish, the academic and the prophetic, the analytical and the mythical. This spellbinding back-and-forth is the secret of his success. His books plait together sober theo-retical observations with near-ecstatic political intimations. (Suggest-ing that the direction of world history is at stake, he can make even discussions of constitutional technicalities glow incandescently.) This striking pattern appears in his famous argument, put forward in *The*

Concept of the Political of 1928, that the essence of politics lies in the distinction between friends and enemies.[7] War is neither the main purpose nor the content of politics. What makes politics special, what lends it its "specific political tension," is the shadow of violent personal extinction cast over all genuinely political action. "The political" lofts citizens above "the economic" by confronting them with a mortal enemy, with the threat of violent death at the hands of a hostile group. (Schmitt did not yet openly associate the economic sphere with Jews, but he already portrayed it as a sordid arena where weaklings scramble to gratify material needs.)

This friend/enemy distinction can be handled affectlessly, as an intellectual tool or a model for historical analysis. Its usefulness for such purposes is beyond dispute. It contains, what is more, a cutting argument against both liberals and Marxists. Liberals generally sort conflict into three types: conflicts of interest, conflicts of ideas, and conflicts of ultimate values. Conflicts of interests, they assume, are resolvable by compromise and negotiation, conflicts of ideas by rational discussion, and conflicts of ultimate values by the privatization of religion. But human strife, Schmitt correctly counters, often takes less tractable forms. Some enmities are so intense and irrational that taking them off the political agenda is just as impractical as resolving them rationally or splitting the difference. In such situations, all parties think confrontationally. It is "them" against "us." Azerbaijan, Lebanon, Northern Ireland, Bosnia, Kashmir, Sri Lanka: it is not difficult to produce recent examples of the Schmittian pattern. (About the social causes for the escalation of manageable conflict into uncompromising enmity, Schmitt has nothing at all to say.[8])

Marx committed a similar fallacy, Schmitt persuasively adds. He reduced all human conflict to the struggle between economic classes, even though everyone can see that conflicts sometimes result from noneconomic cleavages—ethnic, religious, linguistic, national, and so on. Marx also conceived human struggle in the light of a philosophy of history that, in turn, ensured the ultimate victory of those who are morally superior. Schmitt mocked this fairy tale. Conflicts shall persist, he reasonably asserted, so long as humanity endures. In most cases, moreover, not the better but the stronger will win.

These criticisms of liberal and marxist naivete are quite plausible. Unfortunately, Schmitt combines them with quite a different and much less credible kind of argument. He suggests, in all seriousness, that the distinction between friend and enemy is the source of the meaning of life. That is the significance of the cryptic verse he likes to cite: "Der Feind ist unsere eigene Frage als Gestalt" (the enemy is our own question in visible form).[9] We might agree that having an enemy provides a fine reason for getting up in the morning. The innate yearning for set-tos and face-offs is familiar to every student of the human comedy. But Schmitt has little sense of the ridiculous. For him, history is tragedy—or perhaps melodrama. Without the possibility of confronting a mortal enemy life cannot be serious, is devoid of sense. The existential choice between them and us, where physical survival is at stake, gives "the political" its radiance, forges manly men, and permits the politically engaged to soar above the frivolity of everyday life.

While ridiculing their naivete, Schmitt obviously admires the audacity of Marxists-Leninists, especially their willingness, reinforced by a Hegelian philosophy of history, to establish countermajoritarian dictatorships. Unlike liberals, moreover, Marxists understand that human beings need a gripping myth to give weight and significance to life. Myths, as Sorel explained, awaken emotions, create solidarities, tighten muscles, and give people the courage to fight. Communists themselves rely on the myth of a final battle between the forces of good and evil in which the destiny of mankind will be decided. Unfortunately, in Schmitt's view, they also shift the battle line between friends and enemies from the international to the domestic scene. (In healthy societies, according to Schmitt, the only politics is international politics.) With the tools of communist propaganda, Leninists galvanize their followers to kill and die in lethal combat against a hateful "class enemy." By breaking the state's monopoly on the right to designate mortal adversaries, self-righteous leftist revolutionaries have driven Europe backward in history. They have engendered a new pluralistic chaos of sects and estates.

Two Rationales for State Power

This analysis is interesting enough. But the conclusion that Schmitt is a modern disciple of Hobbes (drawn, for example, by Schmitt's American biographer, Joseph Bendersky) remains a half-truth.[10] During the 1920s, admittedly, Germany suffered from *too much* polyarchy: from paramilitarism, group hatreds, and the dangerous ideological polarization of mass parties, not to mention terrifying economic volatility. In response, says Bendersky, Schmitt revived a rationale for autocratic government originally popularized in sixteenth- and seventeenth-century Europe. He reasserted the idea that state power is beneficial because it can impose internal peace on a society that would otherwise consume itself in a civil war of fanatical sects. This interpretation of Schmitt and his times seems plausible at first, and the position sketched does indeed sound like Hobbes.

About tranquility and peace Schmitt is ambivalent, however. He praises dictatorship as a means for establishing civil order. He also views a strong German state as an end-in-itself: "the successful and fully realized state is just as magnificent *(grossartig)* as the failed state is—morally and aesthetically—repugnant and wretched."[11] Such dreams of greatness reveal that Schmitt is not interested exclusively in legal order. At times, in fact, he makes peace seem less important than undoing the public humiliation that the German Reich suffered in the war. The bitterness of the imposed peace may help explain why Schmitt could never be a full-fledged Hobbesian, why he can say that the challenge of disorder is more interesting than the solution of order.[12] After all, manliness flourishes only *in extremis*. Peace, by contrast, is intrinsically boring: it invites people to live lackadaisically and evade responsibility. It is no surprise that bourgeois shopkeepers and cosmopolitan humanitarians, above all others, desire peace.

Schmitt's virulent anti-individualism separates him sharply from Hobbes. Moreover, he was as distressed by decadence and moral flabbiness as by civil war. He was intensely worried about "the general economization of spiritual life," about the disappearance of earnestness, decisiveness, and *virtú* in a pacified world-society made up exclusively of producers and consumers, travellers and entertainers, lawyers and artists. As Leo Strauss points out, Schmitt was at his most un-Hobbesian when he toyed with bellicism. This dimension of his thought is clearly expressed, in the mid-1920s, at the close of the book on parliamentarism: "the value of life stems not from reasoning; it emerges in a state of war where men inspirited by myths do battle."[13] That is Mussolini, not Hobbes.

Contrary to what his apologists believe, then, Schmitt's attachment to "the normal situation" was always counterbalanced by his Maistrean fascination with adrenaline-producing danger and conflict. He greatly admired daring men, tensed for an attack, willing to "renounce the security of the status quo."[14] He was also roused by an existential challenge: to stave off cultural decadence and communist insurgency by creating a strong German state. Schmitt never resolved this fundamental ambivalence in his thinking about state power. What he expected from "the political" was, on the one hand, order and, on the other hand, meaning, national pride, a manly triumph over moral weakness, and a sense of the seriousness of human existence.[15]

Friendly commentators on Schmitt eagerly discuss the period between 1930 and 1932.[16] At that time, Schmitt was urging the Reichspräsident to assume the role of benevolent dictator: Hindenburg and his chancellor should use their extraordinary powers to protect the constitution from extremists on both the left and the right. Is this an accurate description of Schmitt's views at this time? Was he *equally* hostile to the KPD and the NSDAP? We should not forget, when answering this important question, that Nazis and Communists had sharply different attitudes toward the nationalism by which Schmitt was so manifestly bewitched. Thus the suggestion that he was equally hostile to them both (advanced by Schmitt himself after 1945) is not altogether credible. What he feared in the twenties and thirties was not simply pluralism, but the pluralism of militant social groups who saw themselves as incarnations of universalist values. The Nazis were not internationalist or cosmopolitan. They were virulent enough, but they did not conceive themselves as representatives of "humanity" and were therefore not the ultimate danger in Schmitt's eyes. Prior to the seizure of power, it is true, Schmitt considered the Nazis "immature"—able to make Germany ungovernable, but unable to govern it themselves. He disliked them, in fact, because he feared they would create an uproar that Communists, in turn, might exploit. He also opposed attempts to revise the Weimar constitution for this reason, not because he was loyal to it or thought it good (all his constitutional writings are devoted to displaying its fundamental incoherence), but because he feared that upending basic institutions in a crisis could create opportunities for a communist coup and, eventually, foreign domination.

Schmitt's writings should be judged on intellectual grounds, of course, not in the light of his political career. Ignoring his opportunism and worse, I want to analyze more closely six of his most influential works. Taken together, they amply display both the strengths and shortcomings of his antiliberalism.

A Culture of Political Weakness

Originally published in 1919 and expanded in 1921, *Political Romanticism* is concerned with the cultural debility that, in Schmitt's view, led to the humiliating cave-in of the German Reich in 1918. Liberalism and romanticism are far less hostile to one another than many romantics and liberals have conspired to pretend, he argues. For one thing, the romantic sentimentalization of private life would have been unthinkable without the liberal desentimentalization of public life. Moist-eyed expressivism and dry-eyed economism, therefore, are not so much opposites as two sides of the same nineteenth-century coin. This is a provocative historical claim, worthy of study. A more troublesome aspect of the book, however, is Schmitt's identification of both romanticism and liberalism with passive indecisiveness—the purported cause of Germany's ignominious defeat in World War I.

From a historian's standpoint, *Political Romanticism* contains a puzzling silence. Schmitt reduces the content of romantic thought to a narcissistic search for opportunities to express lyrical feelings. This reading of romanticism is historiographically and philologically unsound. So why does Schmitt advance it? One reason may be that it allows him to obscure romantic criticisms of both the *Rechtsstaat* and commercial society—criticisms suspiciously like his own.[17] In fact, Schmitt engages in interpretive acrobatics to distract attention from the romantic and aestheticizing dimension of his own thought. (It is for the same reason, presumably, that he slights romantic nationalism.) Even today, his clever feints permit his apologists to deny his obvious affinities with political romanticism.

The gravamen of Schmitt's case against the romantics—grimly amusing in light of his own subsequent career—is that Adam Müller, the early nineteenth-century German romantic who criticized liberal economic theory in the name of an "organic" conception of society and the state, was a political chameleon. Müller expressed sympathy for revolution or restoration whenever it proved convenient. This tale of spineless adaptation is meant to convince readers that romantics were hopelessly sissyish, noncommittal, and irresolute. At a profound level romantics were just like women! (Schmitt often invokes the distinction between male and female to describe the difference between authority and anarchy.) Even when shorn of metaphysical sexism, however, Schmitt's argument remains faulty: a no-nonsense and *abgehärteter* character such as Talleyrand could also display astonishingly protean traits during periods of rapid political change. And the French ultras were even less self-possessed than the German romantics: most were impractical dreamers, unable to comprehend the realities of the day, embroiled in harebrained conspiracies before 1830 and catapulted out of politics thereafter.

The historical inaccuracies are no more obvious here than in Schmitt's other works: unique about *Political Romanticism* is its shrill censoriousness. This is the railing of the healthy against the sick; and the sick should be liquidated, not cured. Schmitt praises the contempt felt by "the solid man" for whimpering compromisers and prevaricators. His disgust for daydreaming, forlornness, dilatoriness, mawkishness, and heartstring-plucking seems boundless. But what incited these emotional effusions against emotional effusions?

Like Max Weber, whose seminar in Munich he attended during the winter of 1919–1920, Schmitt naturally invoked the austere male virtues of "responsibility" and *Sachlichkeit* when condemning the debility of romantics.[18] Sentimentalists are indecisive because they are "soft." Decisions, by contrast, are "hard," which is why sentimentalists cannot make any. But the concrete political situation to which Schmitt was reacting becomes clear only when he states that romantics lacked the inner strength to hate foreign domination.[19] Germany lost the war because it was infected by the romantic disease. Schmitt also associates romantics with the humiliation of the Peace Settlement and the failure of Germany's middle class to respond to the postwar chaos with a mailed fist. (*The Concept of the Political*, incidentally, contains the poignant claim that reparations payments are worse than tribute. The North American Indians have already been exterminated. Soon the Germans may meet the same fate simply for failing to pay their debts.[20])

"Liberalism," according to Ortega y Gasset, "announces the determination to share existence with the enemy; more than that, with an enemy who is weak."[21] Mushy humanitarianism of this sort is precisely the aspect of liberalism that appalls Schmitt most. Writing of "the liberal origins of this romanticism," he stresses repeatedly that liberalism is fainthearted and nonconfrontationalist.[22] Infected by a concessive liberalism, Germany's middle classes have forgotten how to retaliate when attacked. They are skeptical, relativistic, and timorously apolitical—unable, in short, to distinguish friends from enemies. Liberals have weakened the state in order to protect private property, and

liberalism = feminine

thereby crippled the one force capable of repulsing the socialist threat. Deprived of a guiding myth and in full "flight from politics," the German bourgeoisie lacks the courage to spill blood and is thus no match for resolute Communists. (Strauss, among others, helped familiarize American readers with this diagnosis of sickly and helpless liberalism.[23])

The craven desire to submerge the political into the economic reveals, according to Schmitt, the suicidal nature of middle-class liberalism. No country can maintain its unity as a mere network of consumers and producers—but this is exactly what the demilitarizing clauses of the Versailles Treaty were designed to make Germany become. Moral codes are sticks with which one group beats another.[24] The allies used liberalism to confuse and humiliate Germany while cynically pursuing their own imperialistic designs.

Decisionism

In his Nazi writings Schmitt consistently argued that "a logically consistent liberal democracy locates its ideal in political 'leaderlessness.'"[25] The idea that liberals systematically underestimated the need for political leadership, in fact, goes back to one of his most important early works, *Political Theology* (1922). Liberals place too much confidence, he plausibly argues, in three impersonal mechanisms: the rule of law, the free market, and the inevitable triumph of truth in open discussion. They also fail to appreciate that, in critical moments, decisions may have to be made before a rational consensus has had time to emerge.

This interesting and partly persuasive criticism of liberalism is, as usual, balanced neatly by a penetrating argument against Marxism. Schmitt does not try to replace economic determinism with theological determinism here. But he does assert that the limits to the possible in politics are fixed by human imagination rather than by material resources. What can be imagined is, in turn, a product of religious beliefs. The "proof" Schmitt offers of this dependency relation is the historical coexistence of monarchy with monotheism and of anarchy with atheism. Faith in one God makes monarchical authority self-evident. The belief that God is dead leads inevitably to the idea that power is evil. Especially memorable is Schmitt's claim that nineteenth-century theories of the "nightwatchman state" would have been unthinkable without a prior theological revolution that replaced an interventionist God by a clockmaker God. In other words, economic liberalism is an irrational residue of deistic theology.

In this as in many other instances, Schmitt's two-front attack on liberalism and Marxism has something to be said in its favor. But also characteristically, he quickly swerves onto less reasonable ground. He goes off the rails when he asserts that the modern concept of sovereignty is a secularized version of the theological idea of divine authority. In making this argument he distorts his primary sources. Jean Bodin, the great sixteenth-century theorist of royal sovereignty, knew that a prince, no matter how absolute, had only twenty-four hours in a day and needed to rely, as God did not, on indirect strategies to ensure cooperation. Contrary to Schmitt's assertions, Bodin stated explicitly that the sovereign should rule by and through general laws. (Only by so doing could he make an efficient use of scarce time.) The political decision to declare an emergency situation, Bodin also thought, was precipitated by exceptional events. It was a reactive form of crisis management that had almost nothing in common with God's free production of miracles. The analogy that captures Schmitt's imagination, in other words, is a false analogy.

Whatever his misunderstanding of his sources, Schmitt's own theory is justly described as "decisionism." He scorns bargaining and the rule of law, while apotheosizing "hard" political decisions—the choice of an enemy, for example, or the decision to suspend the constitution and rule by means of the Reichswehr. Arguably, a burning fear of moral skepticism lies at the emotional center of his thought. Bold decisions provide a reassuring alternative to doubt. (Schmitt probably fears moral skepticism even more than does his relentless critic, Jürgen Habermas.[26]) Finally, Schmitt is almost exclusively concerned with the emotional relief provided by authoritative fiats from above. Thus he overemphasizes the doughty character of political decisions, and completely neglects the distinction between intelligent and stupid decisions. Yet sovereigns have been known to destroy themselves by foolish choices. In 1638 Charles I declared an "emergency" (in the ship-money case). Similarly, in 1789, Louis XVI identified the most dangerous enemy of his regime as the French nobility. These were two obtuse and unnecessary decisions. Each one may have eventually cost the sovereign his head. Political mistakes may be easier to repair in constitutional systems than in monocratic regimes, moreover. Schmitt wholly overlooks this possibility in his tendentious criticisms of parliamentary government.

Parliamentarism versus Democracy

The Crisis Of Parliamentary Democracy (1923/1926), too, contains some sharp analysis. What stabilizes a political institution, Schmitt argues, is less the underlying distribution of economic power than a widespread acceptance of the institution's basic rationale. Representative government, for example, is justified on an ideal, not a realistic plane: not as a system for horse-trading among interest groups, but as a forum for rational deliberation among free-thinking deputies striving to achieve a better understanding of what they collectively want. Robust parliamentary debate will foster public learning and will eventually produce enlightened consensus on questions of policy. Unfortunately, according to Schmitt, this beautiful ideology has become totally obsolete. The rise of mass parties, organized interest groups, and plutocratic manipulators, as well as the democratization of the franchise, have exploded the classical liberal conception of representation. Only a madman could think that discussions in the Reichstag might guarantee a triumph of truth. All important decisions are made outside of parliament, by powerful groups, behind closed doors. Unable to integrate the nation through rational debate, the elected assembly has become nothing more than a display case for uncompromising social pluralism.

As a reconstruction of the ideology of parliamentary government and a diagnosis of the stalemate in German politics, this account has a cogent ring. But our second Schmitt, the intoxicated myth-maker, also puts in an appearance. He had not forgotten, presumably, who won the First World War. Yet he explicitly argues that liberal democracies in general, not just in Germany, are feeble, exhausted, and incapable of anything more than "talk." His reconstruction of the rationale for "government by discussion" is designed to make liberalism seem pathetically naive. Liberals, he claims, thought that a single newspaper could abolish tyranny and make government perfect.

Caricatured in this way, liberal principles appear silly and outdated in a realistic age. Schmitt is unsure, incidentally, about whether he wants to portray the rationale for parliamentary government as no longer valid (though it had once been so), or as ridiculous in principle. Was the "discussing class" always indecisive, or did its pitiful waffling begin only recently? His confusion on this point is a natural byproduct of his jeering at "government by discussion" even while he asserts that in the nineteenth century it achieved great political success.

In his constitutional writings of the late 1920s, Schmitt presents himself as an *antiparliamentary democrat.* His principal aim is to "rescue democracy from its overlay of liberal elements."[27] But he defines "democracy," perversely, as the psychological identification of rulers and ruled. To those frustrated with the endless negotiations and unstable, ad hoc compromises of Weimar politics, this appeal to plebiscitary leadership may have sounded attractive. Less easy to accept is Schmitt's explicit claim that democracy has no need whatever for competitive elections. The secret ballot, in particular, destroys the emotional unity characteristic of true democratic government.[28] Opposition, dissent, party competition, distrust of public officials, voluntary citizen groups organized around political issues, a free press critical of government policy, and protests by outvoted minorities are all liberal, and therefore undemocratic. With this in mind, Schmitt declares that fascist Italy and bolshevik Russia are more democratic than Weimar Germany or the United States. Dictatorships provide an opportunity, which liberal regimes do not, for expressing the seamless unity of the popular will.

"Duce sei tutti noi!" was a famous fascist cry. Liberal constitutionalism, with its "banal" separation of powers, aimed to rule out this kind of emotional fusion between rulers and ruled. Freed from liberal shackles, a democratic people will express its will by acclamation, like soldiers smiting their swords against their shields, spontaneously and in deafening unison. In his widely praised treatise on constitutional law (1928), Schmitt wrote that "the natural form for the direct expression of the popular will is the yea-saying or nay-saying shout of the assembled crowd." Acclamation is "a natural and necessary life-manifestation of every people," but liberalism basely tries to make it impossible. Indeed, "the organization of democracy, as it is undertaken today in liberal-bourgeois constitutional states, aims precisely to ignore the assembled people as such." The freedom of assembly enshrined in liberal constitutions has nothing to do with true democracy. For it does not admit "authentic popular assemblies and acclamations." The reason no true democrat would bother to tally votes is that elections are far inferior to the "immediate eruption and expression of the popular will." Not surprisingly, the soccer-stadium democracy that Schmitt already advocates in 1928 requires *das Volk* to exhibit a healthy docility toward its leaders. The serried ranks back their chief thumpingly, but never become dangerously rowdy or out of control. A truly democratic people is not self-organizing like a despicable bourgeois public, but instead adopts whatever behavior the charismatic regime prescribes.

Schmitt refers to the will of the people as *das "formlos Formende"*—a kind of shapeless blob that still exerts a shaping force.[29] This near-Heideggerian salute to the constituent power of the people was hypocritical, though. He plainly assumed that a powerful leader would have total freedom in molding public sentiment and opinion.[30]

Hobbes and the Origins of Jewish Liberalism

Always suspicious of natural science, Schmitt did not endorse racism as a biological theory. Nevertheless, cultural antisemitism was integral to his thinking, not merely decorative or a matter of political opportunism. Long before 1933, and despite his collegiality toward individual Jews, he subtly identified the disease infecting German culture as Jewish liberalism.[31] He continued to think along these lines after 1936. Consider his extraordinary work, *Der Leviathan*, first published in 1938. In his 1965 essay on "The Completed Reformation," Schmitt skillfully but with hindsight glosses his earlier work on Hobbes to make it appear harmlessly liberal in spirit.[32] He summons the unsuspecting witness, C. B. Macpherson, to show that admirers of Hobbes (such as himself), far from being totalitarian, are liberal individualists. And he cites R. G. Collingwood to prove that the very idea of Leviathan is associated with the battle of civilization against the forces of barbarism (such as Hitler). Since Hobbes's intellectual descendents include Pufendorf and Bentham, Hobbes must be considered the progenitor of the bourgeois *Rechtsstaat* with its fundamental norm of *nulla pœna sine lege*. (Coincidentally, Schmitt took a principled stance against retroactive punishment only after 1945.[33]) People may imagine that Hobbesians such as Schmitt sympathize with cruel and tyrannical regimes, but that is only because Hobbes unwisely named his book after a terrifying beast. In truth, Hobbes—like Schmitt himself—was ultimately a liberal, concerned only to guarantee individual freedom by repressing anarchy and enforcing peace.

So Schmitt is a modern Hobbes. Or so he wants us to believe. But his deep differences with Hobbes have already been made clear. Thus it should come as no surprise that the book published in 1938 is not accurately mirrored in the sanitized reconstruction of 1965. In truth, *Der Leviathan* is an attempt to identify the fatal defect in Hobbes's thought by uncovering the roots of the Leviathan-metaphor in ancient and medieval Jewish symbolism. Admittedly, Schmitt defends one aspect of Hobbes's thought: its radical Erastianism, meaning the total subjection of religious to political authority. Internationalist Christianity had to be ruthlessly subordinated to the national sovereign, just as internationalist socialism had to be crushed in Schmitt's own day. Faced with the anarchical religious pretensions of puritans, Presbyterians, and papists, Hobbes naturally divinized the state. To christen the state "a mortal god" was to say that political authority would tolerate no sacralized rivals; that no group within the state could claim privileged access to the divinity or decide independently who was a friend and who an enemy.

Hobbes did not merely describe the state as a mortal god, however. He employed a dizzying array of metaphors: a giant man, a machine, a representative person, a contract, and an enormous beast. Ultimately, Hobbes's failure was due to the disproportionate prominence he assigned to this last symbol. Schmitt's point is not that Hobbes ruined the reputation of the peace-keeping state by naming it after a scary biblical monster (as he claims in 1965). What he stresses, in the original book, is that Leviathan was a *Jewish* interpretation of vital pagan forces, an image implicitly filled with resentment against state power.[34] Hobbes's mistake was to have taken up a Jewish myth.

It is in this context that Schmitt cites his favorite medieval Jewish legend, a story from the Cabbala. History, according to this Jewish fable, was a battle between Leviathan and Behemoth, that is, between sea powers and land powers. Behemoth attacked its enemy with claws, teeth, and horns. Leviathan, by contrast, attacked by holding its enemy's mouth and nose shut. (This latter image of animal suffocation, notes Schmitt, is a splendid symbol for a naval blockade.) The Jews themselves do not participate in these heroic battles. But when the struggle is done, they feed on the flesh of the butchered warriors. Schmitt had already recounted this tale with evident delight, in his book on Hobbes: "the Jews stand nearby and observe how the peoples of the earth kill each other. For them this mutual butchery is lawful and 'kosher.' Accordingly, they eat the flesh of the slaughtered peoples and live off it."[35] This, Schmitt adds, is what the Jews say about themselves!

(Schmitt may well have believed that "the enemy" was not a criminal or a heretic and should be recognized as an equal. In *The Concept of the Political*, he wrote that "the political enemy need not be morally evil or aesthetically ugly."[36] This discriminating approach implies that, while enemy soldiers may be killed, no fanatical attempt will be made to wipe the enemy as a whole off the face of the earth. There will be no final victory, and a peace treaty may be signed after the war. Schmitt's postwar apologists always emphasize this tolerant and humane-sounding argument. But it does not bear much weight. Schmitt viewed the Jew as a bystander and maggot, not as an enemy worthy of manly respect. In the same category he put liberal constitutionalists, cosmopolitan pacifists, and humanitarians—all those who tried to weaken the state or undermine healthy friend-enemy groupings in the name of humanity. They are hypocrites, fighting a covert battle against those who prefer to fight openly. Because Jews, liberals, and the rest are ugly and evil, they can be annihilated in a "final" way.)

By describing the state as a biblical monster, Hobbes made it particularly vulnerable to the destructive efforts of antistatist Jews. The indirect consequence of this imprudent borrowing of a Jewish myth—Schmitt's presentation of the causal link here is obscure—was that Hobbes paved the way for modern Jewish liberalism in the person of Spinoza. As a result, Hobbes's Erastian project miserably failed. His main aim had been to crush factions inspired by universalist (that is, Christian) principles, which were destroying the state from within. The experience of Weimar, where universalist (that is, communist and liberal) factions weakened and abased the state, proved to Schmitt that Hobbes's well-intentioned étatisme had been defeated in modern Europe.

The roots of the disaster, Schmitt argued, lay in the master's own works and go beyond his ineptness at choosing titles. Hobbes did not consistently hold the line against antistatist powers. At the very center of his theory, in fact, he incorporated a distinction between inner and outer, private and public, personal faith and outward confession. He wrote that "internall Faith is in its own nature invisible, and consequently exempted from all humane jurisdiction."[37] Authority-hating liberalism quickly seized this reckless offer of a toe-in-the-door. Hobbes's distinction between public and private "becomes the seed of death that destroys the powerful Leviathan from within and kills the mortal god."[38]

Not long after Hobbes's book appeared, "the first liberal Jew" came along, sharpening his knife and fork. He spied the barely visible crack in Leviathan's carapace, and immediately understood its potential. In Hobbes's public/private distinction Spinoza found "liberalism's great invasion-route," the breach-point where antistatists could enter the state and tear it asunder. Spinoza uncrumpled Hobbes's "internall Faith" outward into a dangerous social world. He made it into a civil society screened from the healthy discipline of state power. He transformed Hobbes's tolerance for invisible inner piety, first of all, into license for visible cults. For Hobbes public peace was uppermost, while freedom of conscience was hardly noticeable. Spinoza reversed the relationship between the two: freedom of religion became central, while the rights of the sovereign were marginalized. Many groups promoted this liberal erosion of political authority for the sake of personal freedom: freemasons, pietists, mystics, "and here again, above all, the restless spirit of the Jews." Every intelligent Jew understood "that such an undermining and subversion of state power would best serve the crippling of other peoples and the emancipation of his own Jewish people."[39]

To redescribe this argument as purely Erastian, as Schmitt did in 1965, exceeds credulity. Sympathizers might argue, admittedly, that a cowardly professor was still trying to sweet-talk some watchful party hacks. But the argument Schmitt advances in *Der Leviathan* is not only morally repulsive; it is also theoretically confused and historically inaccurate. At no point does he even mention Spinoza's basic claim that limited power is more powerful than unlimited power.[40] This crucial liberal idea suggests that liberals were practical-minded, not romantic. It also has the advantage of tallying with reality. (Liberal states have historically proven enormously strong.) Its sole disadvantage is that it contradicts Schmitt's deep conviction that liberalism is inherently *staatsfeindlich*, passionately devoted to the destruction of the state. But how could liberalism be simultaneously so weak and so destructive?

The Paradox of a British World Empire

In *Land und Meer* of 1942, Schmitt struggled openly with this great anomaly of modern history from the antiliberal point of view.[41] Liberalism weakens the state, he firmly believed. But he also knew that, even by his own illiberal standards, liberal states have been tremendously powerful. They have proved themselves able to identify and vanquish enemies, for instance. They won the First World War. Even more impressive, liberal England had accumulated an empire to which none in history could be compared except perhaps the Roman. How could

Great Britain have gone so far if liberalism saps the fighting spirit and is, in principle, allergic to power?

In a few synoptic pages of this rhetorically brilliant pamphlet, Schmitt narrates the entire history of the West, from ancient Crete to World War II. But his focus falls on the origins of Britain's global domination *(Weltherrschaft)*. This is not a schoolboy's assigned theme. The British Empire was a burning issue for Schmitt. It directly involved the past and future place of Germany in the world. Referring to the English-speaking peoples, he dolefully noted: "according to their world-view, the idea that a landpower [such as Germany] could wield world-domination over the entire globe was scandalous and intolerable."[42] The greatest empire held by the British was their empire over German minds. They duped the Germans into believing (until recently) that the British Empire was perfectly natural, while a German one was unthinkable.

Taking a stand against Marxism, Schmitt again urges that history is not the history of class conflict but of conflict between land powers and sea powers.[43] This pattern can be traced from the wars between Sparta and Athens to the wars between Germany and Britain. Schmitt also ridicules marxist pride. Marxists brag about seizing the commanding heights of industry. From a broader historical perspective, however, the confiscation of industry pales into insignificance when compared to the seizure of territory. All great ages begin with a massive, morally unjustified grabbing of land *(Landnahme)*. The key to modern history, in fact, is the forcible European occupation of the globe. Rather than focus on the sideshow of class domination, we should look at the main event, the appropriation of the world by Europe and, eventually, by Britain alone. Modern times can even be defined as "the age of the European land-seizure."[44]

As for liberals, they love to talk about "humanity" and "civilization." But they are hypocritically silent about the cruel behavior of land-seizing Christian nations. Europeans treated the rest of the globe as if it were previously unowned. The British were the biggest hypocrites of all. They spoke and wrote about "free trade" when what they meant was British dominance of the seas. They vaunted their own humaneness, while they invented total war. (Britain's naval blockades hit soldiers and civilians indiscriminately, so blockades were the original form of total war. And not only did the British invent total war, but they had the chutzpah—the word is chosen carefully: Schmitt had a portrait of Disraeli hanging above his desk—to describe their reliance on blockades as a sign of their moral superiority. When women and children die of starvation, Schmitt's imaginary Englishmen brag, no blood can be seen.)

Whatever their moral faults, the British undeniably managed to create an unprecedented world empire. A few years earlier, Schmitt had made the platitudinous contrast between spineless merchants and masculine soldiers, between *Händler* (traders) and *Helden* (heroes). The question he now faced was, how did a despised nation of shopkeepers attain its enormous empire? Britain traversed a unique path of development, he now explains. A feudal kingdom became a world empire without ever having been a state in the continental sense. (It never had a powerful bureaucracy or a land army.) This unparalleled national metamorphosis was highly dramatic. Indeed, the British did something few nations have the courage to do. They made a "manly decision" to turn away from the safety of the land and toward the tumultuous sea.[45] With unbelievable daring, they engrossed to themselves what Locke had called "the Ocean, that great and still remaining Common of Mankind."[46] They lifted themselves up by their bootstraps. By an existential choice, they changed their nature and became sea creatures with lungs. They transformed themselves from shepherds into heroic mariners.

The all-shattering event of modern times, therefore, was not the seizure of lands by various European nations, but the unprecedented British "seizure of the seas."[47] Much of *Land und Meer* is devoted to explaining how this remarkable act of global piracy could have occurred. Schmitt no longer waxes eloquent about Richelieu and other continental state-builders. The hero whose song he now sings is the whaler. His admiration shifts away from orderliness, toward audacity. The whalers were a daring breed. Because of natural timidity, European sailors had traditionally hugged the coastline. To dissolve their primordial ties to the land, they needed a *Führer*. They found such a leader in the whale, the huge, warm-blooded, fellow mammal that breathes with its lungs and, astonishingly, lives in the sea.

Schmitt sees whale-hunting as a dramatic contest between two sea-going mammals. Global expansion was its unintended effect. Neither Columbus nor Drake, but the whale led to the discovery of the new world. In hot pursuit of this colossal beast, Europeans—and especially the British—learned that the world was a ball they could clasp in their hands. Like the whalers, the British corsairs, too, were authentic "children of the sea." The great age of these pirates lasted from 1560 until 1713. They would capture foreign vessels (especially those sailing under the colors of a Catholic nation), kill the crew, and confiscate the goods. "Booty capitalism," Schmitt explains, was the main source of primitive accumulation in sixteenth-century England. Piracy, condoned by the crown, brought an influx of wealth to the island and helped create the first class of wealthy entrepreneurs. The liberal ideology of free trade is a pure myth, designed to dupe naive foreigners. England's economic head-start was a product of trickery and force.

After they had discovered the world, of course, the Europeans decided to make it their own. From Schmitt's perspective, the central fact about the European contest for world empire—won by Britain—is negative. Germany had stood on the sidelines, a pathetic observer. Germany was frozen out of the great land-grab of modern times. It was excluded because of its uniquely miserable historical heritage. Divided internally between Catholics and Protestants, Germany was the Hamlet of nations. Because it was internally riven, it was "poor in deeds" *(tatenarm)*, barred from prancing with its European rivals upon the well-lit stage of history.[48]

By 1942, of course, all this had changed. Britain's relative power had decreased, for one thing. The explanation Schmitt offers for this satisfying decline is amazing. Industrialization led the British to introduce machines onto their ships, he writes. Instead of throwing the harpoon with their arms and shoulders, British sailors began to shoot it with a cannon. Their masculinity was thus undone. They had transformed themselves from sheep-tenders into heroic mariners; now technology turned them into despicable machine-tenders. Between 1890 and 1914, moreover, Germany caught up with and surpassed Britain in industrial productivity. The Germans under Weimar, while technically superior, had still been mentally enslaved, however, for they continued to accept the political superiority of British-style liberal constitutionalism.[49] But this mental enslavement, too, had now been overcome. (Schmitt says nothing about the deleterious effects of technology on the German character)

Land und Meer is a riveting and revealing work. It is authored solely by Schmitt the myth-maker. Schmitt the clear-eyed constitutional theorist is nowhere to be found. What is impressive about the book is not so much the author's analytical acuity or historical erudition, but rather his envy-driven rethinking of modern history. By revealing the imperial designs behind British rhetoric about free trade, he exposes the hypocrisy at the heart of nineteenth-century liberalism. Not his need to mollify the Nazis, then, but simply his German nationalism, forged in the cauldron of World War I, leads him to despise the liberal constitutionalism that originated in England and was imposed on Germany—a symbol of its ignominious defeat. On the other hand, despite his immense learning, he shows himself wholly unable to grasp the underlying causes of liberal political and military power. (If liberal-bourgeois culture is so weak and weakening, why do autocratic nations lose wars to parliamentary democracies?)

A Rebuttal

Schmitt's criticisms of liberalism are often interesting and sometimes persuasive. He points out, for example, that no classical liberal developed an adequate theory of political leadership. The liberal principles of majority rule and equality before the law can operate effectively only within the confines of legitimate territorial borders, yet these principles are totally incapable of creating or justifying such borders. Such criticisms are interesting. But they are not always as decisive as Schmitt believes. For instance, the lack of a liberal theory of leadership has not prevented the emergence of political leaders in liberal societies. Similarly, the lack of a liberal justification for specific territorial borders has not prevented liberal societies from becoming psychologically resigned to the arbitrary and legally unjustified borders that history happened to create.

Many of Schmitt's other criticisms of liberalism, while often clever, simply miss their mark. Here are eight commonsensical rejoinders to Schmitt's main antiliberal claims. First, liberal governments, despite their respect for procedures and reliance on public debate, *do* make and implement binding decisions. They do more than "talk," they decide and sometimes even choose enemies and defeat them. Constitutionalism does not make decision-makers helpless against the tides or laws of history. Liberal political systems are no worse at defending themselves from internal subversion than other known regimes. Schmitt is simply wrong, therefore, when he says that there is no such thing as liberal statecraft, only a liberal criticism of the state. (He is wrong to declare liberalism intrinsically antipolitical even when politics is defined arbitrarily as the act of identifying a mortal enemy; for liberal societies have done this with remarkable success.)

Second, liberal pluralism is not necessarily a license for civil war. The suggestion that limited government produces an armed and anarchical civil society hurtling toward violent self-destruction is obviously exaggerated. Third, liberalism does not wholly metamorphosize all people into private producers and consumers; through electoral politics and a free press, it encourages voluntary and part-time engagement in public life. Fourth, liberals were perfectly aware that groups exert power over individuals and that group hatreds can be wholly irrational. The privatization of religion is a well-known liberal attempt to deal with these irrepressible realities. Fifth, the very existence of the United States seems to refute the assertion that "every democracy presupposes full homogeneity of the people."[50] Liberalism has its own (not wholly ineffective) methods for dealing with social heterogeneity and cultural diversity. Sixth, political impasses can sometimes be overcome by compromise; an authoritative decision from above is not always required. Seventh, although liberals are usually antimilitarists and worry about the physical brutality of government agents, they do not believe that discussion can *wholly* replace force. They prefer economic rivalry and electoral competition to the blood feud, of course. But this preference is not particularly unrealistic. Eighth, liberalism is much more practical than romantic in its origins. For example, competitive elections provide the best known solution to the difficult problem (seldom solved satisfactorily in preliberal or nonliberal political systems) of orderly political succession. Similarly, religious toleration was a response to civil war. Parliamentarism resulted from a fiscal crisis. Judicial independence was a technique for handling governmental overload. And general laws were first introduced as an efficient means for ruling large territories and populations. None of this has anything to do with a dewy-eyed idealization of "endless conversation."

On a more scholarly level, Schmitt's pronouncement that "the exception was something incommensurable to John Locke's doctrine of the constitutional state and the rationalist eighteenth century" should be compared with Locke's own statements that "the Laws themselves should in some Cases give way to the Executive Power" and "a strict and rigid observation of the Laws may do harm." Blackstone, a Lockean in this respect, also argued that it is "impossible . . . in any practical system of laws, to point out beforehand those eccentrical remedies, which the sudden emergence of national distress may dictate, and which that alone can justify." Indeed, liberals typically shared an em-

phatic conception of the exceptional situation. Liberal constitutions do
not abolish executive power, and executive power cannot always operate according to preestablished rules. Liberals assumed that every rule
has its exceptions. They never conceived "the rule of law" as the
sovereignty of abstract, self-applying rules. They viewed it, instead, as
rule by elected and accountable officials *in accord with* publicly promulgated and revisable laws. For this reason and others, personal responsibility for political decisions—which Schmitt pretends to admire—is
more likely to be preserved in a liberal than in a nonliberal political
system. Part of the purpose of liberal constitutionalism, after all, is to
keep rulers accountable, to prevent them from shirking responsibility
and diverting blame.

Finally, Schmitt is wrong to associate liberalism with a naively optimistic anthropology.[51] True, liberals rejected the distinction between
saved and damned; but they certainly recognized the presence of envy,
pride, and malice in human nature. Paine's quip that government, like
clothes, is a sign of lost innocence is wholly typical of this Augustinian
strand within liberal thought. Madison's remark that "if men were
angels, no government would be necessary" is another case in point.[52]
The real liberal innovation was not optimism, therefore, but a *universalization* of pessimism. All human beings have chaos in their souls.
They therefore need to be governed—rulers as well as ruled. Indeed,
naive optimism was less characteristic of liberal thinkers, worried about
abusers of power, than of Schmitt's own *Führer-prinzip*. Anyone who
tries to protect individual security by assigning wholly unlimited power
to a single political leader or group must seriously underestimate the
all-pervasiveness of human sin.

(Liberals deviate from rigid rule-of-law principles, incidentally, because they recognize the need for ordinary citizens to view the government with skepticism and distrust. As Blackstone says, liberal constitutions typically contain "no stated rule, or express legal provision"
for overthrowing a government that betrays the people's trust. Therefore, the remedy must be left up to "the prudence of the time."[53] Why
not conceive the irrepressible right of rebellion as an expression of
liberal decisionism?)

Conclusion

After 1945, perhaps to conceal a residual sympathy for Nazism,
Schmitt affected wholesale hatred for fanatics and nostalgia for a pur-

portedly old and stable European order, where political groups never dreamed of criminalizing and annihilating their worst enemies.[54] The pose was adroit, but not wholly convincing. His pre-Nazi celebration of life-and-death struggles, myth-inflated confrontations, and titanic duels is obviously incompatible with any desire to return to a low-intensity and rule-governed world where conflict would be devoid of ideological drama and where political enemies, unlike criminals and heretics, would be treated with decent reserve. His lasting contempt for a pampered society of producers and consumers gives the lie to this retrospective self-portrayal. Part of what he sought, already in the 1920s, was an intimation of apocalypse found only in the thunderous clash of extreme worldviews.

Schmitt's infatuation with dramatic conflict, incomprehensible to the "shallow" Enlightenment mind, registers his lasting debt to Maistre, among others. And just as he built on the antiliberal past, so he laid the foundation for the antiliberal future. One of the first widely noticed publications of Leo Strauss was a brilliant 1932 review essay of Schmitt's *Concept of the Political*.[55] Strauss's basic argument can be summarized quite simply: Schmitt may despise liberalism, but in the end his thinking remains shackled to liberal presuppositions. For Strauss, then, Schmitt fails to be antiliberal enough. He does not criticize liberalism from a thoroughly nonliberal point of view. This is a stunning assertion. To understand how such an accusation is possible requires us to delve into yet another dimension of the antiliberal mind.

3 / Strauss:
Truths for Philosophers Alone

Quant à celui qui parle ou écrit pour ôter un dogme national
au peuple, il doit être pendu comme voleur domestique.

—*Maistre*

One of the most erudite and intellectually intense of the German-Jewish émigrés of the 1930s, Leo Strauss—who died in 1973—is renowned less for the content of his thinking than for his rare success in establishing a school of political theorists—a school that unfriendly critics call a cult. Professors do not retain disciples without encouraging them, so the phenomenon of Straussianism, at least in the first generation, reveals something interesting about Strauss himself. But annoyance at the worshipful attitude of his acolytes has not favored a balanced assessment of the master's own writings. Indeed, exasperation with his uncritical adulators and frustration at his less-than-transparent style have recently given rise to the myth that Strauss was a sphinx without a secret, an obscure writer whose rhetorical posturing is unjustified by underlying insights or ideas. This criticism is understandable; it is also erroneous.

Strauss mesmerized students by his passionate devotion to texts and his tireless effort to revivify what he called "the Great Tradition." But he was not fundamentally a commentator. He viewed old books as windows onto reality. Thucydides, for example, "makes us understand the nature of human life; he makes us wise. By understanding Thucydides' wisdom, we ourselves become wise; but we cannot become wise through understanding Thucydides without realizing simultaneously that it is through understanding Thucydides that we are becoming wise, for wisdom is inseparable from self-knowledge. By becoming wise through understanding Thucydides, we see Thucydides' wisdom."

61

Strauss wanted us to read his own works in this spirit. Although he dedicated more than a dozen books and scores of articles to the towering figures of political philosophy—ancient, medieval, and modern—he was no ordinary historian of ideas. He sought wisdom above learning. He sought, above all, "a horizon beyond liberalism."[1]

Liberalism, in itself limited and narrow, is also in the throes of crisis. Unlike most intellectual historians, Strauss was obsessed by "the crisis of liberalism." In the same spirit, he warned his readers earnestly about the "crisis of modernity," "the crisis of the West," "the contemporary crisis of Western civilization," "the crisis of the belief in progress," "the final collapse of rationalism," "the decline of Europe," "the danger" currently threatening "the whole Western heritage," not to mention "the one great crisis, the crisis of our time."[2] No ordinary explicator of texts would have focused so single-mindedly on cultural processes of eclipse, impoverishment, and putrefaction. No run-of-the-mill scholar would have suggested that he could help us vanquish our civilization's enemies and remedy our century's ills. No average professor would have suggested that he could answer the burning question left untouched by modern science: how should human beings live? There is an air of drama, perhaps even melodrama, about his writing that smacks of Maistre and Schmitt and that distinguishes Strauss radically from his more timid and bookish colleagues.

Strauss's students praise him for concealing his most interesting ideas and then go on to complain that he is unfairly and incomprehensibly ignored. To take him seriously, of course, we must unlock the secret cabinet, dispel the manufactured fog. Did he claim, for example, that today's liberals have lost a moral truth that was once widely shared? What moral truth was that? Did he view value-free social science as a symptom of a deeper social malady, a sign that liberal society is unable to distinguish right from wrong? Are contemporary Westerners wholly blind to the moral difference between cannibalism and civilization? Were earlier societies, uninfected by social science, much better off? It is also necessary to ask this: if Strauss meant to defend high moral principles against the enervating "relativism" of the age, why did he write so opaquely—disguising his voice, burying his insights, hindering our access to the ethical verities inscribed in nature? These questions are interesting and important, though newcomers to Strauss should start elsewhere.

Savage Truths, Consoling Lies

The correct place to begin is with the political effects of the critique of religion.[3] This was one of Strauss's fundamental concerns. Again and again he posed "the question as to how the unphilosophical multitude will conduct itself if it ceases to believe in gods who punish lack of patriotism and of filial piety."[4] This was a political not a scholarly issue, even though it concerned the politics of books—the politics of publishing books that corrode religion and other ancestral pieties. Like many others before him, Strauss believed that reason, if taken to an extreme, will somersault into unreason. Secular humanism—the worldview underlying political liberalism—brings darkness and destruction on humanity. By undermining religion, secular reason leads directly to personal immorality and political catastrophe. In his view, as in Maistre's, the unhappy consequences of modernization made it plausible to speak of a Dialectic of Enlightenment.

Strauss made his young Jewish-American students gulp by informing them that toleration was dangerous and that the Enlightenment—rather than the failure of the Enlightenment—led indirectly to Adolf Hitler. Far from being a diehard enemy of Enlightenment thinking, however, Strauss was a cosmopolitan nonbeliever, thoroughly convinced that "modern rationalism" had "a number of important insights which cannot be thrown overboard." His question was: how have the great philosophers of the past managed to enjoy the benefits of Enlightenment while avoiding the Dialectic of Enlightenment? It was done through the secret art of writing, the technique of "writing between the lines." Society needs religion while philosophers need freedom from religion. To overcome this dilemma, "science must remain the preserve of a small minority; it must be kept secret from the common man." Philosophers must practice selective dissimulation, feigning devotion to the beliefs of "the herd" while communicating with each other in a clandestine or sub rosa manner: "they will distinguish between the true teaching as the esoteric teaching and the socially useful teaching as the exoteric teaching; whereas the exoteric teaching is meant to be easily accessible to every reader, the esoteric teaching discloses itself only to the very careful and well-trained readers after long and concentrated study."[5] Exoteric teachings underwrite local religious beliefs. But why is religion "socially useful," according to Strauss? There are several reasons, most of which were already identified by Maistre (as well as Dostoevskii and many others).

First, most human beings need to be ruled. Religion habituates believers to passive acquiescence in divine authority, thereby breeding a salutary "deference to the ruling class."[6] Moreover, people will be ungovernable if their desires are allowed to outstrip society's capacity to satisfy them. As a desire-retardant, piety can help prevent a calamitous overtaxing of the political system. Similarly, if religion contains fairy tales about the afterlife, it will encourage obedience to laws by inducing fear of punishment in hell. It will also reconcile the poor to their poverty by giving hope of compensation in heaven. But all these explanations of religion's social utility appear crude and superficial compared to a further point: religion can absorb man's primal anxiety in the face of mortality and the horrifying deafness of the universe's infinite void.

According to Strauss, "the discovery of nature is the work of philosophy." For ordinary mortals, this discovery would be "productive of the deepest pain." But what is nature and why is it so painful? Nature is the cluster of intractable restraints to which human life is subject. The grip of nature is three-fold: personal, political, and cosmic. When the philosopher discovers these stark constraints, he learns that no matter how long individuals manage to extend their lives, they will in no way shorten the amount of time they will be dead. Similarly, reasoning about natural catastrophes plainly suggests that the habitable earth is doomed to extinction and will eventually perish with all traces of mankind. These are among the principal ahistorical truths of Strauss's philosophy. They are not moral imperatives but naked facts, beyond folklore and beyond interpretation. They are brutal and sickening observations about the unchanging human condition. And they must, of course, be kept quiet: "exoteric literature presupposes that there are basic truths which would not be pronounced in public by any decent man, because they would do harm to many people who, having been hurt, would naturally be inclined to hurt him who pronounces the unpleasant truths."[7] Philosophers who can look at these steep truths without squinting have gained permanent distance on their own cultures. In an important sense, they are no longer shaped by their times.

An image that might have seemed inappropriately frivolous to Strauss captures perfectly his main point. Life is like falling off Chicago's 110-story Sears Tower: the pavement-bound travelers will relish their journey only if they abstain from thinking too concretely about where they are heading. We have invented various mythologies to conceal our bleak fate, to make our imminent return to inorganic lifelessness appear to be the beginning of a new life. We dream of a happy end and a divine shepherd. We even prefer frightening tales about vindictive gods intent on punishing us to the realization that the cosmos is "an absolutely terrifying abyss," wholly indifferent to our irreversible obliteration.[8] Focused fear provides an analgesic against existential terror.

A very few supermen are capable of absorbing the hideous truth. These are the unsleeping philosophers. As Allan Bloom writes, summarizing Strauss's position: "*the* uncompromisable difference that separates the philosophers from all others concerns death and dying. No way of life other than the philosophic can digest the truth about death."[9] The philosophers are able to live without comforting illusions. They know that human history is written in water. They are "reconciled to the fact that we live . . . in an infinite universe in which nothing that man loves can be eternal."[10] They take pleasure in their capacity to look savage reality in the face and not blink. The distinction between the few and the many, between the supermen who can live authentically, without myths, and the herd who can swallow reality only if it is sugar-coated—this distinction, too, is ahistorical. The same dualism, already grasped with unrivaled clarity by Plato, can appear in any literate society.

Religion is socially useful because it infantilizes most human beings and anesthetizes them to the anguish an unscreened view of nature would provoke in weak minds. It sweetly deludes them into believing, for instance, that God or the gods actively work to ensure the survival of the habitable earth. Having discovered nature, the philosophical few are immune to such delusions. They can see straight through the childish opinions that hold their fellow citizens in thrall. Philosophers are chronic doubters of shared beliefs and (in thought, not deed) shameless transgressors of inherited taboos. There is nothing "sober" about viewing the world without illusions, as Maistre, too, showed. Indeed, tossing illusion to the winds provides *excessive pleasure* for a select group. If disillusioned philosophers communicate their nonconformism, dubiety, and intellectual lack of moderation, however, they will destroy "the protective atmosphere" that sustains and inhibits most people.[11] If daring philosophical attitudes ever became wide-spread, the bulk of mankind (attached to bodily rather than intellectual pleasures) would behave as if everything were permitted. Mass shamelessness would make social life, and philosophy itself, impossible.

Philosophers Beware

Strauss made an interesting distinction between the early and the mature Socrates. The young Socrates was a typical Enlightenment figure, fascinated by nature, denigrating politics compared to the physical universe, and proclaiming aloud that "Zeus is not," until the sage Aristophanes taught him the error of his ways. If philosophers publicize their knowledge, sons will pummel their fathers and disoriented commoners will set the philosophers' academy ablaze. To prevent social chaos and persecution, philosophers must keep their light under a bushel. They must learn to conceal their drunken thoughts in deceptively sober speech. Socrates absorbed this lesson and began to speak differently to different people, revealing his highly classified thoughts to young men of intellectual promise while paying lip-service to the ancestral pieties before all others. To avoid offending his fellow citizens he went so far as to get married and have children. His philosophical detachment was nevertheless apparent. As Strauss assures us, the mature Socrates completely ignored his children and "behaved like an inveterate bachelor."[12]

Unfortunately, Socrates's conversion to esotericism was too little, too late. In some ways, his trial and conviction were perfectly justified. From the Athenian viewpoint, he was a disloyal citizen who tried to destroy religion. This was no trumped-up charge. Philosophers will *always* be hated on these grounds, and justifiably so: "philosophy is repulsive to the people because philosophy requires freedom from attachment to 'our world'."[13] The execution of Socrates is therefore a lesson for future philosophers. The weak will always resent the strong. The latter must therefore be even more radically secretive about the truth than the mature Socrates managed to be.

According to Maistre, all societies are founded on human sacrifice. More sedately or cynically, Strauss thought that all societies are founded on crime. He agreed with Schmitt, in fact: all nations are built on *Landnahme*, the brutal and illegal seizure of territory: "are cities not compelled to use force and fraud to take away from other cities what belongs to the latter, if they are to prosper? Do they not come into being by usurping a part of the earth's surface which by nature belongs equally to all others?" The answer is yes. That all regimes are built on spoliation is another scandalous truth that must be hidden from peon brains: "a self-respecting society cannot become reconciled to the notion that its foundation was laid in crime." If the bulk of citizens realize that their country's founders are the moral equivalent of a gang of robbers, they will disrespect the laws and refuse to die in war. Traditionally, this problem has been solved by the myth of a divine foundation: society is described as founded by gods or by great legislators who communicated with gods. Consider the American legend of the Founders—morally immaculate figures who believed that "all men" were "endowed by their Creator" with inalienable rights. The uncomely truth, of course, is quite different. The original settlers seized the land and brutally murdered its innocent inhabitants. That was the authentic founding. It is politically necessary, however, for most people to feel an "unqualified commitment" to the moral superiority of their country. All societies must remain "closed" in this sense. They must remain closed to the intolerable truth. Unpleasant reality must always be decently veiled. (Strauss accused social science of having a "corroding influence," weakening liberal democracies in the face of the communist threat.[14] It did so by dispelling national mythologies and suggesting—correctly but imprudently—that unqualified patriotism can never be rationally justified.)

Evil cannot be eradicated from human life. This is not a dangerous truth that philosophers must conceal, but a highly useful truth that wise men, discoverers of a horizon beyond liberalism, should herald as widely as possible. For the sake of political moderation, nature must sometimes be *un*veiled. (Because he focuses obsessively on the phenomenon of harmful truths and beneficial lies, Strauss has nothing illuminating to say about the distinction between beneficial and harmful truths.) Another socially useful truth is the one emphasized by Schmitt: most men are naturally clannish, inclined to identify themselves morally and emotionally with exclusive groups. Universalistic ideologies, such as liberalism and communism, are rooted in modern rationalism. They are therefore fundamentally irrational, placing unrealistic demands on human nature. They are also irrational because they propagate the dream of a world society, a dream that, according to Strauss, could lead to a world tyranny where philosophers would find no refuge from oppression. Both liberals and communists, in any case, deny a fundamental feature of the human condition: the naturalness of exclusive groups.

It is quite fortunate for the maintenance of social order that erotic and prerational identification with one's family can easily be rechanneled into erotic and prerational identification with one's country, even though every such identification implies hostility toward rivals and enemies. Strauss fully accepted the thesis that friend/enemy patterns are a defining characteristic of politics: "the opposition of 'We and They' is essential to the political association."[15] What distinguished Strauss from Schmitt was the former's Platonic insistence that unblinking philosophers, not hard-fisted political rulers, are the real men. Philosophers are truly exceptional. They do not identify morally and emotionally with ethnic, tribal, or national groups locked in mutual hatred.[16] This cosmopolitan detachment or aloofness is another reason why philosophers, throughout history, are distrusted by the herd. They consider the bloody hostilities between exclusive groups and nations to be as foolish as the battle between the big-endians and the little-endians in *Gulliver's Travels*. In any case, nothing can be done to eliminate ridiculous friend/enemy groupings, the naive loyalties and antagonisms of most people. And nothing should be done, since society could not survive without the emotional identification of citizens with their fatherland. For most people, communitarian loyalties supplement fear of punishment and hope for reward.

Consider some other once-hidden truths that have also been unwisely disclosed. When social scientists point out "the irrationality of the masses and the necessity of elites," they are saying nothing Plato did not already know. But their un-Platonic indiscretion is ill-advised. Such unsettling truths, when publicly consumed, will fatally weaken the unqualified commitment of citizens to embattled liberal states. The "relativism" that Strauss saw at the heart of most social science is another case in point. It has led to "complete chaos."[17] Schmitt had attacked liberalism as a spineless doctrine that undercut manly aggressiveness against one's enemies, especially the Communists. Strauss applied the same criticism to his colleagues: the political science they profess has nothing to say against those who prefer surrender to war. Unable to demonstrate conclusively that "we" are right and "they" are wrong, political science condones the inherent halfheartedness of permissive and tolerant societies. Under these conditions, it is not surprising that citizens lose confidence in their collective purposes and display a sickly incapacity to fight back when attacked.

The Ancient Understanding of Natural Inequality

Strauss returns us to the stylized contrast between ancients and moderns. He is famous for having reopened the seventeenth-century "quarrel" and for having suggested, like Maistre, that the ancients knew something profound that the moderns have disgracefully and perilously forgotten. One thing "the ancients" (meaning Plato and Aristotle) knew and that "we" have forgotten is that philosophy and society are irreconcilable. Great philosophers in the classical tradition, such as Al Farabi, worked hard to keep their atheism under wraps. Today, for the first time in human history, atheism, a philosophical truth which is obviously incompatible with "a healthy social life," has become public and widespread.[18]

Ancient and modern philosophers agree about a whole string of riveting truths: there is no afterlife, the habitable earth will eventually perish, all nations are founded in crime, all borders are unjust, and so forth. On these matters, they differ only about the propriety of disclosure. The ancients sagely argued that such truths must be hidden from most people, while the moderns, including all the classic liberals from Spinoza to Mill, rashly assumed that truth is never harmful and must be widely diffused. This is what Strauss means by his implausible-sounding claim that the crisis of modernity is a direct consequence of the eclipse of political philosophy. Political philosophy "means primarily not the philosophical treatment of politics, but the political [i.e., artful] or popular, treatment of philosophy."[19] It is the strategic dissimulation philosophers use when trying to communicate their astonishing wisdom to fellow-philosophers while keeping nonphilosophers in the dark. From this perspective, the decline of political philosophy, identified with the modern crisis, is identical to the fatal disappearance of secret writing.

Ancient rationalism, rediscovered by Strauss, is miraculously invulnerable to crisis, and wholly immune to the loss of confidence that afflicts modern rationalism. That immunity would be incomprehensible, however, if the ancient/modern conflict were only a disagreement about the prudence of mass enlightenment. That is merely one aspect of the contrast. Ancient and modern rationalists also differ in their philosophical perspectives on politics and nature. Modern liberals, to take a narrow example, imagine that human beings are not essentially depraved and do not need to be ruled from above, that coercive institutions will become less and less necessary, that a society can be made to cohere around a doctrine of pure toleration, that mankind can be weaned away from exclusive groups and closed societies, and that war can be eliminated. Ancient sages, not to mention great antiliberals such as Maistre and Schmitt, knew better. Modern rationalists are irrational, and even inauthentic, in a simple sense: they close their eyes to the intractable givens of the human condition.

But Strauss was still more impressed by another way that ancient rationalism outperformed its modern counterpart. Consider how radically Plato and Hobbes disagreed about both nature and philosophy. Plato affirmed, while Hobbes denied, that nature is essentially hierarchical. The very existence of "the low," he believed, is justified only if it subserves "the high." Some souls are nobler, some are baser. Some activities are above, others are below. What has led modern rationalism into an impasse is its egalitarian delusion, its unforgivably malicious attack on the beautiful and all-illuminating high/low and above/below schemes.

Strauss considered natural law to be a benign myth. A law of nature is intelligible only as a "declaration of the will of God."[20] If you do not believe in the existence of a divine lawgiver, you do not believe in natural law. As Strauss was not a religious man, he believed neither in the existence of a divine lawgiver nor in natural law. What he believed in was classical natural right, loosely defined as the totality of what is necessary and inevitable. If we ignore what nature demands, disaster will ensue. (Strauss was unhappy with Weber's fact/value distinction because it implied, among other things, that natural necessity was not morally binding.) Modernity is in crisis because it has attempted, with perverse arrogance, to thwart nature.

Here we come to the nerve point of Strauss's thought. Ancient rationalism taught that *the essence of nature is inequality.* Liberal society is rotten because it has forgotten this sublime truth. We no longer comprehend Plato's distinction between knowledge and opinion. When taken seriously, it inevitably leads to the conclusion that inequality is central to the human condition. To accept the distinction between those who think freely and those who are trapped helplessly in the cave of popular tradition is to reject totally the liberal lullaby that all men are created equal. The gulf yawning between higher and lower types of human being, moreover, is the only moral compass we have. (This is a hierarchy of value, it should be noted, not a law. It distinguishes valuable from valueless lives, but it does not set forth rules to govern behavior.[21]) Liberal aristophobia—the hatred of inequality—has disoriented mankind morally and, if the truth be known, almost destroyed human civilization.

Schmitt was correct, says Strauss, to attack liberalism for ignoring the fundamental structure of human existence. But his criticism of liberalism did not go far enough because it did not reach back to the Greeks for a critical standard: "the critique of liberalism that Schmitt initiated can therefore be completed only when we succeed in gaining a horizon beyond liberalism." This horizon is provided by the thought of Plato and Aristotle. They furnish a way to distinguish "between pleasures which are by nature higher and pleasures which are by nature lower." What "the ancients" taught was that the "complete, perfect, and whole" life is the life of philosophy: "man is so built that he can find his satisfaction, his bliss, in free investigation, in articulating the riddle of being." Contemplating the world, and discussing it at leisure with fellow contemplators, is mankind's *summum bonum*.[22] This resplendent human pleasure, however, is one that only a few can appreciate or experience. Schmitt's basic error was to believe that nature is agonic or that conflict is the law of life. The real law of life, as Plato and Aristotle could have taught him, is inequality.[23] The naturalness of hierarchy—the incontrovertible superiority of philosophers and incontestable inferiority of nonphilosophers—provides the only rational basis for a thoroughgoing criticism of liberal theory and institutions.

The Democratization of Hedonism

The first betrayal of natural hierarchy was epistemological. Plato had believed that science was its own reward: knowledge brings bliss to the knower. Bacon, Descartes, Hobbes, and Locke abandoned the ancient credo that the benefits of knowledge belong exclusively to the knowers. They created and defended a science that could help cure disease, raise food production, ease long-distance travel, and otherwise relieve man's estate. They did it to mitigate the herd's resentment against impious and tradition-belittling intellectuals. Prosperity, they reasoned, would be an even more effective opium of the masses than religion. By using knowledge to improve the lot of the public, deep thinkers could win popular approval and avoid the fate of Socrates, even while remaining nonconformists. Strauss viewed this "deal" as a dreadful mistake. The technological turn, the attempt to "conquer nature," may sate the clamoring crowd for a time. But its ultimate consequences will be catastrophic. The Bible comes close to the truth when it suggests that man's love of knowledge will bring him untold suffering. The pure love of knowledge, on the Platonic model, has no deplorable side effects. But when philosophers pursue wisdom for the sake of mastery over nature, mankind is doomed. Human beings are not wise enough to use well the tools modern science has placed in their hands. And science provides no moral guidance. Ominous references to thermonuclear weapons gives an epic, yet realistic, dimension to Strauss's criticism of modern science here: Faustian man, brimming with knowledge, will eventually cut his own throat.

The power generated by uncloseted science was meant to serve the general ease. In addition to atheism, modernity is characterized also by hedonism. Liberalism in particular has spread the notion that the principal goal of society is to satisfy the desires of most people. For Strauss, as for the other detractors of liberalism discussed in this book, a devastating general moral decline has corresponded to the enthronement of the individual with his urges. By eroding religious restraints upon desire and by promising to exploit nature for human delectation, science has set the stage for an endless explosion of appetites. The modern project was to create a universal and peaceful society in which all desires were satisfied. Since friend/enemy patterns are a permanent feature of the human condition and since desires grow endlessly whenever they are satisfied, the whole "modern project" is absurdly Sisyphean—doomed from the start. The ancients knew this, which is why they were not liberals. They emphatically denied that the purpose of society should be peace and prosperity, universal concord, and the satisfaction of most people's material wants. They advocated a much wiser doctrine, and one more compatible with human nature: hedonism for the philosophical elite, for the "real men" who find pleasure in knowledge; piety and self-sacrifice, in both peace and war, for all the rest.[24] They favored communitarian bonds for the masses, one might say, and individualistic self-fulfillment for the few. Contrary to their official pronouncements, the ancients believed that benefit to one's self is the only natural good. The philosophical cream of the crop find their personal satisfaction and even bliss, harmlessly enough, in theoretical contemplation and conversation. This satisfaction is, by nature, the highest pleasure available to mankind. A good society will guarantee that a few choice individuals have a chance to taste this most delicious experience, without any special regard to what their cloistered happiness costs most people. Such a society would be "according to nature" in Strauss's sense. It would make possible "the good life, the life according to nature," that is to say, "the retired life of the philosopher who lives at the fringes of civil society."[25]

The Worldly Task of Philosophy

Philosophy is the one activity which is self-justifying, an end in itself. But philosophers would be very unwise to retreat into a walled garden and let the rest of mankind govern itself. They need a stable social environment in which to pursue their secret life. And social stability is difficult to mastermind. Even if they knew how to go about it, they could not rule society directly, of course, since the unphilosophical multitude will always distrust philosophers as disloyal citizens and enemies of religion and mock them as absent-minded star gazers. But philosophers can nevertheless perform two socially important functions. If they wear disguises, they can help tranquilize the masses by publicly defending religion and other ancestral myths. And they can exert a kind of secret kingship by privately giving pertinent counsel to the "gentlemen" who occupy high political offices. The content of their behind-the-scenes advice is unclear. It seems that they embolden rulers to deviate from ordinary moral prohibitions whenever rigid adherence would have politically disastrous consequences. But they may also encourage restraint.

Aging philosophers always need fresh recruits; they are always on the lookout for "the young men who might become philosophers." These young men must somehow be convinced that "all practical or political life is essentially inferior to contemplative life." They must learn to look down on politics as something essentially childish. Strauss is impressed by the erotic nature of this secret seduction—the sage few discreetly whispering their dangerous truths into the ears of selected youngsters. Their remarkable generosity, Strauss believes, stems from "the love of the mature philosopher for the puppies of his race, by whom he wants to be loved in turn."[26] (The ungodlike nature of this need for puppy love may bother Strauss less than it should.)

The good society, on this model, consists of the sedated masses, the gentlemen rulers, the promising puppies, and the philosophers who pursue knowledge, manipulate the gentlemen, anesthetize the people, and housebreak the most talented young. Such an ideal, unlike Marx's communist utopia, is compatible with human nature as we know it. It is perfectly realizable, according to Strauss.[27] Unfortunately, philosophers cannot bring it about intentionally, for it depends on "chance" or the fortuitous emergence of amiable gentlemen-rulers willing to listen to the philosopher's secret advice. The recognition that chance cannot be forced is a sign of ancient sobriety and moderation. It should be contrasted with the dizzying ambitiousness of modern citizens, vulgar Machiavellians all, who deny that "fatality is preponderant" in politics, and who suppose that *fortuna* can be subjected to human will.[28]

The Error of Christianity

While Strauss obviously shares a good deal in common with Catholic counter-Enlightenment thinkers such as Maistre or, more recently, Alasdair MacIntyre, he differs from them radically in his conviction that Christianity is almost as guilty for the putrescence of the modern world as secular philosophy itself.[29] The Nietzscheanism of this aspect of his thinking is hard to deny. By teaching that God loves the weak and the ugly, Christianity subverted the supreme rights of the few.

Christianity was universalistic and therefore corrosive of healthy traditions. (Eighteenth-century Enlightenment had the same effect for the same reason.) Jesus spoke to all mankind, slackening people's moral attachment to their exclusive and closed societies. Even more effectively than Machiavelli and Hobbes, moreover, Christianity attacked the Platonic and Aristotelian idea that philosophical inquiry was the highest way of life.[30] In the Islamic and Jewish traditions, philosophers were in a "precarious position," but at least they were free to pay lip-service to ancestral myths while pursuing their own intellectual quest in private. Christianity upset this happy relationship, violating Strauss's most important taboo. It tried to reconcile reason and revelation, thus depriving philosophy of its "inner freedom from supervision." In the Christian Middle Ages, philosophy was "deprived of its character as a way of life."[31] Unlike Al Farabi, Thomas Aquinas was no heroic esotericist. He believed most of what he wrote. There would be nothing amiss if devotion to a jealous God excluded *most* human beings from an erotic love of knowledge for its own sake. But Christianity ensnared people indiscriminately, including the most gifted young men. For this and other reasons, the Christian religion fatally weakened the West, preparing the way for the contemporary crisis.

Modernity Diagnosed

While sometimes arresting, Strauss's style is frustratingly compact and involved. As John Gunnell has pointed out, it is often impossible to determine if he is paraphrasing others or speaking in his own name.[32] He has strong and unusual convictions but does not enjoy exposing them to the light of day. Any attempt to summarize his thought in plain words will violate the spirit of his enterprise. But at least it puts us in a position to ask the question he did not wish to help us pose: what are the fundamental flaws in his position?

Before looking at the basics, a few petty annoyances should at least be mentioned. Consider, for instance, Strauss's hermeneutical principle that the central item in a list is invariably the most important, his unargued premise that there are no cultural limitations to the range of possibilities that great minds can conceive, or his general idea that the history of philosophy has a plot, with heroes and villains, in which noble ancients are tragically vanquished by base moderns. Notice also the banality of his grand political conclusion: not everything is possible and therefore moderation is good. There seems to be a contradiction between his repeated claim that philosophy is an undogmatic or open-ended "quest" and his cryptographical accounts of esoteric "teachings" *(Lehren)* that invariably emphasize doctrinal conclusions or wisdom rather than ideas-in-the-making. His methodological assumptions also entail a score of other perverse consequences: for example, if great philosophers inevitably try to mislead most of their readers, then scholars are always wrong whenever most of them agree.[33] I will pass over such matters and focus instead on four central defects: Strauss's rhetorical posture (borrowed from Nietzsche and Heidegger), the illiberal nature of his elitism, his use of double standards, and his poorly supported causal claims.

Strauss's debt to Nietzsche was profound. Nietzsche, after all, wrote that "the great man is necessarily a skeptic (which is not to say that he has to appear to be one)"; that "every profound spirit needs a mask," and that "what serves the higher type of men as nourishment or delectation must always be poison for a very different and inferior type."[34] He emphatically denied that human beings are equal, of course: "the difference between the exoteric and the esoteric" was "formerly known to philosophers—among the Indians as among the Greeks, Persians, and Muslims, in short, wherever one believed in an order of rank and *not* in equality and equal rights."[35] Similarly, he contended repeatedly that "the will to equality" was the root of the moral catastrophe of modern times. Recall finally that Zarathustra comes down from his mountain to speak not to "the people" but to a few select "companions." He does not want to become "the shepherd and dog of a herd." When Zarathustra lures away society's higher types, we should not be surprised that "the herd shall become angry" with him.[36] These passages provided the seed that eventually grew into Strauss's idea of a perennial conflict between "philosophy" and "the city."

As a student in Germany, Strauss was also profoundly influenced by Martin Heidegger. Heidegger, he later wrote, was "the only German philosopher"; he surpassed "all his contemporaries" in "speculative intelligence"; he taught a whole generation how to think and how to read; he made possible "a genuine return to classical philosophy, to the philosophy of Plato and Aristotle"; compared to him, Max Weber was but "an orphan child"; in the last analysis, he was "the only great thinker of our time." True, Strauss distanced himself from his master in important ways. He found Heidegger's thought fatally tainted by Christianity: "his understanding of existence was obviously of Christian origin (conscience, guilt, being-unto-death, and anguish)." He denied that the search for permanent features in the human condition could be dismissed (as Heidegger dismissed it) as a futile attempt to escape from the perishable world or to take revenge against time itself. And he severely criticized the existentialist idea of "resoluteness" for its own sake. Heidegger's fundamental error, like Schmitt's, was to have ignored the intrinsically superior status of philosophy—a superiority rooted in nature and disclosed by reason. He did not realize that philosophers alone could be authentic, that only a few exceptional souls can go eyeball to eyeball with the fundamental structures of human existence, including death, without blinking. He did not see that philosophizing offered an authentic "remedy" for an otherwise terrifying existential condition. By devoting themselves to a lifetime study of "the riddle of being," philosophers, and they alone, can live "in a state above fear and trembling as well as above hope."[37]

Heidegger was also a historicist. He denied the unchanging importance of the high/low scheme. He slighted the timeless superiority of philosophers and inferiority of nonphilosophers. He repudiated Plato's inspiring conclusion that "the higher is stronger than the lower."[38] To deny hierarchical nature, in this sense, is to extinguish philosophy—to rule out the activity cherished by the best souls. It is not surprising that Heidegger treated authenticity as a subrational "commitment" rather than a rational insight.

Strauss's argument here is stupefyingly paradoxical. Indeed, it is so foreign to our ordinary way of thinking that it is at first difficult to absorb. From a Platonic perspective, it turns out, fascism was excessively democratic and egalitarian. Like Christianity and liberalism, it wholly neglected "the best human type."[39] Fascism did not distinguish between "real men" and lesser breeds. Irresponsible intellectuals like Schmitt and Heidegger, who embraced the Nazi movement, failed to recognize the existence of inborn and natural (although certainly not hereditary) inferiority.

Despite such singular demurrers, Strauss's diagnosis of the "crisis" of modernity reveals the permanence of Heidegger's influence on his thought. A terrible philosophical mistake, he concurred, underlies the fundamental defectiveness of the modern world. Heidegger traced the sorrowful decadence of modern times to *Seinsvergessenheit*, the forgetfulness of being. Adapting this theme to his American audience, Strauss wrote instead of "the oblivion of the most fundamental things." He also echoed Heidegger's famous statement that the United States and the Soviet Union are metaphysically identical, insisting that both societies have the same goal: a universal, prosperous society. (The political differences remain important, of course.) But even more Heideggerian is Strauss's posture as an author. He poses in the same oracular way, and constantly associates himself with the saving power *(das Rettende)* that may rescue humanity from its present danger. With astonishing perspicacity, *he* has seen what almost no one else has seen. He is one of the few who have dared to ask the essential questions. He is one of the few who have recognized the real alternative to modern thought. He is one of the few who have withstood the mental and moral catastrophe of modern times. Almost all others languish in dim caves, while he is one of the few who have broken free of their chains. What makes this posturing so exasperating is not the self-inflation—that is common enough—but the way Strauss combines unstanched pretentiousness with endless references to other people's *hubris* and not wholly sincere protests that he is just a humble nobody, posing a few difficult questions, unworthy of being compared with the great philosophers of the past.[40]

Another aspect of Strauss's rhetorical posture is the suggestion that he and those who follow him are walking time-bombs.[41] Their ideas, far from being bland and boring, are horrifyingly dangerous. What they know could destroy the world. Most intellectuals are plagued by a feeling of impotence, by a sense that their ideas have a relatively limited influence on political events or the course of history. Strauss remedies this malaise when he says philosophers must keep silent, for if their ideas were heard, they would utterly transform the world. A simple slip of the tongue could burn up the nurturing atmosphere that keeps ordinary mortals alive. For desk-bound scholars, this is an extraordinarily flattering idea. To say that the crisis of the West has philosophical origins, moreover, is to imply that it has a philosophical cure.[42] To intellectualize the origins of society's problems is to enhance the social prestige of intellectuals. Something of this self-aggrandizing sort may also have been at the back of Strauss's mind.

Professors are not a notably courageous group. But Strauss allows them to picture themselves as heroes, encamped on the front lines, defending civilization against its enemies. This delusion is laughable, but harmless in itself. It becomes pernicious only when students are drawn into the game. Pedagogically, an invitation to bookworm heroism appears bizarre. There is something perverse, both intellectually and morally, about teaching a young man or woman that the only reason to study the great works of philosophy is to help defend civilization against its enemies, that what he or she should be looking for in classic works is a cure for the crisis of the West. This is to set the student on the wrong track and to promise a Napoleonic "high" that serious scholarship cannot honestly deliver.

A Difference in Kind

The sheep and the goats, the high and the humble, the elite and the vulgar, the wise and the unwise, the thoughtful and the thoughtless, the strong and the weak, the supermen and the herd—Strauss's obsession with this sharp distinction is tedious, of course, and it is also highly unrealistic. The teeming plurality of human types makes it impossible to classify all people by means of a single dichotomy. Strauss's fascination with "real men as distinguished from ordinary human beings"—a division marked by the former's "strength of instinct"—is already prominent in his unpublished Hamburg doctoral dissertation of 1921.[43] When he announces, much later, that "things which are true of the highest intellects are wholly inapplicable to others," he is still underestimating the gradualness of the spectrum running from the less to the more intelligent and wise. He ignores it because of his passion for esotericism. The very idea of a *useful fiction* implies a sharp break between the few and the many, a total separation, with no overlap or continuum, between the producers and the consumers of salutary myths. He calls it "a difference not of degree but of kind."[44] The neatness of this either/or distinction falsifies the world in all its messy variety.

According to David Hume, "to declaim against present times, and magnify the virtue of remote ancestors, is a propensity almost inherent in human nature."[45] Strauss was an ordinary person, with ordinary conceits. Max Weber condemns the common practice of "snobbishly setting one's self off from the 'far too many,' as is maintained by the various and misconceived 'prophesies' which go back to Nietzsche."[46] Likewise, Alexander Kojève criticized Strauss for exaggerating the differences between the few and the many. The few want to be superior, and that is the most common desire of all. (Would they relish their love of knowledge for its own sake if it did not prove them superior to the noblemen who simply want superiority?)

The undemocratic *and therefore unrealistic* dimension of Strauss's thought is clearly displayed at this point. An important premise of democratic theory is not that all men are equal in all respects, but rather that we cannot usually tell in advance who will contribute something important in a public debate. (That is the core of Milton's defense of free speech.) Strauss is undemocratic and illiberal in precisely this sense: he knows in advance that the philosophical few have nothing whatsoever to learn from the unphilosophical many.

Without making it the centerpiece of her thought, Hannah Arendt, too, recognized "the conflict between the philosopher and the polis." She even wrote that "in Plato's political philosophy . . . the whole utopian reorganization of polis life is not only directed by the superior insight of the philosopher but has no aim other than to make possible the philosopher's way of life."[47] Because she did not measure the value of all things by their closeness or distance from philosophy, Arendt may have been criticizing Strauss's one-sidedness here. For what can the vulgar happiness of "utterly incompetent," "dull-witted" and "morally inferior people" mean to Strauss's philosopher? Nothing, of course: "having perceived the truly grand, the philosophers regard the human things as paltry. Their very justice—their abstaining from wronging their fellow human beings—flows from contempt for the things which the non-philosophers hotly contest."[48] This brings us to what we may call Strauss's doormat theory of the overwhelming majority. Most people are not merely inferior to the philosophical supermen. Their lives are utterly valueless and unjustifiable unless they serve to make philosophers more comfortable and secure.[49] Philosophers must return to the cave or the city, even though it is thoroughly beneath them, to ensure an agreeable environment for their own "choiceworthy" activities. (The parasite must keep its host alive.) The philosophical few must teach and tame the gentlemen, or risk being killed for disloyalty, atheism, and so forth.[50] Unfortunately for Strauss, there is no historical evidence that philosophers have ever effectively played such an educative role. Plato himself suggested that the philosopher-behind-the-throne is likely to end up being used and abused by the politicians he attempts to tame.

The Baseness of Liberalism

Strauss did not appear to have a very clear picture of modern science, although he was obviously irked by its "enormous prestige." He thought natural science had less to do with reason, inquiry, problem-solving, discovery, and truth than with catering ignobly to the masses. Modern science aims to satisfy the needs of ordinary people (not of the scientific elite), and those needs, he believed, are by nature unsatisfiable. Aristotle conceived God as "thought thinking itself." Such a divinity neither punished nor came to the aid of lesser creatures. It was wholly self-absorbed. Philosophers should model themselves on this sort of neglectful deity. As Strauss put it: "the life devoted . . . to the service of others is not the life according to nature."[51] Ancient philosophers were never very interested in becoming "benefactors" to mankind. After them, those who tried only unleashed a dangerous torrent of base appetites and eventually produced the atomic bomb.

Against Hobbes, Locke, and the other founding fathers of modern liberalism, Strauss seems to level the same objection that he lodges against modern science. He appears to attack liberals and proto-liberals for lowering the goals of mankind, promoting selfishness, and encouraging the pursuit of material satisfactions. (This is the sort of vulgar Marxist argument that R. H. Tawney apparently found seductive in Strauss.) But Strauss knew that Hobbes and Locke had neither enthroned base passions nor lifted all moral restraints from mankind's shoulders. He was perfectly aware that they required people to restrain themselves, to lay down their arms or abdicate their right to execute the law of nature. He even agreed with liberals and proto-liberals that malice, envy, and the need for revenge were morally "lower" than the desire to live. He also realized that Nietzsche had furiously attacked liberalism on these grounds: liberal society requires individuals to give up their spontaneous wish to inflict pain on others. In other words, Strauss's complaints about low desires and lack of restraint are something of a smoke-screen. His real objection to Hobbes and Locke is another. He deplores their materialism and permissiveness much less than their commitment to a norm—the norm of equality, the prohibition on self-exemption. It is not their moral relativism or aimlessness but their moral absolutism that he rebukes. Their egalitarianism is what he finds most base.

Neither Hobbes nor Locke, for all their differences, believed that the lives of most people should be used as stepping-stones for the pleasures and excellences of a few philosophers. They argued that basic rights should be distributed equally, not in line with "high" or "low" capacities. In this sense, they attacked nature. Building on Christian foundations, liberals and their immediate predecessors declared war on inequality. They did not think that a few supermen should be allowed to exempt themselves from rules applied equally to all. They denied that unyielding hierarchy was a necessity of life.[52] In the end, Strauss is less nettled by modern selfishness than by modern universalism, by the extraordinary idea that all men are made of the same paste.

Strauss passionately believed that "there are politically relevant natural differences among men" and that "some men are by nature superior to others." He made little effort to conceal that he belonged to this peerless breed. But why was he so preoccupied with relations of superordination and subordination? Why was he infatuated by "the superior man," by the individual who was "most high in rank"? Why did he also assume that one of the major preoccupations of great thinkers, such as Thucydides or Machiavelli, was to establish their personal preeminence over competitors, such as Homer or Christ? Was he interpreting others in his own image? Why did he neglect the comic side of the passion to eclipse others, the sheer inanity of the urge to throw rivals into the shade? Why did he tell us on every other page that philosophy is better and higher and more choiceworthy than any other activity? He was obviously enthralled by dreams of a *Stufen-kosmos*, an implacable "hierarchy of beings."[53] But his passion for ranking remains one of the unfathomable mysteries of his mind.

After all his travail, Strauss provides no argument to demonstrate the absolute superiority of philosophers and leaves unanswered a whole range of pertinent questions. What makes him think that even the most talented philosopher could realize anything more than a minuscule range of human excellences? (Weber's value-pluralism was anathema to Strauss, among other reasons, because it suggested that the scholar-thinker had to *give up* something valuable when he embraced the theoretical way of life.[54]) Why should superior capacities imply a right to use others as tools? Why is philosophy self-justifying and why does no other form of life have any but an instrumental value? Why is "philosophy" equated with "reason"? Why should we believe Socrates' conceit that the philosopher is more noble than Achilles? How can an activity which most people do not understand be conceived as "the ultimate aim of political life"? Similarly, why should the desire to live be considered "low"? Is liberal democracy an acceptable regime *only* because it is the best available option from the philosopher's point of view? If philosophers are truly autonomous, why should they stoop to "despising people whose horizon is limited to their consumption of food and their digestion"?[55] And so forth. Finally, Strauss never answered the fundamental philosophical question: how did he know what he pretended to know? Let us suppose, for a moment, that he had no answers to this and other embarrassing questions. In that case, the urgent need to hide his most important thoughts would have been extremely convenient. Such a tantalizing coincidence, of course, proves nothing. But it is suggestive.

Double Standards

Strauss was more lenient to himself than to others. He typically accuses liberals or quasi-liberals such as Weber of lacking the intellectual and moral resources to resist Nazism. But what resources does Strauss himself provide? Reading Plato in Greek will not stop Hitler in his tracks. Can individual conscience, fortified by the wholesome myth of natural law, undo the ravages of hyperinflation, absorb the shocks of industrialization and urbanization, and compensate for the breakdown of political institutions in the face of paramilitary factions? Can religious myths, uncritically imbibed by the many, guarantee political moderation? Social scientists may well be fiddling while the West burns. In the meantime Strauss writes difficult books, teaches a few graduate students, and postures knowingly: it looks a good deal like fiddling. He can encourage a reading of classics in a society that fails to appreciate such study. But can he actually "found an aristocracy within modern mass society"?[56] And even if he could, would it be a reliable barrier against another Nazi maelstrom?

A different sort of double standard is revealed in Strauss's studied neglect of ancient society and culture. He takes the theoretical defects of modern philosophy as a key to the crisis of modern societies. In the case of antiquity, his lack of interest in social or political crises seems total. While contrasting modern society with ancient philosophy is obviously unfair, the correct comparison of modern with ancient societies is never undertaken. Perhaps all societies are in crisis. Perhaps history is one crisis yielding to another. If so (and the evidence is strong), then it is implausible to make modern philosophers appear uniquely guilty as Strauss unremittingly does.

The Power of Ideas

One of Strauss's most rousing suggestions is that the ancients could have invented modern science, but that they refused to do so because they knew it would be "destructive of humanity."[57] This is a historical, not merely hermeneutical or interpretative, claim. Without this sort of bold counterfactual, Strauss would be just another historian of ideas. But even though such assertions are essential to his position, they are never openly discussed or defended. Indeed, they are deftly wedged between paragraphs of dense textual commentary. That way they can titillate his readers without provoking any requests for evidence. (Here we encounter another, perhaps the ultimate, source of Strauss's hostility toward social science. He worried that positivism was sapping the virility of the West. And at the same time as he objected to the plebeian way that modern social scientists tried to influence policy openly and democratically, he was unhappy about the empiricists' embarrassing demand that we provide factual support for our causal claims.)

A similar and more obvious example is Strauss's idea that Machiavelli launched "modernity" by an act of insubordination against the wisdom of antiquity. Would there have been no modern times if Machiavelli had died in his crib? Strauss does not say so. But that is certainly the sort of causal claim on which the rhetorical force of his interpretation depends. Neither economic structures nor political processes, but ideology rules the world—so runs his unfashionably elitist and intellectualist theory of social change. Only great men make a difference. Only they put words into people's mouths. (How the irresistible power of great philosophical opinion-shapers can be reconciled with the rule of "chance" is never explained.)

Most of those who believe in the historical influence of ideas feel compelled to grapple with the mechanisms and intermediaries through which theories and viewpoints shape events. Alexis de Tocqueville, for example, struggles hard to explain how dangerous ideas, once locked safely in the heads of a few philosophers, suddenly "find a welcome among the masses and acquire the driving force of a political passion."[58] Fixated uniquely on heroic thinkers, by contrast, Strauss gives little thought to such intermediary processes, or to accompanying and secondary causes that are less philosophical in nature. The discovery of America, the Reformation and the religious civil wars, the invention of the magnetic compass, gunpowder, the telescope, and the printing press, the emergence of state bureaucracies—none of these factors can be reduced to Machiavellism, though all had a decisive impact on the contours of modernity. To say that Machiavelli single-handedly loosed acquisitiveness on the modern world is to rule out, with little justification, a whole series of other causes for the rise of the modern commercial ethos. This is not to deny the powerful, complex, indirect, tangled, and often unintended influence of Machiavelli, Hobbes, and the others who are said to have revolutionized human life everywhere. But their influence is not disparaged by being put into perspective, as Strauss apparently believed.

Strauss is also making a causal argument about social processes, not offering an interpretation of a text, when he claims that social stability is based on opinion or that a philosophical doctrine, such as the rejection of natural inequality, is "corrupting" or "endangers society."[59] These sorts of assertions, too, give his writing its edge and makes it appear more than merely academic. But, here again, he fails to defend his claims openly. As a result, it is impossible to know exactly what he means. Does he believe, for example, that imposing civil disabilities on atheists actually increases social stability? Under what conditions? Can he prove it? Similarly, can elites be wrong about which myths are "necessary" for society? Do they ever make mistakes on this question, mistakes that just happen to be in their own interest, narrowly understood?

Consider also Strauss's insistence that professed skepticism is dangerous. What does he want to say here? His premise is explicitly Nietzschean: "culture is possible only if men are fully dedicated to principles of thought and action which they do not and cannot question."[60] Skepticism, therefore, frustrates the deep human need for undiscussable truths. But how does the loss of certainty affect the individual? Does it produce listless despair or frantic immoralism? Or perhaps human beings are incapable of living without dogmatic beliefs. In this case, when skepticism demolishes relatively harmless beliefs (such as patriotism and religion), it will drive people to embrace alternative dogmas (such as racial purity) that are much more harmful. In his accounts of the dangers of skepticism Strauss never explains how seemingly contrary processes are related to one another. The price of coy indirection is a deplorable lack of clarity (in his mind, not merely in ours) about his most controversial ideas.

A Final Puzzle

Many non-Straussian intellectual historians would accept the existence of esotericism.[61] Oblique rhetoric and cloaked references, like the censor's search for subversive meanings, are nothing unusual. Everyone knows that the fear of hellfire was long believed to be an indispensable "social cement." It was thought wrong, as a consequence, to attack religion in public. The *libertins érudits* valued their heads and therefore kept their infidelity quiet. In his postwar works Strauss strangely over-taxes this theme—he stretches it into a philosophy of history, a diagnosis of the Great Crisis of the West, a general commentary on the nature of human life. Why does he go so far? A confusing parable enfolded in his discussion of the persecuted philosophers might provide a partial answer. Socrates was attacked as a cosmopolitan outsider or stranger who refused to worship the local gods. The analogy with European Jews, whose "noxious" influence bigots trace back to the Enlightenment, is too close to be accidental.[62] Philosophers can enhance their chances for survival if they do not make waves. They should keep their heads down and refrain from irritating their masters. This advice reinforces the parallel with European Jewry, as does the notion that philosophers should rely on aristocratic gentlemen to protect them from the hostile masses. To complicate matters, Strauss compares Athens, wisely defending itself against the harmful intrusion of universalist ideas, to the closed Jewish community wisely rejecting liberal universalism. But what is the meaning of this curious, convoluted, multilayered, strained, and explosive allegory? Why does Strauss want to arouse and bewilder his readers in this way? We can neither dismiss his parable nor understand it. What did he have in mind? We all want to know. But Strauss's secret art of writing, his self-indulgent abuse of "the specific immunity of the commentator," makes it impossible to guess.[63] (In my view, he did not know what he was trying to say.) We can confidently assume, however, that Strauss's obsession with esotericism and persecution had its roots not in scholarship, but in the unthinkable tragedy of his generation.

Because he believed that some truths remained dangerous in his day, Strauss himself used stealth and frugality in communication. Caution recommends "so involving one's sense that one cannot be easily understood."[64] He apparently thought he was protecting the community by his indigestible prose. But he also protected himself. He had to coddle his readers. So how could anyone complain that he failed to argue for his ideas? But subterfuge may backfire. The sharp disagreement or legacy-dispute now raging among his heirs (known to insiders as "the crisis of the Strauss divided") provides good evidence that, on some questions, at least, no one will ever be able to ferret out his buried treasure.

What Strauss underestimated, perhaps, was the irreparable damage done to philosophy by its need to play hide and seek.[65] Theories are often refined and strengthened by public contestation. (Because he identified science with the attempt to conquer nature, he neglected the importance of this epistemological principle.) Conversely, duplicitous and insulated elites go soft in the head. By shrouding their thoughts in secrecy, philosophers forfeit the stimulus of criticisms, complaints, suggestions, counterarguments, unsettling information, and spirited backtalk. They are never publicly compelled to be perfectly clear. Strauss casually dismissed the thought-provoking function of the right of disclosure and the free flow of information. When an opportunity presents itself, however, even readers of "mean capacities" can helpfully correct a mighty sage. Nature may be hierarchical, but a cat can still look at a king. If ancient rationalism could not face such democratic realities, then it was even less authentic than its modern twin.

Strauss was an exotic flower transplanted from Central Europe to the plains of the American Midwest. It is not surprising that he stood out. True, his spiritedness and originality occasionally degenerate into idiosyncrasy. Even those impatient with his evasive style, however, can come to appreciate the subtlety and strangeness of his mind. Among liberalism's critics, he remains in a class by himself.[66] His total cynicism about religion, especially Christianity, distinguishes him from Maistre. His obsession with inequality distances him from Schmitt. His philosopher's disdain for tribal attachments separates him sharply from the communitarian antiliberals such as MacIntyre. So Strauss is *sui generis*. He was not exactly a philosopher, it is true. And his writings, because of their dubious generalizations, analytical inadequacies, and fundamental lack of clarity, will always irritate most readers. But he will continue to attract the kind of admirers he warmly encouraged and still richly deserves. *?why pull the punch here?*

4 / MacIntyre: The Antiliberal Catechism

La raison humaine ne produit que des disputes

—Maistre

Antiliberals hostile to Enlightenment universalism can be grouped into hardliners and softliners. The former are ruthless, the latter are lax. Hard antiliberals damn liberalism from a wholly nonliberal point of view and dare to draw the shocking political consequences. Soft antiliberals malign liberalism verbally, but when faced with practical choices, reveal a surprising fondness for liberal protections and freedoms. I now turn from hard antiliberalism to one of its milder versions.

Viewed from a distance, Alasdair MacIntyre's position may seem at first close to Schmitt's. There is nothing more important, he agrees, than group loyalty and group life. Unlike Schmitt, however, MacIntyre is wholly silent about conflict between rival groups. And he never associates communitarian longings with conformist bigotry. Similarly, he does not think of his liberal enemies as weak-kneed capitulationists. He never blames liberalism for enfeebling a country militarily. As a soft antiliberal, he does not take enmity between communities as his his central theme.

But might not MacIntyre be described as a Straussian of the left? He does present the central blindness of "liberal modernity" in an uncannily Straussian way. Liberalism, he explains, has repressed the art of secret or selective communication: "the concept of having to be a certain sort of person, morally or theologically, in order to read a book aright—with the implication that perhaps, if one is not that sort of person, then the book should be withheld from one—is alien to the assumption of liberal modernity that every rational adult should be free to and is able to read every book."[1]

But despite this and other parallels, the association of MacIntyre and Strauss too is strained. Strauss was not imbued with Christian piety, for one thing, and would not have proposed, as MacIntyre does, "using the Bible and Augustine to transcend the limitations not only of Aristotle but also of Plato."[2] Strauss favored communitarian attachments and traditional ways of life, it is true, but only for the benighted masses, not for the wise philosophers. And he saw liberal egalitarianism as an expression of the same herd morality that was unleashed on the world by the Christians. Despite a few incautious remarks, MacIntyre does not share this militantly antiegalitarian perspective. Although he has experimented over the years with a variety of theoretical positions, he has never fallen under Nietzsche's spell. He has traveled, basically, from Christianity to Marxism and back. Today he is probably best described as a neo-Aristotelian or neoclerical critic of "modern liberal society." *After Virtue*, his widely praised work of 1981, is written largely from a communitarian point of view. It is a zestful, fighting book. It strives for clarity. It displays enviable erudition and is bursting with strong claims memorably expressed. It also presents a mass of historical material in fresh and interesting ways.

For a student of the antiliberal tradition, however, *After Virtue* is more representative than original. It is a warehouse stacked to the ceiling with well-worn perspectives, accusations, and arguments. Indeed, it is something like a summa of the postwar antiliberal mind, and it begs to be examined in that light. Like other contemporary works, it recycles many of the arguments used earlier by hard antiliberals; but it omits all panegyrics to war, political ruthlessness, natural inequality, and superhuman toughness.

MacIntyre begins by painting Western history as an unremitting process of impoverishment or decay. Past societies were orderly and healthy, while ours is disheveled and sick. History recapitulates the fall from grace. Things used to be good; now they are bad. Once whole, the vase of culture now lies shattered. MacIntyre expresses his discontent with the present, in the traditional manner, by fictionalizing the past: the ancient Greeks simply put us to shame.[3] Judged by "the lost morality of the past," our current situation is a "disaster" and a "moral calamity." Because of a massive cultural catastrophe, "morality today is in a state of grave disorder."[4] People who were once firmly implanted in harmonious communities are now rootless. Vital social relations have been desiccated by arid individualism. A warm, solidary, and emotionally satisfying communal order has yielded to a chilly, egoistical, and morally hollow one. The social faculties of prelapsarian souls have been grievously damaged by Western rationalism. Generosity, friendship, and joy have nearly vanished. Niggardliness and misery are all-pervasive. Idyllic normative consensus has been supplanted by sickeningly endless disagreement. Thick preindustrial forms of social identity have been displaced by thinner and more universal ones. As a result, mankind is clueless about how to live, what to do. "Modernity" has few if any redeeming features, according to the tenets of "deprivation history" in this, its purest form.

Despite his erudition and wide-ranging mind, MacIntyre seems never to have reflected on the history of antiliberal ideology itself. He is a typical antiliberal in this and almost every other way. He apparently battles against moral degeneration all alone. To oppose "liberal modernity," he confesses, "I have step by step deprived myself of very nearly all argumentative allies." Yet he is not so iconoclastic as he pretends. His diagnosis of our grim cultural predicament, for example, culminates in a wholly familiar invitation to follow him along the path of spiritual renewal. Like most communitarian antiliberals, he seems never to have reflected on the drawbacks of the kind of "community" he hopes to establish. He also claims to be one of the "very few" who have understood the scope and depth of the modern crisis. Others cannot see our moral plight because they have been blinded by it. If his theory is true, remarkably enough, "it will necessarily appear implausible."[5] Objections to his book constitute a necessary, though not sufficient, condition for its validity. This style of reasoning allows MacIntyre to "terminate" discussions in an abrupt, if somewhat discourteous, way. Instead of arguing with his opponents and listening to their replies, he can dismiss them peremptorily as a part of the problem he aims to solve.

MacIntyre's stock arguments, slogans, and postures are impressive. He treats "modernity" and "liberalism" as if they were synonyms, neglecting the many fiercely illiberal currents in modern culture. He writes uncritically of "the social world" as if it were a blameless domain where ugly deeds were never done. He contrasts noble community to base individualism, as if group loyalties and collective passions were never morally ambivalent—as if they never produced conflict, for instance. Modern liberal societies glorify instrumental relations between human beings, we are told, as if the abolition of slavery was a negligible affair. MacIntyre also waffles uncontrollably between two inconsistent claims: our communityless or atomistic society is accurately described by liberal political theory, *and* Aristotelians alone understand that our society, deep down, is not atomistic at all. He freely indulges in messianic hermeneutics, suggesting that his critique of intellectual fallacies will usher in a comprehensive social transformation. (The intellectual historian can thus be both a Cassandra of despair and a prophet of hope.) Like other antiliberals, finally, MacIntyre continues "to accept much of the substance" of the Marxist criticism of "liberalism." For example, he disparages "economic self-seeking," deplores "the moral impoverishment of advanced capitalism," expresses nostalgia for "the past before individualism and the power of markets," denounces "impersonal capital" and "institutionalized acquisitiveness," and bewails the "elevation of the values of the market to a central social place."

But Marxism itself, he quickly adds, is a hopelessly flawed tradition. Its principal intellectual defect is its secret kinship with liberal individualism, of course.[6]

Liberalism (Once Again) Diagnosed

But how does MacIntyre describe the liberalism he fears and disdains? He does not accuse it of ignoring harsh or sickening realities—in the manner of Maistre, Schmitt, or Strauss. As a postfascist antiliberal, he makes no reference to our blood-soaked planet, to the inevitability of murderous conflict, or to the need to replace sentimentalism with mental toughness and freedom from pleasing illusions. He is a "soft" antiliberal, and the identifying mark of his position is a fondness for a better world liberalism has purportedly suppressed. Liberalism has failed to comprehend not ugliness, but beauty, not brutal, but comely truths; still, a noxious nescience lies at the heart of liberal thought.

Liberals have no conception of community, first of all. They see the social world as a platform where naked egoisms haggle and brawl. They "treat society as nothing more than an arena in which individuals seek and secure what is useful or agreeable to them." They have no conception of a common good that is "prior to and independent of any summing of individual interests." The motherland has shriveled into a shopping mall. Rather than the collectivity's using individuals, as is proper, individuals now use the collectivity, as is not.[7] For liberals, shockingly, "a society is composed of individuals, each with his or her interest, who then have to come together and formulate common rules of life." Society is created by "the voluntary act of at least potentially rational individuals with prior interests." Indeed, liberals write "as though we had been shipwrecked on an uninhabited island with a group of other individuals, each of whom is a stranger to me and to all the others."[8] Their crude atomistic approach is largely responsible for the bitter loneliness of "modern man."

The ignoble purpose of the social contract is to protect individual rights and foster individual interests. Liberals see nothing inherently defiling in the idea that "each man by nature seeks to satisfy his own desires." As a consequence, liberalism spurns "communities in which men in company pursue the human good." The "modern liberal state" limits itself to "providing the arena in which each individual seeks his or her private good." As a neo-Aristotelian, MacIntyre is perfectly positioned to see the moral bankruptcy of this selfish, antisocial, and unorganic approach: "from an Aristotelian point of view a modern liberal political society can appear only as a collection of citizens of nowhere who have banded together for their common protection."[9] He does not expect uprooted cosmopolitans and conniving expatriates to join him in his quest for genuine communion.

Corrosive Doubt

This pained outcry against liberal theory and society contains nothing new. And a similar carryover of standard antiliberal themes is detectable in MacIntyre's complaints about liberal skepticism. His dislike of "interminable discussion" recalls Schmitt's ironies about *das ewige Gespräch*, for instance. The main pillars undergirding liberal ideology, he concurs, are disagreement and doubt. Liberal societies are the first in human history to permit and indeed encourage the public questioning of inherited dogmas and prejudices. Never before has public disagreement been officially hallowed as a creative force. When MacIntyre laments that "morality is not what it once was," therefore, he means that moral questions are now subject to endless contestation. The total freedom of all citizens to criticize and debate every conceivable orthodoxy results in a terrifying lack of certainty and, of course, in the unhappy "moral pluralism" of liberal societies—what MacIntyre forebodingly calls "the pluralism which threatens to submerge us all."[10] No Pope retains the spiritual authority needed to re-establish a monoethical culture by fiat. No longer can any Church impose simultaneously on all members of society a single obligatory answer to moral questions. No end can thus be brought to excruciating moral debate.

Such pining for unanimity is remarkably unguarded. But MacIntyre is not always so candid with his readers. He begins *After Virtue*, for example, with the lament that "there seems to be no rational way of securing moral agreement in our culture." What we are unable to achieve today is the "rational justification of morality." The clear implication of these passages is that, in other cultures, at earlier times, there *were* rational ways of securing moral agreement. But did "reason" ever rule? Was agreement ever "rationally" attained? MacIntyre mentions various examples of premodern consensus about morality. But he never unearths any moral agreement that was based on something other than custom, habit, or unquestionable authority. From the evidence he presents we might even conclude—following Maistre, Schmitt, and Strauss—that normative consensus has never been achieved by rational argument.[11] When we look closely at his examples, in fact, we might be tempted by the following hypothesis: MacIntyre does not really believe that moral commitments were rationally justified in premodern societies while being rationally unjustified in their modern successors. Rather, he thinks that premodern societies were morally healthy because the question of justifying moral beliefs never arose. Traditional societies were stable and robust because rational justifications were never required. Modern societies, by contrast, are rickety and moribund because they overtax the human capacity for rational vindication. They try to make reason answer questions (how to live? what to do?) that will never be answered in a uniform way unless minds are stringently governed by authority and custom. The Enlightenment project was doomed to fail because no rational foundations for moral consensus can be found.

Admittedly, this is an unorthodox interpretation of *After Virtue* and one against which MacIntyre himself would undoubtedly protest.[12] It makes him sound more like a freemason or a Straussian than like the Thomist he claims to be. He is not a completely consistent writer, it is true. But the interpretation just sketched, while making him more cynical than he ultimately dares to be or is, does account for some important, and otherwise inexplicable, features of his book. For example, while MacIntyre regrets the loss of community, he is equally appalled—precisely in the manner of Schmitt and Strauss—by the collapse of authority and religion.

Authority

Liberalism is as antagonistic to authority as to community. If the truth be known, liberal culture aims to outlaw the very idea of authority. The longing for an authoritative solution to moral conflict is the Schmittian strand in MacIntyre's antiliberalism. He consistently uses the words "authority" and "authoritative" in a reverent way. When trying to convince his readers of the moral value of what he calls "practices," for example, he stresses the need for submission: "to enter into a practice is to accept the *authority* of those standards and the inadequacy of my own performance as judged by them." He even defines a practice as a "shared activity in which one has initially to learn *obediently* as an apprentice learns." From this authority-friendly and obedience-encouraging perspective, liberal societies are fatally flawed. They suffer from "a lack of regulation of individual behavior." His anarchical-sounding diatribes against bureaucracy should not be allowed to distract us here. MacIntyre despises anarchy because it signals a breakdown of spiritual discipline and rule. The function he ascribes to authority, authoritativeness, and authorization is more psychological than social. Authoritative norms, for example, can free an individual from the vexation of ephemeral and mercurial preferences. When fully in the grip of such norms, I recognize gratefully that "how I feel at any given moment is irrelevant to the question of how I must live." Above all, authority can give people "the certitude which the absence of choice provides." This is the main point. Authority can provide an absolute guide, can rescue the individual from the chaos in his soul and his anxiety about difficult decisions. "We are almost intolerably conscious of rival moral alternatives."[13] Reason is unable to pare down this surfeit of possibilities; authority alone can lift mankind's spiritual burden.

The Enlightenment, according to MacIntyre, spreads darkness everywhere. Its attack on superstition and hierarchy kicked out the props from under human civilization. Naively or diabolically, Enlightenment writers misinterpreted "loss" as "liberation." The fundamental problem with modern liberal society is the absence of piety and deference. Enlightened philosophes saw the erosion of devoutness as a sign of moral progress, but it was actually a symptom of moral decay. Intellectual freedom guarantees that "everything may be criticized." This may sound beautiful at first, but it is profoundly corrupting. To live in a society where nothing is sacred is terrifying: "the specifically modern self . . . finds no limits set to that on which it may pass judgment." This lack of firm boundaries is more than just morally disorienting. It leads to universal *anomie*. People need a still point in the turning world. They require a fixed standard, an overpowering principle that is wholly uncriticizable and can squelch irritating debate. Liberal society, however, cruelly frustrates mankind's innate craving for sockdolagers. People seek to kneel down before the indisputable, as the Grand Inquisitor said. But liberalism, addicted to doubt, will not let the human mind have any rest. The worst indictment MacIntyre can level against contemporary societies is: "we possess no unassailable criteria." Incontrovertibility is what he seeks. His longing for community is secondary to, and derivative from, his longing for "ultimate criteria" or unshakable norms. That longing explains his somewhat obscure attempt to resurrect the Aristotelian idea of a human *telos*. A *telos* is a *ne plus ultra*, a terminus rather than a passageway, a state of inaction or repose where movement ceases: "we strive in order to be at rest."[14] Formulated differently, a *telos* is a standard of judgment that cannot itself be judged. Once established, it is unassailable. It puts "an end" to processes of justification in a palpable, experiential sense.

Religion

Sometimes MacIntyre's yearning for a higher authority, capable of settling all disputes and resolving all doubts, seems to have religious roots. The organization and rhetoric of *After Virtue*, however, make it hard to estimate the relative weight of theological and nontheological considerations in the argument. (In later works, as we shall see, MacIntyre becomes more forthright about his theism.) Here he repeatedly explains that not Jesus but Aristotle "is *the* protagonist against whom" he has "matched the voices of liberal modernity." The contemporary crisis began in the period from the Renaissance to the Enlightenment when "the modern world came systematically to repudiate the classical view of human nature." What liberalism destroyed was not the biblical but the classical view of man. That, at least, is what MacIntyre says, but it is not precisely what he means. A sign of prevarication is his implausible suggestion that the Reformation of the sixteenth century represented a more radical break with the past than the rupture between pagan antiquity and the Christian middle ages.[15] This is not true, and MacIntyre does not believe it himself.

In several crucial passages MacIntyre reveals that his ultimate loyalties lie with biblical theology rather than with Aristotelian teleology. One give-away is his repeated denunciation of "secular reason." While he grieves copiously about modern atomism and the crumbling of aristocratic codes of honor, he ultimately identifies the fundamental crime of modernity as secularization.[16] Liberalism, in any case, is apostasy. It destroyed the force that once provided "a shared background and foundation for moral discourse," that is, religion. To celebrate individual autonomy, as liberals do, is to deny human dependency on God. Kant declared that the injunctions of morality were binding regardless of divine commands. Other liberals repeat the same mistake. The "secularization of morality by the Enlightenment" was bound to fail. The same can be said for "the Enlightenment project of discovering the new rational secular foundations for morality" or the attempt at a "rational secular account of the nature and status of morality." Unwisely as well as impiously, the Enlightenment "put in question the status of moral judgments as ostensible reports of divine law."[17] This was a disastrous maneuver because morality has always been (and must always remain) dependent on sanctity. The persistence of moral behavior in a posttheological society proves that human beings may feed parasitically on the carcass of the past. It does not prove that morality can be justified, or sustained in the long run, without religion.

If moral norms could draw support from Aristotle's teleological account of human nature alone, then religion's loss of prestige would not be fatal to morality. Secularization, however, *has* been fatal, according to MacIntyre. It is because there is but a single compelling justification for morality. He implicitly assumes that norms are valid if and only if they are the commands of God. Why keep a promise or repay a loan if the Deity does not enjoin you to do so? The deplorable fact/value distinction can certainly be overcome theologically. From a believer's viewpoint, an "is" leads directly to an "ought." God's commands, *ex hypothesi*, are morally binding. It would not be rational, in any sense, to ignore injunctions and prohibitions of the Almighty.[18]

In religious societies of the past, "rules of morality" were understood as "expressions of an ultimately divine law." This fact alone accounts for the unbelievable conceptual and practical havoc wrought by secularization. Like Maistre and Strauss (but with greater piety than the latter), MacIntyre is dismayed by the unrestrained critique of religion of early modern times. The Enlightenment's attack on faith caused "the language and practice of morality" to fall into a condition of "grave disorder."[19] In making this causal claim, MacIntyre has not deprived himself of "all argumentative allies." Two of his confrères, Maistre and Strauss, have just been mentioned.

Normative consensus is impossible without a shared belief in a divine lawgiver. Public atheism alone explains why "agreement in rules is . . . something which our individualist culture is unable to secure." The general collapse of religious belief has not yet destroyed all residual religious habits of thought and behavior, however. To justify our actions and expectations, we are left, in the wake of secularization, with a few "fragmented survivals" of an earlier time. A theological, as opposed to communalist, interpretation of *After Virtue* would highlight the following statement: today's "moral judgments are linguistic survivals from the practices of classical theism which have lost the context provided by these practices." From sheer inertia, we pretend that hand-me-down normative fragments are "binding." But we cannot justify this anachronistic belief or the behavior based upon it. If the truth be known, "the deontological character of moral judgments is the ghost of conceptions of divine law which are quite alien to the metaphysics of modernity."[20] Like all ghosts, this one too is bound to vanish in the daylight of secular reason.

These are strong pronouncements. They clearly imply that the single most significant trait of modern society is not atomism, but irreligion. MacIntyre's idealization of Aristotle, community, and social roles must therefore be less important than it first seems. The examples MacIntyre gives of moral community surviving in the margins of liberal society, interestingly, are all religious: black and white Protestant communities in the South, Orthodox Jews, Orthodox Greeks, and Catholic Irish. Thus when he says that moral rules were once "embedded in a context which confer[red] intelligibility upon them" readers may well wonder what he means.[21] Is he thinking of the Greek polis and the medieval kinship network, or does he have in mind an unquestioning faith in the biblical God?

Science

After Virtue begins with a shocking fantasy about a society where all natural scientists are barreled off and "lynched." This violent parable is immediately followed by the suggestion that the modern scientific revolution itself was the product of a "Know-nothing political movement," aimed at murdering wise but helpless religious traditions. And this is not the only place where MacIntyre suggests, in a Maistrean vein, that modern science is profoundly immoral, that its practitioners are guilty of some terrible crime. Why does he believe this? Wounded pride may again be relevant. Scientists have usurped the social prestige that formerly belonged to the theologians and philosophers among whom MacIntyre counts himself. And he is concerned, of course, with the way science fosters instrumental attitudes. The crux of his obscure attack against bureaucracy, for instance, seems to be that bureaucrats derive their habits of cynical manipulation from science. But this, too, is a side-line. What MacIntyre really resents is the prominent role science played in destroying theism, in discrediting those religious worldviews on which, he claims, morality itself depends. We have encountered this argument, too, before. The social order was once bottomed solidly on religion. All that is left now, by contrast, is a "physics-based society," and, from a moral perspective, physics is a void.[22] Science cannot tell us how to live. The apple of knowledge is a poisoned fruit. A society where science is revered is a society adrift.

MacIntyre echoes Strauss and other neo-Heideggerians when he indicts modern science for its Promethean ambitions. Science disputes the reality of chance. It does so by suggesting, purportedly, that the human species can somehow replace God. Social science, in particular, hubristically denies "the permanence of *Fortuna*." (This is vintage Strauss.) It was terribly naive for "the thinkers of the Enlightenment" to write "as though fragility and vulnerability could be overcome in some progressive future."[23] But that is what the scientific revolution, with its wild promise that man can ultimately master nature and subject the world to human designs, encouraged them to do.

Functional Concepts

Science, which has destroyed religion and unleashed anarchy, will not improve our lot. The creation or resurgence of "community" would of course. The main argument for community used in *After Virtue* sheds more light on the fundamental tension afflicting MacIntyre's thought: the tension between MacIntyre the theist and MacIntyre the communitarian. Although he can bridge the is/ought gap by invoking the normative force of divine commands, he is not wholly comfortable with this solution. Addressing a secular audience, he prefers to showcase a quite different sort of claim, a "valid argument which moves from factual premises to an evaluative conclusion." This second argument, based on what he calls "functional concepts," is communitarian, not theological.

To explain his basic intuition, he invokes the example of "a good watch." When we use functional concepts of this kind, we are involved simultaneously in description and evaluation. For instance, to say that a watch will not fit in my pocket is to say that it is "bad" in an objective sense. There is no gap here between the "is" and the "ought." An appraisal of value simply characterizes aspects of the world. A descriptive-evaluative statement of this sort is not the mere expression of subjective preferences or attitudes. For one thing, it can be true or false: "to call a watch good is to say that it is the kind of watch which someone would choose who wanted a watch to keep time accurately (rather than, say, to throw at the cat)."[24] Such an example, MacIntyre asserts, exposes the bankruptcy of both emotivist and decisionist theories of ethics.

There is a slight problem with this nimble line of reasoning, however. MacIntyre's watch is "good" only in an instrumental sense. The rationality which decides whether such a watch is good or bad is means-end rationality. No judgment about the value or lack of value of ends is required. Accurate time-keeping itself is presumably valued as a useful means for the pursuit of further yet unjustified ends. As a result, "functional concepts" do not do the job MacIntyre claims they do. They do not demonstrate that morality itself can be rational in a substantive, rather than merely instrumental, sense. The patent feebleness of this argument suggests that MacIntyre would have been unable to sustain his scorn for the is/ought distinction if he did not have a theological ace-in-the-hole. Yet, in *After Virtue* at least, he refuses to lean back and rely wholly on the revealed will of the biblical God.

Social Roles

The need for a usable past is perfectly understandable. But the purposes of nostalgia vary. The watch example helps explain what MacIntyre seeks in his imaginary premodern communities. He projects into archaic societies all the moral certainty, unanimity, and security he misses in his own social world. What he admires most about traditional social orders is the total absence of doubt: "the heroes of the Iliad do not find it difficult to know what they owe one another." They experience no ambiguity about "what is required by the social role which each individual inhabits." (The bounden duties imposed by archaic codes of blood revenge are mentioned here.[25]) Hesitations are unknown when all a person need do is to discharge the obvious obligations associated with his social rank. In a good society, "every individual has a given role and status within a well-defined and highly determinate system of roles and statuses." MacIntyre stresses the heteronomy of primary socialization: "we enter human society . . . with one or more imputed characters—roles into which we have been drafted—and we have to learn what they are in order to be able to understand how others respond to us and how our responses to them are apt to be construed." Duties are clamped on individuals from the outside. Because duties are heteronomous, moral precepts cannot be reasonably assimilated to subjective preferences. Obligations are specified by the social context and cannot be questioned by the individual. In such a situation, "there is an order which requires from us the pursuit of certain ends, an order relationship to which provides our judgments with the property of truth or falsity."[26]

This is a great relief. Indeed, "a man knows who he is by knowing his role in these structures; and in knowing this he knows also what he owes and what is owed to him by the occupant of every other role and status." Moral knowledge is role knowledge, the knowledge of my-station-and-its-duties. Unlike inhabitants of modern liberal societies, therefore, members of preliberal societies have no trouble answering the questions: how to live? what to do? "Nor are such questions difficult to answer, except in exceptional cases. For the given rules which assign men their place in the social order and with it their identity also prescribe what they owe and what is owed to them and how they are to be treated and regarded if they fail and how they are to treat and regard others if those others fail." There was no fact/value distinction in "premodern, traditional societies."[27] Moral questions answered themselves. To know your duty was to know a "fact" that jumped out at you, to know what *in fact* other people expected you to do.

A Wrinkle in the Argument

Conformist reflexes and unquestioning obedience to commands and custom do not seem entirely rational. Yet MacIntyre claims that in traditional social orders moral behavior was the product of reason. As a moment's reflection on the watch analogy reveals, however, "rational" is still being used here in a thin or instrumental sense. Moral precepts simply direct individuals to discharge their roles, that is, to act in the way most profitable for both the survival of their community and the achievement of its collective aims. The "good" individual is the individual who serves his group—just as a "good" watch is a watch that accurately tells the time. A "bad" action, conversely, is an action that frustrates the attainment of common goals. MacIntyre defines the "excellences" of individuals, in a radically anti-individualistic way, as "those qualities of mind and character which would contribute to the realization of their common good or goods."[28] In this sense the value of sustaining the given public order, like the value of telling time, is assumed. That the attainment of collective goals is "good" in a non-instrumental sense is simply taken on authority. That social expectations should be honored is a matter of faith.

Teleological thinking is plausible only in specific circumstances. A watch can be said to have a purpose or function when it exists *within a given context where its tasks are exogenously imposed.* If goals are fixed externally, it is quite reasonable to use evaluative language, such as "good" and "bad," to describe those features of an object which promote or frustrate the attainment of those goals. At his most convincing, MacIntyre writes about human virtues and vices in just this way. Membership in a premodern social group, for example, provides the individual with a reliable moral compass: "I belong to this tribe, this clan, this nation. Hence what is good for me has to be the good for one who inhabits these roles. As such, I inherit from the past of my family, my city, my tribe, my nation, a variety of debts, inheritances, rightful expectations and obligations. These constitute the given of my life, my moral starting point." Obligations are specified by the social context into which individuals are involuntarily socialized. MacIntyre generalizes this idea of contextually specified duties or goals in his conception of a "practice." We need not explore this facet of his theory here. It suffices to note that, at his most persuasive, he defines human virtue by reference to the tasks assigned heteronomously to individuals by their social milieu, by the games they play: "a virtue is an acquired human quality the possession and exercise of which tends to enable us to achieve those goods which are internal to practices."[29]

At this point, MacIntyre's thinking suddenly gets off the track.

Without a word of explanation, he tries to expunge all reference to goal-specifying contexts from his teleological approach to moral evaluation. He turns from human beings who inhabit social roles to man as such. He moves from a contextual (and plausible) to an acontextual (and implausible) form of teleology. He stops referring to externally provided purposes, such as telling time or discharging one's social role, and begins to wax speculative about *the realization of essences.* He would have never dared propose that a "good" watch is a watch which realizes the essence of "watchness" to the highest degree. That would not have impressed his readers as a "valid argument which moves from factual premises to an evaluative conclusion." But this, suddenly, is what he expects us to believe about human beings.

MacIntyre never asks if his watch is "good" apart from any functions which he might want it to fulfill. But that is precisely the question he poses about man. What is "man's true end"? What is a "good man" apart from any social context providing obligations for him to discharge? In one passage, he even redefines "virtue." Instead of being a trait that enables an individual to serve his group or fulfill his social function, virtue surprisingly reappears as a quality necessary for human flourishing in the abstract.[30]

MacIntyre careens off in this new direction, it initially seems, because he is a loyal Aristotelian: "on Aristotle's account . . . virtues attach not to men as inhabiting social roles, but to man as such."[31] To be sure, his attempt to identify the human *telos* apart from any social context is hard to follow. The confusion stems largely from his inconsistent appraisals of the acontextual approach to man. In one passage, he lauds Aristotle for detaching "man as such" from his social roles. In another, he ridicules liberalism for doing the very same thing. This contradiction warrants attention. Liberals destroyed morality in the same way Aristotle saved it, by attempting to conceive human beings outside of social roles: "it is only when man is thought of as an individual prior to and apart from all roles that 'man' ceases to be a functional concept."[32] There is little use trying to discover an underlying coherence here. The argument most prominently advanced in *After Virtue*, implies (despite what MacIntyre explicitly says) that Aristotle, too, is wrong when he claims that "virtues attach not to men as inhabiting social roles, but to man as such." Man is a social animal. In both healthy societies and healthy theories, "the individual is identified and constituted in and through certain of his or her roles, those roles which bind the individual to the communities in and through which alone specifically human goods are to be attained."[33] The decontextualization of humanity, whether done by Aristotle or Locke, spells the end of morality as such.

Or does it? His attack on the decontextualizing tendencies of liberalism is the crux of MacIntyre's argument. Nevertheless, in various passages, and to the mental distress of his readers, he advances his own form of decontextualizing teleology. A watch can be good or bad even in the absence of anyone who needs to tell the time. Not surprisingly, this attempt to define the human *telos* apart from actual social institutions and concrete social demands ends disappointingly. MacIntyre pronounces, in all seriousness, that "the good life for man is the life spent in seeking the good life for man."[34]

How did he stumble into this embarrassment? If morality is always contextual, how can it also be acontextual? If the gravest intellectual sin is to conceive human beings apart from their inherited social roles, why does MacIntyre do it himself? Half-concealed theological commitments again account for the muddle. On the one hand, MacIntyre believes that a man is "good," apart from all social contexts, when he pursues the saving vision of God. It is Christianity, or one version of it, not the last book of the *Nicomachean Ethics*, that leads him to stress a dimension of the human self beyond all social influence. His most proudly exhibited "discovery," on the other hand, is that individuals are socially constituted. From this premise he concludes that treating someone as an individual, rather than as a member of an ascriptive group, can never be morally justified. An individual has value only when he internalizes the rules and goals of the group. (His anti-individualism becomes so radical that, in one passage, he defends the idea of inherited guilt.[35]) There seem to be two MacIntyres: one says that moral obligations derive from concrete social contexts and traditions; the other claims that they are imposed directly by God on the individual soul. This fundamental tension racks and vitiates his thought.

Some Further Inconsistencies

After Virtue bubbles over with other contradictions, large and small. For instance, MacIntyre speaks with contempt of bureaucratic authority but seems devoted to the medieval Church (which embodied precisely such a bureaucratic authority). He attacks the person/role distinction as if it were a modern invention, even though he is aware that the medieval Church relied upon it when claiming the right to depose kings, and even though he knows and approves of the Augustinian doctrine that a priest who is a sinner can nevertheless legitimately perform the sacraments. He pillories the modern figure of "the therapist," while presenting himself as the self-accredited therapist for his entire society. He claims that bureaucratic managers are totally impotent, yet he also says they possess great power. He jeers at both the bureaucrat and the therapist for treating moral ends as "given." But he also recommends obedience to God's commands, admires Homeric heroes for accepting passively the obligations imposed by their social rank, longs for "an order which requires from us the pursuit of certain ends," and even complains that "the peculiarly modern self, the emotivist self, in acquiring sovereignty in its own realm lost its traditional boundaries provided by a social identity and a view of human life as ordered to a *given* end."[36]

Similarly, MacIntyre attacks individual autonomy in the name of piety toward God and reverence toward inherited social traditions, but he defends "rational autonomy" against the threat posed by mechanistic science. He idealizes "narratives" (full of fictions), and scorns "fictions" (organized as narratives). He identifies individualism with the liberalism he loathes, yet eventually finds himself defending the idea of individual moral deserts against both Nozick and Rawls. He writes scathingly of liberals who have "abandoned the moral unity of Aristotelianism," but praises Sophocles for having denied that any such unity exists. Although he claims to admire *Antigone*, he is also able to write that anyone who can imagine conflicting loyalties to his friends and his country has no country, is "a citizen of nowhere." He decries instrumental relations among human beings, yet he sometimes writes as if individuals should be the pliant tools of their social group. He expresses admiration for the Jacobins who regarded "the persistent bachelor . . . as an enemy of virtue"; he praises Jane Austen, just two pages later, for her cool anger at the social disgrace cast on unmarried women. He argues that a sense of *autres temps autres mœurs*, an awareness of "the variety and heterogeneity of moral beliefs, practices and concepts," will undermine Western complacency.[37] Yet he also asserts, along with Allan Bloom, that such open-mindedness is tantamount to moral relativism—the most odious flower of liberal culture. And he declares that there is no moral concord in modern times, only to turn around and attack his contemporaries for *agreeing* about the superiority of freedom and equality over solidarity and hierarchy. His pose as a solitary opponent of unquestionable liberal orthodoxy, of course, fits ill with his complaint about the infinite disputatiousness of modern times.

Another blatant contradiction is also worth noticing. On the one hand, Aristotelianism is rooted firmly in the social context provided by the Greek polis. On the other hand, we can save ourselves if we (who will never lay eyes on a polis) embrace Aristotelianism today. It is interesting to observe how MacIntyre negotiates this perilous transition from sociological relativism to moral absolutism. At one moment, he claims that Aristotle was the philosopher of antiquity, while Nietzsche is the philosopher of modernity. An instant later, he claims that Aristotle is the philosopher of modernity as well. But how can MacIntyre say both? How can he scoot so casually from the idea that Aristotle gives a correct account of a society so wholly different from ours to the idea that Aristotle gives a correct account of our own society as well?

To understand this gambol is also to understand how MacIntyre salvages hope from despair. The implicit pessimism of *After Virtue* is obvious.[38] The book assumes that we want and need ethical unanimity but can never attain it. Unfortunately, "our society cannot hope to achieve moral consensus" and "modern politics cannot be a matter of genuine moral consensus." Previous modern attempts to revive ancient virtue have ended in disaster. Hence "the true lesson of the Jacobin Clubs and their downfall is that you cannot hope to reinvent morality on the scale of a whole nation." Phrased more directly: "we are all already in a state so disastrous that there are no large remedies for it."

Through the prevailing darkness, however, a chink of light appears. The current crisis leaves room for small remedies, at least. And that is exactly what MacIntyre proposes in the book's notorious climax: "what matters at this stage is the construction of local forms of community within which civility and the intellectual and moral life can be sustained through the dark ages that are already upon us."[39] In these terrible times, when all the old hierarchies of value have collapsed, men of good will must band together and retreat to the hills. Previously, the discontented have tried to change society; now they should leave town.

This eye-catching pronouncement should not be given undue importance, however. The invitation to join "a commune for dropouts" is not all MacIntyre has to offer.[40] Indeed, his argument for a renewed Aristotelianism does not underwrite the creation of retreatist subcultures. He asks: "how can Aristotelianism be formulated so as to be a moral presence in a world in which there are no city-states?"[41] The answer has nothing to do with small-scale solutions such as communitarian oases in the liberal desert. Instead, he wants to teach us to perceive the *latent community* which, unbeknownst to us, we all already possess. We can salvage our hidden communal natures, he boldly suggests, simply by looking at ourselves with Aristotelian eyes.

Notice the cautious way MacIntyre formulates this claim: "modern society is indeed often, at least *in surface appearance*, nothing but a collection of strangers, each pursuing his or her own interests under minimal constraints." Modern society is not profoundly atomistic, only superficially so. Underneath the fragmented surface, shared understandings persist. To rescue us from our modern plight, all MacIntyre needs to do is peel away the distorting layer of liberal ideology that blankets our latently communitarian selves. Aristotelianism does not overturn social institutions. It only "restores intelligibility and rationality to our moral and social attitudes and commitments."[42] This seems like a relatively painless procedure. Indeed, transformative politics have never appeared so benign. MacIntyre wants to take our old "moral and social attitudes and commitments" and give them a new "intelligibility and rationality." To enable us to do this, he will provide us with a new language. (To remake society, we need only to redescribe it.) Thus can a philosopher revolutionize the world. By refuting the fallacies of liberal thought (that individuals exist independently of society, and so forth), MacIntyre will save us from ourselves.

Double Standards

In our current and therefore degenerate moral language MacIntyre discovers "an unharmonious melange of ill-assorted fragments" or "ill-assorted conceptual fragments from various parts of our past." Behind this statement lies the implausible suggestion that moral cacophony is unique to the modern world. The image underlying his entire argument is this: the vase was once intact but now lies in shards. But surely this image is misleading. From an archaeological point of view, the vase has always been shattered. MacIntyre disapprovingly remarks that "modern moral utterance and practice can only be understood as a series of fragmented survivals from an older past."[43] But something similar can be said about all known societies.

Almost all our daily locutions originated in a shadowy period about which we know little. Our words swarm with half-understood allusions and connotations. *And this has always been true.* Such is the palimpsest character of every known human culture. No matter how far back we peer into the mists of time, we will discover societies cluttered with poorly understood fossil records of even more remote pasts. Human beings have always muddled along with social codes whose history and full significance were obscure. No one has ever lived in a totally transparent culture. The stubborn persistence of a half-forgotten past is a universal aspect of human civilization. It cannot be convincingly twisted into a critique of modernity or an excuse for despising liberalism. (It might be argued, on the contrary, that modern societies succeed in rinsing out the hauntings of the past much more effectively than traditional societies could ever do.)

MacIntyre is able to depict Western history as a process of degeneration or "moral decline" only because of his typically antiliberal reliance on double-standards.[44] Despite everything he says, modern roles and social expectations provide as much practical orientation to individuals today as did their archaic equivalents in earlier times. As Plato's portrait of Thrasymachus reminds us, there is nothing distinctly modern about the abuse of moral language as a cover for immoral designs. The moral conflicts described by Max Weber are no more "subjective" than the moral conflicts described by Sophocles.[45] If he had lent an ear to those around him, MacIntyre would have discovered that "man" is just as much "a story-telling animal" today as he ever was. The liberal concern for rules never implied a wholesale disparagement of virtues. The notion of friendship is not "alien" to the modern world.[46] Moreover, there *is* a core of moral agreement in modern liberal society. Not even the most extreme reactionary today would dream of proposing the re-establishment of slavery, while the most enlightened Athenian philosophers apparently never dreamed of abolishing it. The taboo against human enslavement, which seems to have emerged in Europe around 1700, is a moral premise shared by all members of contemporary liberal societies. It is exactly the sort of norm that MacIntyre claims cannot now exist. MacIntyre mentions in passing "Aristotle's indefensible defence of slavery"; but, as an unbending opponent of "the morality of modernity," he does not dwell on the subject.[47]

Moral Conflict in the Preliberal World

The past is overflowing with "interminable" or "unsettlable" moral disputes. But, as one critic observes, MacIntyre "never tries to compare the amount of disagreement in our culture with amounts in earlier times."[48] And this lack of comparative analysis seriously weakens his argument. True, his refusal to pursue this matter is easy to comprehend. The best chapters in *After Virtue*, in fact, contain lengthy discussions of premodern moral conflict. That is one of the most arresting, not to say droll, features of the book. MacIntyre's initial premise is that modern moral conflict represents a dangerous decline from previous moral harmony. Readers are therefore taken aback when they are notified of the "general state of incoherence in the use of evaluative language in Athenian culture." Could it be that Athenian morality, too, was in a state of grave disorder? Perhaps "grave disorder" afflicts all societies, past as well as present. In that case, Western history cannot be stylized as a moral Fall. Thus, MacIntyre is contradicting himself. He first says that normative dissonance is uniquely modern, and then adds parenthetically that normative dissonance afflicts antiquity and the middle ages as well. This is not a slight yielding of ground. This is a wholesale retreat or surrender. As if to highlight masochistically his own self-refutation, MacIntyre returns many times to the moral cacophony of Greek antiquity: "the Greek moral vocabulary and outlook is a good deal more incoherent than we find it easy to recognize." At several important junctures, indeed, the hero of the book is identified as Sophocles, not Aristotle, precisely because the author of *Antigone* recognized the permanence of unsettlable moral conflict, while the author of the *Nicomachean Ethics* did not.[49]

MacIntyre's surprising focus on moral disorder and discord in antiquity is complemented by his chapter on the middle ages, devoted almost wholly to "the heterogeneity of medieval thought." Here he describes medieval Europe as "a culture in which human life was in danger of being torn apart by the conflict of too many ideals, too many ways of life." A unified and monolithic Christian culture is a myth, he explains. "Medieval culture . . . was a fragile and complex balance of a variety of disparate and conflicting elements." MacIntyre focuses with special acumen on the deep moral dissonance between Christianity, feudalism, and the surviving fragments of Greco-Roman culture. His more narrow concern is with "the tension between the Bible and Aristotle" which lasted throughout the Middle Ages. A conflict between the two perspectives was inevitable, of course. For one thing, "Aristotle would certainly not have admired Jesus Christ." Christ teaches that we should love the sinner; while Aristotle claims that a good man cannot be the friend of a bad man. Christianity encourages people to forgive the guilty; while pagan philosophers generally advise them to punish those who interfere with collective goals. *Hamartia* does not really mean "sin," and there are no words in classical Greek for repentance or charity either. Aristotle never mentioned patience, would not have considered charity a virtue, and viewed humility as an outright vice. He would have been dumbfounded by the story of the thief on the cross. From a Greek perspective, an individual can be excluded from the good by accidents (ugliness, childlessness, Priam's misfortunes) or low birth; while for the Christians no misfortune can exclude a person from the human good, so long as he does not consent to evil. Similarly, "the notion of a final redemption of an almost entirely unregenerate life has no place in Aristotle's scheme." And so forth. Medieval culture was a discordant hodgepodge of feudal-chivalric, Aristotelian, and Christian ideals. Given the grating disharmony between Greek and Biblical perspectives, it is no surprise that "medieval societies are in general societies of conflict, lawlessness and multiplicity."[50]

This analysis is acute and persuasive. It is also mind-boggling, since MacIntyre *continues* to regret the harmony of the past and the long-lost "framework of medieval agreement."[51] If there was so much conflict in premodern Europe, why talk of a grave cultural loss? If the vase was already shattered, then why blame liberalism for having broken it, for having fractured a beautiful tradition of moral consensus? If both antiquity and the Middle Ages were mongrel cultures, rife with ethical discord, what is unique about modern times? MacIntyre never answers these questions or even asks them in a straightforward way.

Rationality and Tradition

Without being a hero of consistency, MacIntyre is remarkably stead-fast. His missionary zeal does not abate. *Whose Justice? Which Rationality?* of 1988 and *Three Versions of Moral Enquiry* of 1990 are further installments in his apostolic warning against the liberal heresy. All the themes sounded in *After Virtue* reappear. He begins by noting the irresolvability of modern moral debates. He then sets out to explain and solve this problem by providing "an account of what rationality is." He argues, initially, that "there is no rationality as such," and that, as a result, moral reasoning must be buoyed up by inherited concepts and norms.[52] Only "*qua* members" of a group can we reason morally. Only by invoking value-commitments authenticated in a shared culture can we justify our actions. Plucked from the water, a fish cannot swim. Separated from tradition, a moral agent cannot be rational. This sounds like cultural relativism, but relativism is not what MacIntyre has in mind.

He makes his theoretical case, as usual, by way of a commentary on an impressive array of texts—ancient, medieval, and modern. Moral philosophers, he tells us, should be studied historically, in their original settings. But his tone again is polemical, not historical. "Liberalism" remains his principal target, although it is now mentioned less often by name. The "social order of modern individualism" is still associated with moral "degeneration." And the "ghost" of the Enlightenment still needs to be "exorcized." About Kant's endeavor to construct "a morality for tradition-free individuals," MacIntyre is predictably scathing.[53] Liberals both hate tradition and are unaware that it exists. They elevate homelessness and estrangement into moral ideals. (Rawls sins by assuming that "ideal rationality" is what "a socially disembodied being would arrive at," and that justice can be based on traits people have independently of membership in specific communities.)

The Greek polis, we are not surprised to learn, was hospitable to the rational justification of ends, but "20th-century modernity," demoralized by doubt, is not. In our society, "nonrational persuasion displaces rational argument."[54] Evidence that rational arguments played an important role in preliberal societies is never provided.

Whose Justice? Which Rationality? is less about rationality and justice than about the closing of the Western mind, a mind that is so closed because it is so open. While ridiculing the therapeutic culture of "modernity," MacIntyre once again depicts himself as an archtherapist, offering to cure our moral ailments with speculation about tradition.

But what is a tradition? This rudimentary question is answered less satisfactorily than one might have hoped. Traditions are associated, in no particular order, with societies, groups, cultures, languages, sciences, and webs of belief (also with ways of life, including dress and table manners, and lines of research). MacIntyre's discussion assumes that some traditions are marked by naive self-evidence (no questions asked and no alternatives considered), while others are characterized by acute self-awareness and a constant struggle with internal and external critics. But nothing helpful is said about these different kinds of tradition. Generally, but not consistently, MacIntyre tilts toward an intellectual approach: "a tradition is an argument extended through time."[55]

In the final pages of *Whose Justice? Which Rationality?* MacIntyre allows that the prologue is over: he will write his next book as a spokesman for one of the traditions he has just described. And *Three Versions of Moral Enquiry* is, indeed, slightly more forthright about whose side its author is on. But the earlier work is already uninhibitedly partisan. It is already built around the combative assumption that one tradition in particular can defeat its chief rivals. In *After Virtue*, MacIntyre had remarked that Aquinas is "an unexpectedly marginal figure to the history which I am writing."[56] In the two sequels, he gives readers what they expect. He challenges "the cultural and political hegemony of liberalism" in the name of St. Thomas. The tradition MacIntyre himself embraces, although "still in process of construction," now has an authoritative sponsor.

MacIntyre's partisan spirit shines in an acerbic aside about the *New York Times*, "that parish magazine of affluent and self-congratulatory liberal enlightenment." (So far as I can tell, this is the only time he uses the word "parish" in a derogatory sense.) The readers of the *Times* seem to be "just as much a community of prerational faith" as "the congregations of evangelical fundamentalism." Indeed, the former are even less rational than the latter. Unlike those who have been born-again, Eastern establishment liberals miserably "fail to recognize themselves for what they are." MacIntyre writes sympathetically of Protestant fundamentalists, with sincere exaggeration, because the enemy of his enemy is his friend. Liberal society affects tolerance, he charges, but provides "little space . . . for putting liberalism in question."[57] (This a dubious charge, given that the person leveling it is both well-placed and perfectly free to make his case. But its psychological attractiveness should not be overlooked. If there is literally no room for criticism, then the sudden arrival of a critic will be greeted as a miracle.)

MacIntyre sometimes denies that there are neutral, tradition-independent standards that might permit us to choose among traditions. If we harken to his practice, though, rather than to his sonorous preaching, we begin to have our doubts. Implicitly, though obscurely, he himself distinguishes between good and bad traditions on extratraditional or supertraditional grounds. A good tradition, whatever its content, encourages feelings of certainty, terminates endless debate, reinforces social solidarity, gives "unity to life." A bad tradition, whatever its content, is internally inconsistent, irrational in the sense of self-contradictory. Liberalism, for instance, is self-refuting; striving to be broadly cosmopolitan, it ends up narrowly parochial. Liberals also make the empirically false claim that preferences arise by nature, rather than being socially shaped.

The Polis

As a backward-looking cultural critic, MacIntyre continues to use the Greek polis as a large paddle for spanking modern man. The chastisement he delivers is not quite Straussian, of course. He does not invoke Athenian philosophy in contrast to the ordinary beliefs of average Athenians (or at least not at first). Initially, he appeals to Greek community life itself. To study antiquity is to realize how socially degenerate we latecomers are. The picture he paints of the ancient slave republics is correspondingly anodyne. Indeed, some early chapters of *Whose Justice? Which Rationality?* read like a blend of Aristotelian theory and travel brochure: "the polis is human community perfected and completed by reaching its telos."[58] The polis aims at "the good and the best as such." Each citizen seeks excellence, engaged in an "activity for which his or her soul is perfectly fitted," while the city integrates all worthwhile endeavors into a beautifully coherent whole. Once again, friends are not drawn together by anything so flimsy as mutual sympathy or a concern for each other's individuality; rather "each cares for the other primarily because of the relationship of each to the good." And citizens engage in relatively little bargaining, cost-benefit thinking, instrumental reasoning, or conflicts of interest, for they enjoy shared understandings and shared goals.

Unlike contemporary societies, the polis provided a "locus of rationality." It was a pool in which citizen-fish could comfortably swim. It made "reasoning" about moral questions possible, apparently, by buoying-up members, inducting them into a rigid value hierarchy, embedding them within a tautly spun web of social roles. This argument is simply transcribed from *After Virtue*. A my-station-and-its-duties morality gave every citizen, at every moment, unambiguous instructions. That explains how rationality can be "constituted" by membership: "as the self-identified inhabitant of some social role," a person "does whatever his or her role requires." In such a society, "there can only be at any one time one right action to perform."[59] Rationality, thank heaven, means the absence of choice.

The "highest good" of the citizen is wired into his structured activities, not into human nature itself. Goods are activity-specific. As an overarching system of activities, the polis guarantees that "goods are rank-ordered" and that citizens are properly tasked. (Outsiders, by contrast, remain morally unhinged.) MacIntyre again argues that an individual can apprehend the good that gives him reason to act only when he plays a specific role within an organized activity. Noncitizens are unable to understand this good, just as nonscientists today are clueless about disputes in particle physics. Here is a clarifying example: "a hockey player in the closing seconds of a crucial game has an opportunity to pass to another member of his or her team better placed to score a needed goal. Necessarily, we may say, if he or she has perceived and judged the situation correctly, he or she must immediately pass." On someone fully engaged in a social practice, appropriate behavior dawns with "necessity and immediacy"—with the irresistible force of a religious revelation. MacIntyre commends this secular arrangement as only a religious man knows how: "no practical rationality outside the polis is the Aristotelian counterpart to *extra ecclesiam nulla salus.*"[60]

What MacIntyre discerns in the polis, once again, is salvation—specifically, salvation from hesitation. Modern individuals have "too many half convictions and too few settled coherent convictions."[61] They reason carefully about the best thing to do, but then, at the last moment, change their minds. A well-organized tradition prevents such flighty and distracted behavior. It provides an alternative to skepticism, a quietus to doubt. Learning a language "commits" people to authoritative beliefs about virtue and vice. (Of course, languages also make permanently available the chance to say "no" or "I disagree" or "I am not sure," but MacIntyre avoids such flustering thoughts.) Social roles remove disorienting alternatives from sight: the "swineherd" gives the "master" his due, without asking questions. Initially, liberation from struggle is achieved by education in virtue. Through involuntary discipline, raw passion is metamorphosed into virtue and "right desire." Thereafter, virtuous citizens can operate on auto-pilot, never tempted by wrong, always spontaneously choosing the good.

A Surprising Turn (Again)

A particular action may be countenanced by the tradition in which it occurs. But how do we justify the tradition as a whole? Would MacIntyre defend suttee simply because it is traditional? This dilemma already arose, without being resolved, in *After Virtue*, where MacIntyre's definition of a "virtue" is flawed. He described it as a trait that makes it possible for an individual to fulfill his or her social roles. But what about vicious roles? Do we want to call "virtues" those traits that enable a Mafia hit-man to act as a Mafia hit-man is supposed to act? It is possible, of course, to define the "good" and the "bad" by reference to the goals and roles fixed by the society into which we are born. If we conceive of moral judgment exclusively in this way, however, we are prohibited from asking about the goodness or badness of pregiven goals or roles or expectations themselves. We can use "instrumental reason" to identify actions that fulfill the functions assigned to us by our social context, though it is useless for answering the question, is the context itself morally good?

When discussing archaic societies, in *After Virtue*, MacIntyre admitted that "all questions of choice arise within the framework; the framework itself therefore cannot be chosen." As a self-proclaimed spokesman for some higher "reason," however, he could not be satisfied with this limitation. He could not expect people to accept every feature, no matter how vile, of their inherited social identity. So he was compelled to assert that, in an ideal society, community standards of evaluation are themselves subject to evaluation. As it turns out, an Athenian is superior to his Homeric ancestors in precisely this way. He has "standards by which he can question the life of his own community" as a whole.[62] Yet these standards must come from inherited traditions, not from "rationality as such."

MacIntyre returns to this problem and to his unsatisfactory solution in *Whose Justice? Which Rationality?* What is so rational about conforming to a socially given end? Why are we playing hockey in the first place? To answer these questions, and to keep readers off balance, MacIntyre plunges again into an anticontextualist search for "a fundamental standard external to all established practice" or "principles with an authority independent of the social order." This startling about-face is a predictable feature of every "soft" antiliberalism. Having lulled the reader with fantasies about doubt-absorbent tradition, MacIntyre suddenly reverses gears, launching an all-out attack on "values already acknowledged" and "de facto standards upheld by particular groups." After repudiating rootlessness, he now rejects rootedness as well. He now privileges insubordination over subordination, deviants over insiders. Not only can a fish survive out of water, it must be airborne to breathe free. As errant or delinquent citizens, Socrates and Plato were not bogged down in their cultures. They could thus successfully "put in question the beliefs of the ordinary Athenian about the polis."[63] (Here MacIntyre does begin to sound like Strauss.)

Philosophers are deaf to the charms of tradition. They believe that an argument from what has been to what should be has no great force. Independent thinkers argue not by old custom, but true reason.[64] Only crafty rhetoricians, not true philosophers, appeal to community values. The philosopher wants to know "what is good and best, as such, unqualifiedly," independent of the context of a given practice or culture. He must avoid "not error from this or that point of view, but error as such."[65]

Having turned his back on cultural relativism, MacIntyre now describes role structure as a problem, not a solution: "in the best kind of polis the participation of women and of artisans would require a restructuring of their occupational and social roles of a kind inconceivable to Aristotle himself." Culturally embedded forms of rationality are not enough. One must always entertain the conjecture that "one's scheme of concepts and beliefs could be in some way *as a whole* in error." An entire society can be justly condemned for infringing upon tradition-independent taboos. All this sounds fine. In fact, it sounds downright liberal. (Slavery is not morally justified simply because masters and slaves are used to it.) Unfortunately, MacIntyre's attack on inherited norms also explodes his entire project. It destroys the idea that virtue means the discharging of pregiven social roles. If community standards are no longer sacred and uncriticizable, they will no longer serve the purpose he wants them to serve. An open-ended tradition in which "there is and can be no finality" will no longer put an end to interminable debate.[66] The practices into which we are inducted will no longer silence disagreement or absorb doubt.

Traditions in Motion

Ernest Gellner once teased MacIntyre for his capacity "to get on a soapbox and sound like a bishop."[67] Shuttling back and forth between Church and the left, MacIntyre has never been able to decide for long which to eulogize: reverence or impertinence, obedience or rebellion. To relieve the tension (which he bears rather cheerfully), he sometimes indulges in mind-wrenching inconsistency, excoriating the critical spirit in some chapters, apotheosizing it in others. He will first celebrate doubt-absorbent traditions and then praise the subversion of tradition by Socratic doubt. But he also seeks a middle path, a "third alternative." In certain key passages, he reconceives tradition as an unfinished search for "the good." On this model, Socrates's demonstration that community values are bankrupt and incoherent is not an erosion of tradition, but an example of "a tradition in good order," and that means a tradition *en route*, a tradition involved in a never-ending process of self-correction and self-improvement. Unlike a hockey game, "a tradition of rational enquiry" refers to something outside itself, advances truth claims, and is capable of making intellectual progress. As a learning process, such a tradition requires participants to maintain some critical distance. Members are committed "to understand things as they are absolutely, not just relating to some standpoint." But they conduct this search wholly *within* a single framework or tradition. They cannot reach their goal, therefore, but the very striving, mandated by their social roles, gives them "ground for appeals against the social order."[68]

How can we distinguish, according to MacIntyre, between a self-improving tradition and a merely self-satisfied one? If we cannot step outside our categories and culture, if we cannot compare our ideas with uninterpreted reality, how can we recognize progress when we see it? Without "pretheoretical data," how can we be sure that our thinking is adequate to the world? How do we know if an inquiry is being conducted rationally? And how can one research tradition be declared superior to another?

When communities are windowless or autistic, MacIntyre writes (invoking what appears to be a content-neutral or supertraditional standard for success or failure), they can be accused of irrationality, that is, of presifting the evidence from which they draw their conclusions. A rational community, by contrast, has a lackadaisical border patrol and permits unsettling encounters with alien traditions, gate-crasher theories, and confounding situations. Although MacIntyre's writings have nothing good to say about liberal institutions or ideas, he is still a "soft" antiliberal. In the end, therefore, he reverts to the falsificationist theory of truth that Popper inherited from Milton and Mill. Without citing any liberal theorists, he argues that "the beliefs which we have most warrant for, have no safeguard to rest on, but a standing invitation to the whole world to prove them unfounded."[69]

Relativism is false because one tradition of inquiry can collide rudely with another. In the process, some traditions will judge themselves outclassed, even by their own standards. MacIntyre's own tradition, of course, thrives on such encounters: Thomism is a singular tradition. It is uniquely self-revising and dynamic, possessing ample "resources for its own enlargement, correction, and defense."[70] Faced with a competitor, Thomism is capable of "identifying and characterizing the limitations and failures of that rival tradition as judged by that rival tradition's own standards." Compared to all other traditions, then Thomism is "undoubtedly rationally superior."[71] As a Thomist, MacIntyre is buoyed up by a solid tradition, without being blinkered by a culturally relative point of view. Or so he says.

Thomism is a supertradition. This claim is the centerpiece of MacIntyre's argument. It allows him, he believes, to marry custom with reason, to strap authority and reason together. It permits him to be a cultural relativist and a moral absolutist at the same time. On the one hand, he can condemn Enlightenment rationalism for its imperiousness, its refusal to accept the persistence of different traditions and points of view. On the other hand, he can embrace the unstoppable imperialism of Thomistic theory, which has conquered all rivals in the past and will continue to do so in the future. His portrait of Thomism, it must be said, is somewhat muddy. (One problem is that he repeatedly refers to Thomas's own writings as both "essentially incomplete" and "definitive."[72] Thomas is the final authority to which we must always appeal; but he has apparently not yet thought his best thoughts.) But MacIntyre's aim is clear. He wants all the advantages of a supportive culture with none of the disadvantages of a parochial culture. He wants all doubts to be laid to rest *and* all dogmas to be open to question. This ideal would be more attractive if we could understand it.

Conflict and Hierarchy

His unexplained shift from closed to open traditions—from the polis as tournament of games to Thomism as a quest for the final truth— makes MacIntyre's argument difficult to follow. To complicate matters further, he introduces still a third model, one with which we are also familiar: tradition rent by deep conflict. The basic division in the ancient city was not, as historians assume, between the rich and the poor, the clan and the community, or the center and the periphery. It was, instead, a conflict between "two kinds of practical reasoning." Citizens were polarized into parties roughly corresponding to the philosopher's distinction between *Vernunft* and *Verstand*. Some wisely pursued excellence, virtue, and mankind's highest ends; others myopically sought effectiveness, utility, and appropriate means. Associating justice with the perfecting of society and the soul, the teleological party defined it as "what is due to excellence." The instrumental party saw justice merely as "what is required by the reciprocity of effective cooperation."[73]

But the moralist's dichotomy of excellence versus effectiveness is sociologically and psychologically impoverished. It does not provide a useful framework for understanding ancient history. It blinds MacIntyre, for example, to powerful nonconsequentialist motives, such as envy and revenge, stressed by close observers of Greek politics such as Thucydides. It distracts him from the way justice-as-receiving-one's-due fomented turmoil when different cities made incompatible claims about what they were owed. It leads him to claim, inaccurately, that justice-as-righting-wrongs had nothing whatever to do with intercity relations. It allows him to ignore the complex causal role played by religion in the outcome of the Peloponnesian War. It also encourages him to whitewash instrumental relations within the polis, to commend a city in which those with lower goals served as doormats for those with higher ones.

Two MacIntyres

MacIntyre praises antiquity for its aspirations and chastises modernity for its problems. He slights instrumental relations in the polis (for example, slavery) and highlights instrumental relations in modern societies (for instance, bargains), making them sound worse than they are. He announces with indignation that "rank, property, and pride" shaped eighteenth-century English society and ignores the role such forces played in ancient Athens. He shows a touching affection for Plato's pedagogical hierarchy, designed to manipulate the young, but he denounces liberal societies because "the range of possible alternatives is controlled by an elite."[74] He puffs Thomism as "an essentially uncompleted debate," while sniffing at liberalism's "inconclusiveness." He explains with a straight face that "all cultures are of course ethnocentric," but apparently excludes the culture of the Church.[75] When Aquinas makes sexist remarks, he is excused because, given his society, he could not have known better; when Hume adapts to a less-than-perfect status quo, he is pilloried for collaborationism. Theoretically, MacIntyre is committed to a contextualist style of intellectual history. But in practice he oscillates between acontextualism and reductionism, distinguishing at one point between philosophers who think rigorously and those who serve powerful interests. His breathlessly earnest discussion of Aquinas, for example, never descends into thirteenth-century history. Hume, by contrast, is vilified as a traitor to Scotland and a spineless lackey of the dominant English classes of his day.[76]

The contradictions just listed are trifling when compared to the main inconsistency undermining his approach. It is a case of two MacIntyres, and they do not always live on good terms with each other. One is an Aristotelian, the other an Augustinian. (MacIntyre claims, unconvincingly, that his Thomism allows him to "synthesize" these two positions.) One defends a hypersocialized conception of man. The other defends Christianity's idea of the immortal soul.[77] One berates liberals (mistakenly) for their myth of the presocial individual, and the other accepts original sin, a trait clearly imposed "apart from and prior to any particular social and political order." About the cosmopolitan pretensions of the Enlightenment, the first MacIntyre proclaims that the "wider the audience to whom we aspire to speak, the less we shall speak to anyone in particular." But the second MacIntyre refuses to press this sarcasm against Jesus. At times he makes people's worth hinge upon their contribution to their group. At other times, he praises Augustine's counsel to cast off traditional social roles, such as husband and father, and to disentangle oneself from Roman society. The tradition-loving MacIntyre elevates the member/nonmember distinction into the centerpiece of his moral theory, while the tradition-spurning MacIntyre praises *caritas* for inducing a healthy indifference toward group membership. The former urges you to adore your rich local tradition, while the latter assures you that it will mean absolutely nothing when you meet your Maker.[78]

At the same time that he yearns sincerely for moral harmony, MacIntyre enfolds, within his own intellect, the essential disharmonies of Western civilization and finds himself riven helplessly by incompatible traditions. The culture of the West, he explains, was marked for almost two millennia by a sharp tension between pagan and religious ideals, by the conflict, for example, between the glory ethic and the biblical ethic. The observation is not impersonal. For MacIntyre turns his own mind into a battlefield where this war can be ceaselessly waged. He professes undying loyalty both to local custom and eternal truth, both to pagan excellence and to redemption from sin, both to ethnic chauvinism and to the Christian idea of a universal mission. His Janus face is the ultimate secret of his thought. These stubborn duplicities can make his work absorbing, of course. But they are also a form of philosophical incoherence.

No wonder he has theorized at such length about irresolvable moral conflict. His simultaneous commitment to pre-Christian and Christian ideals, to culture-boundness and culture-transcendence, explains why he thinks that "tragic conflict is the essential human condition." And it accounts for the passion with which he discusses "the conflict of good with good" and "the tragic confrontations of good with good." He even interprets his personally intense experience of normative dissonance as evidence that moral conflict is founded in the nature of things: "different virtues appear as making rival and incompatible claims upon us. But our situation is tragic in that we have to recognize the authority of both claims. There is an objective moral order."[79] A more detached view of the vestigial conflict between heroic and biblical ideals might make it appear less cosmic than psychological or personal. It would also make MacIntyre's plea for moral harmony seem like a pained cry for what he, in particular, can never achieve.

MacIntyre writes with admirable vividness, especially in *After Virtue*, his best book. He grapples with large questions and takes risks. But his picture-window nostalgia is unconvincing. His bid for consensus never gets off the ground. His storybook contrast between a sick present and a healthy past is implausible. And his boilerplate portrait of liberalism is almost wholly erroneous. What makes him special is not his need for unanswerable authority and reassuring community. Many antiliberals share this longing. Unique about MacIntyre is his ability to quiet his doubts in mutually repellent ways. An inclination toward moral polygamy explains why his writings, seemingly animated by anxiety and disgust, resonate with self-satisfaction. Long disenchanted with Marxism, he can still feel "at home" with Greek ideals or Christian ones, with absolutism or relativism, in one tradition or another—anywhere, so long as it is not liberalism. If you are nonplussed by such versatility, especially in a devout opponent of "modern pluralism," you underestimate the antiliberal need to believe and to belong.

5 / Anti-Prometheanism:
The Case of Christopher Lasch

Ah! que les sciences naturelles ont coûté cher à l'homme!

—Maistre

Distrust of science and technology is a crucial feature of nonmarxist antiliberalism. This distrust has been mentioned repeatedly in preceding chapters, but never discussed in depth. Consider Carl Schmitt once again. Like Strauss and many others, Schmitt associated liberalism with rising material standards of living, with "a conception of life that makes production and consumption into the central categories of human life." Such an economistic outlook necessarily entails an uncritical attitude toward science. To debase mankind in their crass way, liberals had to embrace "a religion of technological miracles, human achievement, and the domination of nature," for consumerism is unthinkable without the scientific revolution. The "religion of technical progress" produced by that revolution was and is naive, but it has a nearly unbreakable hold upon the contemporary mind: "from its beginnings, the twentieth century has appeared to be an age not only of technology, but of a religious belief in technology."[1] As traditional religions were defeated by secularization, they were replaced by the worship of science itself. It is worth looking more closely at the superstition that has ensnared skeptical liberals and revealed their childlike credulity.

Liberals are said to believe unquestioningly in the magical power of science to sweeten and lengthen life. Here is the liberal dream, summarized ironically by Schmitt:

The uncanny magician transforms the world, changes the face of the earth, and subordinates nature to himself. She serves him, for what purpose is unimportant—for any kind of satisfaction of artificially created needs, for comfort and ease. Men who allow themselves to be fooled perceive only the fabulous effects: nature seems to be mastered, the age of security has begun, everything is taken care of, and clever foresight and planning replace Providence. Modern man, in short, has sold his soul for a few frivolous bodily comforts. The enormous productivity of modern economies reflects the loss of restraining spiritual truths. And the glitz produced by the scientific mastery of nature is hollow. It reveals a profound spiritual failure. The crucial mistake behind this disaster was rationalization itself.

Rationalization is a bastardization of reason. In liberal economies, for example, "the productive mechanism that satisfies any and every material need is called 'rational,' without any question being raised about the rationality of the aim pursued." Means-ends rationality has replaced moral reasoning about the ends of life. The result is predictably catastrophic: "modern technology simply makes itself into a slave of any every need. In modern economies, extremely rationalized production is coupled with wholly irrational consumption. A marvellously rational machinery caters to arbitrary demand, with unswerving seriousness and precision, whether the demand is for silk blouses or poison gas or anything else."[2] Scientific rationality means that human beings seek to know the world only in order to master it. They attend to nature only to satisfy their needs. These needs, however, are low, fluctuating, and mutually inconsistent. Entranced by the prestige of science, we have lost all power to decide rationally what goals to pursue. Liberal tolerationism is the political embodiment of modern science's moral disorientation. Amoralism is the product of an inane and debased ambition.

So thought Schmitt; so Strauss concurred. One source of their teratological approach to modern science and technology was European romanticism—beginning with Rousseau's *First Discourse*. In the early twentieth century, however, no writer had more influence in this regard than Martin Heidegger, a towering figure of counter-Enlightenment thought. Heidegger, too, argues that the development of modern technology is proof that mankind has now "lost its way." Human beings were not always driven by an irresistible desire to master nature and subject it to human will. They once built windmills, for instance, which spun naturally in the breeze. But mankind subsequently became much more aggressive: "modern technology," unlike the rudimentary and now antiquated windmill, "puts nature to the unreasonable demand that it supply energy that can be extracted and stored as such." Nineteenth-century industrialization may have followed the seventeenth-century scientific revolutionary chronologically, but calendar time is deceptive. It was the technological outlook, the hubristic longing to master nature and harness it to human designs, that gave birth to mathematical physics and the other modern sciences. How else explain the way science desecrates nature into a storehouse of energy to be pumped dry by human beings? Here are some of Heidegger's examples: "earth is now set upon to yield ore, ore to yield uranium," and eventually "uranium is set upon to yield atomic energy." Similarly, "the sun's warmth is challenged forth for heat, which in turn is ordered to deliver steam whose pressure turns the wheels to keep a factory running." In the grip of technological thinking, a modern forest-wanderer can apparently see the forest only as a source of profit for the lumber industry. (The lumber industry, in turn, transforms trees into paper for illustrated magazines which, in turn, are consumed by a mindless reading public). A connoisseur of German Romantic poetry, Heidegger is particularly aggrieved by a hydroelectric plant on the Rhine river. He refers to it as "the monsterousness" (*das Ungeheuere*). What he objects to, of course, is that "the Rhine itself appears as something at our command."[3]

How important is this antitechnological syndrome to antiliberals? What role does hostility to science play in attacks on individual rights, political pluralism, and constitutional government? To seek answers from a complex and original figure such as Heidegger would lead us down too many exitless forest paths. Consider instead a relatively simple and imitative one: Christopher Lasch. A popular American writer with a clear and engaging style, Lasch entertains no great philosophical pretensions. This makes him appropriate for my present and narrow purposes. A brief look at his criticism of "progress" will help explain how antagonism to science and technology can be integrated smoothly into a general criticism of liberal institutions and ideals.

The Indictment of Progress

Lasch cites MacIntyre as an intellectual authority, and the posture that he has most recently adopted is closely akin to the one defended in *After Virtue*. In his earlier works, *The Culture of Narcissism* (1979) and *The Minimal Self* (1984), Lasch trained a censorious eye on America's condition, and the social pathologist's report he issued about his decadent compatriots was almost cruel. In *The True and Only Heaven*, on which I will concentrate here, he adopts a similarly churlish tone. As usual, he broods morosely over "our darkening prospects." He writes that "our society has taken a wrong turn" and that we have fallen into "moral and cultural disorder." To his eyes, "the social fabric seems to be unravelling." Wherever he looks, he sees "spiritual disrepair," "moral chaos," "spiritual torpor," and "the loss of moral purpose."[4] These are dispiriting observations. Their accuracy, sensibleness, and implications remain to be seen.

Lasch weaves his account of the contemporary catastrophe into an interesting series of commentaries on writers, mainly American, from Jonathan Edwards to Barbara Ehrenreich. He is interested less in these various thinkers for their own sakes, however, than for the opportunity they provide to develop his own diagnosis of the liberal age. The ease with which he couples the history of ideas to debates on social policy is genuinely impressive. Tending to blur his own voice with that of the authors discussed, he is sometimes cryptic. Still, his dislikes are intense and impossible to miss. Progress, mythical and real, is the main object of his ire. He, too, thinks that an extreme pollyannishness about the future is the distinguishing mark of the liberal mind. Among the most galling features of "progressive" society are sexual permissiveness, moral relativism, contempt for authority, the ethic of enjoyment, open-mindedness, irreligion, the decay of the family, the breakdown of traditional communities, drug addiction, the tendency to shirk responsibility, and "a general collapse of common decency."[5] This list is perfectly familiar. None of these depravities would have come about, he explains, if liberals had not been so absurdly optimistic about mankind.

What finally disturbs Lasch is his contemporaries' restlessness, their impatience with any and every constraint on human freedom. People can no longer see a wall without trying to scale it, a limit without trying to step beyond it. To his litany of general complaints he attaches a bill of particulars: an attack on television, for example, according to which the principal instrument of contemporary cultural transmission "destroys the capacity for respect."[6] Such unqualified chastisements of modern times sound remarkably like those of Allan Bloom and other disciples of Strauss. No surprise, then, that Lasch is easily unmasked as a cultural conservative cloaked in a leftish fleece.

Lasch struggles to distance himself from his conservative look-alikes. He does so, in paragraphs flagged for our attention, by uncovering the capitalist roots of most modern ills. What American right-wingers typically fail to see, he asserts, is the all-corrosive power of a free-market economy: "capitalism itself, thanks to its growing dependence on consumerism, promotes an ethic of hedonism," enfeebling character, undermining the work ethic, shattering communal bonds. Such recoiling from Babylon has never been a monopoly of leftists, to be sure. Schmitt as well as Strauss advanced similar claims. Treading well-worn ground, Lasch even holds capitalism accountable for the contagious spread of narcotics: "the need for drugs—that is, for commodities that alleviate boredom and satisfy the socially stimulated desire for novelty and excitement—grows out of the very nature of a consumerist economy."[7] Bombarded with advertising designed to titillate the senses, teenagers and others naturally gravitate toward addictive substances. As a causal analysis, this statement leaves something to be desired (evidence, for example), but it nicely displays Lasch's penchant for eye-catching, speculative sociological generalizations based on vague intuitions.

Desire Unbound

Guilt for the current crisis lies most heavily on economic growth and natural science. We have dragged our society to the brink of ruin because we are committed to the base goal of unlimited abundance or "prosperity for all." The followers of Adam Smith and Karl Marx quarrel heatedly over tactics, but they concur on mankind's ultimate aim: a cosmopolitan society in which technology is freely deployed to satisfy human needs. Both liberals and socialists maintain that scarcity can be abolished and "the reign of want" overcome.[8] Lasch, by contrast, does not expect that, for most people, material conditions will improve. He does not want them to improve. Like other detractors of industrialization and economic expansion, he vigorously dissents from the ideal of a universal and prosperous world order.

He locates himself, therefore, outside the conventional political spectrum: neither left nor right, neither communist nor capitalist. He speaks in the name of a third force—without reflecting deeply about his predecessors in this endeavor. Neither welfare-state progressives nor free-market conservatives understand that the planet's resources are finite (only the Greens do). The earth is already groaning under the onslaught of "development." The foolhardiness of the modern attempt to achieve prosperity for all is revealed by "the environmental limits to economic growth."[9] If we continue to extend Western lifestyles to the rest of humanity, nature will literally buckle and disintegrate beneath our feet. Lasch's ecological alarmism, it should be said, is never convincingly explained. Sometimes, however, it seems more ornamental than fundamental. He views environmental damage basically as a confirmation of what he had already concluded on other, and more philosophical, grounds; that commercialism and modern science are dire mistakes.

He seems almost gratified that nature is about to punish human beings for pursuing material prosperity.[10] He, Lasch, did not want mankind to embrace "progress" in the first place. Withal, his principal objection to economic growth and technical innovation concerns their effect not on the natural environment but on the human soul. These advances inculcate avarice, an addiction to novelty, an instrumental attitude toward others. Associated with advanced economies, the "love of comfort" erodes virility, heroism, ardor, loyalty, asceticism, the ability to suffer, the spirit of responsibility, the longing for martyrdom, moral discipline, and the capacity for devotion. Progress promotes "the spirit of hedonism and self-indulgence." As a consequence, it makes people incapable of "a tragic understanding of life."[11] Most shocking of all, the age of abundance frustrates our profound yearning for an altar on which we can sacrifice our lives.

Why did mankind set off on the suicidal pathway toward progress? Like other enemies of technical and economic modernization, Lasch traces the current crisis to a philosophical misstep—more precisely, to two grave theoretical errors committed at the outset of the modern age. The first blunder was the emancipation of desire. In earlier periods, human desires were wisely viewed as a source of endless frustration. Desires can never be assuaged into quiescence; human beings invariably clamor for more. Defined as a coincidence of capacities and needs, happiness can be achieved only by an ascetic discipline that restricts wants to a bare minimum. In the modern age, however, humanity's traditional abstemiousness was rudely thrust aside, by Adam Smith especially. Rather than trying to squelch human wants, Smith celebrated their unlimited multiplication. Happiness could still be guaranteed, despite the dizzying proliferation of desires, so long as technological and economic capacities grew apace.[12]

The eighteenth century's positive evaluation of ever-expanding wants was historically unprecedented. It provided the psychological foundation for the take-off of surplus economies in modern Europe and for a new ideology of progress. The energy released by the un-bottling of human desires pulled Western society out of an age-old pattern. Subsistence economies limping along pathetically from famine to famine were replaced by economies of growth and abundance. Yesterday's luxuries became today's necessities. The regime of pleasure was born. The "low" triumphed over the "high" (as Strauss would have said). Moreover, history no longer seemed ruled by fatal cycles of rise and fall. Humanity began to soar short-sightedly in a single direction.

Science

This discussion of economic take-off brings us to our main theme: anti-Prometheanism. "Progress" was motored by capitalism, but behind the unleashing of desires lurked the second cataclysmic blunder of modern times: natural science. Uninhibited curiosity about the workings of nature proved to be a social acid. Without Mephisto-phelian science, moreover, modern economies would never have been able to stay atop the rising tide of human desires. Technology alone makes plausible the modern hope of eliminating scarcity; the "promise of universal abundance" was a promise made, if not wholly kept, by science. The temptation was hard to resist. Modern European philosophers who said "yes" to science (an unpardonable transgression) were seduced by "the intoxicating prospect of man's conquest of the natural world."[13] Not satisfied with improvements in warfare, agriculture, navigation, land travel, and medicine, they were charmed by the expectation that technology might eliminate *all* constraints on human freedom.

Here too Lasch sees eye-to-eye with Heidegger, Schmitt, Strauss, and the more despondent members of the Frankfurt School. He believes that the Enlightenment "gave rise to the dangerous fantasy that man could remodel both the natural world and human nature itself." He conceives science as the expression of impiety, of hubris. Science is a rebellion against natural limitations. It rashly denies "our dependence on higher powers." It embodies humanity's blasphemous hankering to play God. It fosters the illusion of human self-sufficiency: "in the modern world, this illusion finds its characteristic expression in the machines by means of which mankind seeks to liberate itself from toil—that is, from the inescapable constraints of human existence." Enthroning mankind as nature's proud master and possessor, science destroys our "reverence" for the cosmos. It teaches us to "see the world as something that exists only to gratify human desires."[14] It reduces the earth itself to a tool of that collection of earthworms, mankind. Baconian megalomania will inevitably bring punishment down upon our heads (through holes in the ozone, for instance).

In a style that probably derives from Carlyle, but is also redolent of Heidegger, Lasch tells us that technology is deeply alienating. It erects barriers between us and our environment: for example, in modern times, "air-conditioning and central heating" protected the educated classes from the elements, but also "cut them off from the vivid knowledge of nature that comes only to those who expose themselves to her harsher moods."[15] (A reader cannot help wondering whether Lasch puts his preaching into practice. In winter does he do his writing at 55 degrees?) Heidegger's attacks on technology are nowhere cited, but Lasch may be revealing his partial indebtedness to a popularized Heideggerianism when he tells us that the proper attitude toward nature is not one of mastery and manipulation but a "grateful acceptance," a kind of pious letting-go.

The End of Restraint

To give his criticism of science a political twist, Lasch describes "the vision of men and women released from outward constraints" not only as "the core of the belief in progress" but also as "the essence of liberalism." Here is the connection we have been looking for. Science and liberalism are two ends of the same stick. Lasch offers a few grudging words of praise for the liberal political tradition. For the most part, though, he regards liberal politics as a sinister appanage to scientific curiosity, technical innovation, and economic growth. Armed with "an excessive confidence in reason," liberals aim to free mankind from hardship and adversity with the help of science. As militant rationalists and rationalizers, they promote atheism, distrust of authority, moral relativism, excessive tolerance, contempt for traditions, antipatriarchalism, and a cosmopolitan worldview. They support gay rights, women's rights, nonpunitive child-rearing practices, and a "flexible" attitude toward sex roles.[16] They favor educational opportunities and social mobility. They ridicule patriotism and display a "humanitarian horror of violence."[17] (This Maistrean touch, remarkably enough, is meant as a criticism.) Every demand for law and order looks to them like another symptom of the fascist mind, of which they are unreasonably afraid.

Liberals also assert the right to kill fetuses. And, of course, they scorn motherhood as an unworthy profession. His indignation about "the feminist disparagement of motherhood" provides a good example of the way Lasch gives political color to his animadversions against technology. Pro-choice activists, he explains, are simply the latest heirs to the modern ideology of progress: "their insistence that women ought to assume 'control over their bodies' evinced an impatience with biological constraints of any kind, together with a belief that modern technology had liberated humanity from those constraints and made it possible for the first time to engineer a better life for the human race as a whole." His summary of pro-choice thinking here is astonishing. Couples who discover that their unborn progeny has severe and irreversible brain damage demand legal permission to make the tragic choice for abortion because, according to Lasch, they hope to prevent the arrival of children unfit for "success" in the bourgeois rat-race.[18]

His principal concern is not the fetus at all. What offends him about the pro-choice movement is not its heedlessness of fetal life but rather its indifference to the will of nature. The attempt to make pregnancy voluntary is another expression of modern hubris. This background assumption explains why Lasch lets his critique of abortion slide smoothly into a critique of the contraceptive mentality. A condom is just one more technological intrusion, of the sort liberals recklessly admire, into natural processes of reproduction: "the objection that sex and procreation cannot be severed without losing sight of the mystery surrounding both struck liberals as the worst kind of theological obscurantism." He urges compliance with the will of nature, be it noted, from a purely secular (not Catholic) point of view. A limit is a limit. Those who transgress one will inevitably transgress them all. Because he believes this, he even implies, in a bewildering passage, that those favoring birth control are one step away from "far-reaching programs of eugenic engineering."[19]

Ethnic Bonds

According to Strauss, "science is essentially cosmopolitan" or "universal." It is also concerned with results rather than pedigrees. As a result, natural science undermines inherited statuses and traditions. Above all, it "necessarily weakens the power of the national 'philosophies' and therewith the attachment of the citizens to the particular way of life, or the manners, of their community."[20] In the war between scientific rationalism and inherited ways of life, Lasch boldly sides with ethnic community against science. He follows MacIntyre's lead here, but without defending traditional values philosophically against the rationalism of modern times. Rather than making a theoretical case for premodern ideals, he poses as the voice of a neglected, scorned, and humiliated social class. His ideas do not simply rattle around in his head; they have social roots. He is a self-nominated spokesman for "the ethnic worker." And this is surely one of the strangest aspects of his book: to attack the reigning orthodoxy, Lasch hopes to tap the smoldering discontent of lower-middle-class whites.[21]

Those who were once self-employed producers do not swallow the prevailing myth of progress, he explains, for they were the principal victims of economic change. Unlike the rest of us, ethnic workers are comfortable with "limits." They are immune to modern restlessness. They feel no irresistible compulsion to leap across the next horizon. They are ambitionless. Indifferent to the cult of individual achievement, they want nothing more than to retain their way of life. In the nineteenth century they "sometimes sacrificed their children to their passion for home ownership, forcing them into the workplace instead of sending them to school."[22] A teacher by profession, Lasch implies that this was not as "irrational" as liberals might assume. What some would deplore as a failure of imagination, he views as a sign of psychic health. The petty bourgeoisie he holds up for our admiration, in any case, is locally entrenched, morally conservative, committed to family life, respectful of craftsmanship. Its members are staunchly loyal to fellow ethnics. All they want is to be self-employed again, which is precisely what hyperactive capitalism will never allow them to become.

The lower middle classes have their darker side, of course. Lasch mentions narrowness, servility, envy, resentment, parochialism, racism, nativism, and anti-intellectualism. But unlike all other classes, this class can be trusted to keep its destructive impulses under control (though Bensonhurst and Howard Beach do come to mind). At the opposite pole from the ethnic workers are the liberal intellectuals. The most dangerous political enemy of the lower middle class, they are wholly incapable of accepting limits or repressing their malevolent urges. One group is noble; the other is base.

Lasch explains this difference through a mystifying detail: "liberals saw the graffiti scrawled on subway cars as a vibrant new form of folk art, while ethnic workers saw them as part of the crisis of civility."[23] And liberals do not merely poeticize the defacement of public property. They also pour scorn on religion and family values. They live in the suburbs, drive sleek foreign cars, frequent museums and concerts, fly around the world, and eat in posh restaurants. They celebrate self-expression and self-advancement. All this helps to explain their hopeless failure to sympathize with the petty bourgeoisie. They view white ethnic solidarity condescendingly, as an expression of atavistic impulses destined to pale in the sunlight of reason.

For their unbearable arrogance, however, they have paid a heavy price. Their very language has degenerated: they speak an "academic English" that has lost touch with common speech. They can barely understand the regional dialects and "earthy idioms" characteristic of ethnic workers.[24] (This is pure MacIntyre.) Put simply, the typical liberal is a rootless cosmopolitan—an old term of abuse that Lasch finds apt, and that he hopes, unbelievably, to rescue from its purportedly accidental association with fascist and Stalinist antisemitism.

To the suggestion that the resentment of the lower middle class against liberalism is fuelled by racism, Lasch strongly objects. Willie Horton was *not* the tip of an iceberg. The centerpiece of his argument is the antibusing movement. Lasch sees busing, correctly, as an issue on which American progressives are politically vulnerable. He rehearses all the stock arguments, deploring the way that "'limousine liberals' in the suburbs expect the cities to carry the whole burden of desegregation." The white working classes viewed liberal busing policy not only as patronizing, but also as an intolerable invasion of their ethnic enclaves, an attempt to destroy their communities. The fact is, "the burden of busing notoriously fell on ethnic neighborhoods in the cities, not on suburban liberals whose schools remained effectively segregated or on wealthy practitioners of 'compassion' whose children did not attend public schools at all."[25] Liberals are hypocrites, do-gooders at the expense of other people's loyalties, and on the backs of other people's children.

They are not alone in their misdeeds. Martin Luther King Jr. is also guilty for "his ill-conceived campaign for open housing in Chicago." What King failed to see was that "blacks could not hope to achieve their objectives by demanding the dissolution of white communities whose only crime, as far as anyone could see, was their sense of ethnic solidarity." King is explicitly taken to task for "his distaste for anything smacking of separatism." Black communities should be strengthened internally, not dispersed by integration. (Here Lasch comes close to a defense of ethnic and racial fragmentation, a tower-of-Babel version of the American dream.) Lasch's thesis is that "the advantages of community cohesion" far outweigh "the dangers of racial separatism."[26] That liberals oppose balkanization shows how little they understand human nature and its limits.

King's earlier activism had been successful, Lasch opines, because it was firmly rooted in "the regional culture of the South." The farther he moved from tribal politics, the more pitiably his efforts misfired. Thus King made a terrible mistake in trying to transplant the civil rights movement from southern black communities to the secularized and urbanized North. Equally inept was his attempt to forge "an interracial coalition" of disadvantaged groups. This liberal tactic was "morally flawed" because, among other things, it diluted the ethnic solidarity necessary to make the civil rights movement succeed. (Lasch is admittedly unclear on this point, since a few pages later he blames King for having *failed* to create "a biracial coalition" based on joint responsibility instead of common victimization.)[27] This attack on King seems dubious. Might not race relations and community cohesion in the North be in a better state today if King had not died before he was able to work long in the Northern cities?

Lasch endorses group loyalty, local uniformity, and ethnic homogeneity. He sniffs at social mobility and hints that "cultural assimilation" may be a mistake. He even casts doubt, by indirection, on the wisdom of "racial and ethnic intermarriage." Liberals embraced assimilationism, he claims, because of an exaggerated fear of factional strife and a naive faith that human beings are capable of universal sympathies. They made "the misguided attempt to remove the sources of social conflict by discouraging particularism, in the hope that brotherly love would then come into its own." As could have been predicted, this attempt "killed the very possibility of brotherly love by cutting off its roots." Benevolence beyond the boundaries of one's ethnic group is a bloodless ideal, typical of the Enlightenment. Cosmopolitans and universalists offer us the "watery fellowship of humanity in general." This is tasteless gruel. Lasch's sympathies clearly lie with those "advocates of particularism" who "challenged one of the central tenets of enlightened ideology, the equation of progress with the eradication of tribal loyalties and their replacement by an all-embracing love for the whole human race."[28] The heartless assault on tribalism was a natural result of scientific rationalism. It was also liberalism's greatest crime.

Populist Producerism

Somewhat unexpectedly, Lasch tries to distinguish his position from a "vague and milky communitarianism." Indeed, he devotes two important chapters to vague and milky criticisms of ordinary nostalgia for *Gemeinschaft*. He draws a distinction between himself and other communitarian enemies of modernity by emphasizing "honest labor" as well as ethnic solidarity. He sometimes calls his philosophy "populist producerism." This separates him not only from liberals, who distrust working-class radicalism and see human beings exclusively as consumers, but also from namby-pamby communitarians who leave no room for "proprietary independence" and manly work. His goal is "the rehabilitation of work, not the democratization of consumption." He is fascinated by "the ideal of a society composed of small producers" or "a society of small workshops, in which effective control over production remained at the local level." And he is not simply looking backward; a "populism for the twenty-first century," otherwise undescribed, will give pride of place to "the self-governing workshop" and, more generally, to the "democratization of work."[29]

Dazzled by J. G. A. Pocock's account of the civic virtue tradition, Lasch is tempted to project his own version of it into America's pre-industrial past. The key figure in this idealized world (where slavery and rural poverty apparently did not loom large) was the self-employed producer—the moral equivalent to the militiaman-at-arms. Proprietorship gave dignity, responsibility, and manliness to the owner. Unfortunately, Lasch tells us next to nothing about the real people he has in mind, about who they were and how they actually lived. So we get no sense of the kinds of problems *they* had to face. What he lets us know, by way of compensation, is that self-employed artisans and farmers viewed labor as a joyful activity, an end in itself. They had "callings," not jobs. This explains their hostile response to economic development, technical change, and especially the rise of factory production; "populists condemned innovation because it undermined proprietary independence and gave rise to 'wage slavery.'" He even ventures the bold generalization that most or all "democratic movements in the nineteenth century took shape in opposition to innovation."[30] (By exaggerating popular hostility to technical change, he makes it difficult to understand the universal enthusiasm with which all Americans greeted, say, Samuel Morse's fabulous invention.)

It should now be clear why Lasch is almost more hostile to the welfare state than to the economics of laissez-faire. Classical liberalism invented the "cult of consumption." Transfer programs changed nothing essential, accomplishing merely "a more equitable distribution of consumer goods."[31] Under the derogatory term "consumer goods" Lasch apparently includes housing, health care, education, and child nutrition. For him, welfare programs represent just one more encroachment of shameful Enlightenment ideals (such as low food prices for the poor). Like advocates of the untrammeled market, welfare-state liberals see human beings exclusively as consumers of utility, not as exercizers of virtue. This is why Enlightenment do-gooders have always supported automation; they consider work inherently defiling and seek relief from it by means of improved productivity, which generates abundance and thereby cuts down the need for labor.

For Lasch, the gradual abatement of toil is just another strike against science, technology, and economic growth. The reduction of the workday is a "paltry vision" that deserves "contempt."[32] Aghast at physical suffering, liberal intellectuals have betrayed the promise of American life. They have conspired to corrupt and *unman* the worker, stealing away his (and her?) responsibilities and popularizing their own leisure-class values. And predictably enough, the working class's new addiction to material comfort has already extinguished older and more strenuous ideals. ("Populism," it should be said, has seldom been so suffused with contempt for ordinary men and women.)

Defects in the Argument

The True and Only Heaven is something of a mood piece, and the mood is glum. Lasch's antipathy to scientific, technological, and hygienic progress seems to have preconceptual roots. This puts his critic at a disadvantage; you cannot argue with a state of mind. Still, his approach has some remarkable flaws that deserve to be pointed out.

His cultural pessimism is wholly unmitigated by a genuinely comparative perspective. Things are bad, compared with when and where? Despite our presumptuous search for mastery, he claims, we are now more insecure and less in control of our lives than ever. Yet during the greater part of human history disease was rampant, famines periodic, peace rare, and life expectancy shockingly low. What kind of control over their lives have most of humanity ever had?

No question, we lack the political means for deciding which technologies we want and which ones we do not want. This is the core of truth underlying Lasch's argument. Inventions almost seem to thrust themselves upon us, with or without our cooperation. But the failure of politics to guide technical change cannot be blamed on modern liberalism. Communist systems were even worse in this regard, as we have recently learned. Ecologically minded antiliberals walk into a contradiction, moreover, when they proclaim the value of national solidarity: defensive modernization—the uncontrolled development and proliferation of military technology—is rooted in the political division of humanity into rival groups, not in the scientific world view. Similarly, mankind's inability to limit its harm to the planet is due, in part, to failures of cooperation among distinct national units. (Solidarity *within* each nation exacerbates this problem rather than solving it.) Schmitt and others of his generation asked, "what kind of politics is strong enough to take charge of the new technology"?[33] In view of the answer he provided, a political system which modestly admits its impotence in this regard may not be all bad. In any case, the difficulties we have in controlling technology, while serious, do not provide a good reason to reject liberal politics.

Furthermore, Lasch's hostility toward science and technology, to the extent that it reflects ecological anxiety, is pointless. The more serious our environmental problems become, the more we need science and technology (not to mention bureaucracy) to help us deal with them, regardless of how and why the modern scientific worldview arose. You do not sop up an oil slick with natural sponges or stir up public support and government action without employing the powerful means of communication provided by modern technology.

His protest against "the substitution of human choice for the blind workings of nature," if taken seriously, suggests that we should, say, stop vaccinating children or, for that matter, simply close down our hospitals. In an earlier work, Lasch wrote that "all medical technology has done is to increase the patient's dependence on machines" and "medical experts."[34] (Such remarks make one wonder how seriously Lasch wants to be taken after all.)

His sacralization of the concept of "limits" makes it impossible for him to distinguish sensibly between the limits that deserve to be respected and those that deserve to be disrespected. And it lures him into reckless causal claims (contraception today, eugenics tomorrow).

His portrayal of the lower middle class reveals a highly selective vision of the past. For one thing, the American petite bourgeoisie is filled with people who originally came to this country in pursuit of "progress." For another, no social class is as harmless or self-correcting as Lasch makes his ethnic workers appear. A good look at Poujadisme, the French *populist producers'* movement of the 1950s, which had leftish origins but ended up on the xenophobic and antisemitic right, might correct this one-sided account.

His unbalanced assessment of "development" neglects the beneficial effect of economic prosperity on population growth. The richer people become, the fewer children they tend to have. The better educated and more fully integrated into the workforce women become, the more they will choose to limit the size of their families. The earth's carrying capacity is certainly limited, but sliding into backwardness would increase our problems in this regard.

Lasch's unwillingness to weigh the advantages of economic growth and technological innovation against their disadvantages is perverse. "Progress" may have many unpalatable side effects, but it is not vile. Think of literacy; think of sanitation for the working classes. Even "consumerism," the desire for beautiful or useful objects, may have something to do with human dignity. Lasch is right to notice that women's emancipation would have been unthinkable without material progress, in particular, effective contraception, reduced infant mortality, and household work-saving devices—points that should mitigate his exaggerated Heideggerian disgust at science. Lasch's lopsided assessment is especially exasperating here, since he repeatedly warns us that when it comes to tribal loyalties, religious superstitions, and martial virtues, we must not let the bad blind us to the good.

His criticism of nostalgia and the pastoral tradition, while a clever ploy, is theoretically unconvincing. His emphasis on endangered crafts and the dignity of labor makes him stand out among contemporary *Gemeinschaft* theorists. But his thinking remains in the grip of backward-looking communitarian platitudes.

His sympathy with "cultural pluralism" and his doubts about "the assimilationist ideal" remain nebulous in their implications.[35] It sometimes seems that he would favor turning America into an ethnic archipelago, a diverse collection of internally homogeneous subunits. That this is an ill-considered idea is the least that might be said. Strong group pluralism would be tolerable only in the context of a *liberal* system capable of protecting individual rights and fostering national discussion and cross-ethnic cooperation. Yet that is precisely the kind of system he purports to distrust.

His suggestion that fanaticism, intolerance, and superstition are a price worth paying to avoid flabbiness, insipidity, and spiritual desiccation is farfetched. Only an affluent American could write this way. Only a Westerner could dismiss (and even then one wonders how) the problems of disease, famine, poverty, and violence as an obsession of the decadent liberal mind. In a world full of clashes between Armenians and Azeris, Serbs and Croatians, Tamils and Sinhalese, Israelis and Palestinians, Northern Irish Catholics and Northern Irish Protestants, only an American could become larmoyant about the weakening of tribal loyalties and ethnic identifications.

An Antiliberal Miscellany

Viewed as a whole, Lasch's moral perspective—precisely like MacIntyre's—is afflicted with deep and irresolvable inconsistencies. It sometimes seems as if the communication lines among his various chapters have been cut. In retrospect, we can see that he condemns "the progressive mind" on the basis of four wholly distinct traditions or ideals: martial, religious, ethnic, and artisanal/proprietary.[36] The relations among these four value-clusters are never explained or even discussed. But the tensions among them are obvious. His romanticization of the worker, for instance, is not reconciled with the Christian idea that labor is a curse. Likewise, consider his simultaneous praise of the meek and the bold. To his chagrin, liberalism has traditionally disappointed those who seek security *and* those who seek exhilaration. Progress destroyed both dauntless heroism and passive acquiescence; the economy of abundance dampened "virility" and shattered "grateful acceptance"; mankind needs a "taste of battle" and a renewed sense of "sin."

That Lasch draws equally on Georges Sorel and Jonathan Edwards reveals the breadth of his sympathies, not to mention the disheveled eclecticism of his mind. His oscillation between religious and heroic perspectives contributes considerably to the length (not to the clarity) of his book. He sometimes defines virtue as self-abnegation and sometimes as self-affirmation. In one chapter he tells us to submit passively to the universe. In the next he urges us to adopt an "heroic conception of life." We must strive for self-sufficiency, he says, and also accept our totally helpless dependence on a higher power. The Emersonian ideal of self-confidence and self-reliance is noble; the struggle for human autonomy reflected in modern science is base. We must seize back the "control" of our own work and lives, wrested away by capitalism, and also admit that the desire for "control" is blasphemous and even satanic. We must throw off wage slavery while embracing mortality and pain, the wages of sin. We must honor both limits and the heroes who audaciously transgress them. This whipsaw pattern is easier to identify than to understand.

What form would a politics of limits take? What concrete alternatives, in other words, does Lasch propose? He tells us to adopt "a tragic sense of life," but he has no practical suggestions about how to democratize work or revivify ethnic passions. When he remarks that we ought to "try to transform the ghetto into a real community," he is naturally silent about how this alchemy is to proceed. He believes that "a drastic reduction of the standard of living enjoyed by the rich nations and the privileged classes" is inevitable, but he does not tell us how to get there with the least (or the most?) possible pain.[37] He detests large corporations, financial institutions, and national and state bureaucracies, but he does not explain how we could cope with the consequences of abolishing them or how they might be replaced.

A brief autobiographical chapter is titled "The Making of a Malcontent," no irony intended. But malcontentedness is one thing, legal implementation another. Does Lasch want to punish disloyalty and disbelief? Does he favor a *less* equitable distribution of consumer goods? Is all criticism of authority to be suppressed, along with interracial marriage, social mobility, and contraception? Should television sets and credit cards be confiscated and destroyed? Should we revert to small-scale production and abolish paper money? Should all central heaters and air-conditioners be shut down?

In every case, surely, the answer is no. In the absence of decisive positions, however, Lasch's concluding statement is disappointingly academic: "the populist tradition offers no panacea for all the ills that afflict the modern world. It asks the right questions, but it does not provide a ready-made set of answers."[38] He is so reticent here that he does not even tell us what these "right questions" might be. His evasiveness is easy to understand. Answering questions, solving problems, curing ills—these are dangerous activities. They might make things better than they are. They might even threaten to improve our lives. Just imagine people taking the lesson of this book to heart. They might suddenly acknowledge that material abundance is not humanity's greatest good. They might even try to resuscitate tribal connections and bygone crafts. In the face of the possibility of moral advance Lasch concludes with the usual swirl of demurers, to distract us, I think, from the ultimate paradox of his approach. Does he not aspire to "enlighten" his fellows about the dangers of economic growth? Can he sincerely deny his passion for transforming people's lives? What, in the end, does this bitter enemy of improvement have to offer but a renewed, if hopelessly vague, dream of further progress for mankind?

6 / Unger: Antiliberalism Unbound

Liberalism is commonly assailed from two extremes, either for being anarchistic or for not being anarchistic enough. These antithetical complaints are lodged by two distinct types of antiliberal: the *communitarian conservative* and the *countercultural radical*. This dichotomy coincides, more or less, with MacIntyre's lucid distinction between two rival anti–Enlightenment positions (headed by St. Thomas and Nietzsche).[1] Members of the communitarian school see liberalism as a disintegrative force: it loosens social bonds, leaving the individual unattached and bereft of moral support, and wantonly promotes the liberty to do whatever one wants. Adherents to the countercultural view, by contrast, see liberalism as covertly tyrannical: it nails down the otherwise spontaneous individual to rigid rules and coercively enforces an ascetic discipline of conformity and self-denial. The liberal order cruelly prevents people from doing whatever they want (and from acquiring new desires). The former critics see the calculating bourgeois as rootless, nervous, and impious; the latter see him as sedentary, wooden, and boring.

I have already looked closely at some classic examples of communitarian conservatism. For the sake of balance and completeness, I now want to examine countercultural radicalism, as exemplified in the works of Roberto Unger. His *Politics, A Work in Constructive Social Theory* (1987) is marvelously appropriate.[2] His earlier work, *Knowledge and Politics* (1975), presents a hybrid position worth examining for its own sake.[3] While MacIntyre claims that liberal man is too rebellious, Unger, with great clarity, proposes that liberal man is too submissive. For the former, liberalism allows too much room for subjective discretion and choice. For the latter, it does not leave enough room for self-expression and choice. These contradictory formulations nicely summarize two distinct forms of antiliberal discontent.

(Defenders of liberalism will be delighted to juxtapose these two approaches, of course. Both sides have grasped one half of the truth, as it were, and jointly they cancel each other out. Together, they suggest a position close to common sense: liberalism is neither anarchical nor tyrannical. It is both more constricting than communitarian conservatives charge and less constricting than countercultural radicals claim. It is a philosophy of limits as well as a philosophy of freedom. It imposes important constraints on individuals, including prohibitions against violent self-help and against self-exemption from laws that should apply to all. But it also helps preserve the fragile institutional preconditions for personal choice as well as for the democratic correction of collective mistakes.)

In his early works Unger is somewhat torn. To some extent, he tries to hold these two contradictory antiliberal positions simultaneously. The author of *Knowledge and Politics* can thus be read both as a communitarian conservative and as a countercultural radical. No wonder readers of the book are perplexed. In its communitarian passages, it tells us that liberal man is "condemned to dissatisfaction and discontent" and therefore "denied the tranquil possession of self." In its countercultural parts, it explains that liberal man suffers from "resignation" or a passive acceptance of his assigned social position. Which does Unger miss more, tranquility or restlessness?

As a conservative tract, *Knowledge and Politics* attacks both liberalism and modern science for encouraging a "defiance of fate." Science desacralizes the world and thus leads to the liberal "denial of the immutability of nature and of society."[4] As a rebel treatise, *Knowledge and Politics,* far from excoriating hubris and rebelliousness, encourages it. Rather than deplore the free-for-all of a disintegrating order, its author urges us to join it. This time Unger wants us "cherish those *acts of defiance* or genius, of art or play, by which the wholeness of human nature shines for a brief moment upon the world." Instead of being nostalgic about the loss of religious restraints, he bitterly denounces "the sanctification of actuality."[5] Here again Unger admires defiance and regrets it at the same time.

The conservative Unger assures us that "man occupies a place in the order of created things," but that liberalism has uprooted man and denied him his birthright. The rebellious Unger retorts that "man has no predetermined place in nature," but that liberalism has chained man to the galleys of social expectations. The admirer of stability complains that liberalism has created a disheveled society, and he regrets the vanishing of "any stable set of common ends," including a "stable, authoritative Archimedean point." The main sign that liberal society is sick, from this perspective, is "the experience of the precariousness and contingency of all shared values." This situation could be improved only if we introduced "fixed entitlements and duties." Conversely, the champion of instability wants to "make the division of labor less rigid" and even create a society in which the individual can "experiment continuously with different forms of life." A "stable and authoritative sharing of values" is wholly undesirable. Indeed, it is characteristic of despised "forms of hierarchical community."[6]

In line with this second way of thinking, Unger says that he longs for "the disappearance of the distinction" between the extraordinary and the ordinary.[7] What this means is not easy to grasp. (While he claims to repudiate essentialism, he nevertheless makes the essentialist assumption that the term "extraordinary" can retain its meaning even in the absence of its antonym, "ordinary.") But his general idea is clear. As a countercultural radical, he wants to poeticize ordinary life, to democratize the rare. He desires "the expansion of the aesthetic into areas traditionally reserved to the prosaic." Run-of-the-mill events should be suffused with the glow of the exception. We must reproduce the "divine liberation from the everyday" in everyday life itself.[8] It is this hope, I suspect, that leads Unger to compare himself to Archimedes, who "ran naked through the streets of Syracuse to announce his findings."[9] *Knowledge and Politics* contains many such fey moments, as we shall see. But only in the later book, *Politics*, does Unger reveal how truly Archimedean, in the above sense, he is willing to become. I will look at each of these works in turn.

The Basic Stance

Knowledge and Politics reveals some yet unexplored facets of the antiliberal mind. It is second only to MacIntyre's *After Virtue* in examplifying the "soft" or postfascist antiliberalism so widespread in the United States during the 1970s and 1980s. But it is also a unique work. A close analysis of Unger's objections to liberalism will make an appropriate conclusion for my studies of individual antiliberal writers. *Knowledge and Politics* documents once again the irrepressibility of an antiliberal tradition in which well-established complaints and arguments are presented as revolutionary insights. And while Unger is the exemplar of a familiar intellectual style, he is not only that. His position is just as idiosyncratic as that of the other antiliberals with whom he nevertheless shares so much in common.

Unger's fidelity to antiliberal custom is indicated, first of all, by his attitude toward Marx. He denounces class domination, declaring that humanity can be saved only if there is "a victory of the Left over the Right." He flirts vaguely with a wide range of marxist ideas and sentiments, but resolves that this ideology is radically deficient. Marxism is defective, moreover, because it is not antiliberal enough. In Marx's works, "the critique of liberal thought is not carried through to its last conclusions." Despite his best efforts, Marx always remained in the clutches of liberalism. He even shared important intellectual premises with Bentham.[10]

Liberalism exercises an "unbroken tyranny" over the minds of all its conventional critics—including the Marxists. But timidity and half-heartedness is a now a thing of the past. Unger himself is going to crack the frame, make "a break with the whole system of liberal thought." He will not merely discard a few stray aspects of liberalism while surreptitiously accepting important liberal premises or ideas. Unlike Marx, he will "abandon the system of liberal political thought" as a whole, providing "a total criticism of the liberal doctrine." He will present "the most effective critique of liberal political doctrine" ever devised; not resting there, he will let his readers glimpse "the most subversive of doctrines," more subversive than anything fainthearted marxists ever imagined.[11]

In short, *Knowledge and Politics* is an ambitious, aggressive book. Without hesitating, Unger characterizes his own thinking about "the major concerns of human existence" as "deep" and announces his hope "to subvert and destroy" the social order in which less audacious creatures (such as the rest of us) live. A destructive enterprise of this sort is necessary because today's world is a moral "disaster." Our situation has become "urgent." Liberal society is beyond redemption and yet humanity must be redeemed. Any attempt to cleanse the world of liberalism will be "difficult and dangerous," of course. But Unger is willing to run this risk for our sakes. He introduces himself to his readers, interestingly, as a heroic unshackler of the people. He will provide us with "the key that will allow us to escape" from "the prison house of liberal thought."[12]

Liberalism is not just another ideological jailhouse, however. It is the "ruling consciousness" or "dominant mentality" of liberal society. To criticize liberalism effectively, therefore, is to help overturn "its secret empire." Unger allows that he cannot annihilate liberalism entirely on his own. He cannot single-handedly dismantle the prison walls that have kept all citizens of the West incarcerated for the past three centuries. On the other hand, he retains a fairly high opinion of his own capacities. He knows that "a single proud and rebellious individual may show his fellows or his posterity that the truth about the ideal is utterly opposed to what they have imagined it to be."[13] And he casts himself enthusiastically in this David-against-Goliath role. He may not be able to create, simply by publishing a philosophical essay, a wholly nonliberal society, but he can disclose and discredit the rickety intellectual foundations on which the liberal order rests.

He begins confessionally: "I have written this book as an act of hope." His hope is for a radical "transformation of society." Not content with refuting an inadequate theory, how can he, a mere professor armed only with paper and ink, contribute to a massive process of social change? The successful critic of liberal theory can play a world-historical role because of the utmost importance of liberal theory itself. Liberal theory is constitutive of liberal society, not just a bookish doctrine wedged into the skulls of a few scribblers. It is "a dominant form of social organization." Liberal ideas have been "actualized in the main forms of social order today." One result is that a relentlessly abstract book, such as *Knowledge and Politics*, in which no historical dates or country names appear, can provide "a critical understanding of the situation of modern society." A philosophical analysis is simultaneously a sociological inquiry, for citizens in a liberal society live according to liberal norms. While the "liberal image of society" may be impoverished and self-contradictory, it exercises unrivaled power over people's daily lives. Its enormous power, in turn, explains Unger's personal hopes. If he can change the way people see society, he will change society itself. Laying siege to liberalism as a theory is tantamount to attacking "the society of which the liberal doctrine is the theoretical representation."[14]

The "power and greatness of theory" lie in their ability to foster and accelerate social change. Like most antiliberals, Unger bounds athletically from intellectual to social criticism. But he often ends up, as do his fellows, wavering between a criticism of liberal theory and a criticism of liberal society. The two criticisms prove inconsistent. On the one hand, liberalism provides an inaccurate picture of our societies. Our "experience" is much more meaningful than anything captured by "the liberal conception of society as an association of independent and conflicting individuals." By promulgating its "conceptual illusion," liberalism blinds us to the healthy social and psychological reality before our eyes. We seldom focus clearly on our real life "because its design is obscured by the influence of liberal principles."[15]

On the other hand, and concurrently, Unger argues that liberalism has thoroughly mutilated Western societies, flattening them into conformity with its perverse doctrinal premises. While morally hateful, liberalism is, alas, descriptively accurate: "the liberal doctrine is the representation of a certain type of social life." Not only do "the premises of liberal thought describe a form of social existence and social consciousness," but "the seriousness of the political premises of liberalism is a consequence of the accuracy with which they describe a form of social experience." Far from being distortions, "the principles of liberalism draw their power and importance from the fact that they illuminate a historical situation."[16]

This self-contradictory attack on liberalism is as characteristic of *Knowledge and Politics* as it is of *After Virtue* and other works of the genre. On one page liberalism is accused of misapprehending the world, on the next page of having reshaped it in its own image. And Unger, too, again like MacIntyre, is vaguely aware of the corner into which he has painted himself. He tries to wend his way out of this archetypical inconsistency with the usual convolutions. Liberalism, he backtracks, has partly but not wholly deformed our societies: "liberal thought commands our interest and our assent because its principles describe *much of the way* we think and live." We have been mostly, but not wholly deformed by liberal ideology. Because "we are men as well as liberals . . . we have a knowledge of our humanity that the liberal doctrine cannot exhaust." Fortunately, an unspoiled remnant of life uncorrupted by liberal thought exists: "our present way of acting and speaking includes a picture of humanity more complete than the one allowed by liberal premises."[17] This half-perceived, dormant reality has not been destroyed but only hidden by liberalism.

A bad theory produces a bad life because it imposes blinders. Liberalism spoils our lives by concealing from us our most worthwhile potentials. For example, "just as liberal theory is unable to account for the possibility of selfhood, life in modern, liberal society continually denies us the possibility of coherent personality." Liberal citizens, then, suffer personally from the chronic dimsightedness of liberal philosophy. They live divided lives because they interpret their experience through the liberal distinction between reason and desire. Most people are cruelly prevented from having a "full personality," because liberalism coarsely denies that any such personal wholeness exists. By focusing our attention on the vestigial experiences of coherent personality that nevertheless remain available in liberal society (artistic creativity is Unger's favorite example), the critic of liberalism can start the revolutionary process whereby the whole life-impairing liberal system will come crashing down. The counterattack against liberal ideas and institutions "elucidates possibilities already present, and by the very act of elucidation it opens up possibilities not there before."[18]

To open the door to these old/new possibilities, the militant antiliberal—Unger—must simply "provide us with a language" in which we can redescribe our lives. This language will be more descriptively accurate than the liberal language it replaces, because it will correctly depict the undeformed residue ignored by liberal thought. It will also be a force for social transformation, demanding that the rest of society, disfigured by liberalism, be demolished and replaced by a new nonliberal order, modeled on the "residue," on the experience of artistic creativity, and so forth. This argument is tortuous, and the conclusion (about language as an instrument of social change) implausible. But it lets us see what Unger has in mind when he claims, extravagantly, to be presenting a "doctrine of human nature" that can "guide conduct as well as . . . portray reality."[19]

Some Historical Errors

Unger does not limit himself to "the liberal political doctrine" in the abstract. He also refers, more personally, to "the inventors of the liberal doctrine," "the seventeenth-century European thinkers who founded the liberal doctrine," and "the classic liberal thinkers." While he adverts to Spinoza, Locke, Montesquieu, Hume, Bentham, Kant, and John Stuart Mill, he treats them as illustrations rather than as individuals. He asserts that liberals have no sense of history, but *Knowl-*

edge and Politics itself is an ahistorical book. Instead of attempting to describe various liberal works in differing historical settings, it provides its readers with a disembodied reconstruction of liberalism as "a way of thinking." Unger sketches an ideal type that identifies "the core of the political theory of liberalism." No actual liberal ever embraced this "pure" liberal position, he admits. But the thinking of all liberals was nevertheless based upon it. He sees no reason to revise his model of liberalism, therefore, when he discovers actual liberals who contradict its premises. The standard liberal, we are told, believes that "the satisfaction of an individual's wants is his good." This broad generalization is unaffected by Unger's admission that Spinoza and Locke, for example, "also distinguish between what they think is right or proper and what they want." That liberals argue in this way simply proves that they have fallen into "incoherent eclecticism." According to the prefabricated model, the standard liberal defines freedom as the gratification of desire, not as self-realization. When Unger finds Kant and Mill advancing a "view of freedom as the development of the capacities, powers, or talents men possess",[20] he judges them incoherent in that they contradict their own beliefs (as he defines them).

Unger's stylized portrait of "the political theory of liberalism" is meant as a devastating indictment. In fact, it reads like a list of fatal inconsistencies and a sampler of obtuse thinking. (He does not ask how such a bankrupt system of ideas could have survived so long.) The first great liberal mistake was the notion that "groups are less real and fundamental that the individuals who compose them." Liberalism does not admit the existence of "collective subjects" capable of pursuing collective aims. Goals, for liberals, "are always the objectives of particular individuals," never of the social units in which they take part. Liberals affirm "the derivative and artificial character of groups." They denigrate groups in this way, Unger believes, because they aspire to bottom all human community on voluntary consent. This atomizing purpose is the central fault of their way of thinking. Liberal society is "artificial" because liberals strive to transform all social groupings into "products of the will and interests of individuals."[21]

Unger does not explain what it would mean for a group to have aims independent of the aims entertained by the individuals who compose it. Nor does he explore the concrete legal and political implications of conceiving social units in a nonliberal fashion, as "unanalyzable wholes." All we learn is that "the pure liberal" should be condemned for being a reductionist, for dissolving "all wholes into infinitesimal particulars." Is it indeed true that, for liberals, "the characteristics of a group are reducible to the characteristics of its individual members"?[22]

Instead of posing this question to the generic liberal of Unger's imagination, let us ask it of an actual liberal, such as Kant, who is known for his emphasis on individual autonomy and voluntary consent. Did Kant think that the characteristics of the group were reducible to the characteristics of its members? Quite to the contrary, Kant argued that a stable whole could be made out of unstable parts. A population of devils, given appropriate constitutional constraints, can live together harmoniously. In other words, a group can exhibit precisely those traits that are absent in its individual members.[23] This counterintuitive idea is much closer to the standard liberal view than the model proposed by Unger. Montesquieu claimed that England was a happy country even though Englishmen were personally miserable. Hume wrote that "good manners may beget order and moderation in the government where manners and customs have instilled little humanity or justice into the tempers of men."[24] And Madison suggested that "inventions of prudence," that is, constitutional machinery, can compensate for "the defect of better motives" among individual office-holders. The private vices/public virtues model itself clearly implies that the characteristics of a whole need not mirror the characteristics of its parts.[25] It is therefore highly misleading to say that, for liberals, "psychology is more basic than sociology."[26]

Yet Unger accuses liberalism of exactly this form of reductionism. He prefaces his chapter on liberal political theory with a preliminary chapter on liberal psychology. In this way he hopes to introduce readers to the fundamental building blocks of liberalism as a whole. The entire liberal edifice, it turns out, is constructed on a single fatal distinction: "the first principle of liberal psychology states that the self consists of understanding and desire, that the two are distinct from one another, and that desire is the moving, active, or primary part of the self."[27] This single sentence contains Unger's entire diagnosis of liberalism in a nutshell. It must be analyzed in detail.

From the liberal perspective, argues Unger, while "understanding" can never be anything but "a tool of desire,"[28] desire can never be a product of the understanding. Cognitive estimates of the way the world is structured have no effect on human aversions or attractions.

For example, awareness that a certain possibility has become unavailable will not make individuals want it either more or less. Unger's claim, then, is quite strong: liberal psychology is massively obtuse. Indeed, if liberals embraced such a superficial view of the human psyche, they must have been ignorant of the entire history of moral psychology from the ancient stoics to Bacon and Descartes.

Impressive counterevidence is provided by *Democracy in America* and *The Ancien Regime and the French Revolution.* Alexis de Tocqueville was a liberal theorist who devoted his intellectual career to studying precisely what Unger says liberals cannot even imagine: the way understanding shapes desire. Slaves who see no alternative to slavery eventually admire their masters and lose all ambition to cast off their chains. Commoners who begin to perceive their low status as a matter of bad luck, instead of destiny or nature, also begin to hate their local nobles with unprecedented violence. These typically Tocquevillean claims obviously contradict Unger's model. It is interesting to note that Tocqueville learned his "way of thinking" from Montesquieu, among others.

Unger announces dogmatically that "liberal thought cannot provide an account of personality."[29] Yet liberal theorists had many interesting things to say about human psychology. Unger ignores what they actually wrote for the sake of his model. *He* sacrifices concreteness to abstraction. These thinkers' ideas about the interaction between cognition and desire cannot be established simply by citing Hume's remark on reason as the slave of the passions or Hobbes's comparison of thoughts to scouts and spies in the service of appetite. Every major liberal theorist was aware of the Stoics' reflections on the manipulability of desire, on the way passion is susceptible to reshaping by the mind. Adam Smith as well as Tocqueville—both men profoundly marked by neostoicism—made the causal dependency of sentiment on understanding into a major premise of their social theories.

Unger distorts the liberal tradition in other ways. Here is another example: "men are bound together by rules and kept apart by their individual and subjective ends." This assessment is based on two assumptions. First, liberals are presumed to have been unaware that evolving national cultures exist. They thought naively that "personality is independent of history."[30] No liberal could have ever written an *Essai sur les mœurs*. Second, liberals never heard of conformism, imitativeness, xenophobia, collective passions, and other prerational sources of group cohesion. Both assumptions are erroneous.[31]

The Charge of Moral Skepticism

Unger might admit all of the foregoing and say, quite correctly, that he has little interest in what real liberals had to say about human irrationality or the cultural shaping of desire. What concerns him is the key issue of moral philosophy: how to justify desire? Liberals may recognize that understanding affects longing and disgust. They may even grasp the way desires are shaped through cultural stereotypes. Nevertheless they firmly believe that "reason is blind in the world of ends." This is the core of the matter: "liberal psychology admits that desires, as psychic events, can be causally explained. But no operation of the mind can establish what one ought to want." True, "reason can clarify the relationship among ends, but it cannot ultimately tell us which ends to hold." This is a thesis Unger shares with Strauss and MacIntyre: the ancient idea of "practical reason" was "abandoned" by liberals. Indeed, "such an idea of practical reason is unknown to liberal thought and inconsistent with its premises." Although liberals continue to invoke "reason," it is a thin and pathetic substitute for its ancient homonym: "it can inquire into the implications of a novel end," but "it cannot determine whether that end ought to be accepted or rejected." Liberals, in the final analysis, are committed to "absolute moral skepticism."[32]

This is another drastic accusation—the most drastic of all. It implies, first, that liberals furnish no "criteria with which to judge and order our ends." Liberalism "provides no standards for preferring some desires to others." Individuals have preferences in the liberal universe, of course, but these are brute givens, immune to rational evaluation. They are based on gratuitous commitment and groundless choice. For liberals "the good has no existence outside the will."[33] No distinction can be drawn, within a liberal framework, between legitimate and illegitimate desires.

As it stands, this account is unconvincing, since all liberals distinguished between, say, the desire to murder and the desire not to be murdered. Liberalism, therefore, never aimed "to benefit equally everyone's wants." The will of the individual must be strictly subordinated to those behavioral norms required for civilized coexistence and cooperation. Unger mentions this limitation, but dismisses it all too casually. The liberal affirmation of such community-enabling norms "does not truly qualify the principle that values are individual and subjective." In his view, rules against murder and assault represent nothing more that "a convergence of individual preferences." Liberal norms have base origins: "in no way, then, does the idea of sharing of values, as it appears in liberal thought, disrespect the subjectivity of values."[34]

Unger's unwillingness to concede the role of moral principles in liberal thought is especially noticeable in his treatment of Kant. Kantian liberalism, he says, "collapses into" value subjectivism. Universalism simply means that no evaluative distinctions can be drawn between different subjective goals. Kant's morality thus demands that we be "neutral toward the purposes of specific individuals." Kantian freedom, just like freedom in utilitarian thought, is simply "the liberty to do whatever one wants." Liberalism does not even furnish "noninstrumental rules to determine what counts as permissible means." True, liberals sometimes write in moral terms. But their morality is hollow, "capable of accommodating almost any pattern of conduct."[35]

Unger's argument here is so strange that it is hard to bring into focus. He sees quite clearly that at the heart of liberalism there stands an egalitarian norm: "all men are in principle formally equal as citizens and legal persons." But he interprets this norm, bafflingly, as evidence that liberals have no moral beliefs. Although liberals are egalitarians, it is not because they accept a norm of equality. Rather, it is because they are moral skeptics, because they have no criteria allowing them to prize one person's desires over another's. They therefore bow reverently, or attempt unsuccessfully to do so, before all subjective preferences, whatever these happen to be. This is an absurd and impossible way to proceed, since preferences conflict. It is thus impossible to discover "a neutral way to combine individual, subjective values." Liberalism endeavors (but fails) to satisfy equally everyone's wants. It is "destroyed" by its inability to attain the perfect neutrality its skeptical premises demand.[36]

This entire line of reasoning, which we have encountered before, is based on a misunderstanding. Liberals were not value subjectivists. Contrary to Unger, their egalitarianism was not the logical result of their moral skepticism. On the contrary, moral skepticism would have led them to accept self-exemption from general rules—something they steadfastly refused to do. The norm that all people must be treated equally under a single system of law, moreover, cannot be derived from the preferences of individuals (or rather, the derivation is impossible unless we begin by counting all individuals equally, in which case we have simply assumed the norm we want to derive).

Why does Unger, who seems well-read, distort the liberal tradition in this egregious way? One reason is that he interprets it apolitically. He makes no mention of the concrete circumstances that originally gave rise to liberal thinking: religious civil wars, ecclesiastic persecution and censorship, arbitrary taxation and confiscations, problems of political succession, cruel punishments, nightmarish criminal procedures, and so forth. Instead of seeing liberalism as a real response to real problems (within limits imposed by resources at hand), he views it doctrinally, as "a system of theoretical concepts and propositions." He regularly plucks a phrase from a liberal work, composed in response to a concrete situation, and enshrines it as a ponderous metaphysical dogma. It would have been more fruitful to ask about the political implications of theoretical principles. Unger has no trouble finding a few liberals who actually say that "desires are arbitrary from the perspective of the understanding."[37] The question still remains: what does such a statement imply? What did it mean in context? What rival claims did it aim to refute? What was it meant to deny?

True, liberals occasionally wrote as moral subjectivists. They did not write their treatises as professors of philosophy, for scholarly purposes, however; they wrote for political reasons and in pressing circumstances. First, classical liberals were acutely aware of the atrocities committed in the name of ostensibly "objective" values. Why else would they have been so passionately concerned with religious toleration? Second, they recognized that the ancient principle of a hierarchy of desire provided enormous intellectual support for political and legal inequality. Rulers who can distinguish reliably between low and high desires have a perfect excuse for coercively imposing their wishes on the ruled. The readiness of liberals to proclaim publicly that values are "subjective" suggests that this thesis was a forensically irresistible weapon in liberal campaigns against religious persecution and legal inequality. It should therefore not be regarded as the last word of liberalism on moral questions.[38]

Turning Soft

Unger writes with contempt of limited government, the state-society distinction, the rule of law, legal equality, the separation of powers, an apolitical judiciary, periodic elections, representative institutions, and monetary incentives for productive work. He labels these fundamental liberal ideas a "potpourri of platitudes."[39] Such derision confirms the impression that he wishes to reject liberalism totally, not partially. Liberalism, rotten to the core, cannot be salvaged in parts.

But while Unger flirts with such extreme claims, he also hedges. Indeed, in some passages, he simply rescinds his criticisms and embraces a position indistinguishable from the liberalism he elsewhere mercilessly skewers. This dexterous change of positions, it needs no repeating, is a classic symptom of "soft" antiliberalism. Like MacIntyre, Unger refuses to draw any shocking political conclusions from his ostensibly radical criticism of liberal society. He, too, bridles at the kind of ruthless consistency that we find, say, in Schmitt. There is a good reason for this half-heartedness. The 1970s and 1980s were not the 1920s and 1930s. Even when undiscussed, the experience of totalitarianism has had an inhibiting effect on almost all recent critics of liberalism. The years of fascism, as already suggested, led antiliberals to demilitarize their conception of an ideal nonbourgeois order. Knowledge of both Nazi and communist regimes makes it difficult for critics of liberalism to be wholly serious about rejecting government by consent, open public discussion, limits on the police, freedom to emigrate, and other judicially protected individual rights.

When his argument brings him to this point, Unger recants. After disparaging liberalism for its blindness to community values and its failure to appreciate the superiority of "the whole" over "the parts," he suddenly stops in his tracks. He is more of an individualist than a communitarian, he explains. In his view, "theories of community have traditionally suffered from a blend of utopian flavor and totalitarian insinuation."[40] Forcing individuals to conform to a particular community's idea of the good is wholly unacceptable.[41] The chief defect of antiliberal and preliberal political theory is that "it denies any significance to choice" and tends to obliterate "the individuality of persons." Marx's philosophy of history, moreover, is objectionable precisely because "it makes the individual the servant of a future ideal he is unable to realize in his own life." Unger cannot follow fanatical communitarians down such an anti-individualistic path. He therefore announces, to the bafflement of inexperienced readers, that he is not an antiliberal, but simply a nonliberal. He has always assumed, he explains, "the unacceptability of the pure antiliberal doctrine." The liberal empire, it turns out, should not be overturned. It simply needs to be rearranged and improved: "instead of the liberal doctrine upside down, we need the synthesis of liberalism with its opposite."[42] So much for "total criticism."

Unger wants to develop "an alternative to both liberal doctrine and its hypothetical antithesis."[43] As for the essential difference between antiliberalism and nonliberalism, readers who are acquainted with Schmitt and other "hard" antiliberals may be tempted to say that a nonliberal is an antiliberal who does not mean what he says. A non-liberal does not hesitate to use liberal rights while belittling liberal rights; he does not want actually to subvert individual rights, in a Leninist manner. Indeed, he plans to keep his rights in the new, totally transformed, nonliberal society-to-come. A nonliberal is an antiliberal who, after lambasting liberalism on every possible dimension, performs a startling about-face and embraces unhesitatingly all of liberalism's core institutions and ideas. A nonliberal is an antiliberal who does *not* "move beyond liberal thought."[44] In short, a nonliberal is a soft antiliberal. After having "destroyed" liberalism, he simply repeats it.

Despite his dense and abstruse pages about facts and values, wholes and parts, Unger is ultimately satisfied with reiterating Montesquieu's protest against "personal dependence and personal domination." Even "individual freedom," it turns out, must be treated with "reverence." A good society is one in which "certain all but unconditional defenses of the individual against the imposition of the group are respected." The freedoms he has in mind, liberals will be comforted to learn, include "freedom of expression," "freedom of choosing the character of one's work," "freedom of joining and leaving groups," and "freedoms as entitlements to disregard group decisions and shared values." Even the vicious distinction between values and rules, on which Unger lavishes so much disdain, turns out to be worth preserving after all. Lack of it "destroys any support for the belief that individuality ought to be protected." To guard the private sphere, in fact, Unger affirms "the limits to politics." He wants to arrange institutions "to avert the danger to individuality inherent in any tendency to make all life subject to public discourse and political choice." The "effacement" of the liberal distinction between public and private "would corrupt the group." As a result, "there are certain fixed outer limits to the entitlement of the group or of a democratic majority within it to impose measures that embody its shared ends on individuals who dissent from those measures."[45] This parenthetical capitulation to liberal principles would be easier to understand if it did not leave Unger's original excoriation of liberalism untouched. He totally rejects liberalism, but he also accepts it. This to-and-fro is the essential characteristic of "soft" antiliberalism. It would be breathtaking if it had not been encountered so often before.

Unger's self-transformation into John Stuart Mill does not stop here. He tells us that "it is only through communication in society that individuality can be developed and revealed." A community of shared values, he also explains, is not a good in itself. It is good only if these shared values are developed in a certain way. Social consensus is a bad thing unless it is achieved "in democratic circumstances," in conditions where individuals retain their autonomy and through "a process of reciprocal persuasion and collective decision in which one view triumphs by winning more adherents than its rivals." The common purposes that knit such a community together, remember, are valuable only to the extent that they are cosmopolitan or tending to become so. The shared values Unger admires are never the exclusive aims of an exclusive group, as they are for MacIntyre and other communitarians, but always the inclusive aims of all mankind.[46]

One of the central defects of liberal society, Unger explains, is the alienation of the self from others. Because individuals occupy many different social roles (at home, in the workplace, and so forth), they are always viewed from a partial angle. They are never perceived and appreciated as "entire persons," as "unitary and complete." In the course of the argument, however, Unger seems to quiet his anxieties about such fragmentation and alienation and appears more concerned about the opposite. The main problem is a liberal one: to protect the individual's right "to be hidden" from intrusive neighbors and officials. As a result, he openly defends "plural membership," explaining that "the individual ought to be entitled to be a member of various groups."[47] A reader may be forgiven for reflecting here that such an arrangement might require something less that a "total transformation" of liberal society.

After his wholesale surrender to liberalism, Unger nevertheless per-

sists in calling himself a nonliberal. What is the point of this nonconformist pose? He tries lamely to retain his communitarian and therefore antiliberal affiliations by distinguishing between communities and
communities. He dislikes all hierarchical communities of the past but
shows more sympathy for "nonhierarchical communities of shared
ends" that might be developed in the future.[48] He sometimes writes
that hierarchical and egalitarian forms of community are equally inadequate. He claims to be looking for a third way, to be searching for
a nonliberal community in which individuality is nevertheless fully
protected and encouraged. But he cannot finally bring himself to
subject "the utopian socialist or anarchist conception of egalitarian
community" to truly harsh criticisms. His basic objection to the beautiful ideal of nonhierarchical community is that, until now, it has
remained hopelessly vague. Moreover, "the utopian commune provides
an alternative image to the dominant social order and thus an inspiration to change it. But at the same time, by failing to subvert and
destroy that order, it must in the end be subverted or destroyed by
it."[49] This sounds like a plea for radical egalitarians and communalists
to become serious. Do not be satisfied with establishing small communities in which you can realize some of your ideals, Unger appears to
be saying. You must remake the entire social order along egalitarian-
communitarian lines.

A few pages later, not surprisingly, Unger reveals that a call to direct
action was not exactly what he intended. He is a soft insurrectionist,
we might say. Egalitarian community is not meant to be realized. It is
only "a regulative ideal." Attempts to bring it about are ultimately
"vain." Indeed, he distinguishes himself from Marx on precisely these
grounds. Marxists are committed to "the mistaken belief that the ideal
can be realized in history," while Unger (with near-Straussian moderation) recognizes "the impossibility of a full realization of the ideal."
Neither the ideal of the many-sided self nor the ideal of universal
community can be realized "on this earth."[50] Not even an Ungerian
politics of vision and enthusiasm can "wipe away the failings of life."[51]
Modern states, in any case, are too large to allow for face-to-face
interaction among all members.[52] Without such interaction, however,
true mutual understanding is impossible. Territorial expanse and population density alone prove the ultimate unrealism of all communitarian
projects for social transformation.

Unger's self-understanding is strangely diffuse. He thinks of himself

as an anti-utopian militant—a self-contradictory posture that is hard
to fathom. He denies that he is a fatalist, of course. While he suggests
that liberal societies might introduce greater elements of democracy
and equality, it is unclear why such a suggestion should count as
"nonliberal." A criticism of liberal society on the basis of liberal ideas
is by no means radical. Disputes about the degree of democracy and
equality to be fostered in liberal society are the mainstay of political
debate within the liberal tradition. They have nothing to do with a
metaphysical attack on the entire liberal *Weltanschauung* such as that
mounted, however inconsistently, in *Knowledge and Politics.*

Superliberalism

Unger's first attack on liberalism, however unsatisfying intellectually,
is immensely revealing. Its very inconsistency helps clarify an important split within antiliberal ranks. Detractors of liberal society see its
basic shortcomings from two viewpoints. Liberal society can be
blamed, on the one hand, for destroying warm and harmonious community life, for leaving the individual unmoored, for loosening the grip
of group traditions, goals, norms. (This is MacIntyre's complaint,
which Unger once shared.) On the other hand, liberalism can be
indicted for restricting the individual too much, for imposing too many
rules and too many restraints, for placing too many inhibitions on the
creativity and expressiveness of the self. (Unger also advanced this
charge.) These two approaches are logically inconsistent. Having
scoured the landscape and carefully assembled all possible criticisms of
liberal thought, the young Unger could not bear to omit any of them
from his comprehensive attack. He thus decided to weave together
conservative communitarianism and countercultural radicalism in a
single book. This was an audacious, but inherently unstable, choice. It
is no surprise, then, that Unger finally came to abandon his youthful
eclecticism. In his more recent works he has finally opted for one form
of antiliberalism over the other. This strategic repositioning occurs
most voluminously in *Politics, a Work in Constructive Social Theory.*

In this massive treatise Unger jettisons his traditional Catholic form
of antiliberalism. Almost all nostalgia for community, authority, and
religion have disappeared. He focuses instead on the sins liberal society
has committed against the spontaneity of soul. Instead of criticizing
liberal society for its excessive individualism from the communitarian

viewpoint, he criticizes it for not being individualistic enough. To describe his new position he coins the term "superliberalism." The neologism is informative. It expresses his desire to carry liberal individualism to Dionysian extremes. To grasp the peculiarity of this unbuttoned antiliberalism, we must look at *Politics* in some detail.

Replete with historical learning and practical suggestions, the entire book imparts a simple message: the professor of law now hopes to "loosen constraints." The countercultural radical has now left the communitarian conservative behind. To that extent, his position has been simplified. Promulgating a "gospel of plasticity," he advocates flexibility over rigidity, experiment over routine, disobedience over compliance, inventiveness over habit, improvisation over scripts, and the personal over the impersonal. Declaring "war against the tyranny of roles," he exalts the "jumbling" or "permanent confusion" of social and sexual roles. In typical sixties fashion, he finds nothing more abhorrent than the status quo. If we follow his advice, we will combine gaiety and defiance, making everything up as we go along. We will "disrespect and even destabilize custom and privilege," refuse to play by the rules, explode stale conventions, tear down hierarchies, and decline work that discourages the expression of personal uniqueness. To usher in "a transfigured human reality," we must undertake a mischievous activity called "context smashing"—the sabotaging of *all* stable expectations. Our ultimate goal should be a "complete remaking of society."[53]

To carry out "the radical project" we must slip our own chains and "cleanse social life of its taint of enslavement." In depicting his wished-for assault upon "all settled ties and preconceptions," Unger employs a variety of synonyms for "smash," including shatter, break, crack, dismember, pull apart, and trash. He also presses gentler words into service: dissolve, transform, disentrench, remake, revise, shake up, destabilize, wear down, resist, disturb, and even transcend. But his exhortation is always the same. It is to "raise a storm," accepting mankind's "vocation for indiscipline" and "turning subversion into a practical way of life."[54]

This paean to naughtiness is the flip side of Unger's disdain for the establishment and his desire to shock conventional minds. Casting himself as the spokesman for "our unfulfilled longings," he excogitates a social order in which everyday life will become "a condition of experimental freedom," where everything is "up for grabs" and subject to "perpetual innovation."[55] For those who dread, above all else, slipping into a rut, this book provides inspiration and support.

The "repeated liquefaction of entrenched structure" will rinse away the difference between routine and revolution: everyday behavior will radically convulse all basic institutions, habits, and assumptions.[56] Such volatility will enable us to realize both political and personal objectives. For one thing, privileged groups and inherited ethnic divisions will vanish. Politically, Unger's "redeemed society" will assume the form of "a mobilizational democracy committed to open up every feature of the social order to collective challenge and revision and to liquefy all rigid roles and hierarchies."[57] His image of personal fulfillment is equally sloshy and somewhat dreamier, involving not merely the abolition of envy and frustration, but also "the ability to entertain fantasies about possible forms of self-expression or association and to live them out."[58]

Christopher Lasch is sickened by liberal restlessness, by liberal impatience with any and every constraint, by liberal nonchalance about the human need for security. Permissiveness and ceaseless experimentation with forms of life, he claims, are signs of moral decay. The main problem with liberals is that they cannot see a wall without trying to scale it. They cannot see a limit without aching to step beyond it. In *Knowledge and Politics*, Unger had expressed similar views. He condemned liberalism there for promoting perpetual fidgetiness and irreverence toward inherited traditions. But this aspect of his antiliberalism has been dropped. He has now come to admire Prometheus. Far from being too restless, conventional liberal societies are not restless enough. Liberal citizens bump up against limits without trying to leap beyond them. Their craven refusal to overturn all obstacles shows how weak, characterless, and morally despicable they are.

This Promethean turn helps explain why Unger identifies himself as a "superliberal." It is possible "to redeem liberalism through more liberalism," he now believes.[59] The kind of liberalism he hopes to intensify is nicely represented by Locke's statement: "an Argument from what has been, to what should of right be, has no great force."[60] Liberal society can be rescued, Unger thinks, by raising impatience with tradition and insubordination toward authority to an unprecedented pitch of intensity. Liberal reformism should become superliberal super-reformism. The expansion of trade and industry, not to mention the spread of literacy and education, destroyed the self-sufficiency and internal hierarchies of traditional village communities. Government by consent undermined custom-bound styles of existence and unquestioning deference to inherited authority. Conservative-minded antiliberals are distressed by these developments. Not the new Unger; he wants to generalize these dismantling tendencies and apply them uninterruptedly to *all* social structures, especially liberal ones. (Whether liberals will appreciate this hyperbolization of their position remains to be seen.)

In settled liberal societies, human beings are almost "passive automatons" of their cultural contexts and "faceless representatives of predetermined roles." The operative word is almost; individuals, thank heaven, can never be definitively robotized. Personality is always brimming with endless possibilities aching to be realized: "we are an infinite caught within the finite." Our limitedness is due largely to our inadequate social arrangements, which willful spirits can trash. In other words, Unger views society consistently from "the perspective of the will," and thus elevates cabin fever into a way of life. He is interested in revolutionizing the polity and the economy principally as a means for "freeing subjective experience," satisfying the individual's "longing for self-assertion,"[61] and releasing "the implicit boundlessness of personal subjectivity." Liberalism helped individuals define their interests apart from the hierarchical order in which they were born. Superliberalism drives liberal individualism to a heroic extreme. (We are now at the opposite pole, in other words, from the pious self-erasure advocated by antiliberals in the Heideggerian mold.)

Primarily devoted to uninhibited self-assertion, the new Unger also hopes for a "drastic reform" of intimate relations. Although he usually maintains his distance from advanced Western societies such as the United States, he admires our "radical experimentation with personal relations." Intimacy in America remains "tainted," however. To achieve "a heightened condition of plasticity" in personal relationships, we must "make ourselves more fully available to each other"—available as "originals," not as off-the-shelf replicas of social stereotypes. The new intimacy will involve "radical mutual acceptance" and "a heightened mutual vulnerability."[62] Groups as well as couples will be affected.

While flirting with communitarianism, the Unger of *Knowledge and Politics* was already opposed to "the subordination of the individual element in personality to the social one." He even identified communitarianism, where "men occupy fixed social places," with romantic conservatism and with Bonald.[63] A romantic, expressivist, anarchical, or hyperindividualistic strand already distinguished him clearly from MacIntyre and all other antiliberals who long for "roots." This is even more true of *Politics*.

In this later work Unger still writes approvingly about the "cleansing" effects of solidarity. He laments that private law continues "to represent society as a world of strangers." Empowered democracy will foster "a regenerate life in common," that is, a purified form of solidarity that "draws our communal relations closer to love."[64] Purged of any trace of inherited group identity, however, such erotic belonging must never compromise the radical independence of the individual. Group membership is nice, but not essential. If context-smashing requires disloyalty, so be it.

Maistre accused the Enlightenment of destroying healthy illusions. The most important of these noble lies is that society *must* be the way it is. Unger now stands Maistre on his head. Far from praising "false necessity," he condemns it voluminously. While stultifying contexts thwart our potentials, social scientists and historians pile insult upon injury, promoting the "sanctification of existing society," insisting upon the fiction that things have to be the way they are. Under the influence of the Enlightenment, students of society assume that "to explain past or present situations" they must show that "these situations were or are necessary." *Politics* exposes the error of their ways. Diagnosing the present as a necessary stage in a "compulsive sequence," Marx (another child of the Enlightenment) commits the same unpardonable crime against human freedom. Indeed, "the hallucinatory identification of the actual with the possible" is a collective self-delusion of the human race.[65] Here is the theme captured by the title of Unger's middle and pivotal volume: "we talk and act as if the established institutions were natural, necessary, and even holy."

An optimistically interpreted Freud serves Unger as a model in his effort to demolish the "idolatry of the actual" in order to illuminate the darkness and dispel our collective illusions. The theorist-therapist will "demystify society" and thereby set us free. Unger's liberating message is that "everything is politics." (The slogan was revived and made famous by the Critical Legal Studies movement.) He wants us to understand that things can be other than they are. Born again through this revelation, we will cease being the "puppets" and begin to be the "architects" of our milieus.[66]

If "no one context can be our permanent home," it might be reasonable to infer that *Politics* advocates context-hopping as a technique for realizing the multiple facets of our rich personalities. By skillfully plying the airways, for example, one and the same person can be a scholar in Cambridge, Massachusetts, and a political activist in Rio de Janeiro. But double lives are not at all what Unger has in mind. He is much less interested in a series of distinct human potentials realizable in different locales than in a single mighty potential: our astonishing ability to smash contexts. We cannot fulfill our "transformative vocation" by leaving one framework and joining another, but only by shattering and reshaping the framework we are in. Only context-smashing qualifies as real action, adequate to mankind's "longing for greatness."[67]

Once again, Unger's thinking seems more esthetic than political. Without irony, he describes "the transparent, created social world" he yearns to establish as "this joy, this dazzling game, this work of art." He compares a revolutionary's acquiring power while others die on the streets to a poet's trying to pitch upon an elusive word. Among Unger's estheticizing claims none is more eye-catching than the following: in a mercurial and redeemed social order, the "ordinary person" will become "more like the poet, whose visionary heightening of expressed emotion may border on unintelligibility and aphasia." Unger intends this as a positive recommendation, suggesting that he may have already achieved that coveted "freedom from the fear of the ridiculous" characteristic of truly "empowered" individuals.[68]

From Theory to Practice

That these volumes are "visionary" should be clear. Yet Unger also has practical and theoretical ambitions. To people itching for change he wants to offer not merely moral encouragement, but also "a guide to transformative practice" (which we are meant to read, not smash or tear up).[69]

His constitutional proposals, to select one example, reflect his profound distaste for the "banal system of checks and balances" that paralyzes government and precludes bold reform. Our "demobilizing constitutionalism," he laments, makes it "hard for a victorious party to seize the state or, having seized it, to execute its program rapidly and decisively." To escape this frustrating predicament, he proposes a "constitutionalism of permanent mobilization," which will keep society bubbling and somehow guarantee that majoritarianism is consistent with the greatest possible freedom to experiment.[70]

The most striking feature of this constitution is a new branch of government devoted to destabilizing every aspect of social life. Unger does not explain how such a branch could be effective if it were democratically accountable, or how it would be tolerable if it were not. He does say that all citizens will receive an ironclad guarantee of welfare support, untouchable by officials or majorities, almost suggesting (for an instant) that rigidity can be a virtue rather than a vice.

Unger finds markets acceptable only so long as they are power-free, that is, do not permit some people to use their economic resources to influence others unduly. The extent to which he has now succumbed to "the mistaken belief that the ideal can be realized in history" is unclear. In any case, his complex economic proposals include the abolition of inherited capital assets, public control over basic investment decisions, and continuous interventions by a confiscatory state to break up concentrations of wealth. A two-tiered system of lending banks will distribute public funds to teams of entrepreneurs, technicians, and workers. Each team will try to make a profit; but an ever-alert government will reclaim accumulated wealth whenever it swells beyond a certain point. Taking a decentralized form reminiscent of petty commodity production, Unger's ideal economy will also be incredibly innovative and dynamic.

Along with this "guide" to reform, Unger offers "a new understanding of society." The subjects he surveys in *Politics* are surprisingly diverse: marsupials, the crisis of feudalism, tank warfare, the funded public debt, stratography, the analytic-synthetic distinction, nomadic civilizations, Sung dynasty China, the failings of neoclassical economics, Yugoslavia's self-management system (still admired in 1987), Euclidean geometry, the origins of the cosmos, and much, much more. Unsoiled by false modesty, he begins numerous chapters with authoritative remarks about "much of history," "the vast majority of historical situations," "most societies of the past," "all the forms of social life that have existed in history," and "the experience of mankind." From every topic and period Unger pretends to draw encouragement for his radical program. (His lounge-about familiarity with esoteric knowledge is nicely conveyed by the word "remember" in the following sentence, referring to nothing previously discussed in the text: "Remember the

Byzantine military farms—*ktemata stratiotika*, the Ottoman timariots, the Mughal *zamindars* and the Aztec military life-tenants."[71])

Left and Right

As the bibliographies appended to each volume of *Politics* demonstrate, Unger has drawn heavily on conventional historical and sociological research. But the entire work, especially *Social Theory*, reveals a surprisingly unforgiving attitude toward fellow academics. He describes them variously as cowardly, naive, deluded, flaccid, asleep, confused, superstitious, and one-dimensional. They are collaborators, apologists, and traitors to freedom. They are certainly not fire-eaters, as he undoubtedly is. He even calls them sterile and impotent, perhaps to underline his own "fecundity," which is mentioned more than once.[72] Indeed, Unger's portrait of his colleagues diverges in almost every respect from his picture of himself.

It would nevertheless be a mistake to assume that such a polemical work, full of contempt for others, exhibits no intellectual balance. Unger is scrupulously fair-minded about capitalism and communism, arguing that the Soviet Union, at the time, was no freer than the United States. He observes that "both the American and the Russian patterns lie in a twilight zone between craziness and lack of imagination." In any case, it is just as possible to reach "the true republic" by transforming America as by transforming Russia. He obviously feels a greater sympathy for the Third World than for either of the superpowers, however. Unfettered by enduring constitutions, Third World countries display an exemplary instability. Their citizens are especially lucky that rules for attaining political power remain ill-defined. Brazil, in particular, seems full of promise—though Unger's patriotism does not make him wholly uncritical. He is merciless, for example, on the subject of the "pathetic mimicry of foreign ideas" he encounters among Brazil's intellectual elite.[73]

But the edge of his razor is reserved for the United States. What he finds most repellent about America is the trivial nature of our "normal politics" (a phrase meant to echo Thomas Kuhn's "normal science"). Our best politicians seek only worthless changes. We are fixated on necessary but essentially moderate goals such as housing, food, and health care. We may hope to redistribute wealth, to protect minority rights, or to encourage more participation in politics; but we never dream the impossible dream, never attempt a radical transformation of the social order. Indeed, those who strive to improve the welfare state are "tinkerers."[74] Their efforts will only enable the despicable system to survive.

Unger's attitude toward Marxism is more complex. He announces that *Politics* is a "leftist" book (thereby suggesting that the hyperconventional left/right scheme should be accepted uncritically rather than smashed).[75] Like Marx, he admires the antitraditionalist, dynamic, and innovative powers of capitalism. He too suggests that civil society, the everyday world in which we live and work, should realize the universalistic and egalitarian ideals foreshadowed in liberal politics. With Marx, Unger foresees the end of prehistory, the establishment of an unprecedented social world in which human beings become "masters" of their destiny, but he refuses to guarantee that it will arrive.

Marx's gravest blunder is described here somewhat differently than it was in *Knowledge and Politics*. Marx failed because he attributed the coming of communism to iron necessity, thereby turning heroic revolutionaries into the marionettes of history. More devoted to human spontaneity than to inexorable progress, Unger refuses to predict the future. He is so certain of Marx's error on this question that he returns dozens of times, one might almost say compulsively, to lengthy denunciations of "compulsive sequence." Indeed, the mileage he gets out of this obvious and conventional form of anti-Marxism is nothing short of stupefying. A more repetitive attack on repetitiveness is difficult to imagine.

A Few Puzzles

Politics contains obscurities, contradictions, and unanswered questions. A few of the more obvious conundrums and problems follow.

Unger bafflingly identifies breaking a rule with changing a rule, as if disobedience were the same as reform. He advocates "cumulative" change while declaring that everything inherited must be smashed. He expounds on the ways flexibility can enhance survival, intimating inconsistently that endurance is an important value. He alternately admires and deplores capitalism's ruthless approach to failed economic experiments. He despises a society of "placeholders," but hopes to understand himself "as a being with a place." He deprecates inherited group identity, while praising involuntary obligations, including "shared nationhood." He declaims against inflexible arrangements, while inexplicably applauding the "lasting personal commitments" of marriage. He associates "empowerment" with extreme voluntariness and yet remarks, as if it were a bonus, that "experiences of empowerment have an addictive force." Under the umbrella term "naturalistic social theory" he blurs together two quite dissimilar attitudes: the belief that moral ideals are immutable and the belief that actual institutions are immutable. He assumes throughout that context-smashing is inherently leftist, involving a successful demolition of elites, while admitting parenthetically that context-smashing can easily create unprecedented hierarchies of privilege and power. He asserts numerous times that if current arrangements did not have to become the way they are, then they do not have to be the way they are—as if irreversible processes could not be initiated by chance. Monotonously announcing the boldness of his insight into false necessity, he admits in passing that social theorists have always recognized it.[76]

The cascade of contradictions does not cease. While pouring contempt on social theory's traditional appeal to nature, Unger offers "the mutability of human nature" as a moral standard: we must construct a society that embodies and respects man's inborn destructive-creative powers. While spurning social transformation pursued in the name of static ideals, he upholds the "unbiased" decision-procedure as an unchanging goal of reform. He proposes a constitutional scheme for successor generations while striving "to weaken the tyranny of the present over the future."[77] He endorses W. V. Quine's criticism of the analytic-synthetic distinction, while uncritically accepting the closely related form-content distinction. His paradoxical, and therefore interesting idea that "conflict" is a creative force is rendered tautological by his casual admission that "good" conflict must be free of animosity, violence, and a hardening of battle fronts. He makes changing the rules in the middle of the game sound agreeable by neglecting to ask what happens when each player changes the rules in a different manner. He never explains how fellow "transformers" will communicate with each other once they have destroyed the background assumptions that render mutual comprehension, including disagreement, possible. The main reason Unger rejects the status quo is that it does not permit human beings to be all that they could be, but the very same complaint can be leveled at any particular transformative effort: we could always transform the world in *other* ways.

Unger's penchant for idea-jumbling is also illustrated by his attitude toward power. He manages to identify simultaneously with the winners and the losers, crying for the weak and laughing with the strong—an achievement not even Nietzsche could match. On the one hand, he reviles powerful elites who, throughout history, have successfully obstructed change and exploited their feebler companions. On the other hand, especially in the third volume, he indulges in a veritable cult of worldly success, arguing that power is a prize awarded to those most willing to smash their inherited contexts.

Aware of this mind-wrenching disorder, Unger pre-emptively denigrates the value of internal coherence, claiming that "insight can outreach consistency." This is a respectable position, I suppose, but it certainly proves grueling for the reader. The claim that we "can always discover more to be true than we can prove, verify, or even make sense of" implies that discomfort with unintelligible ideas is a sign of intellectual servility. But the difficulties presented by *Politics* cannot all be fairly laid on the poor reader's head. While criticizing innumerable social theorists, for example, Unger almost never names names. (Who actually says that the basic social institutions must remain the way they are?) This omission makes it difficult to gain "critical distance," that is, to exercise one's own small portion of "negative capability" on Unger's speculations.[78]

While trumpeting the extremism of his position, and even claiming that it will fundamentally change our intellectual situation, Unger also retains his disconcerting tendency to lard a text with offhand concessions to common sense. Sober remarks are dropped in passing without being integrated into the basic argument, which would be pointless if it were not shocking. He occasionally straightens his tie, for example, and poses as a sober older brother, offering sage counsel to younger, less seasoned leftists. Anarchistic or infantile "modernists," he bodefully observes, hope to smash one context after another, refuse to "settle down," and forever act "as if everything were up for grabs." He supplements this amicable dissent, confusingly, with outright sympathy for their point of view.[79] The distinction between his own position and the one ascribed to his unkempt brethren is often too subtle to discern. The only serious problem with infantile context-smashers, in truth, is their failure to recognize that we can invent less imprisoning social contexts, that is, institutions that cry out to be smashed and thus allow us to settle down without settling down. The cogency of this idea, distinguishing Unger from the immature anarchist, is less than perfectly clear.

Why would Unger exaggerate his differences with adolescent rebels? Perhaps he is thinking of public relations. His sympathy with the remote, his celebration of infinite possibilities, and his commitment only to social arrangements that have never had a chance to disappoint him—these are all unmistakable symptoms of romanticism, an outlook that, in an age that knows about the consequences of romanticism in politics, begs for a smoke screen. Occasional asides of avuncular chastisement, addressed to the lunatic fringe, may well serve as precisely this sort of distraction or decoy.

A Reply to Superliberalism

The riot of inconsistency and the overdose of rhetoric aside, Unger's positions seems vulnerable to eight basic objections.

First, context-smashing is not an attractive basis for a moral doctrine.[80] The rumpus-room behavior Unger admires can be good or bad, obviously enough, depending on the context being smashed and the replacements available. Playing fast and loose with the rules can spell corruption as well as flexibility. (His suggestion that one context can be superior to another only by being easier to change is equally implausible.)

Second, culture cannot be adequately conceived as an iron lid slammed shut on an otherwise infinite personality. We would not be freer without it—whatever "superliberals" might imagine. The possibilities we value are, in part, creatures of cultural, legal, political, and economic systems. Such possibilities are kept open and available to individuals by institutional means. They cannot be generated spontaneously by the prodigality of the individual soul.

Third, if all stable expectations were smashed, both surprise and nonconformity would become impossible. You can shatter the brittle, but not the fluid. A progressive "liquefaction" of society might have the unintended effect of diminishing opportunities for the exercise of context-smashing powers. Unger concedes as much, though again inconsistently, when he describes modern Western societies as both easier and harder to change than more rigid societies of the past.

Fourth, for young children, the mentally unstable, the homeless, involuntary exiles, and other vulnerable individuals, context-smashing would be harmful, or redundant. The anxieties of rootlessness are real; elementary psychiatry suggests that it is not easy to maintain one's sanity in a condition of total flux. Continuous crisis and convulsion is hard to tolerate. Unger parenthetically concedes that human beings need security, and that nightmarish instability and traumatic dislocation may deprive some people of some options. He also half-accepts the human desire to survive. But Unger—in dramatic contrast to Lasch—displays no mercy at all for the timid wish to maintain one's "way of life." Workers reluctant to retool are viewed with as much contempt as members of ethnic groups who stubbornly cling to an inherited identity. (The fierceness with which he attacks the institution of "job tenure" may tempt some readers to suggest a simple way for the professor to align his practice with his theory.[81])

Fifth, Unger was not the first to notice that "we often mistake for nature what we find established by long and inveterate custom."[82] When a political ruler announces that ordinary citizens *must* go to war or submit to a tax increase, they can be forgiven for expressing their doubts. To that extent *Politics* has a genuinely important, though not earthshaking, lesson to convey. By focusing on advantages reaped by elites, however, Unger makes his account of pseudo-inevitability much less interesting than it might otherwise be. After all, "I cannot help it" is a fairly ubiquitous technique for enhancing individual freedom, as useful to subordinates as to superiors. It is not easy to imagine a human society in which such an excuse would never be deployed.

False necessity may also result from a psychological drive to minimize guilt and frustration. To soothe a bad conscience or to reconcile ourselves to straitened circumstances (that is, to reduce dissonance), we may tend to underestimate the alternatives actually available to us. Alternatively, we may turn a blind eye to various real possibilities because a surfeit of options is psychologically disorienting, impairing our ability to make rational comparisons and choices. Such "self-deception" is independent of plots by the powerful to dominate the weak.

(These are obvious considerations, worth mentioning only because they surface nowhere in Unger's far-from-economical discussion, or rather scolding, of false necessity. We might also ask whether human beings can ever know precisely what can and cannot be done, neither over- nor underestimating the range of alternatives accessible to them. Unger, incidentally, neglects the harmful effects of overly optimistic assessments. He is certainly less worried about trying the impossible than about failing to try the possible. Never mind that scarce resources and even lives can be shamefully wasted when the unfeasible is considered feasible.)

Sixth, sensible and effective reform requires the reformer to gain a foothold in the actual institutions, beliefs, and ongoing social movements that Unger dismissively lumps together as "the given." The civil rights movement invoked constitutional guarantees that had already been secured for the white majority. The women's movement echoes the civil rights movement, trying to build upon the past instead of smashing it. Unger admits, inconsistently, that human beings cannot doubt, distrust, or attack everything at once, but his fundamental claim is that context-smashing is *not* context-dependent. The determined subversive does not defy one part of his context on the basis of another part, but rather defies his entire context (even if not all at once) on the basis of his infinite personality, never appealing to past successes—at most, to past defeats. Surely, such severance of social reformers from the given social world is debilitating rather than invigorating. It even leads Unger to assert, in a Schmittian phrase, that the moral attitude of reformers must be based on "groundless choice." Such "a gratuitous act of commitment" may be compatible with superindividualistic self-assertion, but it does not provide a very promising basis for the society-wide cooperation required for effective reform.[83]

Seventh, the all-important concept of a "framework" presents serious problems. What does it mean to say that a framework "immunizes itself" against change?[84] Does Unger want to suggest that an institutional and cultural context is a conscious agent able to perceive and defend its own interests? His examples themselves raise more questions than they answer. Here is one. Conventional social scientists cannot understand the relation between savings and investment, apparently because they are blind to the formative framework, that is, because they ignore other factors such as confidence in the consistency of government and the form and level of unemployment insurance. There is a core of healthy common sense in this analysis. Nonetheless, why affix a pretentious label such as "the framework" to wrongly neglected "other factors"? Are public trust and unemployment insurance part of the framework because they cannot themselves be influenced by other activities occurring "within" the framework? Do they shape without being shaped in turn? Or are they shaped solely by contextless fighting among context-free context-smashers?

Finally, a stable expectation is not the worst thing one human being can inflict on another. The rigid is not the root of all evil; it can be possibility-creating. That "rigid roles" are far from valueless is obvious to anyone who considers, say, the duties of a lifeguard. Unger may not approve of "rigid divisions" between science and religion and between religion and politics, but reasonable arguments can be adduced in their defense. Inherited hierarchies are useless, but a "rigid" chain of command can be convenient during emergencies, when democratic consultation may hamper prompt action (not to mention its usefulness for the retrospective apportionment of blame). Even "rigid routines," which Unger assails with untrammeled fury, can be liberating, allowing us to focus on what really matters. Most important of all, grammar illustrates the way rigidities create flexibilities. (His interest in zoology apparently never led Unger to contemplate the advantages enjoyed by vertebrates over jellyfish.) *Politics* spurns "disempowering constraints."[85] As many philosophers have pointed out, however, the "rigid rules" of a game or language are enabling rather than disabling. This, at least, is what Locke meant when he argued that "the end of law is not to abolish or restrain but to preserve and enlarge freedom."[86] The same is true of liberal constitutions.

A Nietzschean Strain

Plasticity into Power is largely concerned with the dynamics of state-building. Like Hegel and others, Unger argues that European states became more powerful as their citizens became more free. A mutual reinforcement of individualism and centralized sovereignty occurred in two ways: through the weakening of oppressive local magnates and through the flourishing of a free, monetized economy from which a government could extract funds without exhausting its tax base. His more original thesis, however, involves the uniqueness of the West. Why did European societies "take off" economically, rather than relapse into a miserable "natural economy" as did all great agrarian-bureaucratic empires of the past?

On the basis of a personal survey, Unger has gleaned the following lesson from world history: to prevent economic stagnation, the central government must ally itself with "the vast masses of the population" against predatory elites.[87] That is what happened in Europe. The moral lesson is: if you are good (and join forces with the people), you will succeed. (Here the residual Marxism of *Politics* comes most sharply into focus.) Rephrased for Third World audiences, the lesson reads: national prosperity and power do not require predatory elites or big estates.

The word "militant" is often used by the far left as a euphemism for "militaristic," helping to conceal the bloody-mindedness and addiction to martial virtues characteristic of would-be revolutionaries. As if to confirm our worst suspicions, one-half of *Plasticity into Power* is devoted to a near-rhapsodic chronicle of the strictly military advantages of social plasticity. At one point Unger threatens, in a phrase worthy of a bumper sticker, "plasticity or death." About tradition-bound peoples that fail to adapt, he writes: "their defeat pleases as much as it instructs." He describes Abel Gance's Napoleon as "the great hero, the man of will, embodying to the highest degree the rage of transcendence and the transformative vocation." And he looks forward expectantly to the time when the deviant will become "dominant" and "triumphant."[88]

By recommending a "transvaluation of hierarchies of values" and apotheosizing "the transforming will," he also invokes Napoleon's admirer, Nietzsche. MacIntyre's description of the Nietzschean ideal as "a breaking up of fixed patterns, so that something radically new will emerge" can easily describe Unger's ideal, too. Disclosing the voluntaristic core of his superliberalism, he even remarks that the wearisome reform cycles afflicting capitalism and communist societies alike "insult the primacy of the will." He makes his most interesting Nietzschean gesture, however, during a discussion of the "mobile and warlike peoples" that are able to revitalize faltering agrarian civilizations by conquest. The way he describes this injection of new vitality is quite telling: "the rule of the nomads over the agrarian peoples was sometimes only a predatory extension of dominion over animal flocks to the mastery of human subjects."[89] Unger's superliberalism, it seems, has the same relation to liberalism as Nietzsche's superman has to ordinary men and women.

The mastery that Unger usually endorses, of course, is exercised over social contexts, not over fellow human beings. But his image of "individual and collective self-assertion," superficially peaceful, is deeply colored by his appreciation of conquest. His affectionate reference to "epic grandeur" makes this clear, as does his desire to satisfy "our hidden and insulted longing for greatness." Ultimately, or so the extraordinary concluding sentence of *False Necessity* suggests, he hopes to mingle the excitement of battle with the honey of self-love: "what more could we ask of society than a better chance to be both great and sweet?"[90]

That Unger could resort to such language is deeply disturbing. That he could take the storming will as his starting point, express anger at history, estheticize political violence, declare sobriety a vice, denigrate peace, shower derision on the humdrum and hypocritical bourgeois world, and hope for a dramatic uncorking of stifled human possibilities—all without clearly distinguishing his own position from that of political romantics, not to mention fascists—is simply beyond comprehension.

Up for Grabs

Unger's confusing attitude toward power (why would the historical triumph of predatory elites fail to provide evidence of *their* superior flexibility?) is obscured even further by his book's conclusion, where the resolute transformer predictably retracts much of what he has previously said. Plasticity, it turns out, is not good in itself; it is only capable of producing good results when "harnessed" to a "higher social ideal."[91] Extreme oppression, as well as extreme freedom, may result from the program advocated here. To shatter entrenched structures may be good or bad, depending on what happens next. After jeering at his colleagues for offering so little, Unger serves up the limp claim that radical efforts to improve society do not have to fail. (Superliberalism may seem naughtier than soft communitarianism, in other words, but it is just as harmless.)

Unger initially rebukes "naive historiography" for failing to notice major discontinuities in the course of social evolution. By the end of *Politics*, however, this reproach appears to be a classic case of shooting the messenger. What irks him about historians is not their obliviousness to frameworks, but their failure to provide social activists with grounds for hope. Historians aside, history itself is "narcoleptic." Despite his eagerness to extrapolate moral lessons from a reconstruction of the past, he complains mournfully of "the tedious, degrading rhythm of history."[92] By reporting the past more or less accurately, conventional historians intimate that mankind will probably never achieve a complete mastery over events. They focus on unintended consequences, always an embarrassment to reformers, and they draw attention to the chronological narcissism of revolutionaries who wildly overestimate the degree to which they have broken with the past.

Many expressions of "human potential" can be vile and worthy of repression. A social order that prevents people from expressing everything they feel (for example, racism) may not be wholly inhumane. Recognizing the moral ambiguity of "human potentials," classical liberals affirmed self-restraint. Because he undervalues such considerations, Unger remains an antiliberal, whatever he may call himself. It is not clear why he finds sweet consolation in the thought that everything is possible, and offers the image of society "always . . . at the edge of a cliff" as a promise instead of a threat.[93] There is something baffling about his limitless praise of vertiginous prospects. Consider the casual use he makes of the word "genuinely" in his comment about "those years after World War I when the fundamentals of social life were often genuinely up for grabs."[94] One could infer that the turbulent years between 1918 and 1933 represent the sort of authentic situation to which Unger wants to return. Is this his ideal? Although neither liberals nor Marxists foresaw the rise of National Socialism, the startling genuineness of Hitler's success does not make it welcome. After having delivered predictive social science some near-fatal blows, history no doubt has further surprises in store. But if the "years after World War I" taught us anything, it is this: to view cliff-hanging as an occasion for glee is unquestionably premature.

7 / The Community Trap

Postwar antiliberalism in the United States is richly various, by no means monolithic. While MacIntyre and Unger are two outstanding representatives, they by no means exhaust the field. Having examined their works in detail, I now want to look more generally at a broader school to which both (to varying degrees) belong. The most typical as well as most popular form of antiliberalism in the United States is the theoretical trend known as "communitarianism."[1] MacIntyre is surely the leading member of this school, and he has distinguished company. Not only Lasch and the early Unger, but also Michael Sandel, Charles Taylor, and Robert Bellah (not to mention many others) have written as communitarians or communitarian-sympathizers at some point. A classical example of soft antiliberalism, their perspective plays a significant role in public as well as scholarly debate. Rehearsing its weaknesses, in a brief compass, may be worthwhile. An identical set of theoretical mistakes as well as a number of historical misdescriptions surface in almost all communitarian works. (While theoretically weak, as I have said, communitarianism is not politically dangerous; that is part of what it means to be "soft.") Before turning, in Part II, to the historiographical errors common to all antiliberals, I will explore the six basic fallacies or theoretical failings characteristic of the communitarianism currently in vogue in the United States.

The Phantom Community

No society fully realizes the principles and the aspirations of liberalism. Liberals themselves criticize societies that, while professing liberal ideas, fail in practice to protect rights and satisfy basic needs. The communitarians blame liberal society not for failing to reach but for aiming to achieve liberal goals. The current "crisis" in the United

176

States and other liberal societies resides not in their having achieved justice only imperfectly, but rather in their having become fixated on such a low and colorless ideal. Something more than the legal protection of minorities or an expansion of welfare rights should be achieved by the state. Politics must aim higher, at something more uplifting than justice—more inspiring, more comforting, more spiritual, more erotic.

That something is community. According to the early Unger (and this is a remark that can be fished from almost any antiliberal text), "the political doctrine of liberalism does not acknowledge communal values." MacIntyre agrees that the "notion of the political community as a common project is alien to the modern liberal individualist world." For Sandel, who is perhaps the best-known disciple of MacIntyre and Unger, the citizens of a liberal state are doomed to the miserable isolation of "strangers." For Taylor, inhabitants of a genuinely liberal society will lack "a sense of shared fate" and "a common allegiance to a particular historical community." In actual liberal societies, it seems, "the individual has been taken out of a rich community life and now enters instead into a series of mobile, changing, revocable associations." Lasch identifies modernization with "the collapse of communal traditions" and sees "the essence of liberalism" as the emancipation of individuals from inherited traditions and restraints.[2]

Liberalism is dissatisfying, these critics contend, because it fails to provide what we yearn for most: fraternity, solidarity, harmony, and most magically, *community*. Communitarians invest this word with redemptive significance. When we hear it, all our critical faculties are meant to fall asleep. In the vocabulary of these antiliberals, "community" is used as an anesthetic, an amnesiac, an aphrodisiac. Unger actually calls it, without apparent irony, "the political equivalent of love."[3]

But what is community? What does it look like? What are *its* problems?

Communitarians are divided on these questions. Some locate community in the past, others espy it in the future. The former write *deprivation history*, wringing their hands about the world we have lost. (Their trademark is that melancholy cluster of words, "decay," "breakdown," "decline," "erosion," "impoverishment," "eclipse.") The latter compose *promissory history*, in which anticipation and hope provide consolation for the dreariness or the meaninglessness of the present.

For all their differences, both communitarians of the past and communitarians of the future idealize (bygone or expected) moral consensus. But neither tells us anything more specific about the community we lack. Nebulousness about nonliberal politics is not an incidental feature of communitarianism, moreover; it is an essential one.[4] Antiliberals of this persuasion rhapsodize about neighborhoods, churches, school boards, and so forth; they never provide sufficient detail about the national political institutions they favor to allow us to compare the advantages and disadvantages of illiberal community with the vices and virtues of the liberal societies we know.

All political arrangements involve the use of physical force.[5] Thus, at a minimum, communitarians should be specific about the conditions under which, in their ideal order, sanctions would be applied. Does moral revulsion at "radical separation" among citizens require making divorce and emigration illegal? What does a commitment to "solidarity" or "consensus" imply about the authority of majorities over dissident minorities? Should children of Jehovah's Witnesses be compelled to submit to the community-binding powers of the Pledge of Allegiance? Should nonconformists be legally ostracized or "weeded out"? Would communitarians advocate making *incivisme* into a punishable crime, as it was in France during the Terror? Although they presumably would not, they are reluctant to say so openly, perhaps to avoid being observed defending civil liberties and individual rights.[6]

The Myth of "the Social"

On the face of it, the category "social" should refer to the entire gamut of human motives, actions, and institutions. "Social" is (or should be) a descriptive term. To say that an action or motive is "social" is not to imply that it is necessarily good. While some "social purposes" are morally praiseworthy, others (such as racial purity) are morally repugnant. Members of the Ku-Klux-Klan, too, have "a commonality of shared self-understanding."[7]

Shared self-conceptions or aspirations or allegiances are not thereby intrinsically admirable. Conversely, immoral behavior is not defined by any lack of a social dimension. No asocial atom would strive to humiliate others publicly or seek the envy of inferiors. The blood feud and ethnic animosity do not signal an absence of sociality. The tie of vassalage, too, is a social bond. The relation between master and slave is no less social (though it is less desirable) than relations among intimate friends.

Communitarians do not accept this reasoning. They surreptitiously import moral approval into ostensibly descriptive categories such as "group loyalty," "collective aims," "constitutive attachments," and "social bonds." Sheldon Wolin, another prominent antiliberal, seems to apply the label "the political" solely to political activity that he admires.[8] It is as if "the dental" referred exclusively to healthy teeth. Unfortunately, as history reveals, collective action can be monstrous and "group aims" may include genocide. And the personal identity of a racist or religious bigot is certainly "socially constituted" without being in any way morally laudable.

Put differently, "the social nature of man" is too trite to count as an insight. The social constitution of the individual is worthless as an argument either for or against existing institutional arrangements. If all individuals are socially constituted, then the social self cannot serve as a critical standard to praise some societies and revile others. From the uncontroversial premise that "man is a social animal," communitarians draw the highly controversial conclusion that a warm and solidaristic social order is morally obligatory. But the inference is bogus. They deduce a "value" from a "fact" only by a conceptual sleight of hand.[9]

Human beings are naturally endowed with capacities that can be exercised only in society. Therefore man is "obliged to belong" to society.[10] Liberalism is immoral, for people are morally required to sustain the conditions that allow them to realize their inborn potentials. The weakness of this all-too-common reasoning lies in a tacit and erroneous assumption: that all of the human capacities that cannot be exercised except in society are necessarily praiseworthy. What the communitarian antiliberals consistently forget is that society is a dangerous place in which to grow up. It is only through intense social interaction, for example, that human beings acquire their worst follies and fanaticisms: the capacity for intolerance or racism would never flourish in presocial isolation.

Either/Or

Another infirmity of the new *Gemeinschaft* theorists is an addiction to crude dichotomies, notably to the contrasts of private interest/public virtue and base individualism/noble community. These alternatives are unsatisfactory, first of all, because they obscure the possibility of private virtue. They also suggest that individualism is necessarily antisocial, whereas individualism can involve a heightened concern *for others* as individuals rather than as members of ascriptive groups. The greatest threat to social cohesion, moreover, arises not from individualism but from collective passions, ideological conflict, and inherited rivalries between belligerent factions. In factional settings, solidarity is a problem, not a solution.[11]

Communitarian antiliberals invariably suggest that once people overcome their self-interest, they necessarily act in an admirable and public-spirited way. They assume, in other words, that selfless/selfish segues smoothly into good/bad. But this leaves out of the account the prominent place of selfless cruelty in human affairs. It is much easier to be cruel in the course of acting for the sake of others or for a "cause," than while acting for one's own sake. Those who have homosexuals shot in the name of the Islamic revolution are morally abhorrent, but they cannot be accused of antisocial individualism or base self-interest. There would be no terrorism or nationalistic border wars without selfless devotion to social groupings. In other words, the bloody events we read about every day contain a pertinent refutation of one of the crucial premises of communitarianism. Those who overcome self-interest are not necessarily benevolent or humane.

To and Fro

While trumpeting their own audacity, communitarian antiliberals are not quite exempt from ordinary inhibitions. When striving to catch our attention, they regularly present their indescribable community as an *alternative* to liberal society. Once they succeed in attracting a sufficient number of critical onlookers, however, they nimbly reposition themselves. They tend to retreat to the more modest position that community is merely a *supplement* to liberal society. The first claim is unconvincing while the second is unexciting. The double strategy of thrust and parry, however, should not be underestimated.

It has rhetorical advantages. The built-in option between two claims—one newsworthy but implausible, the other convincing but bland—gives communitarianism enormous resilience and capacity for survival. By artfully shifting weight from one foot to another, communitarian antiliberals can claim both originality and sobriety, taking maximum advantage of whatever audience is at hand. The naive are promised something extraordinary and the doubters are appeased.

But these gains are purchased by the sacrifice of stylistic unity. Communitarian works are typically marred by a schizophrenic tone. A high-pitched jeremiad fizzles into a tiptoed retreat. After *total* criticism of the ontological foundations of liberalism and dire warnings about the collapse of Western civilization, we are treated, say, to limp advice about tightening up pornography laws. This belated retreat into harmlessness is a sure sign of "soft" antiliberalism. After fulminating against liberal society, communitarians inevitably flip-flop into last-minute concessions. They want to inhabit a meaningful community, so long as everyone living there has rights. They inconsistently retract their initial protests, in other words, assuring us that they can continue to benefit, without hypocrisy, from the principles and institutions they otherwise heroically oppose.[12]

The Shifting Target

In the United States, as we have seen, communitarians tend to oscillate between a criticism of liberal theory and a criticism of liberal society. This is a crucial feature of their thought. Sometimes they say that liberalism is simply wrong: liberals are making a factual mistake when they suggest that individuals are pre-existent atomic units and that all social relations are as instrumental as voluntary contracts struck in the market. These "typically liberal" claims are false, runs the argument, because individuals are socially constituted, because wholes are prior to parts, and because what they like to call "constitutive" social relations exist. At other times, however, communitarians advance a contrary line of argument. Liberalism, they mournfully confess, is descriptively correct: modern society has become atomized, social bonds have snapped, instrumental relations are universal, group membership has become optional, that is, derivative from individual wills and subservient to private interests. Mirroring that bleak truth, liberal theory is doomed to be a dismal but not inaccurate science.

This waffle is disorienting, but characteristic. MacIntyre both denies that Aristotle's theory of the social self applies to "atomized" modern societies and insists that it does apply, although neo-Aristotelians alone have grasped the elusive fact. Sandel confusingly asserts that our lives are bad because they enact a theory that fails to describe our lives.[13] It is obviously contradictory to say that liberal individuals do not exist and that the ones who exist are excruciatingly unhappy. Yet this beguiling contradiction is something like the official handshake of the communitarian movement in America. On the one hand, social bonds lie before our eyes even though liberals do not see them. On the other hand, social bonds have been cruelly obliterated, while liberals who report their lack must suffer the fate of all those who bring the bad news—that is, they must be condemned for failing to denounce what they have discovered.

Theory as Therapy

Not surprisingly, some communitarians feel uneasy about switchbacking between such patently incompatible claims. To reconcile the existence of liberal individuals with their nonexistence, they note that a person's self-understanding will decisively affect his behavior. Ways of life are decisively shaped by available idioms and vocabularies. If a person classifies himself as a *croquemonsieur*, this will not make him into one, but it will cause him to act in unusual ways. Analogously, if he thinks he is an atomistic individual, this will not turn him into an atomistic individual, but it will lead him to behave oddly as a liberal citizen, as an economic man. In other words: liberal ideology is true and false. A nefarious theory guides and hides our practice. Liberals ruin the world by misapprehending it. Our impoverished language of radical individualism both distorts our behavior and denies us "access" to our communal selves.

Cognitive mistakes can have important behavioral consequences, of course, and many of them are likely to be bad. As Taylor says, "intellectual errors" can be modes of "self-stultification." Not this uncontroversial premise but only the practical conclusion communitarians draw from it is problematic. As diagnosticians of liberal self-deceit, they claim to be the midwives of our spiritual rebirth. When liberals impugn "the social," it seems, they not only misdescribe human action but also allow the best part of life to wither on the vine. By providing us with a new language, by redescribing human existence accurately (as thoroughly dependent on a nourishing social milieu), communitarians can make it worthwhile once again, or perhaps for the first time.

They promise "to uncover buried goods through rearticulation—and thereby . . . to bring the air again into the half-collapsed lungs of the spirit."[14] They will unearth the hidden treasure, make explicit the implicit, and release the warm human potential half-frozen beneath the ice of liberal ideology. In short, they advocate a transformative politics that is reassuringly benign. (A "soft" antiliberal would never dream of compelling others to change their lives.) Merely by peeling off the misshapen overlay of liberal theory, the hermeneutical sage will accomplish the reform of liberal society. He will "improve" us against our will. And he will do so therapeutically, not coercively, by helping us become explicitly what we already are latently. He will rearticulate the shared understanding that the rest of us have half-forgotten, thereby abolishing loneliness and rendering our lives, again or at last, joyfully communal.[15]

Thought and behavior are interwoven in various ways. But intellectual criticism and social transformation cannot be so effortlessly combined as communitarians appear to believe. A theoretical cause in the past does not guarantee a theoretical cure in the present, because earlier ideas may have set irreversible social processes in motion. (Needless to say, communitarians never provide a causal account of how their language-guided transfiguration of humanity and society might actually come about.) In the United States, to pick one example, racial bigotry is a much greater obstacle to democratization and improved social welfare than is the language of liberalism. As an atavistic form of solidarity and a robust denial of atomistic individualism, racism cannot be overcome by abandoning the language of rights for the language of community.

In any case, the belief that a criticism of liberal theory, by itself, entails a remaking of liberal society speaks volumes about the self-image of communitarians. If social problems arise from theoretical mistakes and linguistic impoverishment, then the counter-theorist who corrects these mistakes and enriches our speech is a great benefactor to mankind. The professional critic is not just another desk-bound professor. His destructive efforts are remarkably creative. He is, or aspires to be, the founder of a beautiful new (or old) world of togetherness and belonging.

Criticism of the critics of liberalism, as I said at the outset, does not imply that liberalism itself lies beyond criticism. To the contrary, liberalism's real defects can be approached with a clear mind only after the misleading attacks launched by communitarians and others are put into perspective. To condemn a social order as irredeemably rotten in the light of wholly unrealizable ideals is not necessarily useful. It makes no sense to develop a style of social criticism that sounds deep and even "metaphysical" but has nothing to do with possible solutions to concrete and urgent political problems.

The communitarian approach suffers from another flaw as well. Its exponents assume that a serious criticism of liberalism must be simultaneously a criticism of liberal theories and liberal societies. This, as I have argued, is a serious error. There are no good reasons to assume that an error in a liberal treatise, say John Rawls's *A Theory of Justice*, will provide a key to the inner sickness of American society.[16] But the principal debility of text-centered antiliberalism is that it inadvertently belittles the criticism of liberal societies in the name of liberal ideals. Liberal observers protest when the voting rights of minorities are not legally enforced, or when the infants of poor blacks suffer high mortality rates because of social bias against the group into which they happen to be born. Those who make liberal ideals responsible for almost all social ills do not take such criticisms seriously.

It would be imprudent, not to say unfair, to claim that these six fallacies, incoherences, or intellectual dead-ends exhaust the theoretical resources of communitarianism in America. But the patterns I have discussed resurface with enough regularity in contemporary works to suggest their permanent importance. In a wide range of liberalism's cultural critics we repeatedly find an unspecified fantasy model of community, a biased treatment of the generic category "social," misuse of the selfish/selfless distinction, tactical ambivalence about the radicalness of the proposed alternative, confusion concerning the descriptive adequacy of liberal theory, and unjustified assumptions about the political power of theoretical criticism. Admittedly, such a generic criticism of communitarianism has only a limited utility. For one thing, it fails to do justice to the colorful variety of views found among its exponents and sympathizers. For another, it conveys almost no information about the theory's intellectual origins and development. Focused on deep argumentative structures, however, such a synoptic view can suggest some underlying weaknesses of this academically fashionable form of antiliberalism. Because the longing for lost community is irrepressible, it may prove useful to keep these fallacies clearly in mind.

Part II / Misunderstanding the Liberal Past

8 / Antiliberals as Historians of Liberal Thought

The portrait of liberalism painted in broad strokes by generations of antiliberals has been absorbed too obligingly into the general stock of commonplaces. According to this proverbial account, entrenched in two hundred years of historiography, classical European liberals ignored the social constitution of the individual, were scornful of the common good, disparaged authority, sacrificed the public to the private, belittled political participation, neglected virtue, idolized economic man, declared values to be subjective, reduced man to a pleasure-pain machine, abolished self-restraint, placed excessive faith in Reason, and generally dissolved all nourishing social bonds. This is a daunting series of allegations. When confronted one at a time with the claims actually defended in classic liberal texts, however, they either seem exaggerated or wrong.

For nearly two centuries antiliberal polemicists have pilloried liberal ideas and institutions. These objects of scorn have been, with some exceptions, imaginary. The inaccuracy of most antiliberal reconstructions of the history of liberalism can be demonstrated by an empirical or case-by-case method. For critical purposes, there is no need to fashion a comprehensive and positive account of the liberal movement as a whole.[1] Historical distortions can be corrected much more economically simply by citing chapter and verse, by juxtaposing hostile accusations with positions plainly defended in a series of indisputably liberal texts. When questioning pejorative models of liberalism, therefore, I will proceed in a largely nominalist manner, employing the word "liberal" not to refer to a clearly defined or logically consistent doctrine, but as shorthand for the political stance adopted by a select group of modern liberal theorists: Spinoza, Milton, Locke, Montes-

187

quieu, Hume, Voltaire, Beccaria, Blackstone, Smith, Kant, Madison, Bentham, and John Stuart Mill.[2]

Controversy is sure to arise about several of these figures. Was Milton really a liberal? And Voltaire? What about Blackstone? And what about Bentham? Locke himself never advocated freedom of the press. Kant notoriously rejected the right of rebellion. Indeed, the incontestable differences among these theorists show that the idea of a single or uniform liberalism is itself doubtful. There are substantial areas of overlap among the positions adopted by these writers, but there is no identity. Given the diversity of historical situations they faced, it is remarkable how many basic principles they shared. They all believed that society can be held together without the fear of God, for instance, on the basis of secular norms and a shared interest in the fruits of cooperation. They all affirmed (though in differing ways) the moral principle of equality before the law—that no individual should be allowed to make an exception of himself. They all asserted, in the teeth of traditional doctrine, that public disagreement is a creative force. And so forth.

By redescribing the positions held by liberals at a sufficiently high level of abstraction, in other words, we can usefully bring out a core of common beliefs. But we cannot, with any fidelity to what they actually wrote, make them perfectly consistent with one another. Divergences among various national traditions and across time remain important. Even without reducing their distinctive views to a single logically consistent doctrine, in any case, we can reveal the general inadequacy of the antiliberal account. However we describe these liberals, we cannot make them resemble the unhandsome portrait painted of them, with unfriendly intent, by their nonmarxist enemies.

Did any of these "liberal" theorists hope to atomize society or to drive each citizen into isolation or a war with all the rest? Did they favor untrammeled selfishness and egoism? Did they thrust aside the common good? They cannot be pigeonholed in this way, not really. In fact, the theses so often described as "typically liberal" were seldom espoused by major liberal thinkers. The gulf that yawns between the legends promulgated by antiliberals and the positions actually defended by a wide variety of liberal theorists is what originally suggested the need for an anatomy of antiliberalism. There is room for legitimate disagreement about how a concept such as "liberalism" should be handled. But one thing is certain: no description of liberalism can be accurate if it applies to *none* of these classical liberals.

In this second part of the book I offer a criticism, along the lines just suggested, of antiliberal interpretations of the history of liberal thought. The evidence assembled for this purpose is merely a sampling, not an exhaustive survey. But once an off-target representation of the liberal past is described, and a refutation suggested, further counterexamples can easily be supplied. Antiliberals habitually distort liberal texts, it should be noted in advance, by reading them apolitically, by wresting pamphlets and treatises from their original historical contexts, disregarding their political and polemical aims, and ignoring the extent to which (as practical men) liberals were driven to scale down their ideals in the face of intractable social realities. Antiliberal falsifications, as a result, can often be set right simply by restoring liberal texts to their original settings. The best corrective to antiliberal misunderstandings is frequently to show, for instance, that the liberals being ridiculed for their absurd "philosophy of man" were actually making specific proposals for resolving concrete historical problems with limited means, and not elaborating a "philosophy" at all.

In the following chapters I examine a dozen of the most common historical misrepresentations perpetrated by the detractors of liberalism. In assembling this catalogue of standard distortions, I have mined the works of many antiliberals, past as well as present. I begin with perhaps the most resilient of antiliberal myths: that classical liberals naively believed in the fiction of a socially uninfluenced individual and advocated a total "atomization" of society.

9 / The "Atomization" of Society?

"In the liberal bourgeois world," according to Schmitt, "the detached, isolated, emancipated individual becomes the middle point, the court of last resort, the absolute." For "all liberal thought," Giovanni Gentile similarly explains, "society remains an aggregation of individual human beings, each one closed in himself, without any necessary relation to others: autonomous and self-sufficient." Strauss concurs: under the influence of liberal theory, "the individual is emancipated from social bonds which antedate all consent or compact." These views are traced back to seventeenth- and eighteenth-century liberals, who purportedly conceived of society as a voluntary compact between preexistent or deracinated persons. For liberals, writes MacIntyre too, "individuals are . . . primary and society secondary, and the identification of individual interests is prior to, and independent of, the construction of any moral or social bonds between them." With childlike credulity liberals swallowed the fiction of the presocial individual. They assumed that a socially uninfluenced individual, before learning a language or being socialized into a culture, could identify his pregiven needs and negotiate contracts to ensure their satisfaction. Charles Taylor, who periodically aligns himself with our antiliberals, could not disagree. Operating with "atomist-infected notions," Locke and other liberals foolishly believed that "men are self-sufficient outside society," he explains. And Robert Nisbet, another well-known antiliberal sympathizer, reproduces the same charge: "the founders of liberalism" asserted "man's fundamental separateness and his self-sufficiency." Liberals regarded the individual "as independent of the influences of any historically developed social organization."[1]

By characterizing the liberal position in this way, both fascist and

190

postfascist communitarians think they have already refuted it. Because "man is a social animal," liberalism is theoretically false and politically bankrupt. Robinsonnades are always implausible. Social relations are not secondary and optional, but primary and necessary. Presocial individuals do not exist. Therefore, Locke was simply dreaming.

Detractors of liberalism often insinuate that the great European liberals were not merely unintelligent but also completely incapable of common sense. Although Taylor does not straightforwardly assert that, according to Locke, an individual could learn to speak English in the absence of social interaction with English-speakers, this is what his analysis of "atomistic" social theory implies.[2] To put aspersions of this sort into perspective, we should recall that Max Weber, Emile Durkheim, and Georg Simmel—to mention only the weightiest of modern sociologists—devoted their careers to studying the *social* basis of individualism. The modern emphasis on individuality, they argued, is a product of a peculiarly modern style of social conditioning. Significantly, those who thought concretely about the social constitution of the individual never imagined that their findings would in any way revolutionize the self-understanding of liberal citizens or bring liberal polities crashing down.

Locke, who is Taylor's premier example of an atomistic liberal, was not unmindful of social life. For example, he wrote that God made man "such a Creature, that, in his own Judgment, it was not good for him to be alone." His treatise on education is impossible to square with charges of liberal ignorance about the processes of primary socialization. He thought that community pressure to conform was overwhelming if not irresistible. And he assumed that an individual's beliefs ordinarily arose from social communication. "Most persons," he wrote, "build up their morals after the manner and belief of those among whom they happen to be born and educated." Similarly, "*Doctrines*, that have been derived from no better original, than the Superstition of a Nurse, or the Authority of an old Woman" may "by length of time and consent of Neighbors, *grow up to the dignity of Principles* in Religion or Morality."[3] The blank-slate theory, in other words, is anything but an asocial approach to how human beings learn.

What was true for Locke was true for all the theorists usually included in the liberal tradition. Hume referred, as if it were totally obvious, to the "social disposition of mankind." He wrote perceptively of human passions, such as pride and envy, that obviously presuppose social awareness and are incompatible with the mutual insensibility of windowless monads. Individuals are always born into families, he agreed with Locke, and they never exist outside a social unit. They are impelled to remain in society by necessity, by inclination, and by habit—because they have to, because they want to, and because they are used to it. According to Kant, too, individuals come into the world with an inborn *nisus* to sociability. Human beings are gregarious animals because their natural faculties can be fully exercised only in society.[4] They cannot be "free" in an isolation chamber or a social vacuum, but only in a community where rights are enforced and possibilities for creative interaction are kept open by institutional means.

It is equally wrong to conclude that the existence of asocial atoms is implied by invocations of an original compact. Liberal ideals and institutions (such as religious toleration, freedom of speech, representative government, and a market economy) are unthinkable in the absence of a dense network of social relations. Textual evidence that political liberalism can be detached from a naive attitude toward the myth of a social contract is provided, again, by Hume. He firmly supported the core institutions of a free society (religious toleration, legal restrictions on the state's means of coercion, representative government, the separation of powers, private property, freedom of the press, and so forth) and no less firmly rejected the idea of an original contract. Political society, he argued, arises not from voluntariness but from the compulsions of natural scarcity and war. Rulership emerged from the imperative of deference in times of tribal conflict rather than out of free consent. In primitive societies, bloody confrontation was an everyday affair that "enured the people to submission." Obsequiousness to warlords developed spontaneously because such subordination helped group members survive in the face of lethal enemies. Eventually, savvy rulers exploited mindless habits of deference to extract a revenue which, in turn, enabled them to build a police force and thereby punish "the refractory and disobedient"—that is, to consolidate their deference-based superiority by force.[5]

The remarkable thing about Hume's realistic and critical account of the origin of government is that liberal contract theorists could have fully accepted it. Despite appearances, Locke's support for government by popular consent did not depend on the historical reality of any original contract. He contended, after all, that "an Argument from what has been, to what should be, has no great force."[6] The way societies began, therefore, is irrelevant to how they should be organized now. Locke's references to a social contract, as a consequence, must be read politically, not descriptively. His state of nature was not a historical description but a model. By giving prominence to this model, he aimed to replace the traditional picture of nature as an inherently hierarchical order. Great preliberal political theorists, from Plato through Aquinas and beyond, had argued that nature was organized as a great chain of being, and that a status pyramid was the natural order of society as well.[7]

Seen against this traditional background, contractualism regains its original radicalness. The force of Locke's idea of an original contract derived from its emphasis on a voluntary agreement among equals. Only this sort of agreement can legitimate the power wielded by some individuals over others. To the extent that he "atomized" human self-understanding, he did so for political purposes—to attack organic chains of dependence and subordination as well as to undermine dangerous clan and sectarian groupings. The state of nature was a condition without dependency, "without Subordination or Subjection." To conceive nature in a traditional fashion, as inherently hierarchical, was to say that social ranks and political superiority require no special justification. A state of nature where individuals were "all equal and independent," by contrast, suddenly puts subjection and subordination on the defensive.[8] State-of-nature theorists, in short, meant to force defenders of hereditary authority and monopoly to explain and justify all deviations from the standard of natural equality. Like other liberals, Locke used the contractualist idea to discredit the strong theory of intergenerational obligations entailed by traditional patriarchalism. His ultimate aim was to dismantle a specific set of involuntary hierarchical relations characteristic of traditional European societies. His proximate aim was to confute those, such as Robert Filmer, who asserted that nature itself had endorsed hereditary monarchy.[9]

Locke's point was not that presocial individuals are fully rational but rather that hierarchy and rulership are legitimate only if ratified by the consent of the subordinated and the ruled. No overlord has an inherent right to impose his will on purported inferiors: "Men being . . . by Nature, all free, equal and independent, no one can be put out of his Estate, and subjected to the Political Power of another, without his own *Consent*."[10] Locke was hoisting a normative standard here, not advancing an empirical or historical claim. By stressing an individual's natural independence, he did not mean to atomize society (what would be the point of that?), but simply to undermine immemorial forms of personal dependency.

Locke defined "want of Liberty" as being "under the determination of some other than himself." To be free, by extension, was to be independent, "not to be subject to the inconstant, uncertain, unknown, Arbitrary Will of another Man." Independence, in this sense, has nothing to do with atomization. Smith, too, defined "liberty and independency" as freedom from "the badges of slavery," for example, the "insolence" of royal tax collectors.[11] The concrete humiliations of dependency, in the seventeenth and eighteenth centuries, should not be underestimated. Uzbek's seraglio, described in the *Persian Letters*, is a vivid reminder of the psychological cruelty of involuntary servitude. The harem is Montesquieu's symbol for an absolutely illiberal community—a community without rights, based wholly on personal dependency and the degradation of inferiors. Women and eunuchs alike stoop, grovel, and beg favors abjectly from their overlords. Montesquieu and other liberals did not want to pulverize society. They wanted to ban seraglio-like abasement, which they considered abhorrent and immoral.

Further textual evidence bountifully supports a normative, rather than naively descriptive, reading of social contract theory. Blackstone, for example, expressly endorses Hume's criticism of the state-of-nature myth. He nevertheless continues to invoke the myth whenever he wants to advance normative claims. In particular, he uses the original contract story to emphasize that "all members of society are naturally equal." The fact that "in a state of nature we are all equal" is meant to provide the moral basis for liberal political and legal arrangements.[12] While assuming that society would always contain important inequalities, Blackstone also declares that such inequalities cannot be justified by an appeal to nature. Human beings are *not* naturally divided into superiors and inferiors. It follows that all inequalities must be justified by invoking common advantage and popular consent.

Kant likewise employs the tale of an original contract not as a historical account but as a standard or ideal which "enables us to conceive of the legitimacy of the state." Kant's contractualism, like Locke's, has a political rather than a descriptive function. It, too, is normative, not empirical. Typically, it aims to delegitimate social castes: "a *hereditary aristocracy* . . . could never be approved by the general will of the people in an original contract, which is, after all, the principle behind all rights."[13] In sum, classical liberals introduced the idea of a state of nature as an invitation to overturn inherited monopolies. They used it consciously to demolish two archaic notions: that membership in a group today implies a moral obligation to remain a member tomorrow, and that social superiority is natural and therefore requires no further justification.

Like all political programs, liberalism was "antisocial" in a trivial sense. It challenged the existence of some widely accepted social institutions. It demanded that certain ongoing practices be changed or abolished. (For example, the practice of confiscating the estates of convicted felons was abrogated on individualistic or "atomistic" grounds—because of the undeserved harm it visited upon innocent children.) Liberals sought to emancipate individuals from relations of heteronomy and subservience. But liberalism can be considered antisocial in a more serious sense only if we identify society with its hierarchical, parochial, and oppressive subforms. That liberals aimed to detribalize or destratify society or to demolish social monopolies does not mean, obviously enough, that they were attacking the essence of human society.

The exaggerated charge of "atomism," however, does contain a distorted echo of the truth. For instance, liberals deny that the value of a person hinges on his or her contribution to the aims of the collectivity. Strong communitarians naturally view women as instruments for reproducing the community. Female members of the group have value if and only if they perform this service. The ostracism or diminished status of childless women is a logical result. Without being "atomistic," then, an individualistic theory such as liberalism revolts against the cruel subordination of individuals to the purposes of the community.

Liberals do not try to destroy all social bonds, of course, but they do encourage personal independence. They consistently urge individuals to think for themselves rather than imbibe thoughtlessly "the Opinions of others."[14] Admittedly, liberalism poses a palpable threat to orthodox and closed communities or traditions. In a liberal society such as the United States, young Jewish men and women will marry outside their religious group against their parents' wishes; and nuns who might have behaved obsequiously if cloistered in more traditional settings may respond saucily to their ecclesiastical superiors. Such subversive behavior is bound to irritate the traditionalists. The liberal stress on legitimation through consent has other unsettling consequences as well. Birth rank and biological characteristics lose prestige in a society organized around voluntary agreements (because individuals obviously do not choose their inherited position or traits). From a liberal perspective, birth status should not be the master key to life. But liberals did not therefore conclude that the human self was factually "disencumbered" of ascriptive particularities; liberals, too, have eyes to see. True, liberal institutions are designed in a special way. They may require a judge to *ignore* the race or church membership of a defendant before the bench, for example.[15] But the attempt to desensitize legal institutions to ethnic traits and religious affiliations does not imply (how could it?) that being black or Catholic has no importance for the life of an individual in a liberal society.[16] The liberal conception of the person as neither black nor white, neither Catholic nor Jew, has a political and legal meaning. It was never intended to deny the obvious reality of primordial attachments.[17]

Antiliberals sometimes identify liberal individualism with epistemological solipsism. About liberalism, Sheldon Wolin writes: "the basic assertion, that each was the best judge of his own interests and hence no outside agency could properly dictate his happiness, rested squarely on the belief that no individual could truly understand another." That liberals have a somewhat more nuanced view is easy to prove. Independence entails neither isolation nor lack of mutual awareness and concern. For one thing, independence is a social practice that presupposes stable rules, institutions, and expectations. For another, classic liberals all believed that one individual could very well comprehend and judge another. How else could they have argued that "no man should be judge in his own case"? Finally, the liberal ideal of independence is universal: it implies that *no one* should be degraded into into a mere instrument of his superiors or his group. Why this prohibition should be considered "solipsistic" is unclear.[18]

Equally implausible is a related charge, leveled by Lasch, among others: "the liberal principle that everyone is the best judge of his own interests makes it impossible to ask what people need, as opposed to what they want." But Adam Smith, for one, had no trouble distinguishing needs from wants. This is why he could argue with such conviction that "it is the luxurious and not the necessary expense of the inferior ranks of people that ought ever to be taxed."[19] Liberals did claim, for example, that privy councillors ordinarily understand less about peasant interests than do the peasants themselves. But their basic point, again, was political or normative, not descriptive. That rulers can sometimes know what is good for citizens better than citizens know it themselves may be a dangerous principle even when it is not always false. No matter how well-founded in some cases, such a principle cannot be safely elevated into a maxim of government. In short, to deny that others can define our true needs or profoundest interests is not to affirm "atomism" or the ultimate privacy of self-knowledge. It is simply to remove a widely abused strategy of justification from the arsenal of public officials.

10 / Indifference toward the Common Good?

Because they defend the right to be different and advocate respect toward strangers, liberals are said to deny the existence of any "genuine shared common good." This accusation, too, is largely unfounded. It flies in the face, for example, of Locke's assertion that "the public good is the rule and measure of all lawmaking." While Locke worried that the government's appeal to the common good might be "a specious show of deceitful words," a lie exploited by wielders of power, he nevertheless consistently invoked "the Publick Good," "the common good," and "the good of the Society" in a positive sense, to define the aims of government. Indeed, would he or other liberals have denounced "the pretense of public good" and the "pretense of care for the public weal" if they had not believed that such a common good existed and was being violated by misusers of power?[1]

Liberal misgivings about the common good must be understood in a political context. They were provoked by the way that concept was traditionally abused. After all, how did governors justify their maltreatment of private citizens if not by invoking overriding public purposes? In the *Politics*, interestingly, Aristotle distinguished the master from the slave by contending that the master had privileged insight into the common good.[2] With his own unaided vision, a slave cannot grasp the rational principle upon which joint advantage depends; he must therefore be instructed and benevolently coerced by his superiors. The common good can be known directly only by a few—the wise and the virtuous. Far from being innocent, therefore, the traditional idea of the common good was deeply implicated in the justification of authority, monopoly, privilege, and social hierarchy. Toward those intimate

198

with the ultimate goals of the community, deference was naturally required. This political background goes far toward explaining the deflationary approach liberals took toward the rhetoric of the common good.

Liberals distrusted the *language* of the common good because it was likely to be strategically misused. They frequently identified the "common good" with dangerous and oppressive values as well. Religious orthodoxy was a common good liberals hoped to live without. Religion aside, the most obvious thing citizens share is a desire for military ascendancy. The more we emphasize the "commonness" of goods, the more we imply that foreigners are to be excluded and perhaps subordinated. As antimilitarists, liberals mistrusted the rhetoric of the common cause, associating it with dynastic wars and "a thousand visionary hopes of conquest and national glory."[3] As anticlericals, they mistrusted the entrenched religious establishment that so frequently invoked the common good to justify sectarian persecution. They also worried that the notion of a single, overarching common good could imply that conflicting opinions about the common good had no legitimate place within the state.

Politically wary of this idea, liberals nevertheless unambiguously endorsed what Madison called "the public good, the real welfare of the great body of the people." Smith likewise wrote that government must actively promote "the general interest of the country," that is, the advantage of "the great body of the people."[4] The right to be different is not necessarily inconsistent with the creation of a common life. Classical liberals may have employed the public interest most often as a standard applicable to rulers rather than as an argument for submission or obedience, but they never doubted that a common good existed. One practical conclusion they drew was that the government is obliged to maintain and improve concrete "public goods," such as highways, education, and the legal machinery necessary for private litigation.

Liberal attitudes toward "civic virtue" will be discussed below, but a preliminary point is worth stressing here. Tolerance for honest differences about the nature of the common good implies the political unreliability or inadequacy of virtue. In a pluralistic society, an individual's willingness to subordinate private interest to what *he* ardently considers "the" common good does not, by itself, resolve society's most urgent political controversies and problems. Indeed, wholly selfless attempts to implement rival concepts of the common good can lead to pointless and viciously destructive civil conflicts.

Despite their doubts, liberals retained an emphatic conception of the common good. Justice, self-rule, and the fruits of peaceful coexistence are all common goods. They are enjoyed by individuals, to be sure, but jointly, not atomistically. As pluralists, liberals discourage the use of force to impose an official set of moral purposes on all citizens, without being hypertolerationists. Certain moral norms, such as justice, should be politically enforced. Although the liberal state does not provide an orthodox definition of "the good life" as opposed to "the bad life," it does administer an obligatory distinction between "right action" and "wrong action." Rightness, to be discussed in Chapter 15, defines the liberal conception of the common good.

An additional piece of evidence supporting this thesis is the persistence, in all liberal theories, of a sharp distinction between crime and tort, between injuries to the community and injuries to the individual. "The true measure of crimes" as Beccaria says, is "the *harm done to society*."[5] In many preliberal societies, it should be recalled (including such admired ones as ancient Athens), offences such as murder were treated as strictly private wrongs, remediable by payment of monetary compensation to the victim's family.[6] Liberal societies, in other words, are built on a broader definition of the common good than are many preliberal ones. Within a liberal framework, as Blackstone, too, makes clear, the very concept of crime is strongly communitarian: "in these gross and atrocious injuries the private wrong is swallowed up in the public: we seldom hear any mention made of satisfaction to the individual; the satisfaction to the community being so great."[7] In the case of murder, he notes, the harm to the community so eclipses the harm to the individual that compensation to the family of the victim is no longer even considered. This is the communitarian or anti-individualistic strain in liberal thought. It is wrongly and perplexingly ignored by virtually all of liberalism's communitarian and anti-individualistic critics.

11 / The Eclipse of Authority?

Antiliberals frequently confuse liberalism with extreme forms of libertarianism. Following Maistre, in fact, they complain that the indiscriminate "hatred of authority" is one of the principal and most deplorable characteristics of modern times. Liberalism, a perfect expression of the modern antipower ethos, is nothing but "an artful system of methods for weakening the state," according to Schmitt. To MacIntyre, for somewhat different reasons, liberal modernity appears to be "a culture to which the notion of authority is alien and repugnant." Contrast these incautious generalizations with Spinoza's assertion that "if government be taken away, no good thing can exist." Obviously enough, classical liberals were neither anarchists nor extreme libertarians, fixated singlemindedly on the dangers of state intervention. The sovereignless or ungoverned society was not their ideal. The common claim that they were virulently antistatist is unwarranted.[1]

Liberals did not believe that all aspects of social life need to be managed from above. They entertained doubts about the coercive-extractive state. But they uniformly affirmed that authority was socially indispensable. Without it, conflicts among individuals would be resolved by "the way of beasts," that is, by force. To learn how human beings behave when unsuperintended by a "common superior" and restrained only by their own consciences, Locke suggested, we should watch an army sack a town. Liberals clung to unified authority, then, because they wanted to avoid "all those mischiefs of Blood, Rapine, and Desolation, which the breaking to pieces of Government bring on a Country." If the government did not have a monopoly on legitimate violence, the strong would ceaselessly victimize the weak. Domestic politics should not replicate the barbaric freedom of the international order where every actor is judge in his own case, the strongest bully gets his way, and no common rules are coercively enforced. To encourage industriousness, moreover, the state must secure to all individuals the fruits of their labor.[2] Such protection requires considerable administrative and judicial capacities. As a result, liberals aimed to constitutionalize authority and make it responsible to the public; they did not wish to destroy or incapacitate the state.

Authority must be continuously susceptible to criticism and guided by law, as well as internally organized to maximize intelligent decision-making and, of course, to prevent tyranny and corruption. It must also be strong and unified enough to impose a single set of rules on all citizens. The textual evidence that liberals were positively inclined toward centralized, law-enforcing state authority is voluminous. Locke, who would never "follow any Authority" in intellectual matters, believed that "Government is hardly to be avoided amongst Men that live together." He was convinced, moreover, that there must always be a "Power within the Community to . . . provide for the Necessities of the publick."[3] Without government, scarcity can never be overcome. Human beings will never act impartially or follow fair rules of conduct if they are not disciplined by political authority.

Hume, too, held that "liberty is the perfection of society; but still authority must be acknowledged essential to its very existence." He added: "it is impossible for the human race to subsist, at least in any comfortable and secure state, without the protection of government." Montesquieu concurred: "without government, no society can subsist." Individual freedom will likewise perish when the central state is excessively feeble, as in Poland. Blackstone gave the same point a Hobbesian flourish: "any government is better than none." One of the most important chapters in the *Wealth of Nations* shows that the emergence of individual freedom was inextricably connected to the process of state-building and the strengthening of centralized institutions.[4] Without a strong state, capable of enforcing contract and property law, no commercial society can exist. *The Federalist Papers* advocate bolstering the effectiveness and capacity to govern of the national government. The first chapter of Mill's *Considerations of Representative Government* and the last chapter of his *Principles of Political Economy* are both devoted to extensive discussions of the positive contribution of state power to liberal freedom. Most classical liberals agreed that the state needs power to provide, among other things, highways, street lighting, and safe water, not to mention public education, poor relief, and the legal apparatus that every private litigant requires.

Kant is renowned for his defense of individual autonomy. He wrote with passion against the authority wielded by priests and other officials over the supposedly immature minds of ordinary citizens. But a repudiation of deference, obsequiousness, and psychological dependency did not make him, any more than Locke, into an antistatist. Far from it; only the state, Kant persistently argued, can create the conditions under which individuals can successfully claim rights, including property rights. (There can be no property without enforceable rules.) Only the power of the state allows individuals to live profitably with one another. With his usual penchant for driving liberal ideas to a memorable extreme, Kant asserted that "man is an animal who needs a master." This illiberal-sounding statement means that every individual would like to exempt himself from otherwise general rules: "he thus requires a *master* to break his self-will and force him to obey a universally valid will under which everyone can be free."[5] The liberal state not only enforces voluntary contracts; it also imposes a uniform system of law and a norm of justice or fairness upon all individuals. (This perspective was expressed with equal force by liberals, such as Locke, who expressed greater sympathy for the right of rebellion.)

It is true, of course, that liberals opposed arbitrary and capricious authority over persons or property. They attacked despotic government or "absolute Dominion." (They were also worried about the venality or corruption of officials.) Montesquieu was especially concerned with the way an arbitrary regime can use the judicial system—"a terrible power among men"—to terrorize and crush its subjects. As a result, it is "on the goodness of the criminal laws that the liberty of the subject principally depends."[6] Liberals were naturally interested in regularizing and controlling state action, especially the power to punish, but they did not excoriate authority in general.

Effective government was necessary and desirable so long as it was conducted according to law and by consent. The liberal theory of "consent," as a matter of fact, is a theory about how to *create authority.* Those liberals who accepted it clearly understood the right of rebellion as including a duty to institute a new legal authority based on public agreement. Their cautious but ultimately favorable attitude toward authority is easy to comprehend. To violate rights in a liberal society, after all, is to defy the authority of the liberal state. Freedoms are protected by laws made by elected legislatures and enforced by the government. This suggests that political power and individual liberty are not necessarily antithetical from a liberal point of view.

Any power strong enough to protect individual rights and promote the general welfare will by the same token be strong enough to violate these rights and serve the private whims of wielders of power. The quandary this presents for liberals was classically formulated by Madison: "in framing a government which is to be administered by men over men, the great difficulty lies in this: you must first enable the government to control the governed; and in the next place oblige it to control itself." This dilemma provides the starting point for all liberal constitutionalism. Kant formulated the same point in the same way. Driven by their inherent partiality, individuals seek to exempt themselves from generally valid laws. Only a coercive power can compel them to behave impartially, as they secretly know they should. In other words, individuals need a "master" to make them just. Unfortunately, "this master will also be an animal who needs a master." Governors will never be godlike. Even worse, an ordinary person elevated to high office will be naturally drawn to abuse his power. How then can the controlling power be controlled? How to find "a supreme authority which would itself be just"? This is "the most difficult of all tasks."[7]

The state must be monitored and controlled without being crippled or weakened until it cannot function, according to both Madison and Kant. To reach this goal the government must, first of all, govern "by promulgated establish'd Laws" and have "the Consent of the People." Its activities must be in accord with legal rules, limited to specified domains, open to public inspection and criticism, and dependent upon public consent, electorally expressed. Laws must be made by an elected assembly and applied equally to all citizens, including the lawmakers themselves. Liberty therefore is inextricably intertwined with authority: "*Freedom of Men under Government*, is, to have a standing Rule to live by, common to every one of that Society, and made by the Legislative Power erected in it."[8] To repeat, freedom means living according to a single system of general rules, enacted by an elected and accountable assembly, predictably enforced by an impartial court, and criticizable by ordinary citizens communicating with each other through an uncensored press.

Liberals were not opposed to power as such but to illegal, unlimited, and irresponsible power. They objected to "a tyrannical concentration of all the powers of government in the same hands."[9] While the power to punish must certainly be monopolized by the government, governmental decision-making authority itself must not be engrossed by a single and unsupervised clique of officials. The separation of powers is obviously a crucial feature of any constitutional system. Separate branches must oversee each other, and each must have an institutional interest in keeping the others free of corruption and operating within legal channels. Important residual powers, moreover, must remain with the voters, especially the power to discuss political affairs uninhibitedly in a free press and the power to oust lawmakers from office in periodic elections. But the separation of powers and representative government are perfectly compatible with a system in which the legitimate use of physical violence is entirely monopolized by public officials. Checks and balances are meant to regularize government, not to paralyze it or destroy its capacity to govern. Hume was explicit on this point: in all free governments there will be "a partition of power among several members." A divided government is more likely than an undivided one to "act by general and equal laws," promulgated publicly and known to all subjects. Distributing power, however, does not necessarily dilute it. When the branches of a free government are partitioned, their "united authority is no less, or *is commonly greater* than that of any monarch."[10]

12 / The Public Realm Sacrificed to the Private?

Liberals thought that certain decisions—such as how to seek salvation or what books to read—were best made by unsupervised individuals rather than governments. They are therefore often accused of being committed to a one-sided expansion of the private sector at the expense of the public. For example, Schmitt asserts that there is "absolutely no liberal politics, only a liberal critique of politics." While they affirm economic competition and intellectual discussion, liberals "attempt to annihilate the political as a domain of conquering power and repression."[1] They want the freedom-encouraging extrapolitical domain to widen and the deadening political sphere to contract.

This account is not quite accurate. Liberals were not so thoroughly antipolitical as to distrust and despise the public sphere and glorify the private sector. Did they really rob from the public to pay the private? Did they consign to private decision-makers important questions that should have been reserved for political officials or assemblies? Not exactly; the picture Schmitt paints of liberal apoliticism is again one-sided. Some counterarguments have already been provided in the chapter on authority above, but much more can and should be said. Liberals were not sympathetic to all things private. No liberal ever expressed support for private courts, private taxation, private armies, or the private right to declare war. As etymology reveals, the liberal attack on inherited privilege was actually an attack on "private laws." Dueling is a voluntary exchange between consenting adults. Vigilantism is private enterprise.[2] Private contracts for murder or assault are struck in the nonpolitical sphere. Yet liberals never hesitated, in cases such as these, to enforce state prohibitions against individual choice. Their antagonism toward dangerous forms of private initiative is also

206

registered in theoretical works. Montesquieu, for example, thought that the superiority of modern over ancient politics was due not to representative government but to the creation of a *public* prosecutor. Fortunately, he wrote, the legal indictment of criminals is now assigned only to public accusers.[3]

By drawing a distinction between the public and the private, liberals did not mean to express a systematic bias for the private and against the public. Often they did just the opposite. They believed that civil society, for example, depends upon "the control of our private inclinations." Similarly, "if individuals were once allowed to use private force as a remedy for private injuries, all social justice must cease, the strong would give law to the weak, and every man would revert to a state of nature."[4] Crucial to the liberal legal order, moreover, is the principle that the judge cannot be a blood relation to either the plaintiff or the defendant. This rule implements a sharp distinction between public and private relationships. Its aim is to contain or weaken the imperialistic private sphere. Liberalism strives to limit the influence of private attachments on public decisions. Montesquieu's entire discussion of punishment revolves around this problem: how to ensure that the criminal law will not become an instrument of private parties pursuing private aims—exacting personal revenge, harassing members of a rival church, or lining private pockets. Vague laws in capital cases are anathema because they furnish a perfect pretext for individual power-wielders who want to liquidate individuals or families they personally despise.[5]

Liberalism might even be defined as a systematic attempt to *restrict the private abuse of public institutions*. Liberals naturally accepted the classical definition of a tyrant as a ruler who treats the state as private property. Locke, for one, warned against "a manifest perverting of Justice, and a barefaced wresting of the Laws to protect or indemnifie the violence of some Men, or Party of Men."[6] Following Montesquieu, Beccaria agreed that law was corrupt so long as it remained a tool of human passion and an instrument for raising revenue. The evidentiary rule requiring two witnesses in court rather than one was designed to complicate the life of malice-driven personal avengers. Punishments for perjury and false accusation had the same function. So did the right to challenge potential jury members. The principle that no judge can benefit financially from either a conviction or acquittal was deliberately erected against the itch for private gain rampant among officials and others. Something similar can be said about the rule that actions alone, not private thoughts, can be punished. If crimes must be observed by third parties, then vengeful liars will have less chance to accuse their personal enemies of heinous acts. According to Montesquieu, the best way to disarm private parties that aim to misuse the law is to decriminalize the whole range of activities—for example, sacrilege, heresy, magic and homosexuality—punished by burning at the stake and extraordinarily difficult to prove.[7]

Liberals do not systematically favor an expansion of the private sector. A good case can be made, on the other hand, for the primacy of publicity in liberal thought. By "publicity" I mean, first of all, the principle that laws should be proclaimed publicly. Laws must be "promulgated and known to the People," "notified to the people" in "the most public and perspicuous manner," well-publicized to "all" subjects. Second, trials—especially criminal trials—should be public. Montesquieu mounted a blistering attack on secret accusations, such as unsigned denunciations of fellow courtiers delivered by stealth to the king.[8] Accusations must be made publicly, with full opportunity for explanation and rebuttal. Third, legislative sessions and government budgets must be open to the public. In this case, liberals conceived of publicity as a stimulant as well as a depressant. Besides curbing abuses and corruption, the "sunlight of publicity" can supply new suggestions, counterarguments, and useful information.

Another important form of liberal publicity, the freedom of the press, has much the same function. According to Wolin, liberals usually identify the public realm with harsh coercion and locate "all worthwhile endeavor" in the private sphere. For Kant, contrary to this suggestion, the public sphere is a place where individuals can freely pursue the eminently worthwhile goal of political reform. A government critic "making *public use* of his reason," Kant writes, must enjoy "unlimited freedom to use his reason and to speak in his own person."[9] Freedom of the press is not only an outlet for individual liberty but also a method by which the collectivity can consider and remedy its own shortcomings. When policies are set publicly and public criticism is encouraged, a government can avoid self-contradictory legislation, discern problems before they get out of hand, and correct its mistakes.

When liberal political systems finally developed firm contours, during the first half of the nineteenth century, three of their basic institutions turned out to be an independent judiciary, a legislature elected by a broad suffrage, and a political opposition. Political opposition is crucial, for a reason that classical liberals had long before made clear: the back-and-forth of public disagreement sharpens the minds of all parties and produces better decisions than any proposals presented at the outset. Spinoza explained the liberal commitment to free debate as follows: "men's natural abilities are too dull to see through everything at once; but by consulting, listening, and debating, they grow more acute, and while they are trying all means, they at last discover those which they want, which all approve, but no one would have thought of in the first place." For the same reason, Locke argued that legislators must make decisions "upon examination, and mature debate." Learning occurs in public by means of public discussion, and public disagreement produces more intelligent decisions. This striking thesis was a staple of liberal theory from Milton to Mill.[10] (It should be contrasted with the romantic and potentially antiliberal notion that, instead of thoughtful policy, public participation produces beautiful or "fully realized" citizens.)

Liberal concern for religious, intellectual, and economic liberty does register a desire to depoliticize certain important areas of life. But classical liberals simultaneously emphasize the importance of public freedoms, such as the right to disagree with governmental decisions, to criticize officials, and to vote in elections and run for office. Unlike emotional identification with particularistic groups, democratic self-rule is a perfectly liberal value. As a result, public freedoms were not marginal but central to liberal thought.[11] In a society where significant religious and ethnic differences exist, democratic cooperation can be achieved only if certain issues of deep personal concern are taken off the political agenda. The liberal distinction between public and private, in other words, may be a necessary precondition for the democratization of public life.[12] Yet the belief that liberal polities wholly sacrifice the public to the private is widespread. What explains this particular antiliberal distortion? Three factors are at work to produce it.

The first is universal suffrage. The democratization of politics has meant that the prestige value (as well as the real importance) of an individual's participation in politics has markedly decreased. When the privileges once enjoyed by a property-holding ruling class are opened to all, they are cheapened in the eyes of some. But how many of those who attack liberalism today for devaluing public life would openly admit that their real complaint is with an egalitarian trend?

Second, the pluralism of values in liberal thought implies that politics is not the only realm in which individuals can serve others and realize their own potentials. The high value placed on social interaction in nonpolitical realms strikes some antiliberals as an implicit denigration of civic participation. But there is no obvious reason why the existence of valuable nonpolitical alternatives should necessarily lead to a total or even a radical devaluation of politics.

Third, before the nineteenth century, classical liberals lived in rather oppressive and censorship-prone societies. As a result, they were intensely conscious of the contribution of secrecy to individual freedom.[13] Many of them published their books anonymously and engaged in covert activities which were not welcomed by wielders of power. They put a special premium on "privacy," therefore. But they valued privacy so highly because of the illiberal nature of their contemporary regimes, not because they wanted private life to hyperinflate and totally eclipse the public realm.

13 / Economic Man?

Lasch's disdain for "the acquisitive individualism fostered by liberalism" is not purely personal. Schmitt too blames liberalism for a "general economization of spiritual life." In the same spirit, Strauss associates liberalism with "the emancipation of acquisitiveness." In MacIntyre's view, "*pleonexia*, a vice in the Aristotelian scheme, is now the driving force of modern productive work." For Sheldon Wolin, "most liberals followed the view that man affirmed his existence through economic activity." It seems that the primary concern of liberal reformers was to assure freedom for economic exchange or to liberate economic egoism. R. H. Tawney even accused liberals of supporting religious toleration primarily because it was good for trade. The abolition of the usury taboo symbolized the tragic loss of the wholesome ethical inhibitions that had so long restrained the possessive individual. Harold Laski, a disciple of Tawney, defined liberalism as "the creed of the Pharisee." He charged this creed with unleashing "an appetite for acquisition which recognized no boundaries to its claims," and argued (after Tawney) that "tolerance came because intolerance interfered with access to wealth," because "a persecuting state meant loss of business."[1] Liberal man is a base economic animal, or perhaps a machine.

To the claim that acquisitiveness is a modern innovation, Max Weber retorted with admirable succinctness: "the impulse to acquisition . . . has been common to all sorts and conditions of men at all times." (Rather than greed, specific to commercial society is the rationalization of greed, the tempering of limitless and pointless hoarding through a methodical style of life, the constraining of hot-headed acquistiveness by cool calculation.) Joseph Schumpeter nicely reinforces Weber's commonsensical point: "pre-capitalist man is in fact no less 'grabbing' than capitalist man. Peasant serfs for instance or warrior lords assert their self-interest with a brutal energy all their own." Selfishness was not invented by liberals; and it is not unique to "modern" societies. The ban on usury, far from expressing an altruistic morality of self-restraint, had itself been an instrument of greed, allowing princes to confiscate the wealth of Jews whenever it proved convenient.[2] But antiliberal diatribes against *homo œconomicus* have other flaws.

Liberalism Is Not Economism

The distinction between economic goals (such as monetary profit) and economic or calculative thinking (which may serve noneconomic goals) does not always register clearly with antiliberal writers. Their blanket charges of liberal economism, therefore, reflect a rather underdeveloped conceptual framework. Analytical confusion is reinforced by a paucity of historical evidence. As the passages cited above indicate, those who blame liberalism for apotheosizing material self-interest are grand reductionists. The liberal desire for religious and intellectual freedoms, they assert, was a mere by-product of the scramble for material prosperity. It is a claim without support. Liberty of discussion and liberty of worship seem worthwhile for other reasons. It is not plausible to assume that freedom of speech and the right to seek one's own salvation in one's own way were valued exclusively, or even primarily, as a means for maximizing wealth. The same reasoning applies, to even greater effect, to the right not to have one's body mutilated by sadistic agents of the state.

While they wished to limit the confiscatory powers of government, both Milton and Spinoza had almost as many contemptuous things to say about "moneying men" as Tawney. Locke, too, wrote derogatorily about "covetousness" and "evil Concupiscence." Even Smith accused merchants of conspiring basely against the public. Indeed, none of the early liberals were morally inspired by merchants who busied themselves exclusively with making a profit, never thinking of religion or politics or science or literature or history. Milton explicitly gave priority not to economic freedom, but to "the liberty to know, to utter, and to argue freely, according to conscience." This freedom should be cherished, he wrote, "above all liberties." Spinoza similarly subordinated economic liberty to the right of individuals "to employ their reason unshackled."[3] Freedom of conscience and discussion and the right to protection against public and private violence are among the core values of liberalism. These values developed independently from, and were more fundamental than, liberty of commerce. Economic man was less essential, for the classical liberals, than religious man or scientific man or man in the grip of physical fear. It is not surprising, therefore, that liberal societies have seldom treated liberty of contract as sacred or unrestrictable, while they have usually regarded, say, religious freedom and the right of the accused to respond in open court to criminal charges in precisely this way.

A reductionist approach to liberalism is inadequate. The liberal campaign against arbitrary arrest, preventive detention, and savage punishments cannot be reduced to a bourgeois strategy for maximizing profits.[4] The attempt to extricate science from ecclesiastical superintendency was not simply an expression of the spirit of capitalism. For Milton and Mill, free and uninhibited public debate came first. For Spinoza, freedom from fear and the development of rational faculties came first. For Locke, toleration, free inquiry, the right of resistance came first. (The unlimited accumulation of knowledge was considerably more important to Locke than the unlimited accumulation of property.)[5] For Montesquieu, legal protections for vulnerable defendants came first. For Kant, "rational self-esteem" was infinitely more valuable than "mere well-being."[6]

This is not to deny that classical liberals tended to have a welcoming attitude toward commercial society. Spinoza and Milton certainly did not consider commerce the worst thing one person could do to another. (Anyone who views commerce this way seriously underestimates mankind's capacity for cruelty.) Smith did not object to trade itself, but only to conspiracies between landowners and merchants. In fact, all classical liberals accepted and indeed endorsed commercialism. There is nothing easier, therefore, than to assemble a line-up of passages in which liberals define the main purpose of government as the protection of property. Locke, for instance, wrote that "Government has no other end but the preservation of Property."[7] Such overcited pronouncements, however, must be understood in context.

To assert that the central aim of government is the protection of property, first of all, is to deny that the central aim of government is to save souls. To make property essential is to help secularize politics and disentangle authority and obedience from religious life. Classical liberals, furthermore, closely associated private property with liberty, both personal and political. Locke notoriously used the word *property* to refer to the lives and liberties of individuals as well as their estates. Human beings have "property" in their own persons. Slaves, by contrast, are deprived of property in themselves and of ordinary property as well. Property might even be defined, politically, as that which tyrants seize without consent. Governments that can confiscate an individual's property at whim are the "Masters, or Arbitrary Disposers of the Lives, Liberties, or Fortunes of the People." If a government whose *sole* purpose is to protect property begins to confiscate and destroy property, subjects need no further reason to resist and rebel. Confiscatory rulers "put themselves into a state of War with the People, who are thereupon absolved from any farther Obedience."[8]

For liberals, then, the political resonance of private property seemed obvious. "No taxation without representation" suggests that the dependence of government on the consent of ordinary citizens is closely associated with private ownership. A legally entrenched property system helps decentralize power. Political opposition is feasible only when some resources remain outside the control of the masters and agents of the state. And so forth.

When they identified the sole purpose of government with the protection of property in the narrow sense, liberals were speaking strategically and hyperbolically. In other passages in the same works they identified the main aims of government in quite different, and less materialistic, ways: personal independence, impartial justice, physical security, the prevention of violence and civil war, the peaceful settlement of controversies, civilized coexistence and cooperation, and the intelligent pursuit of collective well-being. Spinoza expressed what became the liberal consensus when he wrote that "the true end of government is liberty." Locke himself was quite expansive on this question, asserting simply that "the end of Government is the good of Mankind."[9]

The Perennial Problem of Famine

The good of mankind, admittedly, can best be secured by a regulated system of private property where individuals can trade with each other on terms to which they all agree. Classical liberals believed this because they took seriously the intractable problems of scarcity, penury, and starvation. The best way to ensure adequate means of subsistence for all is not state ownership but the widest possible diffusion of private property. Insight into the advantages of individual over common ownership was by no means novel. (Private property was not invented by liberals.) As Aristotle himself had written: "that which is common to the greatest number has the least care bestowed upon it."[10] But liberals were the first to transform this principle into a comprehensive justification for private property. The best method for maintaining and improving the things of this world is to assign property rights to individuals who will suffer directly from dilapidation and who will just as directly benefit from efforts made at upkeep and improvement. The advantages of this arrangement accrue to all, not merely to the owners.

If we focus on Locke's individualistic theory of appropriation, we risk missing his real justification for private property—a justification which explicitly invokes a common good, that is, the elimination of immemorial wretchedness and poverty. The point is that without private property individuals will have little incentive to labor. And without labor we would *all* be eating acorns instead of bread, wearing leaves instead of cloth. Ultimately, private property is justified for one crucial reason: it helps create a surplus in "the provisions serving to the support of humane life." Ten acres in Devonshire, where property is assigned to individuals, produce more than 1,000 acres of American bush, where private ownership is unknown. As a natural result, the clothes, food, and housing of "a day Laborer in England" are superior to those of a tribal chieftain in a primitive society. Private ownership lowers the price of grain (relative to wages) and therefore "does not lessen but increase the common stock of mankind." It is explicitly justified, therefore, by reference to the common good. If citizens are not energized by the hope of bettering their condition, they will be "useless to the public," according to Hume. Smith, too, constructed his entire theory on this Lockean basis: only a free economy based upon private property will provide affordable food prices "to the lowest ranks of the people."[11]

As an antiliberal, MacIntyre does not see it this way. He blames Hume, for instance, for having repudiated the traditional natural-law teaching, once nobly defended by Thomas Aquinas, that theft is permitted in case of dire necessity. Hume rejected the Thomistic stance, we are told, because he did not care about either poverty or the poor. As he abandoned immemorial taboos against excessive inequalities of wealth, Hume was (except for some casual remarks about charity) callously turning his back on starving children. But this is an inaccurate picture of the liberal defense of private ownership. Hume accepted inequality of property for the same reasons that Locke and Smith did—because it was an inevitable byproduct of the quest for prosperity. After considering the conditions for a productive agricultural economy, he concluded that a free market in grain could better satisfy the needs of the poor than any other system. (To accept inequality of property is not to deny the claims of the starving; Hume's *Enquiries*, in fact, contain one of the clearest eighteenth-century restatements of the traditional doctrine that all property rights lapse in cases of dire necessity.[12])

Hume, moreover, did not rely on a labor theory of *initial* appropriation. He did not assume, with Locke, that property arose when labor was mixed with things previously unowned. He and other eighteenth-century liberals recognized, with varying degrees of candor, that most initial appropriations were acts of seizure and were thus impossible to justify. (Current distributions are psychologically acceptable only because initial seizures are concealed by the mists of time.) Later liberals were more forthright than Locke had been about this, stating simply that property is a private monopoly defended by today's government for public purposes.[13] (For liberals property is an institutional arrangement, not a material object. It requires the public observance of enforceable legal rules.) Ultimately, liberals justified private ownership, protected by law, as a *strategy* for defeating immemorial hunger by creating surpluses that could be stored up in anticipation of recurrent famines. They were happy to allow Dutch merchants to enrich themselves by transporting Baltic grain surpluses to Southern Europe where harvests were meager. The threat of mass starvation led them to repudiate the archaic principle that no one should make a profit from the distress of others. They therefore acknowledged, in an unprecedented way, the social utility of "economic man." They did not, however, grant the bargain-hunter and profit-seeker moral primacy of any kind.

Commercialism as a Means, Not an End-in-Itself

Liberals never favored a universalization of market relations. They did not apotheosize pecuniary gain or advocate a society in which everything might be bought and sold. They certainly did not think that freedom of religion or freedom of speech—not to mention freedom of contract—could be traded away. Earlier, kings could sell political rights to the nobility in exchange for money or service. Liberals did not conceive of either citizenship or office in this privatistic way, but rather as potentially universal rights, certainly not as transferable pieces of private property.[14] (Eventually all liberal societies forbade the buying and selling of offices and votes.[15]) The "rise of economic man," in other words, was accompanied by the strengthening of rules that explicitly excluded economic transactions in some important instances. Not only votes and public office, but also exemptions from military service and favorable verdicts in civil and criminal trials were withdrawn from market exchange. Sparsely populated electoral districts (rotten boroughs) could no longer be "owned." Neither could other human beings.[16] Thus liberalism encouraged exchange relations in some areas and discouraged them in others.

Antiliberals endlessly berate their enemies for "instrumental thinking."[17] But they do not clearly explain the evil of producing better goods at a lower cost. Even more strikingly, they seldom mention liberalism's obviously instrumental attitude toward market relations and economic growth. By contrast with religious liberty or the rights of criminal defendants, as mentioned, economic rights were infrequently if ever considered sacred. They were embraced for their results, social and cultural as well as economic. According to Kant, for example, the spread of commercialism would make war obsolete. Montesquieu agreed that "peace is the natural effect of trade" and added that "commerce cures destructive prejudices." Trade teaches people tolerance. It makes people understand that agreement about rules for peaceful collaboration is compatible with disagreement about the meaning of life. A life of business also devalues wild impulsiveness, instils habits of foresight and methodical calculation, and undermines the values (not to mention the economic interests) of the aristocracy. Because it brings citizens into everyday contact with foreigners, commerce also explodes parochialism and promotes an understanding of diversity: "the history of commerce is the history of the communication of people."[18]

Spinoza provides an excellent illustration of the completely instrumental attitude liberals displayed toward commercialism. He poured scorn on "the avaricious. . . who think supreme salvation consists in filling their stomachs and gloating over their money-bags." At the same time he argued that economic freedom increases the stability and power of a regime:

> The city of Amsterdam reaps the fruit of this freedom in its own great prosperity and in the admiration of all other people. For in this most flourishing state, and most splendid city, men of every nation and religion live together in the greatest harmony, and ask no questions before trusting their goods to a fellow citizen, save whether he be rich or poor, and whether he generally acts honestly or the reverse. His religion and sect is considered of no importance.

Voltaire echoed and popularized Spinoza's argument in a famous passage of his *Philosophical Letters:* "enter the Exchange of London, that place more respectable than many a court, and you will see there agents from all nations assembled for the utility of mankind. There the Jew, the Mohammedan, and the Christian deal with one another as if they were of the same religion, and give the name of infidel only to those who go bankrupt."[19]

The sociological insight underlying these two passages is marvelously simple. In sect-riven societies, social cooperation requires an element of mutual indifference. A climate of unbridled religious hatred makes people's ability to cooperate or learn from one another ruinously small. According to Tawney, liberals advocated religious toleration because it was good for trade. But the above passages suggest the contrary claim: liberals supported free trade because it helped foster the peaceful coexistence of rival sects. (Liberals could never have written that toleration is good for trade, incidentally, if they had not *already* decided, on independent grounds, that society can be held together without shared religious beliefs.[20])

Liberals thus valued commerce not only because it lowered the relative price of subsistence goods for the poor, but also because it was a social coolant. Commerce de-eroticizes social bonds. It provides an essential precondition for the exercise of "civic virtue" in multidenominational and multiethnic societies. Arm's-length transactions in the marketplace give members of hostile groupings an apprenticeship in coexistence, preparing the ground for cooperation of a noneconomic sort, including cooperation in political self-rule.

It is in this context that Hume rebuffed the moralistic or "republican" claim that private activity necessarily saps the public will and that self-interest necessarily dissolves civic virtue: "the lower house is the support of our popular government; and all the world acknowledges, that it owed its chief influence and consideration to the increase of commerce, which threw such a balance of property into the hands of the Commons." It is utterly "inconsistent," Hume therefore concludes, to blame commerce "as a bane of liberty and public spirit."[21] Popular government is possible, under modern conditions, only in a commercial society. One important reason is that political dissent is unsustainable without the general security of private property. How much commerce can do for freedom, by shattering monopolies and lowering the relative price of subsistence goods, is also the main theme of the *Wealth of Nations*.

Man as a Pleasure-Pain Machine

The charge of liberal economism is often coupled with the claim that liberalism gave government "the commission to increase pleasure and decrease pain." To indict liberalism for having debased mankind, recent antiliberals (echoing Hannah Arendt) frequently contrast the liberal concern for "mere life" with the Aristotelian concern for "the good life."[22] They assert that liberalism lowered the goals to be pursued by human beings. Base-minded theorists lured citizens into turning away from noble aspirations such as honor and focusing instead on ignoble concerns such as survival and physical comfort.[23] In this way, liberals demeaned their fellow men—perhaps reduced them to the moral status of animals.

This claim may fit Bentham, at least superficially. But it does not apply to most classical liberals. It does not describe Spinoza, who said that liberty was the "true end" of government and that human life was "defined not by mere circulation of the blood, and other qualities common to all animals, but above all by reason, the true excellence and life of the mind." As for Kantian morality, it is both modern and liberal, but it hardly reduces man to a pleasure-pain machine. (Kant repeatedly insisted that man "is *more than a machine*."[24]) There is also the question of what "high values" have been replaced by low ones? Could they be the values of the battlefield or of the Spartan mother who weeps when her sons return from the wars alive? From a comparative perspective, is the desire to live—and for our children to live—really "low"?

The state-society distinction, characteristic of liberal thought, pro-vides a telling rejoinder to complaints about liberalism's degrading of human aspirations. Liberal theorists may have refused to romanticize or consecrate the goals of the state, but that does not imply that they debased the aims of society as a whole. The political goals of peace, security, welfare, and equitable justice were the preconditions for the pursuit of other goals in various nonpolitical but nevertheless social domains. Liberals challenged the old idea that service to the state, especially military service, was the core of moral duty. Self-realization and responsibility toward others, they argued, can also be carried out in a variety of nonpolitical domains. On the basis of a politically achieved order, individuals and subgroups can pursue a number of loftier aims: knowledge, bliss, friendship, salvation, oneness with na-ture, or personal development. Antiliberals, in fact, trip over their own feet when they *both* accuse liberals of having transformed the state into a mere instrument of private parties *and* adduce the lower goals of the state as evidence that liberals have lowered the goals of individuals. Liberal citizens have an instrumental relation toward the state; thus, when they lowered the goals of politics, they did not simultaneously lower the goals of human life.

Antiliberals speak glowingly about willingness to die for one's coun-try. Solzhenitsyn is exemplary in this respect, explicitly berating liber-alism in the name of martial virtue: "to defend oneself, one must also be ready to die; there is little such readiness in a society raised in the cult of material well-being."[25] Historically, it is true, a martial ethos has been the most effective way to discipline citizens and lead them "up" from individualism. Face-to-face confrontations with a deadly enemy, as Schmitt appreciated, help reinforce communal bonds. The practicalities, not to mention the romance, of camaraderie-under-fire forces individuals to extend their interests beyond the boundaries of their skins. This is the context in which MacIntyre, too, mentions "the honorable resort to war."[26] But the desire to die for one's group has always been subordinate to the desire to kill for one's group. Killing turns out to be a more sportive way to soar above mere life than being killed.

Once again, it is useful to situate liberal claims in their historical setting. The view that Bentham expresses in an exaggerated and doc-trinaire fashion can also be explained in a much more practical way. Most liberals who identified good and bad with bodily pleasure and pain were hoping to channel intellectual energies away from sterile theological disputes and toward discovering medical and economic responses to the unrelenting hardships of famine and plague. They aimed to relieve "the many wretches that are at every instant labouring under all sorts of calamities, in the languor of poverty, in the agony of disease, in the horrors of death." Moreover, they wished to draw attention to how, throughout history, the *voluptés* of the few were purchased by the ordeals of the many. They were also engaged in two polemics, one antimilitaristic, the other antireligious. They attacked both glory and asceticism, the shin-guard ethics of the battlefield and the hair-shirt ethics of the monastery. Montesquieu's and Kant's shared devotion to "peace," for example, was based on their shared hostility to war. Smith argued that war-inclined governments impoverish nations. (Why should we kill our customers?) Similarly, liberal devotion to physical health was aimed against Christian abstemiousness, self-mortification, and single-mindedness about otherworldly salvation. Both Smith and Mill ironized about the "melancholy and gloomy humour," the "pinched and hidebound" character typical of religious fanatics who meanly schemed to repress popular entertainments. In Calvinist Scotland, Smith expressly denounced "those absurd and hypocritical austerities which fanatics inculcate and pretend to practice."[27]

Liberals recognized that experiences of pleasure and pain often depend on opinion.[28] They were not physicalists in a crude sense, not even Bentham. They certainly knew, for instance, that human beings feel joy at the death of their enemies and agony at the death of their friends—"there being pleasure and pain of the Mind, as well as the Body."[29] Delights and miseries are not strictly physical in origin. Without either reducing man to a machine or glorifying hedonistic self-gratification, liberals nevertheless consistently stressed physical pleasure and pain. They did so to overcome the denigration of ordinary life in both clerical and aristocratic moral codes.

A Naive View of Preferences

Classical liberals were not given to a reductionist psychology meant to encourage the mindless pursuit of physical pleasure. The notion that they had no idea of the social processes through which individual preferences are shaped and reshaped is also mistaken.[30] Liberalism is not economistic if economism entails treating preferences as given without examining their origins and transformation. Since the French Revolution, it is true, liberals have tended to distrust self-appointed moral legislators bent on "improving" citizens against their will. A politics aimed at transforming souls is not always benign.[31] But the charge of liberal naivete about the way desire is molded by culture and upbringing is without foundation. For one thing, all classical liberals were profoundly affected by the ongoing exploration of the globe. They were fascinated by "the itineraries of travellers" and the discovery of new peoples.[32] Their interest in pre-Christian antiquity, too, sharpened their awareness of cultural variability. They did not think governments should impose an orthodox conception of happiness on its citizens, but they certainly knew that ideas of happiness evolved, decayed, and disappeared.

Locke wrote extensively about "adopted desires" and "acquired habits."[33] Montesquieu described how English laws shape manners and character, how savage penalties barbarize citizens, how Dutch frugality differs from Spartan frugality, and so forth. He even defined man as "that flexible creature, conforming in society to the thoughts and impressions of others."[34] Aware that preferences result from social conditioning, he along with other liberals drew a contrast between "rude" and "polished" nations. Their emphasis on the cordializing and pacifying effects of commerce derives from the same assumption. The liberal virtues extolled by Kant, to pick another example, are obviously acquired by training, not by birth or religious inspiration. Nor does the socially uninfluenced individual make an appearance in *The Wealth of Nations.* Instead, Smith is consistently concerned with the social causes of the surprising emergence of different tastes (especially the taste for useless luxury goods) and different types of personality. A philosopher differs from a street porter chiefly because he was socialized in a different milieu. Having grown up in a bustling environment, a city dweller has a different "temper and disposition" from those raised to bovine drowsiness in the countryside. One of Europe's main contributions to the prosperity of the colonies was the moral character it bequeathed to the colonists.[35]

As these representative claims suggest, liberals were acutely conscious of elementary processes of character formation and preference transformation. Admittedly, they did not think the liberal state should use its coercive powers to remodel human nature according to some inspiring ideal or to impose an orthodox view of salvation. But they agreed that political authorities should discourage the brutishness of human aspirations and encourage the cultivation of the basic liberal virtues, such as self-control and a willingness to listen to others. They favored commercialism, among other reasons, because they thought it would contribute to this end.

14 / The Selfishness
of Rights?

According to MacIntyre, "natural or human rights are fictions," and "every attempt to give good reasons for believing that there *are* such rights has failed." Indeed, "belief in them is one with belief in unicorns and witches." Individual rights, even when they are not conceived as natural or inborn, represent a woeful moral "degeneration." "The arrival upon the social scene of conceptions of rights, attaching to and exercised by individuals, as a fundamental moral quasilegal concept . . . always signals some measure of loss or repudiation of some previous social solidarity."[1] Thus while liberals deplore our failure to enforce rights equitably—such as the voting rights of black Americans—communitarians and other antiliberals argue that we should not be attending to rights at all. In their opinion, these "fictions" are designed only to foster untrammeled egoism.

Antiliberals draw this conclusion because they identify rights primarily with property rights and freedom of contract, that is, with economic self-interest, not with intellectual, religious, or political freedoms. They uniformly interpret the struggle for rights as a scramble for benefits, as if self-interest was the principal motive behind, say, the battle to extend legal fairness and the franchise to persecuted minorities or the effort to redeem the rights of American slaves and former slaves. Antiliberals also assume that liberal rights uniformly protect individuals *from* the state, not noticing that many of them—for instance, the right to litigate or the right to a publicly financed education—give citizens *access to* state institutions. (According to some critics, classical liberals thought naively that "rights" were abstract properties that belonged to individuals and thereby ignored the institutional preconditions for rights. This accusation would seem less plausible, presumably, if more attention were paid to the right to a jury trial or the right to vote.) Finally, antiliberals pretend that liberal rights are designed to create an inviolable zone or private sphere—something like a medieval manor—into which governmental authorities dare not intrude. But this conception, too, is incorrect. The classical liberals consistently argued that individuals can appeal to the law *wherever* they find themselves victimized by force or fraud—be this a private home, club, firm, university, or even a church.[2]

Rights Protect Channels of Social Communication

Antiliberals do not merely dismiss the protection of rights as a bourgeois scam. They belittle the exercise of rights by contrasting it to three allegedly superior alternatives: involvement with fellow citizens, the exercise of virtues and capacities, and the performance of duties. Rights are isolating, sacrifice self-development to self-protection, and elevate selfish concerns above social obligations. Upon examination, all three of these stylized contrasts turn out to be unconvincing.

Liberal rights are *not* inherently asocial or atomistic, though for political reasons they were sometimes presented as "natural" or "presocial." Kings, popes, and other potentates frequently invoked the divine origins of their authority. Countersacralization was a plausible response. Locke focused on the "presocial" origins of property in order to preempt the presocial credentials of confiscation-prone divine right rulers: one *noli me tangere* ideology deserved and provoked another. To this extent, his position was essentially wedded to the theological premises of seventeenth-century political debate.[3]

Liberal rights, moreover, are facilitative. They make possible all kinds of social relations. Freedom of contract makes possible complex forms of cooperation over time. Freedom of association obviously protects group activities. The same can be said about freedom of religion. Locke explicitly described religious toleration as guaranteeing a right to "perform such other things in religion as cannot be done by each private man apart." Similarly, "freedom of debating" keeps open a fragile channel of communication by means of which individuals can collaborate with, and learn from, each other. So does freedom of the press. Conversely, allowing the police to abuse the citizenry at will is not likely to maximize communal involvement. In fact, the more tyrannical the autocracy, the more "atomized" social life becomes, as twentieth-century communist societies have grimly shown. In general, liberals valued individual rights (including property rights) as *preconditions* for all manner of social cooperation. Antiliberals nevertheless continue to assert that rights destroy community and drive citizens into mean-spirited isolation.[4]

Rights Protect the Exercise of Virtues and Capacities

Are liberal rights truly antithetical to the exercise of virtue and the realization of valuable human potentials?[5] This, too, is a lopsided accusation. For one thing, neither preliberal nor nonliberal regimes have ever placed much emphasis on the development of personality. From a comparative perspective, however, liberalism looks exceptionally congenial to individual creativity and self-realization. Historical reasons for special disappointment with liberalism on this ground are therefore scant. While liberals did not believe that an orthodox form of moral perfection should be imposed coercively on all citizens by state power, they did defend rights as a means for encouraging the development of a diversity of talents among mutual tolerant individuals. They were not particularly interested in, or enthusiastic about, *martial* virtues because they considered war a massive waste of a multiplicity of superior, nonmartial capacities.[6] A demilitarized conception of virtue or human potential was obviously central to their thought. Even the extension of the concept of "property" to individuals' talents suggests a greater sensitivity to human capacities than liberalism's detractors have been willing to admit.

Milton eventually became a censor. But in *Areopagitica*, at least, he advocated freedom of the press because it would allow individuals to spread their wings and join the public fray: "I cannot praise a fugitive and cloister'd virtue." The need to develop and exercise one's rational faculties was also one of Locke's leading ideas. All liberals laid special emphasis on education as a necessary condition for the reasonable use of freedom; this shows how important the development of human faculties has consistently been to liberal thought. According to Spinoza, too, the liberal state must protect the rights of individuals "to enable them to develope their minds and bodies in security." Private rights are productive, therefore, not merely protective: they make possible the awakening and improvement of otherwise quiescent potentials. Obligatory, single-minded, and full-time political involvement, on the other hand, would condemn many important human capacities to wither.[7]

In the *Wealth of Nations* Smith analyzes both the development and the thwarting of latent human capacities ("skill, dexterity, and judgment") under conditions of the division of labor. But the best examples of liberal concern for "the development of innate capacities" are Kant and Mill. Mill's case for "the cultivation of individuality" is well known. And Kant, too, wanted all "natural capacities . . . to be developed completely." The state should not forcibly impose self-development on adults, but it should encourage self-development and make it possible. There was nothing asocial about Kant's conception of self-realization: "the development of all natural capacities—can be fulfilled for mankind only in society." While not sociologically naive, Kant's theory *was* explicitly anticommunitarian. He stiffly rejected "an Arcadian, pastoral existence of perfect concord . . . and mutual love" because in such a sleepy society "all human talents would remain hidden for ever in a dormant state." The most favorable condition for the development of human capacities is social competitiveness hedged in by rules of fair play and justice. (True, Kant's enthusiasm for the exercise of human capacities and the realization of human potentials was also tempered by a dose of realism. He stressed unromantically that trade-offs will always be necessary: life is lamentably brief, and an individual can develop one capacity only by forgoing the development of another.[8])

Liberal Virtues

As is well known, Kant also said that even a population of devils could exist cooperatively under a liberal constitution. Less theatrically, Madison argued that institutional devices, such as checks and balances, can supply "the defect of better motives" among citizens and officials. His description does not necessarily suggest that liberals were typically indifferent to "virtue". Indeed, Madison believed that a liberal-republican regime requires some degree of "virtue."[9] Kant himself wrote a *Tugendlehre*. Liberals defended humanitarian and civilian virtues in contrast to harsh and martial ones. They consistently valued moral virtues such as reasonableness, independence, reluctance to resort to violence, tolerance for diversity, a refusal to humiliate others publicly, and a willingness to listen to the other side in an argument. A constitutional government is the only political framework in which these liberal virtues are likely to flourish.

Liberal politics not only fosters such virtues, it also presupposes them. Judges and other public officials in a liberal democracy, for one thing, are required to be honest and fair.[10] Liberals simply recognized that good motivations do not always lead to good outcomes, and bad motives do not inevitably produce bad ones. (This is the realistic assumption behind the somewhat doctrinal theory of an "invisible hand.") If "virtue" means a proclivity to subordinate private advantage to the common good, then virtue is not a wholly trustworthy guide, since different conceptions of the common good may violently conflict. As realists, moreover, classical liberals favored institutions that might survive some ups and downs in the amount of virtue citizens and office-holders bring to public life. The unreliability of virtue does not justify a lawless or harsh government, of course. On the contrary, it requires even more dependable constitutional restraints. Firm and fair procedures are the wisest precaution against a periodic scarcity, but not total absence, of moral motivations.

Liberal Duties

Liberal rights are *not* opposed to duties or obligations. The importance of duties to liberal theory can be demonstrated without reference to the God-assigned duty "to preserve the rest of Mankind" mentioned by Locke. For it is a truism that the rights of some imply the duties of others. According to Smith, moreover, "a sense of duty" is "the only principle by which the bulk of mankind is capable of directing their actions." Admittedly, liberals believed that some duties, such as the duty to seek one's eternal salvation, should not be enforced by the state. And they tended to be unsympathetic toward traditional forms of dutifulness, especially obsequiousness toward social superiors.[11] But they were highly conscious of enforceable duties, including, first of all, the duty to abide by the law.

Liberals conceived the duty to obey the law as both instrumental and conditional, of course. Coercion was not viewed as a good-in-itself, nor was obedience required for its own sake, as appropriate to a corrupt and degraded human species. Liberals favored obedience to the law for the sake of the relatively civilized, just, cooperative, and free order it would help create. Rulers who grossly abused their powers, according to Locke, forfeited their right to popular allegiance. According to Spinoza, nonetheless, "duties toward one's country are the highest man can fulfill." And there is nothing particularly illiberal about this thought. Indeed, the right to participate in making the law—by electing representatives and engaging in public discussion conducted via a free press—implied the correlative duty to obey the law: "for no Government can have a right to obedience from a people who have not freely consented to it."[12] Put the other way, liberal citizens are obliged to follow the law because they, as a collectivity, imposed it on themselves and retain the power to change it.

The obligation to pay taxes, to serve in the armed forces in wartime, and to perform jury duty should obviously be mentioned here. Equally striking is the unanimity among liberals about the duty of parents to care for and educate their children. Consider Blackstone's complaint that "the municipal laws of most countries seem to be defective in this point, by not constraining the parent to bestow a proper education upon his children." And according to Mill, to cite a further illustration, the "duties of parents" in this regard should be strictly enforced: "the State should require and compel the education, up to a certain standard, of every human being who is born its citizen."[13]

Equality and the Abstractness of Rights

These examples demonstrate that social duty and political liberty are by no means incompatible. The second is no less concrete than the first, moreover, even though antiliberals from Maistre to MacIntyre routinely complain about the "abstractness" of rights. *Abstractness* means chiefly this: if I am concerned solely about your rights, I will treat you like a generic person, not as the warm and colorful individual you are, caught up in a tightly knit web of social relations. Sandel's discussion of the unrealism of the liberal conception of the person, what he calls the "unencumbered" self, is a classic example of this approach.[14]

Rights-based thinking allegedly drains significance from human experience. It relentlessly abstracts from the concrete relations that give meaning to life. Liberalism's abstractions wipe out the richness of historical reality: "the language of formal equality is a language of rights as abstract opportunities to enjoy certain advantages rather than a language of the concrete and actual experience of social life."[15] This is a thoroughly Maistrean thought. Since liberalism, because of its universalistic tendencies, is addicted to pale abstractions, to refute it nothing more is needed than greater realism or concreteness about human experience.

It remains obscure how various critics can jettison all abstractions and nonetheless embrace egalitarianism, as Unger, unlike Maistre, still wants to do. When Maistre attacked liberal abstractions he aimed to undermine what he considered the fiction of human equality. His position, while illiberal, was at least internally consistent. Later antiliberals, such as Unger, MacIntyre, and Sandel, renew the Maistrean assault on liberal abstractions even while they attempt to sustain, incoherently, a vaguely egalitarian stance. From a logical point of view, Maistre's position is superior to theirs.

The abstractness of rights is a necessary condition for the universality of rights. Unlike the privileges and immunities formerly monopolized by the landed nobility, liberal rights are extended uniformly to all citizens regardless of concrete differences. This universality of liberal rights is, in turn, based upon an ethical commitment to the equal treatment of persons, a commitment that the classical liberals viewed as a binding norm, not as a subjective preference. Despite his internal inconsistency, MacIntyre diagnoses liberal legalism correctly: the bearer of liberal rights is not born to a specific social rank. Rather than inhabiting a certain social role, he or she is the individual viewed in abstraction from political, economic, familial, and religious roles, as well as from race and gender. In a liberal social order, as a consequence, an individual who claims his or her rights simultaneously affirms the equal rights of all. If I have a right to freedom of conscience, for example, so does everyone else.[16]

Maistre claimed to have encountered Frenchmen, Italians, and Russians, but not "man" as such: "as far as *man* is concerned, I declare that I have never in my life met him; if he exists, he is unknown to me."[17] A liberal might well ask how Maistre could actually see a Frenchman. Was he not always faced with a Breton or a Bordelais? Are national characteristics more real than local, familial, or personal ones? And are they more visible than the traits common to all human beings?

Indeed, who performs the greater *abstraction?* A racist who, seized by a stereotype, ignores the unique traits of the individuals he meets? Or a cosmopolitan who, committed to universalist norms, ignores their national background? All perception is selective. Maistre's Russian is as much an abstraction as is Kant's human being. Who is more shallow? The conflict, in fact, is not between abstraction and concreteness (as antiliberals claim) but between two forms of abstraction. Framed in this way, the universalist perspective enshrined in the Rights of Man does not seem quite so inauthentic as some antiliberals would like us to believe.

Antiliberals ordinarily vilify rights as atomizing and alienating. But they sometimes lapse into the argument that liberal rights are a hollow promise, benefiting only the rich and relieving them of all specific obligation to care for the poor. There is an element of truth in this charge (which, in any case, is more Marxist than antiliberal in my sense), even though there is no evidence at all that the destruction of rights-based legal systems would improve the standard of living for most people. The valid insight buried in the antiliberal charge is that rights cannot be exercised in the absence of means. Freedom of the press, for example, is meaningless if the government controls all paper and ink supplies. In the same way the right to run for office is only selectively useful when political campaigning becomes exorbitantly expensive. If the costs of litigation mount too high, similarly, one casualty is likely to be equal access to the law.

There is nothing about this dependency of rights on resources that would have shocked the classical liberals, however. Paper rules are obviously futile unless society can produce the means necessary to put them into effect. That is just another reason that liberals so strongly favored a competitive market, organized around property rights and freedom of contract. They correctly anticipated that poverty would not be typical of liberal regimes. A dynamic economy produces resources without which noneconomic rights would necessarily be empty. (In my view, however, a productive economy alone—without any allocative decisions on the part of government—cannot ensure the reality of liberal rights for all.)

15 / Moral Skepticism?

In his communitarian phase Unger announced disapprovingly that "the teachings of liberalism must be, and always have been, uncompromisingly hostile to the classic idea of an objective good" and he singled out the monstrous "liberal view that choice is the province of arbitrary will." Liberals embrace the randomness of choice because they believe that facts are one thing, values another. This fact/value distinction, in turn, registers "the moral impotence of reason." Despite Kant's inept theorizing about impersonal reason, liberalism is committed to a "morality of desire," to the idea that desires are surds and cannot be justified or criticized. Liberal morality is therefore "inconsistent with the attribution of any normative significance to reason." To attribute normative significance to reason is to bring the liberal empire down. The task is urgent, for if we fail to bridge the gap between "is" and "ought," mankind will be hurled into the abyss of "the subjective view of value." Thus the enemies of liberalism must strive mightily "to throw off the shackles imposed by the liberal contrast of understanding and evaluation."[1] These sentiments of Unger's can be found in the works of MacIntyre and others as well.

How persuasive is this common argument? Liberals favored religious toleration and freedom of speech, it is true. They thought a society could be stabilized even without a "correct line" being imposed from above, even when its members quarrelled about theological questions and disagreed about the road to personal happiness. In certain contexts they distinguished between legality and morality. Within legally defined limits individuals should be allowed to pursue their own moral ideals, even if their neighbors consider these ideals repulsive or wrong. As a result of these beliefs and others, liberals are often inculpated for advancing "absolute moral skepticism." They are sometimes even described as nihilists of a particularly spineless sort.[2] From the

232

same hostile perspective they are blamed for dissolving the healthy forms of moral restraint that preliberal societies wisely imposed upon individuals. Having had a profound impact on liberalism's public reputation, these charges deserve a separate treatment.

The Limits of Liberal Individualism

The classical liberals were "individualists" in several senses of that elusive word. They did not think it a crime for people to enjoy life or to improve their lot. For nature's bounty to be beneficial, they argued, it had to benefit individuals, for there is no collective stomach. They favored private ownership because they were convinced that unambiguously assigned property rights enhance individual responsibility for the waste or misuse of scarce resources. They claimed that "the care of each man's salvation belongs only to himself." (This suggests that their individualism was not necessarily materialistic.) They wanted to decentralize the authority to define personal happiness, dispersing it into the hands of unsupervised individuals. They denied state authorities the right to suppress all moral differences. They believed that blameworthy individuals—not hated classes or groups such as Jews or aristocrats—should be punished. (This suggests that their individualism was not necessarily selfish.) From the standpoint of humanistic individualism Montesquieu argued that victorious soldiers may have a right to destroy a nation, but they certainly have no right to destroy the individuals who populate its territory. In a moderate government the life of even the least citizen is deemed important ("la tête du moindre citoyen est considerable").[3]

So liberals were individualists. But they were not hyperindividualists. The "fundamental principle" of liberalism was not, as Schmitt claimed, a "sphere of unlimited possibility for the individual."[4] It is true that Montesquieu, say, valued *independence*. He despised a society of grovelers where social underlings kiss boots and beg for favors. Nevertheless, he could also write that "the independence of individuals is the end aimed at by the laws of Poland, thence results the oppression of the whole." Totally unfettered individualism was a catastrophe, in other words. Like all classical liberals, Montesquieu stipulated the limits of individualism in simple language: political liberty does not consist in doing whatever one wants. Liberty is *not* defined as the satisfaction of one's desires, whatever they happen to be. On the contrary, from a liberal perspective some desires are legitimate and others are not. Thus "liberty can consist only in the power of doing what we ought to will, and in not being constrained to do what we ought not to will." The primacy of moral norms over subjective inclination could not be expressed more clearly. This is what Locke, too, meant when he distinguished between liberty and licence, or between proper and improper interests. It is why he argued that the very purpose of government was to restrain "the partiality" of human beings.[5] Filmer was simply wrong to define (and dismiss) liberal freedom as a form of whim, as behaving however one pleases. Liberals did not advocate licentious self-indulgence. The rule of law, after all, must be coercively enforced.

Political versus Moral Skepticism

Strauss noticed that liberals sometimes described value judgments as simply a matter of subjective preference, as if "conscience" were merely "opinion." But liberal remarks to this effect must be understood contextually. Rather than try to destroy all moral inhibitions, liberals sought to subvert the pretensions of priests, censors, and other moral authorities who retained coercive powers over the life of the mind. Before he joined their ranks, Milton cut censors down to size by emphasizing the subjectivity of the standards they applied: "any subject that was not to their palat, they either condemned in a prohibition or had it strait into the new Purgatory of an Index." Spinoza condemned the religious bigot for trying "to make the rest of the world live according to his own fancy." Locke wondered if it could be right for men "to impose their own inventions and interpretations on others as if they were of Divine authority." Mill, too, deliberately redescribed religious commitment as subjective preference on the grounds that most people will be unwilling to persecute others cruelly for a mere point of view. Horrible atrocities can be easily justified, on the other hand, by invoking supposedly objective values.[6] An egalitarian emphasis on the "subjectivity" of value judgments, in short, helped deflate moral imperialisms. It was not meant to destroy morality itself.

Most liberals valued freedom of thought not because they were moral skeptics but, on the contrary, because they saw such freedom as an indispensable condition for discovering the moral truth.[7] Antiliberals afraid of public disagreement, such as Schmitt or MacIntyre, are in some ways more skeptical about moral questions than were Locke and Mill. Liberal skepticism, moreover, to the extent that it existed, was more political than moral. (Soft antiliberals, at least, slide over this distinction because they ignore questions of justified legal compulsion.) Liberals assumed that public officials cannot always be trusted to codify and enforce the distinction between the moral and immoral—particularly when this distinction retains a strongly religious flavor. This mistrust is what led Beccaria not merely to distinguish between "divine justice" and "political justice," but also to demand that this distinction be put into practice.[8] Democratization, moreover, powerfully reinforces the liberal separation, for some purposes, of morality from legality. In representative regimes, the outvoted minority must accept the legal bindingness of the majority's decision, but (by the right of opposition) can continue to debate the goodness or rightness of legislative decisions and to protest morally.

From liberal distrust of office-holders and commitment to the rights of a legal opposition, however, we cannot logically conclude that liberals denied the reality or importance of a substantive distinction between the moral and the immoral, or the relevance of this difference to the foundation of an acceptable legal order. Liberals certainly cannot be accused of subjectivism when they argued, as they consistently did, that it is "unreasonable for Men to be Judges in their own Cases."[9] Asserting that slavery is a "vile and miserable" condition, the opening sentence of Locke's *Treatise* suggests a commitment to a nonarbitrary distinction between good and bad. Voltaire, for all his skepticism, claimed that "one morality," humanistic in content, is inscribed "in the hearts of all men."[10] That Kant's deontology and Mill's utilitarianism are incompatible with "absolute ethical skepticism," not to mention nihilism, should go without saying, though that is exactly what antiliberals commonly charge.

If moral subjectivism elevates naked preferences into an ultimate justification for behavior, then liberals have never been moral subjectivists. For the same reasons, it is a mistake to assume that liberalism involved a rash unleashing of base passions or total collapse of self-restraint. Nietzsche, who attacked liberalism from the opposite direction, provides a useful corrective here. He abhorred liberalism because of the egalitarian straitjacket it imposed upon the individual's will to power. He denounced liberalism as a crippling form of herd morality. It was a victory of the weak over the strong, the sick over the healthy.

It continued the Christian attempt to eliminate the master races from the earth. Why else would liberals have erected "restraint from mutual injury" into the fundamental moral principle of modern society?[11] In his typical anemic way, Locke had written that "no one ought to harm another in his Life, Health, Liberty, or Possessions." He claimed that the essential purpose of government is "to restrain the partiality and violence of Men." Liberalism, Nietzsche concluded with some justification, was a philosophy of self-renunciation. Every single liberal insisted that "the right of making war, which by nature subsisted in every individual, is *given up* by all private persons that enter into society, and is vested in the sovereign power."[12] From a Nietzschean perspective, then, liberals failed to relish the natural splendor and ferocity of the highest types. Liberals clung to "security," which noble pagans scorned.

Even those, such as Mill, who valued self-expression and self-development more than security, still asked strong members of society to suppress their yearning to inflict physical pain on people they despised. All individuals can and should seek personal advantage, but not in physically aggressive or murderous ways. Nietzsche adopts a different view. To do away with innocent butchery, to prevent the strong from stomping on the weak, is to stifle the spontaneous expression of human instinct. Life is essentially a matter of rapaciousness, violence, voluptuous cruelty.[13] Liberalism is thus a clever but craven repudiation of vital human instincts. It is a denial of natural hierarchy. It has led to the diminution and leveling of European man. Liberalism defangs. The disheartening result of its cultural triumph, for Nietzscheans, is that modern individuals no longer bite.

Ultimately, Nietzsche's representation of liberal self-crippling is no more satisfying intellectually than the idea of liberal restraintlessness propagated by conservative-minded antiliberals. But it does draw attention usefully to the restrictive, or even anti-individualistic, element within liberalism itself. The myth of the state of nature is a monument to the liberal belief in self-restraint. To live civilly, each individual has to surrender his primordial "Right to . . . be Executioner of the Law of Nature." The crucial difference between the state of nature and civil society is that members of society are sometimes politically coerced to do what they do not want to do. The compact would be meaningless if individuals were bound in society only to do what they personally wanted or, at a given moment, judged right. As Kant put it, individuals must resign their "barbarous freedom" in order to attain tranquility and security in a legal-constitutional state.[14] Paradoxically, the ideal of moral autonomy can be realized politically only if individuals give up anarchical habits of self-help. Self-legislation does not imply an automatic acquiescence in naked preferences. Human beings can begin to think for themselves, for example, only after they stop avenging or pre-empting injuries by themselves.

Upending the traditional claims of conservative antiliberals, Nietzsche inadvertently demonstrates that self-restraint is fundamental to both liberal theory and liberal society. (This is the same unintended lesson, of course, that we culled from Unger's *Politics*, a book of Nietzschean inspiration.) Indeed, the existence of liberal self-restraint is, or should have been, obvious. Liberal citizens are not allowed to persecute weak groups on religious grounds, print libelous stories about each other, or shout "fire" in a crowded theater. Those who lose elections must accept decisions they do not like and, above all, must refrain from violence. Individuals cannot decide to disobey a law simply because they find it stupid or unwise. Finally, social order is possible despite conflicting ideas of happiness because all groups practice forbearance. (In a comparative, and still Nietzschean, vein, we should recall that preliberal societies were not exactly images of self-restraint; even today, in nonliberal societies, unhinged male aggression, on a massive scale, may frequently be observed.)

The Self-Exemption Taboo

Respecting the equal right of others to be different and to seek the moral truth in their own idiosyncratic ways requires enormous self-control. Indeed, the many limitations placed upon liberal citizens by the liberal state cannot be overlooked. Yet antiliberals such as MacIntyre and Strauss seem to deny the existence of liberal self-restraint. Under the influence of liberalism, Strauss argues, "the satisfaction of wants is . . . no longer limited by the demands of the good life but becomes aimless."[15] From the assumption that subjective preferences are the ultimate touchstone of value, MacIntyre tells us, liberals concluded that all human desires were of equal worth.[16] This last point, in fact, is the decisive one. MacIntyre reproduces here a fundamental thesis of one antiliberal school. Liberals, he writes, promulgated the idea that "the desires of every individual are equally to be taken into account in deciding what is right to do." The crucial word is "equally." We are indebted to MacIntyre for being so forthright. What he objects to, in this case, is not the subjectivity of values, but the moral equality of human beings. This is even more true of Strauss.[17]

For once, the accusation sticks. Liberals have always subscribed to "general and equal laws." The state must equitably and coercively apply a single system of law to all citizens. The "fair and impartial execution of the laws" is incompatible with laissez-faire and requires that the liberal state provide important resources that enable private citizens to exercise their rights. One obvious example is publicly financed education. Another is an easily accessible legal system. For example, Blackstone boasts, in a liberal spirit, that "the king's courts are open for all persons to receive justice according to the laws of the land."[18] Equal access to the law, provided by the state, may be the British tradition. It has been preserved, admired, and imitated abroad because it is morally right.

Underlying liberal legalism, in fact, is not local custom, but a substantive norm of fairness. All classical liberals acknowledge that the tenet of equality before the law is an uncompromisable moral principle. They make room for conflicting personal ideals (the good), but they insist on a single, enforceable social norm (the right).[19] It is quite unreasonable, therefore, to describe them, in the antiliberal manner, as radical subjectivists or "absolute moral skeptics." Like most liberal works, Locke's *Two Treatises* can be read as a manifesto against partiality. From a purely self-interested standpoint, it would be preferable to benefit from the self-restraint of others while enjoying one's own lack of self-restraint. "If it were possible," writes Beccaria, every one of us would prefer that the compacts binding others did not bind us; every man tends to make himself the center of his whole world."[20] But that self-centered or hyperindividualistic arrangement is explicitly ruled out by the strong norm at the heart of liberal morality: *the self-exemption prohibition.* Here lies the ethical center of liberalism: each citizen must play by rules that apply equally to all. There is nothing anarchistic or nihilistic or selfish or atomistic or wantonly permissive about this principle of right. Locke articulates liberal universalism or the norm of impartiality in the simplest terms: "no man in civil society can be exempted from the laws of it." This includes, of course, the king. Not allowing self-exemption is a norm of reason in this sense: no individual can provide a reason why *he* should be exempted from general laws that could not, with equal plausibility be invoked by any other individual.[21] That may be what Locke meant when he wrote that *"Reason must be our last Judge and Guide in every Thing."*[22] The political consequence is that "legislators "are to govern by promulgated establish'd Laws, not to be varied in particular Cases." Morally required is "*one Rule* for Rich and Poor, for the Favorite at Court and the Country Man at Plough."[23]

Montesquieu formulated the self-exemption prohibition as follows: "if a citizen could do what [the laws] forbid, he would no longer be possessed of liberty, because all his fellow-citizens would have the same power." This is a moral argument, not an empirical prediction. It means this: a citizen who violates the law has *no justification* for the claim that others should obey the law. A liberal legal system, according to Blackstone, demands "a general conformity of all orders and degrees to those equitable rules of action, by which the meanest individual is protected from the insults and oppression of the greatest." And Smith, too, praised "that equal and impartial administration of justice which renders the rights of the meanest British subject respectable to the greatest." No one may claim a right for himself which another may not claim with just as great a justification. Once again, Nietzsche attracts attention to this moral core of liberalism by attacking it. He execrates John Stuart Mill in this way: "I abhor his vulgarity, which says: 'What is right for one is fair for another.'"[24]

The charge that liberals were value subjectivists has always appeared egregious in the case of Kant. In truth, Kant deviates little from his liberal predecessors on this question: "no-one can put anyone else under a legal obligation without submitting simultaneously to a law which requires that he can himself be put under the same kind of obligation by the other person." That is the crux of the matter. Man is a partly rational animal, Kant argued, and hence all human beings inwardly recognize that laws should apply equally to all. In thought, at least, they accept "the principle of legal *equality* for everyone (as citizens)." No matter how unequal people are in material possessions, "they are all equal as subjects before the *law*." But man is not wholly rational (in a substantive rather than instrumental sense); he also lives under the sway of irrational passions and "abuses his freedom in relation to others of his own kind." Indeed, "he is misled by his self-seeking animal inclinations into exempting himself [sich selbst ausnehmen] from the law where he can."[25] Such inborn partiality must be corrected or deterred by intelligently applied pressure from the liberal state.

All liberals explicitly subordinate self-interest to a binding and enforceable norm of fairness. The primacy of the right in liberal thought means the primacy of the injunction against self-exemption. Far from sanctifying naked preferences, or abandoning all "restraint of the appetites," liberals viewed given desires with an amicable but unfailingly skeptical eye.[26] Rather than leaving instinctive human partiality to its own devices, the liberal state should control it coercively, applying an egalitarian norm. To repeat: the rule that you cannot make an exception of yourself is not a subjective preference. It is not a value which can be chosen or not, as atomistic individuals please. The prohibition against making an exception of oneself is a standard by which liberal citizens are required to judge and curb their own first-order desires.[27]

Universalistic norms may sound nebulous, but they have concrete legal and political consequences. Equality before the law includes the principle that "no member of the commonwealth can have a hereditary privilege as against his fellow subjects."[28] The ban on hereditary monopolies is simultaneously an affirmation of equality of opportunity. Universal education is another political embodiment of a liberal commitment to the norm of equality. The same can be said for universal suffrage. Majoritarian decision-making also reflects the fundamental liberal norm. For these reasons, the disallowance of self-exemption constitutes *the* moral core of liberal constitutionalism.

Is Procedural Neutrality a Sham?

Ignoring this moral norm at the heart of liberal theory, antiliberals frequently attack liberalism for its amoral legalism. "It is a remarkable phenomenon," writes Schmitt, "that the European liberal state of the 19th century portrays itself as *a neutral and agnostic state* and can see its existential justification precisely in its neutrality." The thin legalistic principle that *pacta sunt servanda*, he argues, cannot hold society together, reinforce a common cultural identity, or introduce order into the chaos of conflicting loyalties. According to Solzhenitsyn, too, liberalism worships empty formalities, "the soulless and smooth plane of legalism," and neglects the moral and emotional attachments that really count.[29] Liberalism coolly sacrifices the spirit to the letter, vital substance to brittle forms. Laws do not constitute a way of life, yet liberals focus obsessively on legality and the rule of law. (It does not follow that they are therefore indifferent to ways of life.)

From the antiliberals' viewpoint the primacy of contractualism and proceduralism in liberal thought has many regrettable consequences. One is that the liberal state pretends to be "neutral" toward conflicting ideas of happiness. It does not openly endorse an orthodox conception of the good but tries hopelessly to forge a *modus vivendi* among rival groups following incompatible ideals. According to Unger, liberalism strives to frame "a procedure for lawmaking to which any man, no matter what his values, would have reason to agree." Thus it seeks to adopt "the posture of neutrality among the desires of the individual and among the desires of different individuals." This high-minded "neutrality" is a sign of both liberalism's moral bankruptcy and its political naivete, for there is no such thing as "a neutral, Archimedean point." Every regime, however committed to neutrality, "prefers some values over others." Sandel argues in exactly the same way. Contaminated by liberalism, he tells us, America has degenerated into a "procedural republic."[30] As political science or social history, this claim is difficult to understand. As a protest against some unspecifiable moral decay programmed into society by Kantian theory, it has an obvious appeal for some.

When assailing "liberal neutrality" in this way, antiliberals frequently cobble together two contradictory claims. One is that neutrality toward conceptions of the good life is impossible: liberal regimes favor some alternatives and disadvantage others. The other is that neutrality is pernicious, an ignominious collapse into wishy-washiness, fence-sitting, and moral disorientation.[31] Liberals are unable to be morally neutral (they take a stand), and they are unable to be morally engaged (they do not take a stand).[32] Antiliberals reconcile these two seemingly incompatible charges in the usual way. A liberal regime is bad, they argue, because it fails to understand its lack of neutrality and thus fails to enforce its underlying commitments vigorously enough. Liberalism fails to *understand* itself and thus fail to *be* itself in a healthy sense. But this acrobatic afterthought does not lead antiliberals any closer to common sense.

Perhaps the concept of "neutrality" should be reserved for foreign affairs. While Switzerland may claim to be a neutral country, the decisions reached by the courts in a liberal state are not really neutral between contending parties. After all, one side wins, and the other loses. Strictly speaking, therefore, Unger is right; neutrality is impossible: "as soon as we reach the level of concrete regulation of conduct, we are forced to prefer some values to others."[33] Nevertheless, impartiality or fairness is well within human powers. There is nothing particularly naive or unrealistic about Hume's or Smith's case for "the *impartial* administration of justice."[34] Neutrality, in a feasible sense, must be understood not abstractly but in specific contexts, as impartiality among or fairness toward specific parties. A Protestant whose property was saved by the promulgation of the Edict of Nantes would not have been impressed by a philosophical "proof" that impartiality is logically impossible.[35]

It is true that liberals placed great emphasis on "the set forms of justice." They favored a procedural republic in this modest sense. Parties will always feel frustrated by the procedural delays in any liberal court of law, Montesquieu wrote. But time-consuming proceduralism is the price citizens pay for liberty. Such exasperating delays provide an indispensable chance for reconsidering legal principles, double-checking facts, correcting first impressions, and cooling turbulent emotions. Legal snags and hurdles help irrational and biased creatures to be somewhat less irrational and biased when deploying the full force of the state to crush an individual's life.[36]

As this example suggests, it is incorrect to say that liberals embraced proceduralism to the exclusion of substantive moral principles. Pure majority rule, while embodying an egalitarian norm, is a method of choice compatible with many conceivable decisions. Majoritarianism, however participatory, *is* procedural. One of its principal attractions is that it does not stipulate in advance the content of the decisions that will eventually be made. To the extent that it contains a strong dose of majoritarianism, liberalism, too, refuses to endorse specific policies ahead of time. Instead, it creates a constitutional structure within which citizens can debate, choose, and rethink their goals.

Liberalism, however, is neither wholly majoritarian nor wholly procedural. It imposes important constraints on majority rule. (For example, a majority cannot silence outvoted minorities or prevent them from criticizing majority decisions and attempting legally to have past votes reversed.) It should not be surprising, therefore, that the procedures adopted by liberals, far from being amoral or morally neutral, are meant to influence in important ways the moral content of decisions taken. James Harrington's story about the two girls who have baked a cake is perfectly illustrative of liberalism in this sense. One girl cuts the cake in two pieces; the other chooses first which piece to take. This procedure is itself fair; it is also designed to produce an *outcome* that is fair. Liberal impartiality, far from being hollow, content-less, or morally vacuous, then, is another powerful expression of liberal commitment to an egalitarian conception of the right.

Liberal arguments for the separation of powers reinforce this point. The separation of powers is not meant simply to limit the power of government. It is also meant to influence the *kind* of decisions govern-ments will take. When government functions are divided, each branch can act only with the cooperation of the other branches. It can gain this cooperation, in turn, only when its actions are equitable and in accord with acknowledged law. Both Locke and Montesquieu are ex-plicit about this. If legislators also wielded the power to enforce the law, they might feel free to make oppressive and unfair laws. By separating legislation from execution, liberal constitutionalism aims to head off the enactment of such laws. Because someone else wields the law-enforcing power, legislators will presumably not make laws they do not want to have applied to themselves. Separation of powers, therefore, while formalistic or procedural, makes self-exemption less likely. Its purpose is moral, in a substantive sense. It is designed to produce laws that are more moderate and just.[37]

Antiliberal attacks on the idea of neutrality, besides being histori-cally inaccurate, also imply a sordid message. To inflict tolerance on the intolerant is a form of intolerance, and one form of intolerance is worth another. It is the government's obligation, Kant wrote, "to stop anyone forcibly hindering others from working as best they can to define and promote their salvation."[38] Antiliberals deny that there is anything impartial about such action. There is no difference, they suggest, between an individual's imposing his beliefs on others by force and a democratic government's forcibly preventing him from imposing his beliefs on others by force. We may not want to say that the latter is perfectly "neutral," granted. We may throw away the word "neutral-ity." If we do so, however, we will simply have to find another word ("impartiality"?) to capture the important distinction at stake.

In the *politique* tradition, in addition to unfairness, liberals worry about how to prevent moral conflict from igniting into mass violence. They offer two solutions: the secularization of politics and the equality of all citizens before the law. Different groups can define happiness in different ways, so long as everyone accepts the core liberal norm of fairness: no self-exemption. To a limited extent, this means that the liberal state tries to impose personal ideals on its citizens: reasonableness, acceptance of diversity, and reluctance to resort to violence in settling disputes. On the other hand, individuals and groups are given wide latitude to seek happiness by particular routes.

Fairness is possible, even though perfect or pure neutrality is not. There is nothing logically inconsistent or politically unstable about *selective neutrality*. Liberal regimes abstract from some moral questions, but not from others. On the one hand, the government is constitutionally constrained to be indifferent about an individual's choice of the church he joins (the good). On the other hand, the government is not at all neutral or impartial or indifferent about a whole set of other moral choices individuals must make (the right). To return to the most obvious example: murder is wrong, both morally and legally. The liberal state does not adopt a stance of "neutrality" toward the preferences of murderers and their victims. It does not keep "hands off" or follow the hypersubjectivist principle of *chacun à son goût*. Liberals did not believe that the taste for murdering was just as respectable as the taste for not being murdered. As Locke put it, the murderer "hath by the unjust Violence and Slaughter he hath committed upon one, declared War against all Mankind, and therefore may be destroyed as a Lyon or a Tyger, one of those wild Savage Beasts, with whom men can have no Society nor Security."[39] The "neutrality" of the liberal state, then, is far from absolute. It is consciously and intentionally selective. Those who violently exempt themselves from the common rules are not treated indulgently by liberal authorities. Tolerance toward diverse ideas of happiness is wholly liberal. Intolerance toward those who reject liberalism's core norm, toward those who make flagrant exceptions of themselves, is wholly liberal as well.

The Primacy of Instrumental over Moral Relations?

According to Taylor, "procedural liberalism" is "the formula for an instrumental society." This rebuke, too, is common. Unger, for instance, agrees that a "manipulative view of action" follows from "the instrumental conception of knowledge" embraced by liberal thought. In other words, "instrumental rationality" leads to "an increasing technical control of nature and social relations." Similarly, "the manipulative posture toward the natural world," characteristic of modern science, encourages the "manipulative posture toward society" that is congenial to liberalism. MacIntyre has something of the sort in mind when he denounces the "dominance of the manipulative mode in our culture."[40] In a truly liberal society, we are asked to believe, individuals do not communicate with each other as equals, share experiences, grow old together, or cooperate in the achievement of common moral aims. Instead they eye one another meanly, as tools for their selfish and usually materialistic purposes. The association of liberalism with an increase in instrumental or manipulative relations, however, is unsatisfying from several points of view.

For one thing, instrumental relations were not originally introduced into society by liberal theorists or even by admirers of modern science. A characteristic example is 1 *Corinthians* 11:3–16: "Neither was man created for woman, but woman for man." Liberals did not invent domination, exploitation, intimidation, arm-twisting, or terror. Likewise, they did not invent war, where individual lives are calculatingly expended for the pursuit of political goals.[41] Finally, slavery can plausibly be considered the most instrumental of all human relations. But predatory groups reduced their weak and conquered neighbors to serviceable chattel long before liberalism was on the scene. It was liberals who condemned this ancient social practice.

Locke's politics, in fact, was rooted in a denial that "we were made for one another's uses." Parents do not own their children, he emphatically explained. Similarly, when punishing a crime, a person has no right "to *use* a Criminal . . . according to the passionate heats, or boundless extravagancy of his own will." No reader of Montesquieu's *Persian Letters* would gather that liberals admired instrumental relations. Usbek's eunuchs are depicted there as pure tools and therefore as the quintessence of human abasement. Smith argued explicitly that you cannot treat people like "pieces upon a chessboard." Kant's injunction to regard another "never simply as a means, but always at the same time as an end," because perfectly anti-instrumental, was also perfectly liberal.[42] All the classical liberals agreed that citizens should not be treated as mere instruments or materials in the hands of their rulers.

Indeed, no political ideology has ever taken so severe a stance against instrumental relations as liberalism. Individuals should not be pawns to their family, group, church, state, or social superiors. A young woman has moral value, for instance, even when she does not serve her group by bearing children. This de-instrumentalization of the individual is what Taylor derides as "atomism." But there is nothing viciously self-centered about it, contrary to what he claims, because it is meant to apply to all individuals equally.

Antiliberals fall into incoherence, moreover, when they accuse liberalism of favoring instrumental relations and, at the same time, blame it for defending individual rights and promoting skepticism. Antagonism toward liberal rights cannot be reconciled with a sincere abhorrence of manipulation.[43] After all, rights were designed to prevent unwanted and oppressive manipulation, while political skepticism was aimed against the intrusive manipulations of censors and other self-assured overlords of the mind.

The association of liberalism with instrumental thinking does contain a pale reflection of the truth. Liberals regularly derided monks and aristocrats who never contributed anything *useful* to society. More generally, liberals admired the useful as opposed to the wasteful, the sacred, and the merely traditional. They also stressed means-ends thinking as a technique for restricting and rationalizing the arbitrary powers of the state. Locke wrote: "if a thing be not useful to the commonwealth . . . it may not presently be established by law."[44] Religious intolerance has no political utility and therefore is wholly out of bounds. In other words, Locke coupled instrumental thinking with limited government.[45]

The only legitimate reasons for punishment, to cite another example, are "*Reparation* and *Restraint.*" Punishment should be useful to the public. It should never become a conduit for private hatred and should always be applied in a dispassionate and calculating spirit. This is one of the main themes of Beccaria's *On Crimes and Punishments*. To demand that punishments be *useful* was to demand that they become less arbitrary and less severe. (Beccaria was careful to define utility in a negative way: it is not divine goodness, but goodness from a strictly human and thus limited point of view.) This instrumental approach to punishment was balanced by noninstrumental considerations. All liberals, including Beccaria, agreed that punishment can be inflicted only on someone who has violated the law. Kant formulated this anti-instrumentalist point with exceptional clarity: "judicial punishment can never be used as a means to promote some other good for the criminal himself or for civil society, but instead it must in all cases be imposed on him only on the ground that he has committed a crime."[46]

16 / The Crimes of Reason?

Antiliberals often associate liberalism with extreme rationalism. Rationalists are said to believe that human reason is powerful enough to construct a workable blueprint for the best possible social order and that people can be persuaded by rational argument to accept this blueprint. The critics of such hyperrationalism argue that reason is too feeble for such a task, given the complexity of social life, and that people are more likely to be swayed by passion and interest than by rational argument. The most direct answer to this charge is that liberals were not hyperrationalists. Indeed, some were antirationalists in precisely this sense, especially the followers of Hume, such as the American framers. To give a fuller reply, however, we must look at the two most popular versions of the charge, one aimed against the Enlightenment in general, the other against natural science in particular.

Dialectic of Enlightenment

The Enlightenment is profoundly hypocritical, according to Schmitt: "today the most terrible war is waged in the name of peace, the most awful oppression is carried out in the name of freedom, and the most terrible inhumanity is inflicted in the name of mankind." The ideals of liberalism, it seems, result in exactly opposite practices. It is no use arguing that liberals *intended* to create a decent society; what they actually brought into being was a human disaster.

This paradoxical claim, which has profoundly influenced the debate about liberalism, has modest and extreme forms. An extreme version was already advanced by Rousseau. In Strauss's paraphrase of the *First Discourse:* "enlightenment paves the way for despotism." Another source for the charge that rationalism engenders political disaster can be found in both Maistre and Louis de Bonald. They were effective

247

propagandists, successfully promulgating the myth of a direct causal link between the activity of the eighteenth-century philosophes and the Reign of Terror. It is amazing what a grip this implausible idea has had on later antiliberals. Consciously or inadvertently, for instance, Lasch echoes these Catholic counter-Enlightenment theorists. He agrees that "the revolutionary terror" was "perhaps the most enduring legacy of the Enlightenment." Once this idea of a "dialectic of Enlightenment" was launched, it was able to sustain itself, apparently by an air of paradoxical profundity. As a more self-conscious heir to this nineteenth-century Catholic tradition, Unger asserts an underlying kinship between rationality and brutality. He writes coolly that "legalism and terrorism, the commitment to rules and the seduction of violence, are rival brothers, but brothers nonetheless."[1] Michel Foucault's suggestion that the physical and psychological mistreatment of the mentally ill was a logical consequence of the modern idea of reason is another, even more notorious, example of this common claim.

On the American scene, arguments for a dialectic of Enlightenment take many forms. In one version liberalism destroys religion, channeling man's innate idealism into political utopianism, that is, into the kind of revolutionary violence which destroys liberal institutions. The individual, freed from religious restraints, runs amok. According to another version, scientific progress leads to specialization; specialization leads to a neglect of fundamentals; a neglect of fundamentals leads to an erosion of civilization and thus to an end of progress.

MacIntyre's version of the dialectic of Enlightenment is typical of many. Those who criticize inherited group identity and unquestioned religious beliefs, he says, cannot replace what they tear down. Kant and others tried to establish universal moral principles, addressing all rational human beings, regardless of their cultural heritage or social group. But their antilocalism asked too much (or too little?) of human beings and was bound to fail. After the inevitable defeat of liberal-cosmopolitan ethics, the average "post-Enlightenment person," having been rudely dislodged from his traditional cocoon and deprived of traditional moral guidance, was naturally propelled toward nihilism. Reason's capacity to destroy moral norms but not to create them explains why Nietzsche followed Kant with such unseemly haste.[2]

In a Maistrean vein, Unger accuses empirical science of debasing mankind. He also explains that liberalism was born "in revolt against the ancient claims of theology." Militant secularism therefore triggered a dialectic of Enlightenment. By emptying heaven, liberalism paved the way for "the deification of mankind."[3] Unger discovers this vice in Marx, just as Maistre had decried it in Robespierre. Liberalism leads naturally to unspeakable human arrogance and, eventually, to Terror.

Is it necessary to take seriously the claim that, when the Enlightenment is taken too far, something terrible must occur? This conclusion is not quite so compelling as antiliberals pretend. First of all, the Terror of 1793–94 followed on the heels of a *defeat* of the liberal forces in France. To make liberalism guilty for Jacobinism comes close to blaming the victim.[4] French liberal writing after 1793, moreover, had little trouble criticizing Robespierre with purely Enlightenment categories: he was a secular priest, a fanatic, a zealot, an enthusiast. As a matter of fact, the leading Jacobins exhibited few signs of excessive, or even modest, rationality. Viewed clearly, the counterrevolutionary assimilation of freedom and terror, of reason and barbarism, amounts to a *post hoc, ergo propter hoc* fallacy. Although the Terror came after the Enlightenment, it had other causes than the Enlightenment's success. It may even have resulted from the failure of the Enlightenment to take root.

With regard to the erosion of religion, the accusers claim that skepticism toward religious norms has destroyed social trust. To answer them we must ask: when and where did social trust flourish? How stable and orderly were the traditional communities "annealed" by religion? During the many centuries of the Middle Ages, it seems, masses of people were sincere believers, in the firm grasp of tradition. Yet their lives were far from idyllic and peaceful. Did they never go on rampages? Were the perpetrators of the Inquisition or Saint Bartholomew's Day massacre secularized folk who had lost their moral anchorage in the traditional faith? To pose these questions is to answer them and realize that the faith-doubt distinction cannot be mapped neatly onto the distinction between moderation and immoderation, as antiliberals often assume. The reason is easy to grasp. Religious and irreligious human beings have a roughly equal proclivity to violence. If anything, religious skepticism is more likely to function as a social sedative than is religion, as Nietzsche explained.[5] Has anyone ever met a dangerous skeptic? (Montaigne, for one, was not a threatening man.) Conversely, certainty has never been completely harmless, and doubt has seldom been more dangerous than fanaticism and violence. Moreover, most people, most of the time, are incapable of withholding judgment. Psychologically, skepticism is an unstable attitude, difficult to sustain for long periods. Thus mass skepticism will probably never be a major social problem. This, at least, is the liberal premise: blind credulity and passionate certainty will always cause more trouble to mankind than doubt.

Finally, the antiliberals raise the charge of specialization: liberalism has impoverished human life by encouraging an excessive focus on mindless jobs and thus leading to a general neglect of the most important questions. The best answer to this is found in the *Wealth of Nations*. Liberal theorists were not wholly unaware of the problematic side effects of developments they nevertheless, on balance, continued to favor. According to Smith, for example, the division of labor (stimulated by the opening of new markets capable of absorbing manufactured goods) had human costs as well as human benefits. His discussion of the subject is a good example of the higher realism of the liberal tradition, wrongly neglected by its antiliberal critics. The division of labor brought enormous gains in productivity, making individuals more responsible and better able to perform their tasks. But this was not the whole story. According to Smith, "the man whose whole life is spent in performing a few simple operations, of which the effects too are, perhaps, always the same, has no occasion to exert his understanding, or to exercise his invention in finding out expedients for removing difficulties which never occur. He naturally loses, therefore, the habit of such exertion, and generally becomes as stupid and ignorant as it is possible for a human creature to become." Economic development is purchased at the expense of the worker's "drowsy stupidity" and even his "mental mutilation, deformity, and wretchedness." Overspecialized workers are "incapable of relishing or bearing a part in any rational conversation," unable to make judgments about private duties, and totally in the dark about "the great and extensive interests of his country."[6] In response to these problems Smith did not advocate abolishing the division of labor, of course. What he proposed instead was a state-subsidized system of public education. This proposal is an apt symbol for the real dialectic of Enlightenment, the liberal attempt to solve liberal problems by liberal means, quite unlike anything the antiliberals have in mind.

Blaming Modern Science

A scientific outlook of the sort Smith admired encourages detachment from particularistic communities. It will cause no surprise, therefore, that many of the antiliberals discussed above express deep distrust for science. They sometimes present liberalism, interestingly enough, as a political expression of the scientific world view.[7] Maistre and Schmitt write this way, as do MacIntyre, Unger, and Strauss. Their quarrel with scientific rationality, wholly foreign to Marxism, is an essential aspect of their dislike of liberal politics and ideas. Science destroys meaning, they claim, or at least deprives mankind of comforting illusions. Because it claims universal validity, science uproots people from their inherited ways of life. What antiliberals most resent in science is what they take to be its arrogant deification of man. Scientists, they announce, are trying to play God. According to Martin Heidegger, for instance, man in the technological age "exalts himself to the posture of lord of the earth."[8] Solzhenitsyn, in the same spirit, associates the scientific revolution with "anthropocentricity." Modern rationalism, which culminates in natural science, attributes sovereignty to the subject and assumes that "man is above everything." The sin of science lies in its implicit humanism. It implies that "I—Man with a capital M—am the crowning glory of the universe."[9] (The erroneousness of this charge has already been discussed.)

Unger accuses science of leading liberal citizens to see nature as nothing but "a fund of means capable of satisfying his cravings," a set of "external objects whose value lies in their capacity to satisfy human desires." In so saying he speaks for all the others. Science is nothing but a struggle for power, driven less by curiosity about the world than by a need for the "prediction or control of events."[10] It is not surprising, then, that "the progress of science increases rather than diminishes the strangeness of the natural world." In liberal-scientific thought, "man stands before nature and society as the grand manipulator." He senses no limits, feels no awe. The intolerable arrogance of this posture needs no comment. And the danger of going over the edge with genetic engineering is self-evident: "even birth, death, and the physical forms of human life may be changed in conformity to willed objectives."[11] As the natural consequence of science, the uncontrolled proliferation of technologies reveals that modern rationalism does not respect "the sanctity of nature." It is also morally repugnant: "technology is the instrument and external expression of the manipulative relationship to nature and to society." The ultimate degradation is "the subjugation of nature to human will."[12]

These words of Unger's could just as well have been any other antiliberal's. None of them, it should be said, make fine discriminations among the sciences. They do not explain, when impugning science in general, if they have theoretical physics, meteorology, evolutionary biology, geology, or medicine in mind. But they do repeatedly announce that modern science is morally useless, unable to tell people how to live or what to do. They sometimes go farther, suggesting that science is essentially immoral.

Is it really plausible to claim that science swaggers with Promethean self-importance?[13] Not exactly. The Enlightenment was a limits-of-reason and limits-of-knowledge tradition, teaching humility before the facts. Writing in this tradition, the classical liberals believed that man is a limited being, subject to ignorance and error. The scientific method, like the formalities of liberal proceduralism, was designed, in part, to compensate for the weaknesses and imperfections of the mind. The main theme of a liberal work such as Voltaire's *Philosophical Dictionary* is the inability of reason to answer certain large questions. The nature of matter and the soul are inscrutable to the human mind. Scholastic attempts to penetrate to the essence of things failed because they asked too much of human cognitive capacities. In contrast, science demands and produces the ability to tolerate our inevitable ignorance. Admirers of the scientific revolution considered modesty to be an intellectual duty, for the human mind will always be fallible; certitude is not a proof of certainty.[14] We should always listen to our critics, who may turn out to be right. Arrogance is reasonably ascribed to religious puppeteers, posing as depositories of rare wisdom, presuming to tell individuals how to save their souls. Not Galileo and Newton, but *Genesis* 1:28 tells human beings to subordinate nature to their uses. Finally, doctors experimenting tentatively but persistently with inoculations against smallpox are not so megalomaniacal or overweening as antiliberals would, for some reason, have us believe.

17 / Antonym Substitution

Antiliberals do not merely decontextualize liberal thought. They also provide a false context of their own making, one that imparts a very different meaning to the principles being attacked. Thus the final mark of an antiliberal approach to the history of liberalism is the fallacy of antonym substitution. Polemicists with a bias against liberal thought regularly distort the significance of central liberal ideas by replacing the counterconcepts that originally bestowed political significance on liberal principles with antonyms of their own choosing, which were either ignored or explicitly rejected by the early liberals. The liberal idea of competition, for example, is routinely subjected to a denigrating contrast with brotherly love. For the classical liberals, however, the principal antonym of competition was not love but monopoly. And monopoly has nothing to do with love—as anyone knows who has studied, say, the relation of the Irish landlord to his local peasantry. By way of antonym substitution, then, antiliberals have concealed the moral and political motivation for the original liberal embrace of the principle of competition. By such a conceptual sleight-of-hand, one might say, the nineteenth and twentieth centuries have conspired to make the seventeenth and eighteenth centuries unintelligible.

Examples of antonym substitution are legion and well worth pondering. To begin with, antiliberals misleadingly counterpose skepticism to moral wisdom. The original antonyms of liberal doubt, however, were false certainty and enthusiasm. Private property is unfavorably compared to charity, while liberals saw it as an alternative to princely confiscation. Instrumental attitudes are disparagingly contrasted with moral attitudes, but they seem more attractive when opposed, as they were in the seventeenth and eighteenth centuries, to wastefulness and status display. Similarly, rights are prejudicially contrasted with duties, an opposition that makes the former seem mean-spirited and selfish. The original opposites of rights, however, were tyranny, slavery, and cruelty. Why the liberal crusade against oppression should be considered selfish has never been clear.

In their attempt to discredit liberal theory, antiliberals unfairly contrast contract or exchange to reciprocal altruism. But the opposite to mutual exchange was not solidarity but a relation in which one party was wholly sacrificed to the other.[1] Similarly, detractors of liberalism oppose the adjustment of interests to rational consensus—a contrast that makes anyone wonder how a person of good will could ever have advocated the former alternative. The original antonym of interest-based compromise, however, was not rational agreement but civil war. Viewed as an alternative to ideal-driven slaughter, interest-driven accommodation seems much less ignoble. That is precisely how it seemed to European liberals in the seventeenth and eighteenth centuries.

Antiliberals expose the purportedly liberal maxim "I can do whatever I want" as nihilistic self-indulgence by contrasting it misleadingly with the reassuring precept "I shall do whatever morality requires." But the original antonym of "I will do what I want" was "I must do whatever my master or my social rank demands." Antiliberals contrast liberal freedom with authority in general, but liberals were hostile only to arbitrary authority. Rule-governed authority they assumed to be essential for the creation and maintenance of a just social order. Finally, antiliberals belittlingly contrast liberal individualism with community *tout court*. Individualism was never counterposed to all forms of community, however, only to stifling or authoritarian kinds, such as sects, clans, caste systems, and parochial village life.[2] By reducing the levels of xenophobia and intolerance, liberalism aimed to facilitate the free expression of cultural identity in heterogeneous societies. Far from being anticommunal, therefore, liberals strove to create a specific kind of community, one in which citizens could enjoy the cooperation, interaction, and mutual stimulation made possible by a system of uniformly enforced individual rights.

By using antonym substitution, antiliberals make the past difficult to understand. They obfuscate the motives of intelligent and reform-minded theorists. By decontextualizing liberalism, they deradicalize it and obscure its initial appeal. The most noteworthy victims of antonym substitution have probably been the crucial categories of *self-interest* and *self-preservation*. To discredit these concepts, antiliberals contrast them with benevolent concern for others, public-spiritedness, and devotion to moral ideals. Almost universally neglected are the antonyms that would have occurred first to liberal writers (and that suggest themselves naturally to common sense): self-hatred, self-destruction, self-mortification, self-effacement, and *incuria sui*—a failure to take an interest in oneself. These, too, are "habits of the heart." Subject to a combined assault by religious, authoritarian, romantic, militaristic, and socialist traditions, the concept of self-interest acquired, by the end of the nineteenth century, a totally unmerited infamy. Most outlandishly, self-interest is now routinely depicted as the opposite of the public interest, as if doing something for oneself were necessarily a failure of patriotism or a betrayal of one's fellow man.

Despite the prevailing mythology, no liberal ever affirmed self-interest as an *alternative* to the public interest. All liberals expressed deep concern about "sinister interests," meaning private interests opposed to the fair treatment of all. They prized self-interest only so long as it was regulated by a norm of justice and, even then, only because—as Albert Hirschman has shown—they conceived it as a practical alternative to various malevolent passions and conceits as well as to the fraudulent display of benevolent motives.[3] To understand the relatively friendly attitude liberals displayed toward self-interest, we need only think more deeply about the original antonyms of the idea. Religious self-disgust and self-effacing obedience to God's inscrutable will were not the only attitudes liberals hoped to overcome. Equally important antonyms of self-interest were privilege, paternalism, blood revenge, envy, military glory, and the grandeur of the state.[4] Liberals who expressed sympathy with self-interest were not endorsing radical selfishness. To a large extent, they were simply suggesting that individuals should assert themselves in nonaggressive, nonviolent, nonbrutal ways.

Antonym substitution, I hasten to add, may be a reflection of deep social transformations. It is not *merely* an intellectual fallacy. It is not always due to the obtuseness or maneuvering of antiliberals but often results simply from the evolution of language and human concerns. In many cases, its plausibility can be historically explained. For example, the contrast between markets and barbarism, while almost universally accepted in the seventeenth and eighteenth centuries, fell out of fashion in the nineteenth. Such a significant cultural shift is easy to understand. The commercialism/barbarism antithesis lost its original self-evidence because of the Industrial Revolution. Civilized industrial societies themselves began to display some unpleasantly "barbaric" traits. The Enlightenment commonplace that commerce replaces war and tyranny was also rudely undermined by subsequent experience. Thus, although the nineteenth century misinterpreted the eighteenth, these misinterpretations can sometimes be comprehended as a natural expression of a shifting scene. Even when convincingly explained, however, historiographical distortions remain distortions.

The idea of antonym substitution, finally, may suggest that liberalism once played an important historical role but that it has now outlived its usefulness. It helped overturn superstitions, break up monopolies, shatter cruel traditions, and so forth. But once liberalism's original enemies have been vanquished, does it retain a *raison d'être?* The answer is simple: liberalism gains new enemies every day while it keeps many of its old ones. Religious fanaticism has not vanished from the earth; nor have authoritarian government, judicial cruelty, political censorship, rigged elections, and repression of minorities. The defeat of fascism and the collapse of communism have not left the world in the hands of liberals. This is all the more reason to be clear about the illiberal forces with which liberalism has been confronted in the past and with which it will continue to be confronted in the future.

Conclusion

The foregoing study has been lamentably selective and incomplete. The handful of theorists chosen for analysis do not represent every important school or camp within nonmarxist antiliberalism. But a close examination of their writings tends to buttress my initial thesis. In these incarnations, at least, the nonmarxist assault on liberal thought and institutions has sufficient cohesion to qualify as a tradition. Its exponents display a common sensibility and circle back relentlessly to a single set of core ideas. Laid side by side, their books resemble a protracted argument rather than a disconnected series of complaints. Like liberalism itself (and, indeed, like most powerful traditions), nonmarxist antiliberalism contains a rich diversity within its overall unity. Formulated and reformulated by many authors, it has varied significantly over time and from country to country. But this variation is perfectly compatible with eye-catching historical continuities and similarities among the attacks against liberalism that have been launched, independently or through mutual influence, in distinct national cultures.

Unity and Diversity in the Antiliberal Tradition

Antiliberals (using the term in my sense) unfailingly adopt a gloomy or "pathogenic" approach to the emergence of the modern world. They present themselves as root-and-branch critics, moreover, assailing liberalism relentlessly and from a position purportedly uncontaminated by liberal ways of thought. They do not urge that liberal societies become more egalitarian or more democratic (that the poor really be given "equality of opportunity" for instance), as do many liberals themselves. On the contrary, they ordinarily trace the current ills of their societies to an infection, sometime in the past, with the theoretical errors of an egalitarian-democratic philosophy. In this way, they associate their own ruthless exposés of liberalism's flaws with a campaign for social salvation. As dismantlers of a defective intellectual framework, they will not merely controvert the theories of their liberal enemies. They will also lead the rest of us to some healthier, profounder, more anchored, or perhaps more exciting world.

To highlight variations on antiliberalism's traditional refrains, I have relied on two typologies. Some antiliberals are "hard," I have argued, and others are "soft." (The former berate liberals for ignoring bitter realities, the latter for ignoring sweet possibilities.) Furthermore, some critics attack liberalism for loosening restraints, while others attack it for tightening restraints. The first are anti-individualists, the second superindividualists. Although they are sometimes combined in a clumsy way, anti-individualism and superindividualism pull in opposite directions. The differences are obvious. Anti-individualists worry about liberal permissiveness; superindividualists worry about liberal conformism. Anti-individualists complain about a terrifying lack of restraint in liberal society, while superindividualists warn about a surfeit of restraint. The former say that liberal man is impious or too free, the latter that he is boring or not free enough. The former praise conventional social roles for providing moral orientation and a sense of place, the latter condemn social roles as inauthentic masks. Yearning for depths of authenticity or heroic self-expression, superindividualists argue that the liberal legal order flattens the individual with rules and proceduralisms and submerges him in everyday banalities. Longing for security or place, by contrast, anti-individualists blame liberalism for releasing all normative constraints and comforting social bonds, leaving people undirected and unmoored. Finally, superindividualists associate liberalism with the death of nonconformist doubt and dissent, while anti-individualists blame it for the collapse of real consensus.

Consider again the anti-individualists, hard and soft. Severe and affable enemies of individualism alike claim that liberals are blind to the importance of group life. But anti-individualists of the two persuasions have different reproaches to make and different groups in mind. "Hard" antiliberals—such as Schmitt—see groups as a source of danger. "Soft" antiliberals—such as MacIntyre—see groups as a source of warmth and meaning. The former focus on the harsh realities that cosmopolitan liberalism ignores at its peril. The latter emphasize the morally consoling attachments that cosmopolitan liberalism slights and thereby erodes. The hardliners see violent conflict among solidaristic groups as the principal reality of political life. The softliners (or communitarians) poeticize lost "roots" without giving much thought to the problems that rival and hostile communities may pose. Tough anti-individualists always think of insiders in relation to outsiders. They never forget the shadow side of solidarity: neglect of, or hostility toward, nonmembers. They recognize that an enhanced concern for loyalty implies an enhanced sensitivity to treason. Easygoing critics of individualism, by contrast, imagine their beloved community located peacefully in an unpopulated void. They never mention the fate of nonmembers and ignore violent conflict between hostile groups. But the omissions are more innocent than sly. Appealingly, and in tacit response to fascism, soft communitarians demilitarize the ideals of "virtue" and "community," using these watered-down terms where their predecessors would have invoked "manliness" and *das Volk*. They therefore appear naive or harmless in a way that hard anti-individualists do not.

In the superindividualist line of attack, liberalism is said to ignore greatness, self-development, virtue, the unfolding of potentials, and the exercise of capacities. "Hard" superindividualists—such as Strauss —argue that the talents of the exceptional man are undernourished in a liberal society where egalitarian norms demand that no one make an exception of himself. They subordinate right action (stressed by liberals) to a personal ideal of the good life, achievable by only a select few. "Soft" superindividualists—such as Unger—also protest against the rule of law in the name of self-assertion and self-expression. But they suggest, generously but naively, that everyone should be a hero; that superiority can exist without inferiority. Thus they never ponder the shadow side of the heroic life and never consider the fate of nonheroes. Soft superindividualists, too, put the distinction between "good life" and "bad life" on a moral plane above the liberal contrast between "right action" and "wrong action." Unlike hard superindividualists, however, they do not have a clear understanding of the antiegalitarian implications of the good life/bad life distinction. They do not see that, taken seriously as the basis for a political order, this distinction implies political inferiority for those unable to grasp "the good" or who fail to realize it in their lives. Soft superindividualists sweetly ignore all this. They therefore appear naive or harmless in a way that hard superindividualists do not.

These two sets of dichotomies have proved helpful for classifying and comparing the theorists studied here, although they represent only a beginning. To probe more deeply into the simultaneous unity and diversity of the antiliberal tradition, it is useful to ask how our cultural critics would react to a broad range of controversial subjects. What is their attitude toward hedonism and consumerism, toward science and technology? Other important topics on which their opinions can be sounded include cosmopolitanism, ethnic identity, the sacred, awe, authority, violence, and sacrifice.

With this list in mind, we can easily begin a more fine-grained comparative analysis. Schmitt favors authority, while Unger opposes it. MacIntyre is religious and thinks we need divine assistance to perfect our natural virtues, while Strauss would disagree on both points. Schmitt prefers the man of decisive action, Strauss the man of deep thought. (They disagree about which one is truly made of steel.) MacIntyre praises inherited traditions, Unger scorns them. Maistre is obsessed with violence, while communitarians normally write as if coercion barely exists. Unger worries about the subordination of the individual to the group; MacIntyre does not give the subject any thought. Maistre attacks the abstractness of liberal rights (logically) in order to discredit the norm of equality; MacIntyre and Unger attack the abstractness of liberal rights while (illogically) defending the norm of equality. Indeed, the closer we look at our antiliberals, the more striking their differences become.

And the more striking are their resemblances as well. Despite their obvious dissimilarities, the antiliberals discussed above share a common style of argumentation as well as a common enemy. They all adopt a teratological approach to modern society, despise hedonistic materialism, and spurn abstract universalism. They all associate liberalism with spiritual anemia and a loss of meaning. All, even the superindividualists, suggest that modern science represents a sickening deification of mankind. And all of them imagine that gross theoretical errors bear primary responsibility for massive social ills. (They thereby associate their own unveiling of intellectual mistakes with efforts at social salvation.) Most of them would agree with Solzhenitsyn's warning about "the disastrous deviation of the Enlightenment." He means here, as they do, "the calamity of an autonomous, irreligious humanistic consciousness." Secular humanism is the root of the liberal disease. At the onset of the modern age, "a total emancipation occurred from the moral heritage of Christian centuries," from "the heritage of the preceding one thousand years." To this "deviation" most antiliberals trace liberal society's dismaying ills.

Solzhenitsyn, to be sure, is a unique figure. Unlike the authors discussed above, he draws inspiration from nineteenth-century Russian critics of Westernization. Yet his works bristle with formulations that readers wholly ignorant of Slavophile thought will nevertheless find eerily familiar. For a final example, consider his attack on materialistic euphoria: "we have become hopelessly enmeshed in our slavish worship of all that is pleasant, all that is comfortable, all that is material—we worship things, we worship products." Because of humanistic liberalism, "everything beyond physical well-being and the accumulation of material goods, all other human requirements and characteristics of a subtler and higher nature, were left outside the area of attention of state and social system, as if human life did not have any higher meaning."[1] The identical claim, in strikingly similar words, can be discovered in the books of Maistre, Schmitt, Strauss, MacIntyre, and Unger. Their amazing uniformity of thought and vocabulary on this subject suggests that, regardless of their many differences, these antiliberals are profoundly akin. To put it another way, they are representatives of a single tradition. That tradition speaks through them, with or without their knowledge.

Liberalism Clarified by Its Enemies

However critical, a study of such a resilient and multiform tradition cannot be merely an exercise in demolition. By hammering out responses to the principal charges advanced against liberal theory by its most merciless critics, we can learn a great deal about liberalism itself. In fact, we can come to see liberalism with new eyes.

Maistre, for example, teaches us to appreciate the metaphysical radicalness of liberal thought. From the perspective of preliberal or Christian political theory, he explains, the concept of human self-rule is incoherent. Mankind is heteronomous by nature. This becomes clear when we reflect on the principle that the power to bind entails the power to loose. This maxim implies that no society can effectively bind itself. Only a superhuman force can compel human beings to limit themselves, keep their promises, and obey the law. Liberal constitutionalism, from this perspective, represents a hopeless bootstrap operation, a futile attempt by prideful human beings to tie themselves down to a political framework without the help of a cosmic enforcer or "binding god."

Maistre was wrong to predict that secularization would spell the laughable instability and quick demise of constitutional regimes, but he was right to emphasize the boldness and originality of the liberal idea. Without significant support from God or religious myths, individuals with imperfect reasoning powers have proved capable of jointly limiting themselves, in a relatively stable manner, and binding themselves to a constitutional framework, which is difficult to change, for the sake of cooperation, coexistence, and common interests. A society created in this manner, as Maistre recognized, has a wholly untraditional principle of legitimacy. Laws and rulers are not accepted because they are sacrosanct or immutable. On the contrary, laws and rulers are accepted *because they can be changed.*[2] Maistre's scoffing commentaries call our attention to the audacity and unexpectedness of this wholly novel basis for political consent.

From a critical reading of Schmitt, too, students of liberalism have a great deal to learn. For one thing, his relentless insistence on the military weakness of liberal regimes directs our thoughts to precisely the opposite: the remarkable capacity of liberal societies to mobilize resources for military and other collective ends. Parliamentary regimes, as history demonstrates, can do a great deal more than just talk. Similarly, Schmitt's tendency to link liberalism to anarchism inadvertently alerts us to the positive attitude toward lawful state power shared by all classical liberals. His claim that liberal constitutions aim exclusively at weakening government in the name of individual rights leads us to emphasize the contrary point: liberal constitutions attempt to design state power in such a way as to maximize the free flow of information and enhance the thoughtfulness and appropriateness of the decisions made. Similarly, Schmitt's linkage of liberalism to romantic ideas such as "endless discussion" reminds us of the dry-eyed and practical nature of most liberal aspirations, including, for instance, the minimizing of governmental corruption. Finally, his repeated assertion that liberal politics is based on an optimistic anthropology or a denial of original sin helps clarify the particular kind of pessimism at the heart of liberal constitutionalism. Liberals are not optimists but *universalistic* pessimists: not the governed alone, but also the governors need to be ruled.

Provoked by Strauss, too, the student of liberalism learns to appreciate, again, the radicalness of liberal secularism. In the teeth of traditional political theory, which stressed the unifying power of religious belief, liberals claimed that society can be "held together" by secular norms and common interests. The open society, advocated by liberals, turns out to have, at the very least, the same imperfect capacity for self-defense as the regretted closed societies of the past. Strauss also unintentionally leads us to see the centrality of the self-exemption prohibition in liberal thought. He considered the imposition of a single system of norms on all individuals, including philosophical supermen, to be morally debased; hence he interpreted the liberal norm of impartiality as a form of moral nihilism. But this necessitates that we identify morality with partiality to the philosopher over the nonphilosopher, to the strong over the weak. The main importance of Strauss for the study of liberalism lies in his unintentionally disclosing the centrality of the moral norm of impartiality to liberal thought and society. He also helps us feel the psychological allure of those strong inegalitarian fantasies for which liberalism gives no outlet. On the other hand, his attack on value pluralism reminds us (contrary to what he suggests) that liberal societies are quite open to a modest striving for superiority, so long as this occurs along a variety of incommensurable dimensions and does not justify the political power of some over others.

Along similar lines, MacIntyre's taste for consensus reminds us that liberals valued both political disagreement and the privatization of religious disputes. His vivid anti-individualism focuses our attention on what we might otherwise have forgotten: the human proclivity to bandwagoning and group-thinking against which all classical liberals vigorously fought. His attack on the abstractness of rights drives home the intimate connection between individualism and universalism in liberal thought. Contrary to Schmitt, moreover, MacIntyre never asks about the relation of different communities to one another. His silence on this vital point directs our attention to it and helps us understand why liberals have also hesitated to encourage unlimited loyalty toward kith-and-kin. At its most radical, communitarianism demands the physical sacrifice of the patriot for his *patrie*. This sounds noble, but it also involves killing counterpart patriots defending rival fatherlands. In contrast, liberal citizens may have feelings of dutifulness toward their country, but they are not inclined to blood brotherhood, are not eager to sacrifice their lives or to kill others for particularistic goals. (They may be willing to die, however, for universalistic values, such as individual freedom and dignity, equality before the law, and democratic self-rule.)

Finally, despite conservatives' claims to the contrary, Unger teaches us the degree to which liberalism is a philosophy of limitation and self-limitation. Liberal norms, for example, demand that human beings give up some of their more powerful urges, such as the desire to inflict physical pain on people they hate. By elaborating obsessively and voluminously on the constraining features of liberal society, Unger unwittingly helps us resist those who criticize liberalism for having recklessly swept aside every stabilizing limit. His superliberal aspirations reveal what is wrong with the traditional Catholic idea that liberalism has lifted all restraints off human beings and exposed them, unguided, to an infinite field of choice.

All in all, therefore, liberalism's severest critics can make an important contribution to the self-understanding, not to mention the self-confidence, of liberals themselves. Despite their Herculean efforts, nonmarxist antiliberals have failed to prove that liberalism is especially debased or debasing. For many contemporary problems, such as violently contested state borders, classical liberalism furnishes no practical solutions. But blaming liberalism for the never-ending "contemporary crisis" is not particularly realistic or helpful. Admittedly, there are many aspects of, say, American society today, including the deplorable condition of inner cities and the notorious weaknesses of social welfare policy, that provoke legitimate anxiety or even anger. But how many of these shortcomings have been *caused* by liberalism? To the extent that libertarianism, as opposed to liberalism, expresses doctrinaire hostility to state intervention in the market, it may needlessly impede the solution to some social problems. Yet the damage even libertarianism has done to America does not compare, say, to that done by racism—a classical expression of anti-individualistic thinking. In a world of resurgent tribalisms and clashing xenophobias, we are beginning to see more clearly the unholy side of solidarity. Contemporary detractors of Enlightenment universalism, addicted to an old polemic, are now being forced to contemplate a disorderly array of societies in which primordial group loyalties blend with anti-Westernism into an explosive antiliberal mix. The longer they ponder these examples, we may safely predict, the "softer" or more evasively apolitical their antiliberalism will become.

Notes

Index

- I75 south
- Off in Flint on M21
- west about 20-30 m.
- will bring in into Owosso
- past Town Hall on rt
- past big downtown
  intersection

- left
- 2 blocks after TB
  on Ball St
- rt on Ball
- 4 blocks + to
  604 Ball.
  (on rt)

Notes

Preface

1. Another influential book in the MacIntyre-Unger mold is Michael Sandel's *Liberalism and the Limits of Justice* (Cambridge: Cambridge University Press, 1982). Sandel decorates his summary and criticism of John Rawls's position, which he conceives as a criticism of American society, with lyrical celebrations of "loyalty" and "allegiance" to "this family or community or nation or people," and he chastises liberalism in general for loosening ethnic, religious, and social "bonds."

2. Schmitt's works are discussed in Chapter 2. For Giovanni Gentile, see *Che cosa é il fascismo* (Florence: Valecchi, 1926); and *Genesi e struttura della societá* (Florence: Sansoni, 1946).

3. Alasdair MacIntyre, *After Virtue*, 2nd ed. (Notre Dame, Indiana: University of Notre Dame Press, 1984), p. 25; Roberto Mangabeira Unger, *Knowledge and Politics* (New York: Free Press, 1975), pp. 20, 229; Gentile, *Genesi e struttura della societá*, p. 65.

4. MacIntyre, *After Virtue*, p. 172; Unger, *Knowledge and Politics*, p. 211; Charles Maurras, *De la Politique naturelle au nationalisme intégrale* (Paris: Vrin, 1972), p. 103; Maurras's antiliberal tirade is remarkably resilient. It resurfaces even today, almost word for word, in the musings of naive American journalists completely unaware of its impeccable fascist pedigree: "eighteenth-century rationalism tried to envision humanity stripped of such supposed inessential attributes as cultural, ethnic, and class particularities" (George Will, *Statecraft as Soulcraft* [New York: Simon and Schuster, 1983], p. 143).

5. MacIntyre, *After Virtue*, 59; Sandel, *Liberalism and the Limits of Justice*, p. 180.

Introduction

1. A fine example of this attitude is Carl Schmitt's claim that "American financiers and Russian Bolsheviks join forces in fighting for the triumph of economistic thought" (Schmitt, *Römischer Katholizismus und politische Form* [Stuttgart: Klett-Cotta, 1984], p. 22).

2. Zeev Sternhell, *Neither Right nor Left: Fascist Ideology in France*, trans. by

David Maisel (Berkeley: University of California Press, 1986); see also, by the same author, *Maurice Barrès et le nationalisme français* (Paris: Seuil, 1972); *La droite révolutionnaire: Les origines françaises du fascisme 1885–1914* (Paris: Seuil, 1978); and, with Mario Sznajder and Maia Asheri, *Naissance de l'ideologie fasciste* (Paris: Fayard, 1989); Andrzej Walicki, *The Slavophile Controversy: History of a Conservative Utopia in Nineteenth-Century Russian Thought* (Oxford: Oxford University Press, 1975); and his *A History of Russian Thought: From the Enlightenment to Marxism* (Stanford: Stanford University Press, 1979).

3. The success of authoritarian socialism in underdeveloped countries may stem in part from Marxism's blend of traditionalism and modernity: its "neotraditionalism" is modern enough to reject inherited monopolies, but archaic enough to retain the traditional taboo on new economic inequalities.

4. Adam Smith, *An Inquiry into the Nature and Causes of the Wealth of Nations* (New York: Modern Library, 1937), p. 11; this argument is the classic example of what John Rawls has called "the difference principle," the liberal norm that inequalities are justified not by analogy with some cosmic hierarchy of values or beings, but only by the palpable advantages they bring to the worst-off members of society. (Obviously enough, the liberal ideal of a society freed from both poverty and dependency remains imperfectly realized today.)

5. For a more detailed account of the liberal tradition, see Stephen Holmes, *Benjamin Constant and the Making of Modern Liberalism* (New Haven: Yale University Press, 1984), and my *Rediscovering Liberal Democracy* (Chicago: University of Chicago Press, 1994).

6. Francis Coker, "Some Present-Day Critics of Liberalism," *American Political Science Review*, 47 (March 1953), p. 12.

7. Alexander Solzhenitsyn, *Warning to the West* (New York: Farrar, Straus and Giroux, 1976), pp. 79, 127, 146; and his *A World Split Apart* (New York: Harper and Row, 1978), pp. 47, 51, 53, 57.

8. See, for instance, Alasdair MacIntyre, *After Virtue*, 2nd ed. (Notre Dame, Indiana: University of Notre Dame Press, 1984), p. 200; Roberto Unger, *False Necessity* (Cambridge: Cambridge University Press, 1987), p. 581.

1. Maistre and the Antiliberal Tradition

1. Joseph de Maistre, "Quatre chapitres sur la Russie," in *Œuvres complètes* (Lyons: Vitte et Perrussel, 1884), vol. 8, p. 291.

2. Maistre, *Considérations sur la France* (1797), ed. by Pierre Manent (Paris: Editions Complexe, 1988), p. 87.

3. Maistre, *Les Soirées de Saint-Pétersbourg* (Paris: Trédaniel, 1980), vol. 1, pp. 351, 373; vol. 2, p. 91.

4. Isaiah Berlin, "Joseph de Maistre and the Origins of Fascism," *The Crooked Timber of Humanity* (New York: Knopf, 1991), p. 127.

5. Carl Schmitt, *Political Romanticism* (Cambridge, Mass.: MIT Press, 1986), p. 122.

6. Maistre, *Soirées*, vol. 2, p. 167; Maistre, *Considérations*, pp. 23, 26, 31, 137, 160; Jacques Godechot, *The Counter-Revolution* (London: Routledge and Kegan Paul, 1972), p. 94; cf. *Soirées*, vol. 2, p. 166; *Considérations*, p. 30.

7. Richard Lebrun reports on his personal attempt to unearth traces of liberalism in Maistre's private diaries, letters, and early works (*Joseph de Maistre: An Intellectual Militant* [Montreal: McGill-Queen University Press, 1988]). He produces some interesting evidence. Maistre occasionally wrote sympathetically of moderate monarchy, ruling in accord with custom, hemmed in by the power of hereditary magistrates, and amenable to mild reform. It was a vision more or less akin to Montesquieu's. In most of Maistre's writings, however, this moderate strand is swamped by its polar opposite. His justly famous works are not so disappointingly bland as Lebrun—in a misguided effort to improve his hero's reputation—wants us to believe.

8. *Soirées*, vol. 2, p. 109; *Étude sur la souveraineté*, in *Œuvres complètes*, vol. 1, p. 346; *Souveraineté*, p. 376; ibid., p. 355.

9. Louis de Bonald, "Théorie du pouvoir politique et religieux dans la société civile," *Œuvres complètes* (Paris: Migne, 1859), vol. 1, p. 123.

10. *Souveraineté*, p. 329; *Soirées*, vol. 2, p. 12; *Souveraineté*, p. 316–318, 321.

11. *Souveraineté*, p. 313; *Considérations*, p. 39; Maistre, *Essai sur le principe générateur des constitutions politiques* (1814), reprinted in *Considérations sur la France*, p. 274.

12. Maistre, *Éclaircissement sur les sacrifices*, in *Œuvres complètes*, vol. 5, p. 326; *Souveraineté*, p. 357; *Considérations*, p. 159, 78, 27; *Constitutions politiques*, p. 272; *Soirées*, vol. 2, p. 227; "murderous egoism encroaches remorselessly on public spirit and makes it retreat" (*Souveraineté*, p. 409).

13. Schmitt, *Political Romanticism*, pp. 134, 32, 23, 32, 115, 142, 144, 121, 116, 144; Schmitt, *Political Theology* (Cambridge, Mass.: M.I.T. Press, 1985), p. 66; see also Schmitt's review of a German translation of the *Considérations* and *Le Principe générateur* in *Zeitschrift für die gesamte Staatswissenschaft* (1925), pp. 727–28.

14. *Souveraineté*, p. 424; *Du Pape*, in *Œuvres complètes*, vol. 2, pp. 338–339, 168; *Souveraineté*, p. 324; *Soirées*, vol. 1, p. 108; *Du Pape*, p. 6.

15. *Constitutions politiques*, p. 256; *Soirées*, vol. 1, p. 72; *Du Pape*, p. 167.

16. *Considérations*, p. 121, 135; *Soirées*, vol. 1, pp. 68–69; *Du Pape*, p. 167; *Soirées*, vol. 1, 13; *Souveraineté*, p. 449

17. *Soirées*, vol. 1, p. 21; cf. 35; *Du Pape*, p. 170.

18. *Considérations*, p. 60; *Soirées*, vol. 1, p. 288; *Constitutions politiques*, p. 274; *Soirées*, vol. 2, p. 109.

19. *Soirées*, I, 76; *Constitutions politiques*, 229

20. *Du Pape*, p. 342; see also Judith Shklar, *After Utopia* (Princeton: Princeton University Press, 1957), pp. 19, 21.

21. *Considérations*, p. 136; *Soirées*, vol. 1, p. 287; *Souveraineté*, pp. 320, 375; *Soirées*, vol. 1, p. 12.

22. *Constitutions politiques*, pp. 259, 238; *Souveraineté*, pp. 329, 425; *Considérations*, p. 154; "Quatre chapitres sur la Russie," p. 290; *Souveraineté*, p. 353; *Constitutions politiques*, p. 212.

23. *Constitutions politiques*, pp. 237–238, 242; "there exist mysterious laws which it is not good to divulge which must be covered in a religious silence and revered *as a mystery*" (cited in Massimo Boffa, "Maistre," *A Critical Dictionary of the French Revolution*, eds. François Furet and Mona Ozouf (Cambridge, Mass.: Harvard University Press, 1989), p. 969.

24. Ibid., p. 970; *Considérations*, p. 70, 54, 84; *Constitutions politiques*, p. 212; *Souveraineté*, pp. 354–355;

25. *Soirées*, vol. 1, pp. 15, 277, 225; vol. 2, p. 185; vol. 1, p. 214; *Constitutions politiques*, p. 249

26. *Soirées*, vol. 1, p. 272; vol. 2, p. 108; vol. 1, p. 11, 214, 224, 108; "Quatre chapitres sur la Russie," pp. 297–308.

27. *Soirées*, vol. 1, pp. 290, 374; vol. 2, p. 180; *Souveraineté*, p. 416; *Considérations*, p. 67;

28. *Considérations*, p. 75; *Soirées*, vol. 2, p. 128; *Constitutions politiques*, p. 249; *Considérations*, p. 93.

29. *Souveraineté*, p. 408

30. The imaginative suggestion that liberalism somehow heightened personal anxiety, although purportedly based on Locke's theory of innate human "restlessness," is also dubious. According to Wolin, "anxious man emerges as the creation of liberalism" (Sheldon Wolin, *Politics and Vision* [Boston: Little, Brown, 1960], p. 324). Actually, tolerance for public disagreement and political contestation, typical in liberal societies, suggests a relative freedom from primal anxiety. Compared to traditional autocrats, liberal leaders are remarkably unrattled by dissent. Public willingness to censure and criticize government, moreover, depends on the underlying confidence that such attacks will not cause the indispensable law-enforcing powers of society utterly to collapse (Adam Smith, *The Wealth of Nations* [New York: Modern Library, 1937], p. 668).

31. *Soirées*, vol. 2, p. 163; *Considérations*, p. 160.

32. *Souveraineté*, p. 376; *Soirées*, vol. 2, p. 172.

33. *Souveraineté*, p. 376, my emphasis.

34. *Soirées*, vol. 1, p. 87; *Souveraineté*, p. 359; *Considérations*, p. 137; *Soirées*, vol. 2, p. 116; *Constitutions politiques*, p. 231; the core of Maistre's *Considérations*, according to Schmitt, is "the rejection of the idea that law could result from the methodical activity of individual human beings" (Schmitt, *Political Romanticism*, p. 109); human planners typically achieve the exact opposite of what they want: "the efforts of the people to attain their objective, are precisely the means that it [Providence] employs to drive them away from it" (*Considérations*, p. 127); see also *Du Pape*, p. 175 and *Souveraineté*, pp. 351–352; Albert Hirschman has shrewdly analyzed the basic structure of this enduring conservative argument, with pointed references to Maistre, in *The Rhetoric of Reaction* (Cambridge, Mass.: Harvard University Press, 1991).

35. To explain why men will never be able to govern themselves, as liberals hope, Maistre invokes a technical distinction between "reglèment" and "loi." A *reglèment* is a pact or settlement which various individuals or groups make with each other. Such a pact, therefore, is necessarily self-enforcing. It does not rely on an external enforcer, since the parties keep their promises for reasons of self-interest. This means, however, that they keep these promises just as long as they like, and no longer—obviously a precarious arrangement, given the fluctuating nature of human preferences. It is certainly not suitable for the basic ground-rules governing all social interactions. A *loi* is superior to a pact in this decisive way: it is a contract that all parties honor because defection or reneging is punished by an irresistible superior power. It is impossible for secular liberalism to find such an overriding authority. Liberal constitutionalism is a boot-strap operation, an attempt to create a higher law above the popular will, while expressly denying the existence of any power superior to the popular will (*Constitutions politiques*, p. 212).

36. In a more empirical vein, Maistre attacks the notion that representative government is a form of popular government; even in the most democratic form of representative system, "the people remain wholly foreign to the government." In France, Paris will always be in charge, and a small group will do the actual ruling. In effect, "in every republic of a certain size, what is called liberty is nothing but the total sacrifice of the large number of individuals to the independence and pride of the few." Or, again, " a republic, by its nature, is the government that gives the greatest rights to the smallest number of men, called the sovereign, and that takes these rights away from all the others, called subjects." This cynical or "elite" theory of democracy, reminiscent of Gaetano Mosca, is not necessarily compatible with Maistre's suggestion that democracy is indistinguishable from anarchy (*Considérations*, pp. 63, 141; *Souveraineté*, pp. 452, 501, 466).

37. *Considérations*, pp. 90, 98–99; *Souveraineté*, p. 352; *Considérations*, p. 99.
38. *Considérations*, p. 53.
39. *Soirées*, vol. 2, pp. 13–14.
40. Ibid., pp. 32–34, 36.
41. Ibid., pp. 13, 25, 18.
42. *Souveraineté*, p. 332.
43. *Soirées*, vol. 2, p. 2; vol. 2, p. 27; *Considérations*, p. 42.
44. *Soirées*, vol. 1, pp. 32–34.
45. To cite another example of Maistre's dubious realism, this renowned defender of political authority published, toward the end of his life, a book arguing that the Pope should have the power throughout Catholic Europe to release subjects from allegiance to their monarchs (*Du Pape* [1819], in *Œuvres complètes*, vol. 2. At the beginning of the nineteenth century, this plan can hardly be considered an expression of hard-headed *Realpolitik*.
46. Burke, *Reflections on the Revolution in France* (Harmondsworth: Penguin, 1968), pp. 171–172.
47. Jeremy Bentham, "Principles of Legislation," *The Theory of Legislation* (Bombay: N. M. Tripathi, 1979), p. 5; David Hume, "Of the Populousness of Ancient Nations," *Essays Moral, Political, and Literary* (Indianapolis: Liberty Classics, 1985), pp. 377–464.
48. Michael Howard, *War and the Liberal Conscience* (New Brunswick: Rutgers University Press, 1989).
49. *Soirées*, vol. 2, p. 10; *Souveraineté*, p. 449.
50. *Soirées*, vol. 1; pp. 22, 25; vol. 2, 23–24.
51. Ibid., vol. 2, pp. 4–5.
52. Ibid., p. 14; *Considérations*, p. 42.
53. *Eclaircissement sur les sacrifices*, p. 300; *Considérations*, p. 52.
54. Many commentators have noted that Maistre's Christianity is not entirely orthodox, that it slights brotherly love, for example, as well as the role of Christ as a universal savior, emphasizing instead Christ as "the sanguinary sacrifice demanded by the offended Deity—like Iphigenia or Jephthah's daughter" (Georg Brandes, *Revolution and Reaction in Nineteenth-Century French Literature* (New York: Russell and Russell, n.d.), p. 112).
55. *Soirées*, vol. 1, p. 68; Maistre writes: "we are indulged by modern philosophy, which has said that everything is good, even though everything is contaminated and, in a very real sense, everything is evil because nothing is in its place" (*Considérations*, p. 53).
56. *Soirées*, vol. 2, pp. 18, 25; *Considérations*, p. 50.
57. *Considérations*, pp. 36, 49; *Soirées*, vol. 2, pp. 84–85; vol. 1, pp. 226, 228.
58. *Soirées*, vol. 1, pp. 20, 36, 27, 229; for a liberal account of the distinction between injustice and misfortune, see Judith Shklar, *The Faces of Injustice* (New Haven: Yale University Press, 1989).

59. *Soirées*, vol. 1, pp. 27, 290, 228; vol. 2, p. 82.
60. Ibid., vol. 1, pp. 20–22, 194, 202.
61. Isaiah Berlin, *The Hedgehog and the Fox* (New York: Touchstone, n.d., p. 76).
62. *The Federalist Papers*, #1, p. 33.
63. *Considérations*, p. 29.

2. Schmitt: The Debility of Liberalism

1. *Telos*, 72 (Summer 1987), p. 14; for an even more favorable introduction to Schmitt, see Günther Maschke, "Drei Motive im Anti-Liberalismus Carl Schmitts," in *Carl Schmitt und die Liberalismuskritik*, edited by Klaus Hansen and Hans Lietzmann (Opladen: Laske and Budrich, 1988), pp. 55–79.
2. Carl Schmitt, "Der bürgerliche Rechtsstaat," *Abendland* (1928), p. 202; arguing along these lines, Schmitt claims, paradoxically, that liberalism can be simultaneously impotent and destructive. It cannot replace friend-enemy groupings with universal cooperation, but it can permanently injure Germany by subjecting German minds to naive pacifist, humanitarian, and antistatist temptations in the interests of aggressive allied powers.
3. Schmitt, "Wesen und Werden des fascistischen Staates" (1929), in his *Positionen und Begriffe im Kampf mit Weimar-Genf-Versailles* (Hamburg: Hanseatische Verlag, 1940), p. 114; Schmitt, *Staatsgefüge und Zusammenbruch des zweiten Reiches: Der Sieg des Bürgers über den Soldaten* (Hamburg: Hanseatische Verlagsanstalt, 1934), p 49.
4. "Die Verfassung der Freiheit," *Deutsche Juristen-Zeitung* 19 (1 October 1935), p. 1136; "Neutralität und Neutralisierungen" (1939), *Positionen und Begriffe*, pp. 275, 293; "Der Führer schütz das Recht," *Deutsche Juristen-Zeitung* 15 (1 August 1934), p. 946; for Schmitt's deep hostility toward federalism—which, he thought, prevented the Wilhelminian Reich from becoming a real state—see "Reich-Staat-Bund" (1933), *Positionen und Begriffe*, p. 196.
5. "Die deutsche Rechtswissenschaft im Kampf gegen den jüdischen Geist," *Deutsche Juristen-Zeitung* 20 (15 October 1936), pp. 1193–1199; Nicolaus Sombart has now definitively refuted the claim that Schmitt's antisemitism was merely a matter of political opportunism between 1933 and 1936 (Sombart, *Die deutschen Männer und ihre Feinde: Carl Schmitt, ein deutsches Schicksal zwischen Männerbund und Matriarchatsmythos* [Munich: Carl Hanser Verlag, 1991]). Sombart's persuasive argument on this point should not be overshadowed by his controversial and—in my view—arbitrary (not to say eccentric) psychoanalysis of Schmitt.

6. "Interrogation of Carl Schmitt by Robert Kempner," *Telos*, 72 (Summer 1987), p. 103–104.
7. Schmitt, *The Concept of the Political* (New Brunswick: Rutgers University Press, 1976).
8. His "explanation" seems to be the same as Maistre's: life simply *is* conflict.
9. Schmitt, *Ex Captivitate Salus* (Cologne: Greven Verlag, 1950), p. 90.
10. Schmitt was a Hobbesian, in my judgment, only to the extent that he was a Maistrean. For example, he endorsed Maistre's implausible view, which (in turn) echoed Hobbes, that "all government is absolute; and from the moment when anyone can resist it on the pretext of error or injustice, authority no longer exists" (Maistre, *Du Pape*, in *Œuvres complètes* [Lyons: Vitte et Perrussel, 1884], vol. 2, p. 2; also ibid., p. 170).
11. "Staatsethik und pluralistischer Staat" (1930), *Positionen und Begriffe*, p. 144
12. "The exception is more interesting than the rule. . . . In the exception the power of real life breaks through the crust of mechanism that has become torpid by repetition" (*Political Theology: Four Chapters on the Concept of Sovereignty* [Cambridge, Mass.: M.I.T. Press, 1985], p. 15).
13. "Das Zeitalter der Neutralisierungen und Entpolitisierungen" (1929), reprinted in *Der Begriff des Politischen* (Berlin: Duncker und Humblot, 1963), p. 83; Leo Strauss, "Comments on *Der Begriff des Politischen* by Carl Schmitt," reprinted in Schmitt, *The Concept of the Political*, p. 88; his *The Crisis of Parliamentary Democracy* (Cambridge, Mass.: M.I.T. Press, 1985), p. 71.
14. "Das Zeitalter der Neutralisierungen und Entpolitisierungen," p. 93.
15. It was this second aspect of his thinking, evidently, that predisposed Schmitt toward collaboration with the Nazis once they had gained power. George Orwell helps illuminate what must have attracted Schmitt to the NSDAP: "Whereas Socialism, and even capitalism in a more grudging way, have said to people 'I offer you a good time,' Hitler has said to them 'I offer you struggle, danger and death.'" (Orwell, book review of *Mein Kampf*, in *The Collected Essays, Journalism and Letters* [Harmondsworth: Penguin, 1970], vol. 2, p. 29.).
16. Joseph Bendersky's indispensable biography, *Carl Schmitt: Theorist for the Reich* (Princeton: Princeton University Press, 1983), is to be read with some skepticism on this and other delicate topics, because of the author's acquiescence in Schmitt's own postwar self-presentation.
17. For comments on Schmitt's own romanticism, see Karl Löwith (pseudonym, Hugo Fiala), "Politischer Dezisionismus," *Internationale Zeitschrift für Theorie des Rechts* (1935), 2, pp. 101–123.
18. Weber, "Politics as a Vocation," *From Max Weber*, eds. H. H. Gerth and C. Wright Mills (New York: Oxford University Press, 1946), pp. 126–127.

19. The "political hatred and outrage over the injustice of foreign domination," Schmitt writes, "is missing in every romantic utterance" (*Political Romanticism* [Cambridge, Mass.: M.I.T. Press, 1986], p. 129; this passage is in the third chapter, first published separately in 1920 and incorporated into the 1925 edition of the book).

20. *The Concept of the Political*, pp. 55–56; 31.

21. José Ortega y Gasset, *The Revolt of the Masses* (New York: Norton, 1957), p. 76.

22. *Political Romanticism*, p. 192.

23. According to Solzhenitsyn, similarly, "liberalism was inevitably pushed aside by radicalism, radicalism had to surrender to socialism, and socialism could not stand up to communism" (*A World Split Apart* [New York: Harper and Row, 1978], p. 55). The "inevitability" that some antiliberals ascribe to a communist victory over "tolerant" liberalism may reflect a deep wish for its punishment.

24. This reductionist conception of morality derives from Thrasymachus in Plato's *Republic* and from Nietzsche (the quintessential anti-Hobbes), who argued in *The Genealogy of Morals* that the idea of justice was a weapon used by resentful Jews and Christians against their hated enemies, the noble pagans.

25. *Staat, Bewegung, Volk*, p. 36.

26. See Jürgen Habermas, "The Horrors of Autonomy: Carl Schmitt in English," in his *The New Conservatism* (Cambridge, Mass.: M.I.T. Press, 1989), pp. 128–139.

27. "Der bürgerliche Rechtsstaat," p. 202.

28. Opinions expressed in the privacy of a voting booth do not deserve the name of public opinion, Schmitt explains. "The consistent implementation of the secret ballot is not democratic because it takes the single citizen out of the public sphere and transforms him into a private person." In fact, "the method of individuals voting in secret is not democratic, but an expression of liberal individualism." Schmitt adds that "the secret vote of the individual means that the voting citizen in the decisive moment is isolated." With the ballot "the connection between the assembled people and the suffrage is fully broken apart. The people participates in an election but does not vote as a people" (*Verfassungslehre* [1928], [Berlin: Duncker and Humblot, 1970], pp. 245–246); "the remarkable thing is that in our democratic constitution the assembled people nowhere appears"; but this is radically antidemocratic because "the people exists only as the assembled people" ("Der bürgerliche Rechtsstaat," p. 202). The weakness of this line of reasoning becomes clear when we ask: what does it mean, in a concrete case, for the people to act not as individuals, through elections, but as "the assembled people"? Schmitt admits that such acclamatory arrangements give enormous decision-making powers to those

political puppeteers who can psychologically manipulate strategically placed minorities.

29. *Verfassungslehre*, pp. 83–84, 244, 279, 81.

30. In other words, Schmitt toyed with plebiscitary techniques for legitimating authoritarian rule; but his democratic professions were insincere. To grasp this point it is enough to recall that he fully accepted Maistre's description of democracy as the political equivalent to atheism and, therefore, as intrinsically evil.

31. See, for example, *Political Theology*, p. 55.

32. *Der Leviathan in der Staatslehre des Thomas Hobbes: Sinn und Fehlschlag eines politischen Symbols* (Cologne: Hohenheim, 1982); "Die vollendete Reformation, Zu neuen Leviathan-Interpretationen," reprinted in ibid., pp. 137–178.

33. For his earlier view, see "Der Weg des deutschen Juristen," *Deutsche Juristen-Zeitung* 39 (1934), p. 693.

34. Ibid., p. 18.

35. *Der Leviathan*, p. 17–18

36. *The Concept of the Political*, p. 27.

37. Hobbes, *Leviathan* (Harmondsworth: Penguin, 1968), chap. 42, p. 550.

38. *Der Leviathan*, pp. 86.

39. Ibid., pp. 86, 92–93.

40. Liberalism guarantees, for example, that political decision-makers are exposed to embarrassing or troublesome but useful information; it also helps the state mobilize the decentralized resources of citizens for solving common problems.

41. Schmitt, *Land und Meer: Eine weltgeschichtliche Betrachtung* [1942], (Cologne: Hohenheim, 1981).

42. Ibid., pp. 88–89.

43. Ibid., pp. 16–17.

44. Ibid., pp. 71, 75.

45. Notice again that Schmitt associates "decisionism" here not with the repression of anarchy and creation of social order, but with masculinity, human freedom, and an existential escape from meaninglessness.

46. Locke, *Two Treatises of Government* (Cambridge: Cambridge University Press, 1988), II, 30.

47. *Land und Meer*, p. 89; again, a Marxist revolution in the ownership of the means of production dwindles into insignificance when compared to "the revolution in the concept of planetary space" that accompanied the establishment of British naval dominion around the globe.

48. Schmitt, *Hamlet oder Hekuba: Der Einbruch der Zeit in das Spiel* [1956], (Stuttgart: Klett-Cotta, 1985), pp. 54–55; *Land und Meer*, p. 80

49. *Land und Meer*, p. 104.

50. "Der bürgerliche Rechtsstaat," p. 203.

51. *Political Theology*, p. 56.

52. *The Federalist Papers*, #51, ed. C. Rossiter (New York: Mentor, 1961), p. 322.

53. Locke, *Two Treatises of Government*, II, 159; Blackstone, *Commentaries*, vol. 1, pp. 244, 238.

54. Schmitt, *Der Nomos der Erde im Völkerrecht des Jus Publicum Europaeum* (Berlin: Duncker and Humblot, 1974), originally published in 1950.

55. Strauss, "Comments on *Der Begriff des Politischen* by Carl Schmitt."

3. Strauss: Truths for Philosophers Alone

1. Leo Strauss, "Comments on *Der Begriff des Politischen* by Carl Schmitt" (1932), reprinted in Schmitt, *The Concept of the Political* (New Brunswick: Rutgers University Press, 1976), p. 105.

2. Strauss, *Thoughts on Machiavelli* (Glencoe, Ill.: Free Press, 1958), p. 120; *The Rebirth of Classical Political Rationalism*, ed. Thomas Pangle (University of Chicago Press, 1989), pp. 90–91, 17, 31, 234, 239, 245; "Preface" to Strauss's *Spinoza's Critique of Religion* (New York: Schocken Books, 1965), p. 9; "The Crisis of Our Time," in *The Predicament of Modern Politics*, ed. Harold Spaeth (Detroit: University of Detroit Press, 1964), p. 43.

3. Shadia Drury makes this point in her marvelously clear overview of Strauss's work, *The Political Ideas of Leo Strauss* (New York: St. Martin's Press, 1988), to which I and all students of Strauss are greatly indebted.

4. Strauss, *Liberalism Ancient and Modern*, New York: Basic Books, 1968, p. 100

5. Strauss, *The Rebirth of Classical Political Rationalism*, p. 234; *Persecution and the Art of Writing* (Glencoe, Ill.: Free Press, 1952), p. 24; *Natural Right and History* (Chicago: University of Chicago Press, 1953), pp. 260, 220; *What Is Political Philosophy?* (Glencoe, Ill.: Free Press, 1959), pp. 221–222.

6. *Thoughts on Machiavelli*, p. 231.

7. *Natural Right and History*, p. 81; *Liberalism Ancient and Modern*, p. 85; *Persecution and the Art of Writing*, p. 36.

8. "Preface" to *Spinoza's Critique of Religion*, p. 11.

9. Allan Bloom, *The Closing of the American Mind* (New York: Simon and Schuster, 1987), p. 285.

10. *Natural Right and History*, p. 113.

11. *What Is Political Philosophy?* p. 222.

12. Strauss, *Xenophon's Socrates* (Ithaca: Cornell University Press, 1972), p. 178; as Strauss wrote in a private letter of 22 April 1957, "I do not believe in the possibility of a conversation of Socrates with the *people*." In another context, "the relation of the philosopher to the people is mediated

by a certain kind of rhetorician who arouses fear of punishment after death" (*On Tyranny*, ed. Victor Gourevich and Michael Roth [New York: Free Press, 1991], p. 275).

13. *Natural Right and History*, p. 113.

14. Ibid., p. 106; *On Tyranny*, p. 35; *What Is Political Philosophy?* pp. 222, 18.

15. Strauss, *The City and Man*, Chicago: Rand McNally, 1964, p. 111.

16. In Strauss's view, "science or philosophy is essentially universal. Science or philosophy necessarily weakens the power of the national 'philosophies' and therewith the attachment of the citizens to the particular way of life, or the manners, of their community. In other words, whereas science is essentially cosmopolitan, society must be animated by a spirit of patriotism, by a spirit which is by no means irreconcilable with national hatreds" (*Natural Right and History*, p. 257). This contrast between traditional xenophobia and a scientific outlook helps explain why many antiliberals associate science so closely with political liberalism.

17. *The Rebirth of Classical Political Rationalism*, p. 12.

18. *What Is Political Philosophy?* p. 22.

19. Ibid., p. 93.

20. *Natural Right and History*, p. 202.

21. To employ the language of John Rawls, Strauss assumes the absolute priority of the good over the right.

22. "Comments on *Der Begriff des Politischen* by Carl Schmitt" (1932), in *Spinoza's Critique of Religion*, p. 351; *Natural Right and History*, pp. 75, 249–250.

23. Put differently, both Schmitt and Strauss denounced liberalism as evasive or inauthentic: for Schmitt it was a form of conflict avoidance, for Strauss a form of inequality denial. A reference to the "esoteric" truth known only by an initiated few occurs in Schmitt's *Ex Captivitate Salus* (Cologne: Greven, 1950), pp. 50–51.

24. *On Tyranny*, p. 95; for Strauss's comments on "the wholly unnatural life" to which ordinary men and women are doomed, see *Natural Right and History*, p. 113.

25. *Natural Right and History*, p. 113.

26. *The Rebirth of Classical Political Rationalism*, p. 64; *Persecution and the Art of Writing*, p. 36.

27. That is, "no miraculous or nonmiraculous change in human nature is required for its actualization; it does not require the abolition or extirpation of that evil or imperfection which is essential to man and to human life" (*Natural Right and History*, p. 139).

28. *The Rebirth of Classical Political Rationalism*, p. 88.

29. For MacIntyre, see the next chapter.

30. For Christians, keyed to salvation and the beatific vision, "the end of man

cannot consist in philosophical investigation" (*Natural Right and History*, p. 164). Essentially, Strauss is twisting an eighteenth-century commonplace into an attack on the Enlightenment itself; both Hume and Gibbon assumed that the conversion of the Roman world to Christianity in the reign of Constantine spelled not only an eclipse of religious toleration but also a decline in the prestige of learning and intelligence together with an end to freedom of inquiry.

31. *Persecution and the Art of Writing*, p. 21; "The Mutual Influence of Theology and Politics," *The Independent Journal of Philosophy*, 3 [1979], p. 113.

32. See note 42.

33. Here is another eye-catching paradox, though not a contradiction. Strauss attacks historicism vehemently, yet few doctrines are as historicist as the theory of secret writing: philosophers are always dodging local authorities, adapting to local circumstances, responding to local crises, taming local elites, and seducing the most gifted local youths away from politics and toward the contemplative life (*The Rebirth of Classical Political Rationalism*, p. 62). As a result, context controls most of what philosophers have to say and the way they say it—even while their "highest and purest thoughts" remain completely unchanged from one millennium to the next.

34. Friedrich Nietzsche, *The Will to Power*, trans. Walter Kaufmann and R. J. Hollingdale (New York: Vintage, 1968), sec. 963, p. 505; *Beyond Good and Evil*, trans. Walter Kaufmann (New York: Vintage, 1966), sec. 40, p. 51; 30, p. 42.

35. *Beyond Good and Evil*, sec. 30, p. 42; Like Strauss, Zarathustra says: "I do not want to be mixed up and confused with those preachers of equality. For, to *me* justice speaks thus: 'Men are not equal. Nor shall they become equal'" (*Thus Spoke Zarathustra*, translated by Walter Kaufmann [Harmondsworth: Penguin, 1978], book II, sec. 7, pp. 100–101); unlike Nietzsche, of course, Strauss never made the leap from favoring inequality to favoring cruelty.

36. *Thus Spoke Zarathustra*, Prologue, sec. 9, p. 23.

37. *The Rebirth of Classical Political Rationalism*, pp. 28–29, 38; *Natural Right and History*, pp. 113, 75; *The Rebirth of Classical Political Rationalism*, p. 251.

38. *The Rebirth of Classical Political Rationalism*, p. 100.

39. *What Is Political Philosophy?*, p. 36; admittedly, Schmitt too distinguished between "essentially distinct human types" *(wesensverschiedene Menschentypen)*; but what he had in mind was the distinction between the decisive and the indecisive man, between the soldier and the bourgeois (*Staatsgefüge und Zusammenbruch des zweiten Reiches: Der Sieg des Bürgers über den Soldaten* [Hamburg: Hanseatische Verlagsanstalt, 1934], p. 13). Strauss's dichotomy of strong and weak or hero and antihero was not martial, of course, but intellectual.

40. *The Rebirth of Classical Political Rationalism*, pp. 102, 29.

41. Stressing the way secret-keeping inflates the self-esteem of the secret-keeper, Georg Simmel may help us understand some of the subtle psychological attraction exerted by Strauss upon his followers. For example: "the secret is surrounded by the possibility and temptation of betrayal; and the external danger of being discovered is interwoven with the internal danger, which is like the fascination of an abyss, of giving oneself away" ("Secrecy," *The Sociology of Georg Simmel*, ed. Kurt H. Wolff [New York: Free Press, 1964], p. 334).

42. This point has been forcefully made by John G. Gunnell, "Political Theory and Politics: The Case of Leo Strauss and Liberal Democracy," *The Crisis of Liberal Democracy*, eds. Kenneth L. Deutsch and Walter Soffer (Albany: SUNY Press, 1987), pp. 68–88; see also, by the same author, "The Myth of the Tradition," *American Political Science Review*, 72 (1978), pp. 122–134; *Political Theory: Tradition and Interpretation* (Cambridge, Mass.: Winthrop, 1979); "Strauss before Straussianism: The Weimar Conversation," *The Vital Nexus*, 1 (May 1990), pp. 73–104.

43. *On Tyranny*, p. 96; "Das Erkenntnisproblem in der philosophischen Lehre Fr. H. Jacobis," typescript, Preussische Staatsbibliothek, Berlin, pp. 7, 63.

44. *What Is Political Philosophy?*, p. 224; *The Rebirth of Classical Political Rationalism*, p. 68.

45. Hume, "Of Refinement in the Arts," *Essays Moral, Political, and Literary* (Indianapolis: Liberty Classics, 1985), p. 278.

46. Weber, "National Character and the Junkers" [1917], *From Max Weber*, edited by H. H. Gerth and C. Wright Mills (New York: Oxford University Press, 1958), p. 393.

47. Hannah Arendt, *The Human Condition* [Chicago: University of Chicago Press, 1958], pp. 12, 14.

48. *On Tyranny*, p. 203; *Liberalism Ancient and Modern*, p. 107; *The Rebirth of Classical Political Rationalism*, p. 66; *The City and Man*, p. 125.

49. Cf. John Rawls, *A Theory of Justice* (Cambridge, Mass.: Harvard University Press, 1971), p. 25.

50. To use Nietzsche's distinction, Strauss's philosopher is not a shepherd but a master: "the former [is] a *means* of preserving the herd; the latter an *end* for which the herd exists" (Nietzsche, *The Will to Power*, sec. 902, p. 479).

51. *The Rebirth of Classical Political Rationalism*, p. 241; *Natural Right and History*, p. 113.

52. Strauss does not merely argue, like Schmitt, that liberalism is too weak politically to resist militant egalitarian movements such as Bolshevism. He also suggests, however obscurely, that liberalism *leads* to communism by its own inherent logic.

53. *On Tyranny*, p. 211; *Natural Right and History*, p. 135; *The City and Man*, p. 51; *Liberalism Ancient and Modern*, p. 131; *On Tyranny*, p. 96.

54. Max Weber, *The Methodology of the Social Sciences* (New York: Free Press, 1949), p. 53.
55. *The Rebirth of Classical Political Rationalism*, p. 60; *What Is Political Philosophy?* p. 21.
56. *Natural Right and History*, p. 42; *Liberalism Ancient and Modern*, p. 5.
57. *On Tyranny*, p. 178; *What Is Political Philosophy?* p. 37.
58. Alexis de Tocqueville, *The Old Regime and the Revolution* (New York: Anchor, 1955), p. 139.
59. *Thoughts on Machiavelli*, p. 10; *What Is Political Philosophy?* p. 221.
60. *The Rebirth of Classical Political Rationalism*, p. 25.
61. For more imaginative and commonsensical approaches to the subject, see Annabel Patterson's "New Introduction" to the paperback edition of her *Censorship and Interpretation: The Conditions of Writing and Reading in Early Modern England* (Madison: University of Wisconsin Press, 1990); David Wooton, *Paolo Sarpi: Between Renaissance and Enlightenment* (Cambridge: Cambridge University Press, 1983) and Perez Zagorin, *Ways of Lying: Dissimulation, Persecution, and Conformity in Early Modern Europe* (Cambridge, Mass.: Harvard University Press, 1990). That esotericism had become an exoteric doctrine by the eighteenth century is demonstrated entertainingly by the entry on "Fraud: Should Pious Frauds Be Practiced on the People," in Voltaire's *Philosophical Dictionary* (Harmondsworth: Penguin, 1983), pp. 212–215.
62. For the close association of "l'illuminisme" with "des Juifs," see also Joseph de Maistre, "Quatre chapitres sur la Russie," in *Œuvres complètes* (Lyons: Vitte et Perrussel, 1884), vol. 8, pp. 335–336, 345.
63. *Persecution and the Art of Writing*, p. 14.
64. *Natural Right and History*, p. 209.
65. Kojève warned against the uncritical group thinking that is likely to emerge when a few philosophers cloister themselves with their secrets and refuse to join public debate ("Tyranny and Wisdom," reprinted in *On Tyranny*, p. 155); as Kant warned: "it is very harmful to propagate prejudices, because they finally avenge themselves on the very people who first encouraged them" ("An Answer to the Question: 'What is Enlightenment?'," *Kant's Political Writings*, ed. Hans Reiss [Cambridge: Cambridge University Press, 1970], p. 55).
66. While he was just as anticosmopolitan as Alasdair MacIntyre, Strauss was a communitarian only for the masses, not for the philosophical elite. He criticized Heidegger and Schmitt. He viewed public pressure as inimical to private excellence. He thought that liberal democracy, while morally base, was safer (for philosophers like himself) than any other system likely to emerge under modern conditions. Admittedly, he thought liberalism's horizon was constricted. But does he really belong to the antiliberal tradition discussed in this book? His disciples will say no. I say yes.

He belongs here, for one thing, because of his plea for a total, rather than merely partial, criticism of liberal thought. As he wrote in his essay on Schmitt, to criticize liberalism properly one must occupy a standpoint wholly untainted by debased liberal ideas. (His return to Platonism was an attempt to find such unspoiled ground.) The radicalness of Strauss's questioning of liberalism, his textualist approach to social problems, his hostility toward cosmopolitan and egalitarian norms, and his obsession with "the one great crisis" of modern times—all these factors reveal his kinship with the other antiliberals scrutinized here. More evidence includes the forms of esotericism advocated by Maistre and Nietzsche, and the several fascinating parallels between Strauss and Schmitt.

The similarities (which do not exclude important differences) extend beyond these three cases. For all his iconoclasm, Strauss belonged to a larger tradition. Powerful confirmation that his thinking is representative as well as original comes from an unexpected source: Roberto Unger. On the surface, none of the thinkers treated in this book are more dissimilar than Unger and Strauss. For example, Unger warns repeatedly against "the danger of elitism." He even describes "the exercise of power by the higher talents over the less gifted" as one of the truly repulsive features of liberal-bureaucratic society. Never pained by elitism, Strauss seemed to lodge the contrary complaint: liberal society is decadent because it fails to honor the higher types. Unger also looks forward to the way a morally pure and heroic struggle to eliminate "domination" from society will lead naturally toward "a world state" (*Knowledge and Politics*, pp. 257, 266, 173, 284). This, of course, is exactly what Strauss feared.

Yet despite their surface differences, it is their unexpected similarities that stand out. For instance, they share a crucial premise. As Unger puts it: "beliefs that at one moment are hidden in the heads of a few thinkers may at another become a ruling vision of society." Liberalism was "at first the possession of a tiny band of thinkers," but "increasingly became the common property of broader social groups and the basis of the modern social sciences." As always, this Straussian principle has a transfiguring effect. By declaring social problems to be the logical outcome of political ideas, it elevates the historian of political theory into an instant expert on the crisis of the West.

Like Strauss, Unger tantalizes his readers with references to the forgotten wisdom he has excavated from "the philosophy of the ancients." His daring criticism of liberalism has "preliberal" roots. He, too, has managed to retrieve bygone wisdom even though it was treacherously suppressed by "the modern theory of natural right." Liberalism "has almost managed to stamp out" earlier truths inherent in "the metaphysical systems of ancient and medieval Europe," including "Plato's ethics." Plato's philosophy, however, has become completely "alien to our ways of thinking." To help us fathom what "the ancients" once knew, therefore, Unger wants us to refocus radically our intellectual and moral lenses (*Knowledge and Politics*, pp. 149, 5, 76, 41, 71, 111, 113, 31, 32, 41, 143).

This long-repressed wisdom includes the perennial conflict between philosophy and politics and even "the ancient view of philosophy as the most exalted of human activities." The main insight is "the belief in a single human nature all men have in common regardless of the society to which they belong or the age during which they live" (*Knowledge and Politics*, pp. 294, 200, 193.). For moral philosophy, two crucial lessons can be drawn from the ancient concept of invariant human nature.

The first lesson is this: it is absurd to define "the good" in a crass hedonistic way as the satisfaction of bodily wants. The reason is simple: every time a human desire is satisfied, a new desire is born. Human nature, in other words, has guaranteed that materialistic striving will remain futile (*Knowledge and Politics*, p. 67). This was Strauss's analysis exactly. A hedonistic theory of the good has given birth to a hedonistic society in which individuals are condemned to the joyless quest for joy. And the fateful slide into mass hedonism would never have occurred if philosophers had not allowed ancient teachings about human nature to fall into oblivion.

The second vital insight of ancient thought, as Strauss too explained, was the idea of a natural hierarchy of desires. The crime of modern liberalism was its declaration, made in a fit of egalitarianism, that all desires are of equal worth. According to liberals, "nothing makes one man's goals worthier of success than another's" (*Knowledge and Politics*, pp. 51, 66). Things would be different if some desires were naturally superior to others, as "the ancients" said. If, to use Strauss's example, the desire to philosophize was naturally superior to the desire for glory or wealth, then people could take guidance from nature when deliberating about how to live, what to do.

But liberals deny that the human good is inscribed in nature. They see it, instead, as a matter of naked preferences or choice. To find an alternative to the liberal principle of subjective value, Unger advises us to look to "the philosophy of the ancients," to Plato who advanced "the opposing conception," that is, "the idea of objective value," for "objective values are standards and goals of conduct that exist independently of human choice." If we could perceive such values, "they would become the true foundations for the social order" (*Knowledge and Politics*, p. 76). This sounds Straussian, and it is. To be sure, referring to the doctrine of objective value, Unger adds: "I think it is false." He also announces that his "purpose is not to return to the classical idea of an essential human nature impervious to the course of history" (*Knowledge and Politics*, pp. 77, 246). While rejecting the ideas of an unchanging human nature and an objective hierarchy of value, Unger inexplicably retains his criticisms of liberal theory and society based wholly on this idea. This incoherence or softness distinguishes him from Strauss. Both of them criticize universalistic morality in the name of personal self-assertion. But Strauss is more coherent, embracing the inegalitarian consequences of his Platonism. Unger pulls up short, pretending that his brand of heroism has no victims or losers. These important differences should not distract us from an extraordinary convergence: Unger and Strauss diagnose the philosophical core of the modern "crisis" in almost identical terms. Their writings should therefore be studied together, as two variations on a common theme, as two versions of the single tradition: antiliberalism.

4. MacIntyre: The Antiliberal Catechism

1. Alasdair MacIntyre, *Three Rival Versions of Moral Enquiry: Encyclopedia, Genealogy, and Tradition* (Notre Dame, Ind.: University of Notre Dame Press, 1990), p. 133. MacIntyre's nostalgia for esotericism as a lost illiberal social practice becomes even more interesting when juxtaposed to some of his other Straussian-sounding claims. He, too, describes secularization as the principal source of the modern "crisis," for instance. He suggests that social consensus depends upon prerational habits and identifications and simultaneously praises Socrates and Plato because they were able to "put in question the beliefs of the ordinary Athenian about the polis." And he denounces social science for hubristically denying "the permanence of *Fortuna*." Most impressive of all, he states that the best city will retain "a hierarchical order." Indeed, he advocates a pedagogical, not a power-based hierarchy, where good citizens teach virtue to the young. The ultimate purpose of the polis—its highest good—is philosophical contemplation. Only a few people can perfect their souls by imitating divinity. MacIntyre has never been a Nietzschean, but when he says that the city exists "for the sake of that in human beings which links them to the divine," he implies, exactly like Strauss, that nonphilosophers exist for the sake of philosophers (MacIntyre, *Whose Justice? Which Rationality?* p. 124; *After Virtue*, p. 105; *Whose Justice? Which Rationality?* pp. 105, 143; such antiegalitarian passages, arguably, run against the grain of MacIntyre's general approach.)
2. MacIntyre, *Three Rival Versions of Moral Enquiry*, p. 141.
3. This was also a theme of certain German romantics; see Friedrich Schiller, *Über die ästhetische Erziehung des Menschen* (Stuttgart: Philipp Reclam, 1973), p. 18.

4. Alasdair MacIntyre, *After Virtue*, 2nd ed. (Notre Dame, Ind.: University of Notre Dame Press, 1984), pp. 22, ix, 256.

5. Ibid., pp. 4, 263, 3, 4.

6. Ibid., pp. ix, 239, 262, 227, 254, x.

7. This item in the antiliberal catechism was clearly expressed in a Papal Encyclical of Pius XI, *Divini Redemptoris* (19 March 1937), which blames "liberal economics" for undermining religion and thereby making the workers vulnerable to the charms of communism. It also explains that "liberalistic individualism . . . subordinates society to the selfish use of the individual."

8. *After Virtue*, pp. 156, 25, 236, 250–251.

9. Ibid., pp. 229, 160, 160–172, 156.

10. Ibid., pp. 22, 156, 226.

11. Ibid., pp. 6, 39, 111–112; see also p. 244; notice that MacIntyre's stress on "narratives" or story-telling also reveals an implicit skepticism about the scope of rational argumentation.

12. He attacks Pascal and the Jansenists, from the standpoint of Aquinas, for developing a theology reconciled to modern science and for asserting that "the power of reason was destroyed by the fall of man" (*After Virtue*, p. 53).

13. Ibid., pp. 42, 68, 190 (my emphasis), 258 (my emphasis), 35, 41, 42, 127, 43.

14. Ibid., pp. 92, 61, 31, 8, 33, 137.

15. Ibid., pp. 146, 165, 173.

16. MacIntyre overplays the transition from belief to unbelief in early modern Europe, and underemphasizes the shift from religious homogeneity to religious pluralism. Schmitt was more realistic when he blamed multidenominationalism rather than atheism for moral disorder in modern Europe. Modern philosophy fled from theology into science because the former was widely perceived as a "zone of conflict," an arena of rationally irresolvable disputes (Schmitt, "Das Zeitalter der Neutralisierungen und Entpolitisierungen," reprinted in *Der Begriff des Politischen* [Berlin: Duncker and Humblot, 1963], p. 88). In brief, Schmitt saw secularization as a response to the problem of moral conflict, while MacIntyre believes (much less plausibly) that secularization caused this conflict.

17. *After Virtue*, pp. 50, 56, 117, 60, 256, 60.

18. Although he puts less emphasis on faith, Roberto Unger agrees with MacIntyre, that religion may turn out to be the best way to overcome the fact/value gap: "the contrast of understanding and evaluation is foreign to the religious consciousness, for its beliefs about the world are simultaneously descriptions and ideals." In fact, "the view that the understanding of what we ought to do is part of a comprehension of what the world is

really like is a well-recognized characteristic of religious ideas." Religious traditions at once provide a picture of the world and tell us how to behave: "religion starts with the notion that the realm of values is somehow grounded in the reality of things." In other words, religious traditions explain how the world *is* organized and how we *should* act: "a theology both states a view of the world and defines an ideal of the good" (*Knowledge and Politics*, pp. 41, 157–158, 41, 248, 112, 109). Secularism therefore inflicted a terrible wound on the human spirit: it has caused "desire" to become refractory toward "reason."

19. *After Virtue*, pp. 62, 3.

20. Ibid., pp. 244, 257, 60, 111.

21. Ibid., pp. 252, 112.

22. Ibid., pp. 1, 36, 94.

23. Ibid., pp. 96–97, 105, 103.

24. Ibid., pp. 58–59

25. One might argue against MacIntyre, of course, that Achilles's ditherings reflect his questioning of the heroic ethic and his doubt about whether he should play his socially prescribed heroic role.

26. *After Virtue*, pp. 125, 128, 124, 122, 216, 145.

27. Ibid., pp. 120, 123, 33.

28. Ibid., p. 151.

29. Ibid., pp. 220, 191

30. Ibid., pp. 53, 162

31. Ibid., p. 184.

32. Ibid., p. 59; as societies change, conceptions of the "self" also change. For example, as inter- and intragenerational social and job mobility increases, it becomes less plausible to ascribe any permanent characteristics to the self. In the course of modernization, therefore, we can trace an evolution from the concept of the self as a substance (with fixed traits, such as an inborn *telos* or original sin) to an "open" conception of the self. In "the transition into modernity," MacIntyre explains, "the distinctively modern self was invented." Today, "the self is 'nothing,' is not a substance but a set of perpetually open possibilities." It can therefore constantly readjust to changing social expectations. Given high rates of role mobility, it is quite useful that "from the standpoint of individualism I am what I myself choose to be." MacIntyre, of course, is not satisfied with explaining conceptual change sociologically. He must also take a moral stand. Subtly but surely he denounces what he discovers: "this democratized self which has no necessary social identity can then be anything, can assume any role or take any point of view, because it *is* in and for itself nothing" (*After Virtue*, pp. 61, 220, 32). This is more of a pastoral admonition than a historical observation, however.

33. Ibid., p. 172.
34. Ibid., p. 219.
35. Ibid., p. 220.
36. Ibid., pp. 158, 172, 28, 75, 107, 30, 145 34 (my emphasis).
37. Ibid., p. 85, 249, 156, 238, 240, ix.
38. MacIntyre explicitly disclaims the name of pessimist, to be sure: "pessimism too will turn out to be one more cultural luxury that we shall have to dispense with in order to survive in these hard times" (ibid., p. 5).
39. Ibid., pp. 252–253, 238, 5, 263.
40. Benjamin Barber, "The World We Have Lost," *The New Republic*, 13 September 1982, pp. 27–32.
41. *After Virtue*, p. 163.
42. Ibid., pp. 250–251 (my emphasis), 259
43. Ibi., pp. 10, 256, 111.
44. Ibid., p. 18
45. Charles Larmore persuasively argues this in *Patterns of Moral Complexity* (Cambridge: Cambridge University Press, 1987), pp. 36–39.
46. *After Virtue*, pp. 216. 119, 236, 257, 135; MacIntyre defines friendship, incomprehensibly, as collaboration among teammates. Friendship is "a relationship defined in terms of a common allegiance to and a common pursuit of goods" (ibid., p. 156). Liberal society is decadent, he implies, because its citizens feel affection for people who have aims quite different from their own.
47. Ibid., p. 162.
48. J. B. Schneewind, "Moral Crisis and the History of Ethics," *Contemporary Perspectives on the History of Philosophy*, vol. 8 of *Midwest Studies in Philosophy*, ed. P. French, T. Uehling, and H. Wettsetin (Minneapolis: University of Minnesota Press, 1983), p. 529.
49. *After Virtue*, pp. 131, 135; Aristotle is "blind to the centrality of opposition and conflict in human life" (ibid., p. 163).
50. Ibid., pp. 177, 165, 166, 177, 184, 175, 176.
51. Ibid., p. 173.
52. Alasdair MacIntyre, *Whose Justice? Which Rationality?* (Notre Dame, Ind.: University of Notre Dame Press, 1988), p. 352. For a more charitable interpretation of this book, see the review by Charles Larmore, *The Journal of Philosophy* (1989), pp. 437–442.
53. MacIntyre, *Three Versions of Moral Enquiry*, pp. 193, 171; *Whose Justice? Which Rationality?* p. 334.
54. *Whose Justice? Which Rationality?* p. 343.
55. Ibid., p. 12.
56. *Three Versions of Moral Enquiry*, p. 117; *Whose Justice? Which Rationality?* p. 178.

57. *Whose Justice? Which Rationality?* pp. 5, 392.

58. Ibid., p. 97.

59. Ibid., pp. 141, 210, 141.

60. Ibid., p. 140–141.

61. Ibid., p. 397.

62. *After Virtue*, pp. 126, 133.

63. *Whose Justice? Which Rationality?* pp. 230, 220, 124.

64. Cf. Locke, *Two Treatises of Government* (Cambridge: Cambridge University Press, 1988), II, 103, 158.

65. *Three Rival Versions of Moral Enquiry*, pp. 127, 200.

66. *Whose Justice? Which Rationality?* p. 105; *Three Rival Versions of Moral Enquiry*, p. 121; ibid., p. 125.

67. Ernest Gellner, "The Belief Machine," in his *The Devil in Modern Philosophy* (London: Routledge and Kegan Paul, 1974), p. 195.

68. *Three Rival Versions of Moral Enquiry*, pp. 17, 116; *Whose Justice? Which Rationality?* pp. 81, 285.

69. Mill, "On Liberty," in his *Essays on Politics and Society*, ed. J. M. Robson (Toronto: University of Toronto Press, 1977), p. 232.

70. *Whose Justice? Which Rationality?* p. 402.

71. *Three Rival Versions of Moral Enquiry*, pp. 181, 5.

72. Ibid., pp. 25, 30, 124; since the truths of faith do not change, the dynamism that MacIntyre attributes to the Thomistic tradition must result from its founder's need of correction.

73. *Whose Justice? Which Rationality?* pp. 43–44.

74. Ibid., p. 345

75. *Three Rival Versions of Moral Enquiry*, p. 28.

76. "Hume's Anglicizing Subversion" is the most memorable chapter of *Whose Justice? Which Rationality?* Here MacIntyre defends not rationality but nationality. The sheer cattiness of this attack on Hume is bemusing. In his eagerness to increase the importance of loyalty in society, MacIntyre is also preoccupied with treason. He complains peevishly that Hume broke with the "dominant Scottish tradition" and nearly destroyed the "distinctive Scottish cultural identity." Born in Scotland, Hume was nevertheless a turncoat, an Anglophile, a base defector from his "inherited culture." As "a thoroughgoing assimilationist," he aped English manners and accent and even "changed the spelling of his name." He found Scots law "nauseous," refused to read Scottish poetry in dialect, wrote of Scotland "as if it were a foreign country," and generally showed no emotional susceptibility to his roots. Despite this treachery, Hume never succeeded in sounding like a proper Englishman: his idioms were always slightly off. MacIntyre even votes thumbs-down on Hume's candidacy for the Edinburgh chair in moral philosophy: "Hume did indeed have to be excluded

from any part in educating the young" (ibid., pp. 259, 283, 320, 322). Despite his sensitivity to disloyalty, interestingly enough, MacIntyre never mentions those Catholic priests who, throughout modern Europe, found it natural to serve a foreign prince.

77. As Montesquieu wrote, "love of country is not a Christian virtue" (*Spirit of the Laws*, p. lxxi). Tocqueville, too, explained why religiosity and ethnic chauvinism are difficult to reconcile since "common to all religions is an interest in the human personality, the man-in-himself, irrespective of the trappings foisted on him by local traditions, laws, and customs" (*The Old Régime and the Revolution* [New York: Doubleday, 1955], p. 11).

78. *Whose Justice? Which Rationality?* pp. 210, 393–394; *After Virtue*, p. 137.

79. *After Virtue*, pp. 157, 163, 224, 143.

5. Anti-Prometheanism: Christopher Lasch

1. Carl Schmitt, "Das Zeitalter der Neutralisierungen und Entpolitisierungen" (1929), reprinted in *Der Begriff des Politischen* (Berlin: Duncker and Humblot, 1963), p. 83–84.

2. Carl Schmitt, *Theodor Däublers "Nordlicht". Drei Studien über die Elemente, den Geist und die Aktualität des Werkes* (Munich: Georg Müller, 1916), p. 66; and *Römischer Katholizismus und politische Form* (Stuttgart: Klett-Cotta, 1984), p. 24–26; this book was originally published in 1923.

3. Martin Heidegger, *The Question Concerning Technology*, trans. William Lovitt (New York: Harper and Row, 1977), pp. 12, 14–15, 16, 21–22; Heidegger notoriously concedes that the Rhine remains a landscape, but "in no other way than as an object on call for inspection by a tour group ordered there by the vacation industry" (ibid., p. 16).

4. Christopher Lasch, *The True and Only Heaven: Progress and Its Critics* (New York: W. W. Norton, 1991), pp. 225, 23, 518, 171, 22, 279, 508.

5. Ibid., pp. 507, 31, 495.

6. Ibid., p. 524.

7. Ibid., p. 521.

8. Ibid., pp. 335, 220; interestingly, Lasch argues that the socialist tradition is infected by liberalism in another way: Marx despised capitalism because it obstructed the full development of human *individuality* (ibid., p. 152).

9. Ibid., p. 14.

10. Cf. Sheldon Wolin, *Politics and Vision* (Boston: Little, Brown, 1960), p. 317.

11. *The True and Only Heaven*, pp. 516, 90, 89, 522, 80.

12. This entire argument echoes Strauss's sharp commentary on "the joyless quest for joy," to which liberal theorists have ostensibly condemned us all (*Natural Right and History*, p. 251); in the same spirit, Roberto Unger

denounces liberal society for "the deadening hedonism of consumption" (*Knowledge and Politics*, p. 59).

13. *The True and Only Heaven*, p. 528.

14. Ibid., pp. 446, 239, 39, 239, 527; but see *Genesis* 1:28, which commands human beings to "subdue" the earth.

15. Ibid., p. 467.

16. As we shall see in the next chapter, some antiliberals (who draw inspiration primarily from Nietzsche rather than from Heidegger) criticize liberal society for not taking this "flexibility" far enough.

17. *The True and Only Heaven*, pp. 76, 261, 34, 308.

18. Ibid., pp. 489–490.

19. Ibid., p. 491; in earlier works Lasch expresses his commitment to reproduction as the natural purpose of intercourse by castigating "the fascination with oral sex" purportedly prominent among his contemporaries (*The Culture of Narcissism* [New York: Norton, 1991], p. 50; *Haven in a Heartless World*, p. 183). This pious invocation of "nature's law" might be usefully compared with the appeals to nature in Schmitt and Strauss.

20. Strauss, *Natural Right and History* (Chicago: University of Chicago Press, 1953), p. 257.

21. He does not explain why they would care to read his books, however.

22. *The True and Only Heaven*, p. 487.

23. Ibid., p. 495.

24. Ibid., pp. 466, 467.

25. Ibid., pp. 478, 506, 409.

26. Ibid., p. 402, 403.

27. Ibid., pp. 395, 387, 405, 406, 409.

28. Ibid., pp. 354, 355, 359, 193, 360.

29. Ibid., pp. 303, 346, 226, 360, 531, 335, 532, 328, 345.

30. Ibid., pp. 226, 213.

31. Ibid., p. 321.

32. Ibid., p. 305.

33. Schmitt, "Das Zeitalter der Neutralisierungen und Entpolitisierungen," p. 94.

34. Lasch, *The Culture of Narcissism*, p. 42.

35. *The True and Only Heaven*, p. 355.

36. Ibid., p. 531.

37. Ibid., pp. 402, 529.

38. Ibid., p. 532.

6. Unger: Antiliberalism Unbound

1. Alasdair MacIntyre, *Three Rival Versions of Moral Enquiry* (Notre Dame, Ind.: University of Notre Dame Press, 1990), pp. 32–57, 170–215.

2. Roberto Mangabeira Unger, *Politics, A Work in Constructive Social Theory* (Cambridge: Cambridge University Press, 1987). The book has three volumes: *Social Theory: Its Situation and Task; False Necessity: Anti-Necessitarian Social Theory in the Service of Radical Democracy;* and *Plasticity into Power: Comparative-Historical Studies on the Institutional Conditions of Economic and Military Success.*

3. Roberto Mangabeira Unger, *Knowledge and Politics* (New York: Free Press, 1975).

4. Ibid., pp. 53, 195, 61–62, 153, 152. Liberal ontology can be summarized in the precept: "being implies no sanctity"; it assumes impiously that everything can be changed: "the manipulative posture toward the world takes the form of a denial of the immutability of nature and of society" (pp. 159, 152); the hubris of this stance is overwhelming.

5. Ibid., pp. 277 (my emphasis), 194.

6. Ibid., pp. 206, 202, 101–102, 97, 102, 103, 96, 275, 171.

7. Ibid., p. 232.

8. Ibid., pp. 233, 232; his way of writing here, admittedly, sounds somewhat ominous: "the features of commonplace life that make it profane and prosaic *must* be changed" (p. 233, my emphasis). Who is going to prevent us from speaking prose? By what means? And do they need our consent? But Unger's evident dreaminess makes it clear that he intends nothing coercive or violent here.

9. Ibid., p. 192.

10. Ibid., pp. 252, 274, 316, 11, 15, 40–41.

11. Ibid., pp. 5, 88, 102, 290, 133.

12. Ibid., pp. 289, 106, 252, 27, 119, 4, 137.

13. Ibid., pp. 24, 149, 6, 281.

14. *Knowledge and Politics*, pp. v, 4, 23, 141, 231, 250, 59, 149, 229, 118, 151. This intellectualization goes so far that a talented admirer of *Knowledge and Politics* can present his criticism of John Rawls's *Theory of Justice* as if it were automatically a criticism of American society (see Michael Sandel, *Liberalism and the Limits of Justice* [Cambridge: Cambridge University Press, 1982]).

15. *Knowledge and Politics*, pp. 28, 74, 77, 120, 212, 197.

16. Ibid., pp. 145, 140, 103, 140.

17. Ibid., pp. 146 (my emphasis), 198, 197.

18. Ibid., pp. 58, 69, 140; surprisingly enough, "schizophrenia brings to light the hidden truth of the moral condition liberal psychology describes" (p. 58).

19. Ibid., pp. 195, 231.

20. Ibid., pp. 63, 30, 40, 80, 119, 124, 8, 63, 67, 301, 88.

21. Ibid., pp. 128, 81, 211, 76, 78, 81.

22. Ibid., pp. 123, 129, 63.

23. Unger takes it for granted that the category "group" is much more sophisticated sociologically than the category "individual." But this is far from obvious. The most interesting forms of social interaction (love, science, religion, law, education, entertainment, and so forth) cut across group borders—including national ones—and are not wholly controlled by the norms of any single group.
24. Hume, "That Politics May Be Reduced to a Science," *Essays Moral, Political, and Literary* (Indianapolis: Liberty Classics, 1985), p. 25.
25. *The Federalist Papers*, #51, ed. C. Rossiter (New York: Mentor, 1961), p. 438.
26. *Knowledge and Politics*, p. 82.
27. Ibid., p. 39.
28. Ibid.
29. Ibid., p. 303.
30. Ibid., pp. 111, 81.
31. Unger himself mentions the possibility of an irrational form of social consensus, but he attributes this pathological form to "domination," an assumption which suggests that he continues to suffer from a residual marxist proclivity toward conspiracy thinking (*Knowledge and Politics*, pp. 242–243).
32. Ibid., pp. 120, 119, 135, 50, 97, 52.
33. Ibid., pp. 53, 52, 68.
34. Ibid., pp. 86, 78, 79.
35. Ibid., pp. 68, 53, 88, 135, 54.
36. Ibid., p. 165, 86, 87.
37. Ibid., pp. 107, 42.
38. Liberals separated reason from desire, incidentally, to reveal that superior intellect, because it is no guarantee of good will, confers no right to rule. A similar contextual account can be given of liberal "reductionism," the principle that the whole is equal to the sum of its parts. The liberal tendency to view the group as a mere "means" for the individual should also be understood politically. In preliberal European societies, after all, the vast majority of individuals were treated as expendable means for the pursuit of the purposes of elites (who conceived of themselves, by a convenient synechdoche, as equivalent to the whole). To desacralize "the whole," and reduce it to all of its "parts," therefore, was to put this pattern into question and thus to undermine aristocratic dominance. Such an argumentative strategy, needless to say, did not commit liberals to a naive belief that a society can have no characteristics not previously possessed by its individual members in isolation.
39. *Knowledge and Politics*, pp. 151, 268, 271, 151.
40. Ibid., p. 289.

41. Ibid., p. 278; most unpalatable is the enforcement of shared norms "regardless of the means by which it is exacted." This phrase suggests not only that Unger has inwardly reconciled himself to the means-ends distinction, but also that he is subliminally aware, all protests to the contrary, of liberalism's commitment to "noninstrumental rules to determine what counts as permissible means" (p. 135).

42. Ibid., pp. 77, 140, 194, 140.

43. Ibid., p. 229; why hypothetical? Was fascism just a thought experiment?

44. Ibid., p. 290.

45. Ibid., pp. 167, 318, 281–282, 279, 140, 277, 272, 272, 279; admittedly, Unger is inconsistent here, since he also says that these limits should *not* be "fixed" (p. 274).

46. Ibid., pp. 280, 188, 267, 188, 220, 225, 242–244, 261.

47. Ibid., pp. 184, 173, 204, 280; see also p. 283.

48. Ibid., p. 178. Unger's double standards, incidentally, are quite apparent in this preference for egalitarian community: he can provide no rational justification for his norm of equality that was not already used by the liberals he scorns.

49. Ibid., pp. 249, 252.

50. Ibid., pp. 260, 224, 231, 284, 224, 260, 290. This phrase suggests the Christian element in Unger's anti-utopianism: Christ will not come again until history is over and done.

51. Ibid., p. 237; see also pp. 221, 242.

52. Ibid., p. 286.

53. *Plasticity into Power*, p. 2; *False Necessity*, pp. 293, 563, 566, *Plasticity into Power*, p. 81; *False Necessity*, pp. 468, 303, 451. Already in *Knowledge and Politics* Unger's hyperindividualism leads him to attack "the playing of roles" in general as a "universal pantomime." He hates "the sanctity of one's station and its duties." He identifies social roles and adaptation to community norms with inauthenticity and moral phoniness. His differences with Alasdair MacIntyre are most obvious on this point: he writes sneeringly of roles as masks. Acquiescing in the expectations of others obliterates personal "uniqueness." About social roles in general, he says "all of them will seem, and they will be, to a greater or lesser extent, a diminishment of what I shall describe as the attributes of the self." He explicitly rejects the idea that "each way of being human is inseparable from a particular form of social life." Individuals must exist beyond their social roles, if they do not want to abandon "the idea of a virtually many-sided personality." There is nothing more immoral than a situation in which "the person is completely absorbed in his concrete social position and identified with it" (*Knowledge and Politics*, pp. 195, 20, 26, 179, 60–62, 229, 156, 174, 194, 179, 223). Caught up in a social charade, individuals

lose their multidimensionality. Acquiescing in group norms, they sacrifice the gaiety of life.

54. *Social Theory*, pp. 12, 206; *Plasticity into Power*, pp. 160, 2; *Social Theory*, p. 16; *False Necessity*, p. 589.
55. *Social Theory*, pp. 150, 197, 169.
56. Ibid., p. 47.
57. Ibid., p. 158.
58. *False Necessity*, p. 579.
59. Ibid., p. 613.
60. John Locke, *Two Treatises of Government* (Cambridge: Cambridge University Press, 1988), II, 103.
61. *False Necessity*, pp. 364, 12; *Social Theory*, pp. 24, 1; *False Necessity*, p. 528.
62. Ibid., p. 566; *Plasticity into Power*, p. 11; *False Necessity*, 35; *Social Theory*, p. 214; *False Necessity*, pp. 564, 519, 562.
63. *Knowledge and Politics*, pp. 267, 237, 188, 229, 177, 319.
64. *False Necessity*, pp. 537, 568, 594.
65. Ibid., p. 291.
66. Ibid., p. 513; *Social Theory*, pp. 138, 196, 171, 5.
67. *False Necessity*, p. 12; *Social Theory*, p. 12; *False Necessity*, p. 584.
68. *Social Theory*, p. 214; *False Necessity*, pp. 566, 583.
69. *False Necessity*, pp. 625, 56.
70. Ibid., pp. 454, 459, 462.
71. Ibid., pp. 323, 87–89; *Plasticity into Power*, p. 22.
72. *Social Theory*, pp. 118, 139, 127.
73. *False Necessity*, pp. 111, 413; *Social Theory*, p. 75.
74. *False Necessity*, 12; *Social Theory*, p. 118.
75. *False Necessity*, p. 25.
76. Ibid., p. 127; *Social Theory*, pp. 158, 212; *False Necessity*, pp. 569, 562, 528; *Social Theory*, p. 233.
77. *False Necessity*, pp. 56, 572.
78. *Social Theory*, p. 184–185; *False Necessity*, p. 277.
79. In his earlier book Unger had already criticized adolescents who "imagine themselves as occupants of the greatest possible variety of life situations and practice the cult of the fullness of 'experience'" (*Knowledge and Politics*, p. 224); the striking similarity of this youthful stance to Unger's own may explain his recurrent need to distance himself from infantile leftism.
80. The identification of freedom with wanton acts of destruction, of course, has more psychological plausibility in some contexts than in others. The historical dominance of entrenched elites in South America probably has something to do with Unger's attraction to such an incoherent view; this is probably what Rorty means by his uplifting claim that Unger's "natural

audience may lie in the Third World—where his book may someday make possible a new national romance" (Richard Rorty, *Essays on Heidegger and Others* [Cambridge: Cambridge University Press, 1991], p. 187).

81. *False Necessity*, p. 529.

82. William Blackstone, *Commentaries on the Laws of England* (Chicago: University of Chicago Press, 1977), vol. 2, p. 11.

83. *False Necessity*, p. 365; in his earlier book, Unger had poured scorn on the very idea of "a society governed by law." This was not the only way in which he resembled Carl Schmitt; like Schmitt, Unger declared that liberal legalism is a pious fraud. The "rule of law," viewed concretely, is the rule of those individuals and groups who are strategically situated to make, interpret, and use the law. Unger even singled out Schmitt's archenemy, Hans Kelsen, as a quintessential liberal. Kelsen absurdly believed that abstract rules could solve the problem of "the eternal hostility of men to one another." More generally, "society, as it appears to the liberal, is held together by rules. Rules are the main devices for establishing order and freedom," but they are wholly inadequate for maintaining social order. Thus, as could have been predicted, "the program of organization by impersonal rules cannot be carried out." Despite these Schmittian themes, Unger was quite anti-Schmittian on one point: he chastised liberals for believing that "the good has no existence outside the will." He definitely wanted to provide a rational foundation for decisions, going beyond "choices that cannot be justified." Values, he wrote, have cognitive content and are not merely a matter of preference or whim (*Knowledge and Politics*, pp. 63, 56, 303–304, 67, 83, 169, 68, 103). In *Politics*, however, he has abandoned this position and therefore comes even closer to Schmitt. He has become a superliberal, among other reasons, because he has now been converted to ethical voluntarism. Like Schmitt, in fact, Unger-the-superliberal claims that we can "never succeed in emptying our normative ideas of a large and ineradicable residuum of choice"; it is interesting, therefore, that he also praises a high-adrenaline life and counsels strong executives to take "decisional initiative" (*False Necessity*, pp. 360, 447).

84. *Social Theory*, p. 152.

85. *Plasticity into Power*, p. 93.

86. Locke, *Two Treatises of Government*, II, 57.

87. *Plasticity into Power*, p. 16.

88. Ibid., pp. 162, 165; *False Necessity*, pp. 581, 336.

89. *False Necessity*, pp. 570, 296; MacIntyre, *Three Versions of Moral Enquiry*, p. 43; *False Necessity*, p. 52; *Plasticity into Power*, pp. 70, 73.

90. *False Necessity*, pp. 209, 584, 595.

91. *Plasticity into Power*, p. 212.

92. *Social Theory*, p. 118; *False Necessity*, pp. 510, 1.
93. *Social Theory*, p. 205.
94. *False Necessity*, p. 73.

7. The Community Trap

1. See Amy Gutmann, "Communitarian Critics of Liberalism," *Philosophy and Public Affairs*, 14 (Summer 1985), pp. 308–322.
2. Roberto Unger, *Knowledge and Politics* (New York, Free Press, 1975), p. 76. Unger announces that "the formulation of an ideal of community is the highest calling of political theory"; liberalism's critics, moreover, should put their aspirations into practice by promoting "the actual spreading of communities of shared ends" (ibid., pp. 249, 115); Alasdair MacIntyre, *After Virtue* (Notre Dame, Ind.: Notre Dame University Press, 1984), p. 156; Michael Sandel, *Liberalism and the Limits of Justice* (Cambridge: Cambridge University Press, 1982), p. 183; Charles Taylor, "Cross Purposes: the Liberal-Communitarian Debate," in *Liberalism and the Moral Life* ed. Nancy Rosenblum (Cambridge, Mass.: Harvard University Press, 1989), pp. 171, 176; Taylor, *Sources of the Self* (Cambridge, Mass.: Harvard University Press, 1989), p. 502; Christopher Lasch, *Haven in a Heartless World* (New York: Basic Books, 1977), p. 168; *The True and Only Heaven: Progress and Its Critics* (New York: W. W. Norton, 1991), p. 76. Summarizing his reading of antiliberal literature, Robert Paul Wolff accurately writes: "the severest criticisms of liberal society, both from the left and the right, focus on the absence of community in even the most efficient and affluent liberal capitalist state . . . What is it that conservatives and radicals alike miss in liberal society? . . . *the social values of community*" (*The Poverty of Liberalism* [Boston: Beacon, 1968], pp. 183–184).
3. Unger, *Knowledge and Politics*, p. 261; also pp. 220, 225, 233; it is impossible to understand communitarianism fully without seeing it as a response to the moral skepticism feared by all antiliberals. Contrary to the asocial premises of liberal individualism, human beings can gain moral orientation by looking to the demands of their "social practice," where meanings are shared and descriptive and evaluative terms coincide. In other words, "the moral question about what ought to be done need no longer be abandoned to unjustifiable choice; it can be answered by a study of the traditions or institutions of a nation, a class, or a group." People can rescue themselves from excruciating doubt by clinging to "group values that are neither individual nor subjective." Communitarianism, in other words, provides a middle way between objective and subjective values, between theology and nihilism, between one-right-answer Platonism and any-

thing-goes liberalism. From a communitarian perspective, values are neither subjective (based on whim) nor objective (inscribed in nature). They transcend the individual without being etched into any sort of eternal order of things. The norms inculcated by social groups have a powerful grip on behavior. They tell the individual what ends he should hold, and how he should act in particular situations. To understand these norms, fortunately we need not make any dubious theological and metaphysical assumptions about everlasting or objective values. Group norms and goals are thoroughly down-to-earth and yet they furnish what Unger, MacIntyre, and the others most ardently desire: a plausible "alternative to the principle of subjective value" (Unger, *Knowledge and Politics*, pp. 287, 220, 178, 261, 285, 287, 283, 108, 121, 102, 52, 54, 85, 100).

4. Curiously, Taylor finds Sandel's radical criticism of liberal premises especially useful because, in his mind, it has no political implications whatsoever (Taylor, "Cross Purposes: the Liberal-Communitarian Debate," pp. 161–163).

5. Schmitt's charge that liberals do not recognize the existence of evil and, therefore, the necessity of force, can be applied more reasonably to MacIntyre or Unger than to Locke or Montesquieu.

6. Unlike communitarians, liberals view community discriminatingly. Solidarity is good or bad, they believe, depending on its results. Group identification is morally welcome when it supports the universalistic distribution of individual rights to all individuals regardless of their place of birth, race, ethnic group, religion, gender, and so forth. It is unwelcome when it inhibits such a liberal distribution of rights.

7. Sandel, *Liberalism and the Limits of Justice*, p. 182.

8. This separates Wolin from a hard antiliberal such as Schmitt.

9. For a useful analysis of the confusions resulting from the communitarian postulate that some forms of social life are more social than others, see Bernard Yack, "Does Liberal Practice 'Live Down' to Liberal Theory: Liberalism and Its Communitarian Critics," in *Community in America: The Challenge of 'Habits of the Heart,'* ed. Charles Reynolds (Berkeley: University of California Press, 1988), pp. 147–169.

10. Charles Taylor, "Atomism," in his *Philosophy and the Human Sciences* (Cambridge: Cambridge University Press, 1985), pp. 198, 200.

11. As mentioned above, "hard" antiliberals—such as Maistre, Schmitt, and Strauss—were acutely aware of violent hostility between solidaristic groups; this distinguishes them sharply from MacIntyre, Unger, and the other gun-shy postwar communitarians.

12. For one example among many, see Charles Taylor, *Sources of the Self*, p. 532; Taylor, in any case, is more interested in personal "fullness" than in community.

13. Michael Sandel, "The Procedural Republic and the Unencumbered Self," *Political Theory*, 12 (1984), p. 82; even "hard" antiliberals sometimes argue in this confusing way. Schmitt himself claimed that the abstract idea of "humanity" both falsifies reality, because individuals always live in exclusive groups, and dangerously erodes concrete communities ("Staatsethik und pluralistischer Staat," *Positionen und Begriffe: im Kampf mit Weimar-Genf-Versailles* [Hamburg: Hanseatische Verlagsanstalt, 1940], pp. 138–142). As Strauss correctly notes, Schmitt cannot decide if "the political" is irrepressible or threatened ("Comments on *Der Begriff des Politischen* by Carl Schmitt," reprinted in Schmitt, *The Concept of the Political* [New Brunswick: Rutgers University Press, 1976], p. 94).
14. Charles Taylor, *Sources of the Self*, pp. 504, 520.
15. The key communitarian notion of "latent community" is persuasively discussed and criticized by Nancy Rosenblum in "Moral Membership in a Postliberal State" (*World Politics*, 36 [July 1984], p. 589).
16. This is Sandel's thesis.

8. Antiliberals as Historians

1. For the beginning of such an account, see Stephen Holmes, *Rediscovering Liberal Democracy* (Chicago: University of Chicago Press, 1994).
2. The word "liberalism" entered European languages at the beginning of the nineteenth century, but antiliberals and others continue to project it backwards into the past. I will follow their practice in order to argue more effectively against their conclusions.

9. The "Atomization" of Society?

1. Carl Schmitt, *Political Romanticism* (Cambridge, Mass.: M.I.T. Press, 1986), p. 99; Giovanni Gentile, *I Fondamenti della filosofia del diritto* (Florence: Sansoni, 1961), p. 106; Leo Strauss, *Natural Right and History* (Chicago: University of Chicago Press, 1953), p. 248; Alasdair MacIntyre, *After Virtue*, 2nd ed. (Notre Dame, Ind.: University of Notre Dame Press, 1984), p. 250; Charles Taylor, "Cross Purposes: The Liberal-Communitarian Debate," *Liberalism and the Moral Life*, ed. Nancy Rosenblum (Cambridge, Mass.: Harvard University Press, 1989), p. 181; and Taylor, "Atomism," in his *Philosophy and the Human Sciences* (Cambridge: Cambridge University Press, 1985), p. 200; Robert Nisbet, *Community and Power* (New York: Oxford University Press, 1962), pp. 225–226; Robert Bellah et al., *Habits of the Heart: Individualism and Commitment in American Life* (New York: Harper and Row, 1985), p. 143–144; Taylor, "Atomism," pp. 198, 200.

2. Charles Taylor, "Atomism," pp. 187–210.

3. John Locke, *Two Treatises of Government* (Cambridge: Cambridge University Press, 1988), II, 77; *The Educational Writings of John Locke*, ed. James Axtell (Cambridge: Cambridge University Press, 1968); *Essays on the Law of Nature*, ed. W. von Leyden (Oxford: Clarendon Press, 1954), p. 129; *An Essay Concerning Human Understanding*, ed. Peter H. Nidditch (Oxford: Clarendon Press, 1975), p. 81 (on conformism, see p. 356). True, Locke urged people to think for themselves, but Taylor (no friend to heteronomy) criticizes Locke primarily on descriptive or "metaphysical" grounds, for offering an inaccurately asocial picture of "the self," not because he favored thinking for oneself.

4. David Hume, "Of the First Principles of Government," *Essays Moral, Political, and Literary* (Indianapolis: Liberty Classics, 1985), p. 33; "Of the Origin of Government," ibid., p. 37; Immanuel Kant, "Idea for a Universal History with a Cosmopolitan Purpose," *Kant's Political Writings*, ed. Hans Reiss (Cambridge: Cambridge University Press, 1970), p. 44. Notice that Kant is making two distinct claims here, both of which antiliberals ignore: that man's social nature is *inborn*, and that the principal worthwhile characteristics of human personality are *products of social interaction*.

5. Hume, "Of the Original Contract," *Essays Moral, Political, and Literary*, pp. 465–487; "Of the Origin of Government," ibid., pp. 39–40.

6. Locke, *Two Treatises of Government*, II, 103.

7. See Samuel H. Beer, *To Make a Nation* (Cambridge, Mass.: Harvard University Press, 1993), chap. 1; liberals also deployed the state of nature as a deft piece of anti-Christian mythology, an alternative to biblical versions of the origins of society and government. According to Montesquieu, for example, "the idea of a Creator" does not occur to individuals in the state of nature *(The Spirit of the Laws*, trans. Thomas Nugent [New York: Hafner, 1949], I, 2, pp. 3–4).

8. Locke, *Two Treatises of Government*, II, 4, 6.

9. As a matter of actual prehistory, Locke agreed that "Government commonly began in the Father" (ibid., II, 105), but he dismissed this observation as politically irrelevant.

10. Ibid., II, 95.

11. Locke, *An Essay Concerning Human Understanding*, p. 264; Locke, *Two Treatises of Government*, II, 22; Adam Smith, *An Inquiry into the Nature and Causes of the Wealth of Nations* (New York: Modern Library, 1937), pp. 374–375, 549.

12. William Blackstone, *Commentaries on the Laws of England* (Chicago: University of Chicago Press, 1977), vol. 1, pp. 48, 43.

13. Immanuel Kant, *The Metaphysical Elements of Justice* (Indianapolis: Bobbs-

Merrill, 1965), p. 80; Kant, "Perpetual Peace," *Kant's Political Writings*, p. 99.

14. According to Locke, "there cannot be a more dangerous thing to rely on, nor more likely to mislead one" than the opinions of others, "since there is much more Falshood and Errour amongst Men, than Truth and Knowledge" (*An Essay Concerning Human Understanding*, p. 657).

15. According to Blackstone, "the law of England acts upon general and extensive principles: it gives liberty, rightly understood, that is, protection, to a jew, a turk, or a heathen" (*Commentaries on the Laws of England*, vol. 1, p. 413).

16. Justice's "blindfold" can be understood as the institutional counterpart to John Rawls's "veil of ignorance." When Sandel asks us to take the concrete characteristics of the person into account, he is inadvertently and unwisely calling for an intensification of race consciousness in the allocation of society's benefits and burdens. For a liberal response, see Rawls's "Justice as Fairness: Political Not Metaphysical," *Philosophy and Public Affairs*, 14 (1985): 223–251.

17. Industrialization, urbanization, mass literacy, and improvements in communication and transportation (not to mention modern warfare) have all contributed to the weakening of traditional localisms and regionalisms. To blame this massive social transformation on "liberalism" is to mistake analogical reverie for causal reasoning.

18. Sheldon Wolin, *Politics and Vision* (Boston: Little, Brown, 1960), p. 341; Locke, *Two Treatises of Government*, II, 13); Blackstone, *Commentaries on the Laws of England*, vol. 4, p. 8; *The Federalist Papers* (New York: Mentor, 1961), #10, p. 79.

19. Christopher Lasch, *The True and Only Heaven: Progress and Its Critics* (New York: W. W. Norton, 1991), p. 209; Smith, *Wealth of Nations*, p. 839; taxes on "the necessaries of life" are "a curse equal to the barrenness of the earth and the inclemency of the heavens." Notice that Smith employed a simultaneously cultural and biological definition of needs here: "by necessaries I understand, not only the commodities which are indispensably necessary for the support of life, but whatever the custom of the country renders it indecent for creditable people, even of the lowest order, to be without" (ibid, pp. 432–33, 821).

10. Indifference toward the Common Good?

1. Alasdair MacIntyre, *After Virtue* (Notre Dame, Ind.: University of Notre Dame Press, 1984), p. 170; John Locke, *A Letter Concerning Toleration* (Indianapolis, Ind.: Bobbs-Merrill, 1955), pp. 16, 36, 40, 50; Locke, *Two Treatises of Government* (Cambridge: Cambridge University Press, 1988), II, 3, 110, 131, 159, 215.

2. Aristotle, *Politics*, 1254b, 20–22.
3. Adam Smith, *An Inquiry into the Nature and Causes of the Wealth of Nations* (New York: Modern Library, 1937), p. 872.
4. *The Federalist Papers*, #45 (New York: Mentor, 1961), p. 289; Smith, *Wealth of Nations*, pp. 579, 582; see also the references to "the real interest of the community," "the general advantage of the public," "the universal good of the nation," and "the benefit of the people" in William Blackstone, *Commentaries on the Laws of England* (Chicago: University of Chicago Press, 1977), vol. 1, pp. 48, 121–122, 239, as well as his Lockean warning that "the mask of justice and public spirit" may sometimes be used to conceal "private spite and enmity" (ibid., vol. 3, p. 126).
5. Cesare Beccaria, *On Crimes and Punishments*, (Indianapolis: Bobbs-Merrill, 1963), p. 64.
6. Interestingly, Aristotle describes assault as a wrong against an individual. His example of a wrong against the community is the refusal to do military service (*Rhetoric*, I, xiii, 3–4).
7. Blackstone, *Commentaries*, vol. 4, p. 6.

11. The Eclipse of Authority?

1. Joseph de Maistre, *Étude sur la souveraineté*, in *Œuvres complètes* (Lyons: Vitte et Perrussel, 1884), vol. 1, p. 525; see also *Du Pape*, vol. 2 in *Œuvres complètes*, p. 170; Carl Schmitt, "Wesen und Werden des fascistischen Staates," *Positionen und Begriffe im Kampf mit Weimar-Genf-Versailles* (Hamburg: Hanseatische Verlag, 1940), p. 110; see also Schmitt, *The Concept of the Political* (New Brunswick: Rutgers University Press, 1976), p. 70; Alasdair MacIntyre, *After Virtue* (Notre Dame, Ind.: University of Notre Dame Press, 1984), p. 42 (MacIntyre is referring more to authoritative traditions, it should be said, than to authoritative decision-makers in the style of Schmitt); Benedict Spinoza, *A Theologico-Political Treatise and A Political Treatise*, trans. R. H. M. Elwes (New York: Dover, 1951), p. 249; Hannah Arendt, *The Human Condition* (Chicago: University of Chicago Press, 1958), p. 31; Sheldon Wolin, *Politics and Vision* (Boston: Little, Brown, 1960), p. 317; note that antistatism was the ideology of ecclesiastics, while anticlericalism was a pivotal element in liberal thinking.
2. John Locke, *Two Treatises of Government* (Cambridge: Cambridge University Press, 1988), II, 181, 230; Adam Smith, *An Inquiry into the Nature and Causes of the Wealth of Nations* (New York: Modern Library, 1937), p. 376; Locke, *Two Treatises of Government*, II, 21; Smith, *Wealth of Nations*, p. 576.

3. Locke, *An Essay Concerning Human Understanding*, ed. Peter H. Nidditch (Oxford: Clarendon Press, 1975), p. 100; Locke, *Two Treatises of Government*, II, 105, 219.

4. David Hume, "Origin of Government," *Essays Moral, Political, and Literary* (Indianapolis: Liberty Classics, 1985), p. 41; "Of the Original Contract," ibid., p. 466; Montesquieu, *The Spirit of the Laws* (I, 6), p. 6 (my translation); (XI, 5), p. 151; William Blackstone, *Commentaries on the Laws of England* (Chicago: University of Chicago Press, 1977), vol. I, p. 123; he goes on to say that even tyranny should preferred to anarchy; Locke disagreed (*Two Treatises of Government*, II, 225), providing the very slim basis for Schmitt's association of liberalism with anarchism; Smith, *Wealth of Nations*, book III, chap. 3.

5. Immanuel Kant, "Idea for a Universal History with a Cosmopolitan Purpose," *Kant's Political Writings*, ed. Hans Reiss (Cambridge: Cambridge University Press, 1970), p. 46.

6. Locke, *Two Treatises of Government*, II, 174; Montesquieu, *The Spirit of the Laws*, trans. Thomas Nugent (New York: Hafner, 1949), p. 153 (XI, 6), and p. 184 (XII, 2).

7. *The Federalist Papers*, #51 (New York: Mentor, 1961), p. 322; Kant, "Universal History," *Kant's Political Writings*, p. 46.

8. Locke, *Two Treatises of Government*, II, 142, 175, 22.

9. *The Federalist Papers*, #48, p. 313.

10. Hume, "Of the Origin of Government," *Essays*, p. 41, my emphasis.

12. The Public Realm Sacrificed to the Private?

1. Carl Schmitt, *The Concept of the Political* (New Brunswick: Rutgers University Press, 1976), pp. 70–71; similarly, "the efforts of the bourgeois constitutional state are directed toward suppressing the political" (Schmitt, *Verfassungslehre* [Berlin: Duncker and Humblot, 1970], pp. 41).

2. The seeming unconstitutionality, in the United States, of national controls on the possession of guns reveals a strikingly illiberal feature of the American polity.

3. Montesquieu, *The Spirit of the Laws*, trans. Thomas Nugent (New York: Hafner, 1949), VI, 8, pp. 80–81.

4. William Blackstone, *Commentaries on the Laws of England* (Chicago: University of Chicago Press, 1977), vol. 1, p. 122; vol. 3, p. 4.

5. A vaguely worded criminal statute "may furnish a pretext to take away a man's life, and to exterminate any family whatsoever" (Montesquieu, *The Spirit of the Laws*, XI, 7, p. 190).

6. John Locke, *Two Treatises of Government*, II, 20.

7. Cesare Beccaria, *On Crimes and Punishments* (Indianapolis: Bobbs-Merrill,

1963), pp. 22, 39, 92; Montesquieu, *The Spirit of the Laws*, XII, 5–6, pp. 187–190; "the Laws do not take upon themselves to punish any other than overt acts" (ibid., XII, 11, p. 193); note the simultaneously positive and negative, welcoming and suspicious, attitude toward privacy in Montesquieu's argument here. If homosexual acts are considered a *private* matter, then the state's immense judicial powers will not be used as an instrument of *private* hate.

8. Locke, *Two Treatises of Government*, II, 131); Blackstone, *Commentaries*, vol. 1, pp. 45–46, vol. 4, pp. 44–50; David Hume, "Of the Origin of Government," *Essays Moral, Political, and Literary* (Indianapolis: Liberty Classics, 1985), p. 41; Montesquieu, *The Spirit of the Laws* (VI, 8), pp. 80–81; (XII, 24), pp. 202–203; Montesquieu, *Persian Letters* (Harmondsworth: Penguin, 1973), letter 9, p. 52.

9. Sheldon Wolin, *Politics and Vision* (Boston: Little, Brown, 1960), p. 291; Immanuel Kant, "An Answer to the Question: 'What is Enlightenment?'," *Kant's Political Writings*, ed. Hans Reiss (Cambridge: Cambridge University Press, 1970), p. 57; for the duty of the government to make public the principles behind its policy choices, see Kant, "Perpetual Peace," ibid., p. 126.

10. Benedict Spinoza, *A Theologico-Political Treatise and A Political Treatise*, trans. R. H. M. Elwes (New York: Dover, 1951), p. 376; Locke, *Two Treatises of Government*, II, 222; George Sabine, "The Historical Position of Liberalism," *American Scholar*, 10 (1940–41), pp. 49–58.

11. This is true, even though liberals described political participation as a means to good government as well as to private liberty, rather than as an end-in-itself providing the majority of citizens with a reason for living.

12. The public/private distinction is the majoritarian way to combine democracy with diversity; the nonmajoritarian alternative is consociationalism.

13. Montesquieu expressed his ambivalence about the public realm on many occasions: "I know a woman who walks quite gracefully, but she limps as soon as anyone looks at her" (*Persian Letters*, p. 39); more seriously, Usbek inflicts unspeakable crimes on the women in his harem in response to *public* humiliation.

13. Economic Man?

1. Christopher Lasch, *The True and Only Heaven: Progress and Its Critics*, p. 15; Carl Schmitt, "Das Zeitalter der Neutralisierungen und Entpolitisierungen" (1929), reprinted in *Der Begriff des Politischen* (Berlin: Duncker and Humblot, 1963), p. 83; Strauss, *Natural Right and History*, p. 242; MacIntyre, *After Virtue*, p. 227; Sheldon Wolin, *Politics and Vision* (Boston: Little, Brown, 1960), p. 300; R. H. Tawney, *Religion and the Rise*

of Capitalism (1927; Gloucester, Mass.: Peter Smith, 1962), pp. 57, 207. The personal ties between Tawney and Strauss were symptoms of a significant intellectual sympathy; see Ross Terrill, *R. H. Tawney and His Times* (Cambridge, Mass.: Harvard University Press, 1973), pp. 83–84; Harold Laski, *The Rise of European Liberalism* (London: Unwin, 1962), pp. 105 102, 87. Laski not only asserted "the economic necessity of religious toleration," he also argued belittlingly that the main achievement of English constitutionalism was to guarantee that "the English merchant may sleep comfortably in his bed" (pp. 169, 69).

2. Max Weber, *The Protestant Ethic and the Spirit of Capitalism* (New York: Scribner's, 1958), p. 17; Joseph Schumpeter, *Capitalism, Socialism, and Democracy* (New York: Harper and Row, 1950), p. 123; Montesquieu, *The Spirit of the Laws*, trans. Thomas Nugent (New York: Hafner, 1949), XXI, 20, pp. 364–365.

3. John Locke, *Two Treatises of Government* (Cambridge: Cambridge University Press, 1988), II, 32–34, 111; John Milton, *Areopagitica* in *Complete Prose Works of John Milton* (New Haven: Yale University Press, 1959), vol. 2, p. 560; Benedict Spinoza, *A Theologico-Political Treatise and A Political Treatise*, trans. R. H. M. Elwes (New York: Dover, 1951), p. 259.

4. Judith N. Shklar, "The Liberalism of Fear," *Liberalism and the Moral Life*, ed. Nancy Rosenblum (Cambridge, Mass.: Harvard University Press, 1989), pp. 21–38.

5. Strauss claims that Locke consigns man not to free contemplation, but to joyless labor, "the life dominated by the pain which relieves pain" (Strauss, *Natural Right and History*, p. 250). He thus wholly misses a fundamental aspect of Locke's and indeed of all liberal thought.

6. Immanuel Kant, "Idea for a Universal History with a Cosmopolitan Purpose," *Kant's Political Writings*, ed. Hans Reiss (Cambridge: Cambridge University Press, 1970), p. 43.

7. Locke, *Two Treatises of Government*, II, 94; The Federalist Papers, #10 (New York: Mentor, 1961), p. 78.

8. Locke, *Two Treatises of Government*, II, 124, 123, 27, 76, 193, 221, 222; government is dissolved when its officials invade the property of private individuals (ibid, II, 221).

9. Ibid., II, 57, 76, 101, 211, 227, 239; Spinoza, *A Theologico-Political Treatise and A Political Treatise*, p. 259; Locke, *Two Treatises of Government*, II, 229.

10. Aristotle, *Politics*, 1262^b, 33–34.

11. Locke, *Two Treatises of Government*, II, , 42, 37, 41; cf. Adam Smith, *An Inquiry into the Nature and Causes of the Wealth of Nations* (New York: Modern Library, 1937), p. 12; Locke, *Two Treatises*, II, 37; David Hume, "Of Refinement in the Arts," *Essays Moral, Political, and Literary* (Indian-

apolis: Liberty Classics, 1985), p. 272; Smith, *Wealth of Nations*, p. 11; the elimination of poverty also loosens the bonds of personal dependency, since fear of starvation naturally encourages the obsequiousness of workers toward employers.

12. David Hume, *Enquiries Concerning the Human Understanding* (Oxford: Clarendon, 1962), p. 186.

13. Even the ultra-cautious Blackstone allows that "all property is derived from society" (William Blackstone, *Commentaries on the Laws of England* (Chicago: University of Chicago Press, 1977), vol. 1, p. 289.

14. Guido de Ruggiero, *The History of European Liberalism* (Boston: Beacon, 1959), p. 2; Montesquieu favored the sale of offices, admittedly, but for complex liberal reasons having to do with counterweights to royal authority.

15. Blackstone explained the selective liberal allergy to buying-and-selling as follows: "no public office shall be sold, under pain of inability to dispose of or hold it. For the law presumes that he, who buys an office, will by bribery, extortion, or other unlawful means, make his purchase good, to the manifest detriment of the public" (Blackstone, *Commentaries on the Laws of England*, vol. 2, pp. 36–37).

16. Kant's definition of marriage as a form of mutual possession, while genuinely weird, should not be misinterpreted as a transformation of the family into a market relationship. Such an interpretation is incorrect because, in a Kantian marriage, a bilateral monopoly is enforced, there is no right of resale, and the sexual acts of one's spouse cannot be purchased for money, but can be enjoyed only on the basis of in-kind exchange for one's own sexual acts (Kant, "Die Metaphysik der Sitten," in *Kants Werke* [Berlin: Walter de Gruyter, 1968], vol. 6, p. 278). The *mutuality* of the Kantian marriage contract must be understood as a protest against the asymmetry, at the time, in nonmarital relations—an asymmetry that favored males. He favored an "exchange relation" over a relation based on the "sacrifice" of one party to the other. Though it may be emblematic of a new "bourgeois" mentality, therefore, Kant's theory of marriage does not signal a universalization of market exchange.

17. See Chapter 15 below.

18. Kant, "Perpetual Peace"; see also *Kant's Political Writings*, p. 114; Montesquieu, *The Spirit of the Laws* (XX, 2), p. 316, and (XX, 1), p. 316; according to Montesquieu, "the spirit of commerce is naturally attended with that of frugality, economy, moderation, labor, prudence, tranquillity, order, and rule" (V, 6, p. 46; XXI, 5, p. 334).

19. Spinoza, *Theologico-Political Treatise*, pp. 262, 254; Voltaire, "Lettres philosophiques," *Mélanges* (Paris: Pléiade, 1961), pp. 17–18; an intermediary between Spinoza and Voltaire was Addison's *Spectator*: "there is no Place

in the Town which I so much love to frequent as the *Royal Exchange*. . . . Sometimes I am lost in a Crowd of *Jews;* and sometimes make one with a Groupe of *Dutch-men*. I am a *Dane, Swede,* or *Frenchman* at different times" (*The Spectator,* No. 69, 19 May 1711, in Joseph Addison and Richard Steele, *Selected Essays*, ed. Daniel McDonald [Indianapolis: Bobbs-Merrill, 1973], pp. 237–238).

20. It would be difficult to show how this fundamental change in belief itself could have an explanation based on economics, as the result of a desire to get rich.

21. Hume, "Of Refinement in the Arts," *Essays Moral, Political, and Literary*, p. 278.

22. Arendt, *The Human Condition;* George Will, *Statecraft as Soulcraft* (New York: Simon and Schuster, 1983), p. 72; cf. Unger, *Knowledge and Politics*, p. 38; Charles Taylor, "Atomism," *Philosophy and the Human Sciences* (Cambridge: Cambridge University Press, 1985), p. 201.

23. This charge conflicts, it should be said, with the equally widespread antiliberal claim that liberals had *no* steady goals but were obsessed solely with the most efficient means to whatever ends happened to cross their minds.

24. Spinoza, *Theologico-Political Treatise*, pp. 259 and 314; Kant, "What is Enlightenment?," *Kant's Political Writings*, p. 60.

25. Alexander Solzhenitsyn, *A World Split Apart* (New York: Harper and Row, 1978), p. 45.

26. MacIntyre, *After Virtue*, p. 200.

27. Adam Smith, *A Theory of Moral Sentiments* (Oxford: Clarendon Press, 1976), p. 139; Spinoza, *Theologico-Political Treatise*, p. 228; Adam Smith, *An Inquiry into the Nature and Causes of the Wealth of Nations* (New York: Modern Library, 1937), p. 748; John Stuart Mill, "On Liberty," *Essays on Politics and Society*, ed. J. M. Robson (Toronto: University of Toronto Press, 1977), p. 265; Smith, *Wealth of Nations*, p. 760.

28. Andrzej Rapaczynski, *Nature and Politics: Liberalism in the Philosophies of Hobbes, Locke, and Rousseau* (Ithaca, N.Y.: Cornell University Press, 1987), pp. 150–170.

29. Locke, *An Essay Concerning Human Understanding*, p. 258; Bentham wrote, in the same spirit: "when I say *physical,* I mean the pains and pleasures of the soul as well as the pains and pleasures of sense" (Jeremy Bentham, "Principles of Legislation," *The Theory of Legislation* [Bombay: N. M. Tripathi, 1979], p. 2).

30. Taylor, "Atomism," p. 209.

31. Before the revolution, liberals could be more blasé about this: "all plans of government, which suppose great reformation in the manners of mankind, are plainly imaginary" (Hume, "Idea of a Perfect Commonwealth," *Essays Moral, Political, and Literary*, p. 514).

32. Locke, *Essays on the Law of Nature*, 141.
33. Locke, *An Essay Concerning Human Understanding*, p. 262.
34. Montesquieu, *Persian Letters*, p. lxix.
35. Smith, *Wealth of Nations*, pp. 15, 384, 556; the best known illustration of Smith's pervasive concern for character formation occurs in his discussions of the division of labor (pp. 8–9, 735).

14. The Selfishness of Rights?

1. MacIntyre, *After Virtue*, pp. 69–70; MacIntyre, *Three Versions of Moral Enquiry*, pp. 184–185. He explicates this claim by adding: "rights are claimed *against* some other person or persons; they are invoked when and insofar as those others appear as threats" (p. 185).
2. As Beccaria wrote, "within the confines of a country, there should be no place independent of the law" (Cesare Beccaria, *On Crimes and Punishments* [Indianapolis: Bobbs-Merrill, 1963], p. 60); while the liberal state can intervene in all social domains, it can do so, of course, only on the basis of a standing law.
3. It is thus anachronistic and obfuscatory to speak, for example, as does Robert Nozick, of a sacred or inviolable or natural right to property in a society where government no longer boasts a divine sanction.
4. John Locke, *A Letter Concerning Toleration* (Indianapolis, Ind.: Bobbs-Merrill, 1955), p. 35; Locke, *Two Treatises of Government* (Cambridge: Cambridge University Press, 1988), II, 215; the depiction of rights as "atomizing" is one of the few points of intersection between marxist and nonmarxist critics of liberal society; see Karl Marx, "On the Jewish Question," *The Marx-Engels Reader*, ed. Robert Tucker (New York: Norton, 1978), pp. 26–46.
5. MacIntyre attacks liberal morality for its obsession with "what rules ought we to follow?" and its neglect of the ancient question "what sort of a person am I to become?" (*After Virtue*, p. 118). Unger elaborates on this theme in his *Politics* (see Chapter 6), but the most famous development of the contrast between obeying rules and developing virtues is found in the later Foucault. Like Strauss and MacIntyre, Foucault flails modernity in the name of the ancient world. Characteristic of *The History of Sexuality* is the idea that the Greeks had no concept of the subject in the modern, debased sense. The ancient Greeks developed an ethics without subjectivity, an ethics of the individual, and thus an ethics of freedom as opposed to an ethics of law. At the center of ethical life they placed "care for self" or cultivation of personal uniqueness. Their ideal was the beautiful life. To achieve high pleasures and sculpt his life into a work of art, an ancient Greek gentleman had to master his wayward appetites. But the emotional prohibitions, the "techniques of austerity" he imposed on himself were

part of an ethics of self-affirmation, not of self-denial. What the Greeks lacked, and what distinguished them happily from later Europeans, was the idea of universal norms in line with which people in general were encouraged to judge censoriously the behavior of others. Foucault denied that the morality of aesthetic self-cultivation, reserved for the aristocratic few, was an attempt to normalize the population, as was the modern idea of universal norms. The liberal infliction of general norms entailed a cruel standardization and suffocation of personal uniqueness. He scorned Enlightement morality because it was acceptable to *everyone*, in the sense that everyone should submit to it (Michel Foucault, *The Use of Pleasure* [New York: Random House, 1985]; and *The Care of the Self* [New York: Random House, 1986]); but there is something hypocritical about this opposition to universalism, since Foucault ends up criticizing the ancient republics for holding slaves and otherwise violating the abstract norm of equality.

6. Liberals sometimes favored citizen militias, principally for the sake of "negative liberty," to keep the dangerous tool of a professional army out of the hands of political rulers. Belief in the character-building power of military service, overemphasized by some commentators, was marginal to their thought (see Immanuel Kant, "Perpetual Peace," *Kant's Political Writings*, ed. Hans Reiss [Cambridge: Cambridge University Press, 1970], pp. 94–5); for Kant's argument that warfare stunts the development of important human talents, see "Universal History" (p. 49).

7. John Milton, *Areopagitica* in *Complete Prose Works of John Milton* (New Haven: Yale University Press, 1959), vol. 2, p. 515; Benedict Spinoza, *A Theologico-Political Treatise and A Political Treatise*, trans. R. H. M. Elwes (New York: Dover, 1951), p. 259; the most celebrated example of a liberal political theory based on the personal ideal of self-realization is Wilhelm von Humboldt's *The Limits of State Action* (Cambridge: Cambridge University Press, 1965); citing Humboldt, Charles Taylor admits that some forms of liberalism, at least, are "inspiring," namely those based on "the post-Romantic view . . . that each person has his own original form of self-realization" (Taylor, "What's Wrong with Negative Liberty," in his *Philosophy and the Human Sciences* [Cambridge: Cambridge University Press, 1985], pp. 216, 229).

8. Adam Smith, *An Inquiry into the Nature and Causes of the Wealth of Nations* (New York: Modern Library, 1937), p. 3; Kant, "Idea for a Universal History with a Cosmopolitan Purpose," *Kant's Political Writings*, p. 44; John Stuart Mill, "On Liberty," *Essays on Politics and Society*, ed. J. M. Robson (Toronto: University of Toronto Press, 1977), chap. 3; Kant, "Universal History," *Kant's Political Writings*, pp. 42–43, 45.

9. Kant, "Perpetual Peace," *Kant's Political Writings*, p. 112; *The Federalist Papers*, #51 and #55 (New York: Mentor, 1961), pp. 322, 346.

10. Locke, *Two Treatises of Government*, II, 131.
11. Strauss, *Natural Right and History*, p. 248; Locke, *Two Treatises of Government*, II, 6; Adam Smith, *The Theory of Moral Sentiments* (Oxford: Clarendon Press, 1976), p. 162. The psychology of duty, outlined by Montesquieu, reflects liberal skepticism about the impulse to obey: "how comes it that monks are so fond of their order? It is owing to the very cause that renders the order insupportable. Their rule debars them from all those things by which the ordinary passions are fed; there remains therefore only this passion for the very rule that torments them" (Montesquieu, *The Spirit of the Laws*, V, 2, pp. 40–41).
12. Spinoza, *a Theologico-Political Treatise*, p. 249; Locke, *Two Treatises of Government*, II, 192.
13. Locke, *Two Treatises of Government*, II, 183; William Blackstone, *Commentaries on the Laws of England* (Chicago: University of Chicago Press, 1977), vol. 1, p. 439; Mill, "On Liberty," p. 301.
14. Michael Sandel, *Liberalism and the Limits of Justice* (Cambridge: Cambridge University Press, 1982).
15. Unger, *Knowledge and Politics*, p. 74.
16. In criminal law, incidentally, abstractness has other advantages. It allows us to respect Charles Manson's rights, for instance, even though we obviously cannot respect him as a person; rights-thinking, in other words, is well adapted to the permanent scarcity of human sympathy stressed by Hume.
17. Joseph de Maistre, *Considérations sur la France* (1797), ed. Pierre Manent (Paris: Editions Complexe, 1988), p. 87.

15. Moral Skepticism?

1. Unger, *Knowledge and Politics*, pp. 77, 255, 52, 42, 138, 248, 254.
2. Ibid., p. 52; compare the criticisms of Max Weber along these lines by Strauss (*Natural Rights and History*, p. 42) and by MacIntyre (*After Virtue*, pp. 26–27, 114–115, 143–144).
3. John Locke, *A Letter Concerning Toleration* (Indianapolis, Ind.: Bobbs-Merrill, 1955), p. 46; Shirley Letwin, *The Pursuit of Certainty* (Cambridge: Cambridge University Press, 1965), pp. 127–188; Montesquieu, *The Spirit of the Laws*, trans. Thomas Nugent (New York: Hafner, 1949), X, 3, p. 135; ibid., VI, 2, p. 74.
4. Schmitt, "Der bürgerliche Rechtsstaat," *Abendland* (1928), p. 201.
5. Montesquieu, *Spirit of the Laws*, XI, 5, pp. 150–151; ibid., XI, 3, p. 150; "Law, in its true Notion, is not so much the Limitation as the direction of a free and intelligent agent to his *proper Interest*, and prescribes no further than is for the general Good of those under that Law" (Locke,

Two Treatises of Government (Cambridge: Cambridge University Press, 1988), II, 57), my emphasis; see also II, 6, 13.

6. Strauss, *Natural Right and History*, p. 222; John Milton, *Areopagitica* in *Complete Prose Works of John Milton* (New Haven: Yale University Press, 1959), vol. 2, p. 503; Benedict Spinoza, "The Ethics," in *The Chief Works of Benedict de Spinoza*, trans. by R. H. M. Elwes (New York: Dover, 1955), vol. 2, p. 212; Locke, *Letter Concerning Toleration*, p. 22; John Stuart Mill, "On Liberty," *Essays on Politics and Society*, edited by J. M. Robson (Toronto: University of Toronto Press, 1977), p. 230.

7. This point is persuasively argued in Will Kymlicka, *Liberalism, Community, and Culture* (Oxford: Clarendon Press, 1989).

8. According to Beccaria, "once these essentially distinct principles are confounded, there can be no further hope of correct reasoning in public affairs. It pertains to theologians to determine the boundaries between the just and the unjust with regard to the intrinsic wickedness or goodness of an act; to determine the relation of the politically just and unjust pertains to the statesman" (Cesare Beccaria, *On Crimes and Punishments* [Indianapolis: Bobbs-Merrill, 1963], p. 6).

9. Locke, *Two Treatises of Government*, II, 13.

10. Voltaire, *Philosophical Dictionary* (Harmondsworth: Penguin, 1983), p. 322; everyone knows it is immoral to convict and punish a defendant without allowing him to defend and explain himself, Voltaire asserts. This principle is neither subjective nor arbitrary nor a matter of personal inclination. It is a universally valid moral rule.

11. Friedrich Nietzsche, *Beyond Good and Evil*, trans. Walter Kaufmann (New York: Vintage, 1966), sec. 259, pp. 203–204.

12. Locke, *Two Treatises of Government*, II, 6, 13; William Blackstone, *Commentaries on the Laws of England* (Chicago: University of Chicago Press, 1977), vol. 1, p. 249.

13. Cruelty is a spice that seasons all pleasures. Here lies the heart of Nietzsche's own peculiar form of antiliberalism: "to see others suffer does one good, to make others suffer even more . . . . Without cruelty there is no festival" (Nietzsche, *The Genealogy of Morals*, trans. by Walter Kaufmann (New York: Vintage, 1967), Book 2, 6.

14. Locke, *Two Treatises of Government*, II, 8, 97; Immanuel Kant, "Idea for a Universal History with a Cosmopolitan Purpose," *Kant's Political Writings*, ed. Hans Reiss (Cambridge: Cambridge University Press, 1970), p. 49.

15. Strauss, *Natural Right and History*, p. 250.

16. It is telling, in this regard, that MacIntyre consistently uses the word "democratic" in a derogatory sense. His attack on the "democratization of moral agency" is a typical example. In liberal society, he writes, "anyone and everyone can thus be a moral agent, since it is in the self and not in

social roles or practices that moral agency has to be located." Liberal rights are assigned to persons, not to social ranks. For liberals, therefore, "the moral agent" is "anyone and everyone not actually mentally defective." Aristotle would never have democratized moral agency in this way. He did not believe in "the moral agency of everyone." He understood, presumably, that true moral agency was the monopoly of a few (*After Virtue*, pp. 220, 32, 155, 256). Since MacIntyre, in contrast to Strauss, drops repeated hints about his egalitarian-socialist sympathies, it is all the more striking that he can bring himself to write in this antidemocratic way.

17. MacIntyre, *Whose Justice? Which Rationality?* p. 98. See also Unger, *Knowledge and Politics*, pp. 63–103; Taylor, "Atomism," *Philosophy and the Human Sciences* (Cambridge: Cambridge University Press, 1985), p. 201; and Sheldon Wolin, *Politics and Vision* (Boston: Little, Brown, 1960), p. 332. Robert Nisbet, too, helps us focus clearly on this point. Liberalism dissolves social bonds, he writes, and "inequality is the essence of the social bond" (*Twilight of Authority* [New York: Oxford University Press, 1975], p. 217).

18. David Hume, "Of the Origin of Government," *Essays Moral, Political, and Literary* (Indianapolis: Liberty Classics, 1985), p. 41; Locke, *Two Treatises of Government*, II, 220; Blackstone, *Commentaries*, vol. 1, p. 400.

19. Situated between communitarians and superindividualists, liberals accept the social importance of two distinctions: loyalty/treason and good life/bad life. However important, these distinctions have a subordinate role to play in every liberal society. For political purposes, they must take a back seat to the liberal dichotomy of right action/wrong action. Only in an illiberal society do the differences between loyalty and treason, on the one hand, and good life and bad life, on the other, have greater *political* importance than the distinction between right and wrong. (These words are admittedly slippery: we can plausibly argue that justice itself is a good and that loyalty to the constitution is perfectly liberal. But the goodness of justice and of loyalty to liberal ideals are not what the antiliberal advocates of goodness and loyalty have in mind.)

20. Cesare Beccaria, *On Crimes and Punishments* (Indianapolis: Library of Liberal Arts, 1975), p. 11.

21. Locke, *Two Treatises of Government*, II, 76, 94, 5.

22. Locke, *An Essay Concerning Human Understanding*, ed. Peter H. Nidditch (Oxford: Clarendon Press, 1975), p. 704; the principle of self-consistency alone means that Lockean "reason" is not merely instrumental. Locke repeatedly invokes the standard of consistency, for example, in his arguments against the persecution of religious minorities. If the magistrate in England has the right to punish those who adhere to a minority sect, then

the magistrate in Istanbul has a parallel right to persecute Christians. The only way to avoid this unacceptable but logical conclusion is to abandon a politics of persecution. Toleration within politically determined limits is the moral decision that "reason" (which is more than means-ends rationality) demands.

23. Locke, *Two Treatises of Government*, II, 142, my emphasis.

24. Montesquieu, *The Spirit of the Laws* (XI, 3), p. 150; Blackstone, *Commentaries*, vol. 1, p. 6; Adam Smith, *An Inquiry into the Nature and Causes of the Wealth of Nations* (New York: Modern Library, 1937), p. 576; Nietzsche, *The Will to Power*, trans. Walter Kaufmann and R. J. Hollingdale (New York: Vintage, 1968), sec. 926, p. 489.

25. Kant, "Perpetual Peace," *Kant's Political Writings*, p. 99; "On the Common Saying: 'This May be True in Theory, But It Does Not Apply in Practice'," ibid, p. 75; "Universal History," ibid, p. 46; the key principle in Kant's moral philosophy is "I ought never to act except in such a way that I can also will that my maxim should become an universal law" (Kant, *Groundwork of the Metaphysic of Moral* [New York: Harper and Row, 1956], p. 70).

26. Compare Strauss, *Natural Right and History*, p. 248, with Locke, *An Essay Concerning Human Understanding*, 75.

27. This prohibition can be redescribed, once again, in a derogatory or Nietzschean way: cretinized by liberal morality, modern Europeans lack the aristocratic chutzpah (if we can put it that way) to say that an action is "good" simply because they want to do it. Liberals are too crippled by a guilty conscience to embrace forthrightly the subjectivity of values.

28. Kant, "Theory and Practice," *Kant's Political Writings*, p. 76

29. Schmitt, "Das Zeitalter der Neutralisierungen und Entpolitisierungen" (1929), reprinted in *Der Begriff des Politischen* (Berlin: Duncker and Humblot, 1963), p. 87; "Staatsethik und pluralistischer Staat" (1930), *Positionen und Begriffe*, pp. 134–137; Aleksander I. Solzhenitsyn, *A World Split Apart* (New York: Harper and Row, 1978), p. 37.

30. Unger, *Knowledge and Politics*, pp. 54, 86–87; Michael Sandel, "The Procedural Republic and the Unencumbered Self," *Political Theory*, 12 (1984).

31. Such antiliberal zig-zagging is the equivalent to the double complaint: this food is inedible *and* there is not enough of it.

32. This putative contradiction is also ascribed to liberals by, among others, MacIntyre in *Whose Justice? Which Rationality?* pp. 326–348.

33. Unger, *Knowledge and Politics*, p. 85.

34. Hume, "Of the Origin of Government," *Essays Moral, Political, and Literary*, p. 39; Smith, *Wealth of Nations*, p. 681. The umpire at a baseball game, to take a mundane but easily grasped example, cannot be perfectly neutral: he must enforce the rules. Moreover, winners and losers are determined

at least in part by discretionary decisions. But would anyone want to claim that a referee *cannot* be impartial between rival teams? (Umpiring, admittedly, does not provide an adequate model for the judicial function in a liberal state. But this homely illustration does help refute the common antiliberal charge that impartiality is impossible.)

35. It was in the wars of religion, it should be said, that the idea of impartiality among specific rival groups first emerged as a widely held political ideal. It remains valuable today, when political authorities must deal with the heirs of the parties that participated in those wars. The liberal state may still wisely and successfully refuse to embroil itself in a discrete set of social or moral controversies. (The government reserves the right to intervene in cases of public danger, but the case must be proved.) For a cogent defense of the liberal idea of neutrality along these lines, see Charles Larmore, *Patterns of Moral Complexity* (Cambridge: Cambridge University Press, 1987), pp. 40–68.

36. Montesquieu, *The Spirit of the Laws*, VI, 2, p. 73; VI, 5, p. 77.

37. It is inaccurate to say that liberalism is hostile to any conception of social purpose, concentrating exclusively on side contraints or rules of the game; rather, liberals had goals, but they were *limited* goals.

38. Kant, "What Is Enlightenment?" *Kant's Political Writings*, p. 58.

39. Locke, *Two Treatises of Government*, II, 11.

40. Charles Taylor, "Cross Purposes: The Liberal-Communitarian Debate," p. 172; Unger, *Knowledge and Politics*, pp. 20, 152, 168, 228, 177; MacIntyre, *After Virtue*, 107. Note that Taylor, in some passages, distances himself from communitarian critics of proceduralism: "it is quite possible to be strongly in favor of a morality based on a notion of the good but to lean to some procedural formula when it comes to the principles of politics." He adds, by way of clarification, that "the political issue is, indeed, quite distinct from the nature of moral theory" (Taylor, *Sources of the Self* [Cambridge, Mass.: Harvard University Press, 1989], p. 532). Needless to say, the wider the gap between moral and political theory, the more implausible it becomes to criticize liberal *politics* in the ordinary communitarian way.

41. As Kant ironized: "the glory" of a country's ruler normally "consists in his power to order thousands of people to immolate themselves for a cause which does not truly concern them, while he need not himself incur any danger whatsoever"; see also his comments about mercenaries: "the hiring of men to kill or be killed seems to mean using them as mere machines and instruments in the hands of someone else (the state)" (Kant, "Perpetual Peace," *Kant's Political Writings*, pp. 103, 95).

42. Locke, *Two Treatises of Government*, II, 6, 8, my emphasis; Montesquieu, *Persian Letters* (Harmondsworth: Penguin, 1973), p. 48; Kant, *Groundwork*

of the Metaphysic of Morals (New York: Harper, 1956), p. 96; Locke, *Two Treatises*, II, 6; Smith, *The Theory of Moral Sentiments* (Oxford: Oxford University Press, 1976), p. 234 (VI, ii, 2); Kant, *Metaphysical Elements of Virtue* (Indianapolis: Bobbs-Merrill, 1965), p. 97.

43. There is no contradiction between sincere abhorrence of manipulation and the instrumental justification of rights in a rule-utilitarian framework.

44. Locke, *Letter Concerning Toleration*, p. 36.

45. He does so on the grounds that "nothing [is] necessary to any society that is not necessary to the ends for which it is made"; a sergeant can "command a soldier to march up to the mouth of a cannon," but given the express purpose of his office, he cannot "command that soldier to give him one penny of his money." Power, in other words, "is not arbitrary by being absolute." It is strictly limited by the aim for which the power was granted (Locke, *Two Treatises of Government*, II, 47, 139).

46. Ibid., II, 8; Beccaria, *On Crimes and Punishments*, pp. 65–66; Kant, *The Metaphysical Elements of Justice*, p. 100.

16. The Crimes of Reason?

1. Schmitt, "Das Zeitalter der Neutralisierungen und Entpolitisierungen" (1929), reprinted in *Der Begriff des Politischen* (Berlin: Duncker and Humblot, 1963), p. 94; Strauss, "On the Intentions of Rousseau," *Hobbes and Rousseau*, ed. Maurice Cranston and Richard Peters (Garden City, N.J.: Doubleday Anchor, 1972), p. 267; Lasch, *The True and Only Heaven*, p. 308; Unger, *Knowledge and Politics*, p. 75.

2. MacIntyre, *Whose Justice? Which Rationality?* p. 353.

3. Unger, *Knowledge and Politics*, pp. 160, 213.

4. Counter-Enlightenment writers seldom use the word "terror" to describe the slaughter of peasants or heretics under the old regime. Group murders are terroristic, from their point of view, only when committed upward on the status ladder, only when lower classes dare lay a hand upon those who symbolize the social order.

5. Friedrich Nietzsche, *Beyond Good and Evil*, trans. Walter Kaufmann (New York: Vintage, 1966), sec. 208, p. 128–129.

6. Adam Smith, *An Inquiry into the Nature and Causes of the Wealth of Nations* (New York: Modern Library, 1937), pp. 734–735, 739.

7. This is a curious identification because, among other reasons, natural science has no particular regard for human freedom—a condition that is presumably of some interest to liberals.

8. Martin Heidegger, *The Question Concerning Technology*, trans. William Lovitt (New York: Harper and Row, 1977). p. 27.

9. Alexander Solzhenitsyn, *A World Split Apart* (New York: Harper and Row, 1978), pp. 48–49, 59; *Warning to the West* (New York: Farrar, Straus and Giroux, 1976), pp. 130–131.

10. Unger, *Knowledge and Politics*, pp. 25, 179, 204, 32. Unger combines this argument, as does Lasch, with the opposite complaint: that liberalism has deprived mankind of the "mastery of its own future" (p. 59).

11. Unger, *Knowledge and Politics*, pp. 201, 153. He wrote this, needless to say, before he presented going-over-the-edge as a moral imperative.

12. Unger, *Knowledge and Politics*, p. 229, 176, 112. How did we land in this catastrophic situation? The origin of our fall, as readers of Maistre will know, was secularism or a loosening of religious restraints: "the conception of nature and society as possible and proper objects of unlimited manipulation becomes available when the world is regarded as profane rather than as the embodiment of the sacred." Secular humanism is a sacrilege. It abets science by abolishing the traditional "conception that many of the phenomena of nature are sacred and therefore must be respected by man" (pp. 19, 159, 153). Unger also echoes Heidegger's criticism of "the rationalist claim to make the world transparent to the mind" (pp. 320).

13. That some of the instruments produced by modern science are terribly dangerous is a very different, and wholly indisputable, claim.

14. William Blackstone, *Commentaries on the Laws of England* (Chicago: University of Chicago Press, 1977), vol. 1, p. 47; Locke, *An Essay Concerning Human Understanding*, ed. Peter H. Nidditch (Oxford: Clarendon Press, 1975), p. 120; Voltaire, *Philosophical Dictionary*, trans. by Theodore Besterman (Harmondsworth: Penguin, 1972), p. 297.

17. Antonym Substitution

1. This is the reasoning that led Kant to describe marriage as an exchange (see note 16 in Chapter 13 above).

2. Liberals denied that individuals were "part" of one another for quite concrete political purposes—to abolish the very idea of inherited guilt, for example. They did not seek thereby to destroy enduring human relations.

3. The original antonym of egoism, we might say, was not altruism but irrational violence; Albert Hirschman, *The Passions and the Interests: Political Arguments for Capitalism before Its Triumph* (Princeton: Princeton University Press, 1977).

4. See Chapter 1 of Stephen Holmes, *Rediscovering Liberal Democracy* (Chicago: University of Chicago Press, 1994).

Conclusion

1. Alexandr Solzhenitsyn, *Warning to the West* (New York: Farrar, Straus and Giroux, 1976), pp. 146–147, 49; *A World Split Apart* (New York: Harper and Row, 1978), pp. 57, 51.
2. Only politicians who expose themselves publicly to the possibility of electoral defeat, for instance, acquire legitimacy in this system.

Index

Abortion, 130
Absolutism, 81, 105, 117, 121
Acquisitiveness, 91, 211
Act of Toleration (England), 3
Adorno, Theodor, xi
Al Farabi, 69, 74
Altruism, 254, 315n3
Anarchy, 157, 168–69, 237, 276n45; association with liberalism, 302n4; and atheism, 46; and authority, 44, 94; and democracy, 21, 271n36; and liberalism, 35, 50, 51, 58, 141, 201, 262, 302n4; and science, 98
anomie, 95, 156, 231
Anthropocentricity, 251
Anti-authoritarianism, 15, 21
Antibourgeois sensibility, 13
Antibusing movement, 132
Anticlericalism, 15, 199, 301n1
Anti-individualism, 42, 258–59, 263, 264; and outsiders, 259
Anti-intellectualism, 131
Antimilitarism, 199
Antipatriarchalism, 129
Anti-Prometheanism, 122–40. *See also* Lasch, Christopher
Antisemitism, xiv, 38, 50, 132, 137, 273n5
Antistatism, 51–53, 201, 203, 273n2, 301n1
Antonym substitution, 253–56
Aquinas, Thomas, xii, 74, 111, 118, 119, 141, 193, 215, 285n12. *See also* Thomism
Archimedes, 143, 241
Arendt, Hannah, xi, 79–80, 219
Aristocracy, 4, 83, 96, 195, 217, 233; and codes of honor, 96
Aristophanes, 66
Aristophobia, 71. *See also* Inequality

Aristotelianism, 89, 91, 92, 96, 102, 104, 109, 181, 211, 219; and Christianity, 74, 119; and Greek polis, 105, 106, 112, 113. *See also telos*
Aristotle, xii, 69, 71, 76, 89, 97, 102, 115, 215, 301n6; vs. Christianity, 109; conception of God, 80; and modernity, 95, 105; and moral agency, 311n16; *Nicomachean Ethics*, 103, 108; *Politics*, 198; theory of social self, 181
Asceticism, 127, 141, 221
Assimilationism, 138, 288n76; and fear of factional strife, 133
Atheism, 14, 21, 46, 69, 72, 80, 97, 129, 276n30, 285n16
Atomism, 90–91, 96, 97, 106, 181, 182, 189, 190–97, 200, 225, 246; and disintegration of society, 6; and doubt, 18; and liberalism, xiii, 17, 92, 148; and rights, 231, 307n4. *See also* Enlightenment; Individualism
Augustine, 13, 89, 120
Augustinianism, 59, 104, 119
Austen, Jane, 104
Authenticity, 258
Authority, xii, 22, 36, 37, 94–95, 158, 260, 272n45; vs. anarchy, 44; arbitrary, 254; bureaucratic, 103; creation of, 203; criticism of, 139; divine, 18–19, 46, 47, 64; eclipse of, 93, 201–5; guided by law, 202; hatred of, 14, 18, 26, 37, 52, 125, 129, 160, 187, 201, 203; liberal view of, 201–5; need for, 25, 121; rebellion against, 20, 116, 142, 161
Autonomy, 139, 237; individual, 9, 96, 104, 149, 190, 203; rational, 104

Bacon, Francis, 14, 71, 129, 150
Beccaria, Cesare, 188, 200, 207, 235,

317